Original Nation Approac

MW00852105

"A bold shot across the bow of orthodoxy where conceptions of world order are concerned, *Original Nation Approaches to Inter-National Law* is sure to stimulate reconsideration of a range of past assumptions regarding the legitimacy and even the viability of the prevailing statist system of global dominion. In offering clear alternatives, this book is not only timely but urgently needed."

—Ward Churchill, *author of* Struggle for the Land *(1993)*, On the Justice of Roosting Chickens *(2003), and* Kill the Indian, Save the Man *(2004)*

"This book results from the most profound and well-illustrated research that diverges and goes beyond traditional and TWAIL discourses, which remain paralyzed on the state as a canonical unit of geopolitical analysis. His ONAIL approach is a catalyst for a much-needed theoretical and practical change of mindset and behavior that prioritizes non-state-centric perspectives and is designed to treat the ecology and environment as indispensable elements of theoretical tenets that negate the human-centric, Anglo-American, and European historical narratives. It is a perfect example of the way a dissenting theory can foster innovation and accentuate largely unheard voices."

—Denis De Castro Halis, *Professor of Law, Estácio de Sá University, Brazil*

"A powerful manifesto for a true 'Inter-National' law against the hegemonic 'international' system of states and a resounding reminder that human emancipation cannot be separated from ecological justice."

—Chulwoo Lee, *Professor of Law, Yonsei Law School, Korea*

"Packed with horrifyingly compelling examples from a range of geographical and historical contexts, this comprehensive volume goes beyond reminding us of the massacres, epidemics, land appropriations and ecological disasters that continue to ravage ancestral nations to this day to enjoining us to question the legitimacy and utility of the state-based political order that has come to control the planet with increasingly destructive consequences. This book argues that for humanity to survive a legal and cognitive transformation in 'international law' is required that puts collaboration among original nations at its heart."

—Richard Powell, *Professor at the College of Economics, Nihon University, Japan*

Hiroshi Fukurai · Richard Krooth

Original Nation Approaches to Inter-National Law

The Quest for the Rights of Indigenous Peoples and Nature in the Age of Anthropocene

Hiroshi Fukurai
Legal Studies and Sociology
University of California Santa Cruz
Santa Cruz, CA, USA

Richard Krooth
Department of Sociology
University of California Santa Cruz
Santa Cruz, CA, USA

ISBN 978-3-030-59275-2   ISBN 978-3-030-59273-8   (eBook)
https://doi.org/10.1007/978-3-030-59273-8

This Palgrave Macmillan imprint is published by the registered company Springer Nature Switzerland AG
The registered company address is: Gewerbestrasse 11, 6330 Cham, Switzerland

This book is dedicated to the "rebels," "terrorists" and allies of the original nation, who continue to dedicate their lives to restoring dignity, sovereignty, and rights to self-determination all across the globe.

PREFACE

This book introduces the Original Nation scholarship to examine the history of the nation's struggles against the state in the world. We assert that a fundamentally different portrait of history, geography, and politics emerges when the perspective of the nation and peoples is placed at the center of geopolitical analysis of global affairs. In contrast to traditional and canonical state-centric narratives, the Original Nation scholarship offers a diametrically distinct "on-the-ground" and "bottom-up" portrait of the struggle, resistance, and defiance of the nation and peoples. It exposes persistent global patterns of genocide, ecocide, and ethnocide that have resulted from attempts by the state to occupy, suppress, exploit, and destroy the nation. The Original Nation scholarship offers a powerful and widely applicable intellectual tool to examine the historical genealogy of resilience, emancipatory struggles, and collective efforts to build a vibrant alternative world among the nation and peoples across the globe.

Let us apply the Original Nation approach to Santa Cruz, California, U.S., where we have lived and worked for decades. Santa Cruz was once known as a sleepy retirement enclave for the wealthy and privileged. Santa Cruz is also known as "Surf City," given Jack O'Neill's nearly 60-year association with the town, as an iconic surfer and businessman as a first inventor of the wetsuit. Santa Cruz is also known as the home of the yellow banana slug, often seen in the redwood forest in the University of California, Santa Cruz which made it a campus mascot.

Behind the familiar façade lies the historical struggle of the original nation and peoples in Santa Cruz. Prior to the arrival of Spaniards and European settlers in the 1700s, Santa Cruz had been the home to the Awaswas people, one of the tribal communities of the Ohlone Nation, whose self-sustaining culture supported them in this beautiful coastal bioregion of the Monterey Bay for more than 12,000 years. The Awaswas shared the territorial space with other Ohlone people in the southern Bay Area region, including the Ramaytush to the north, the Tamyen to the east, and the Mutsun and Rumsien to the south. The Awaswas' ancestral homeland was surrounded by the deep ancient redwood forests of the Santa Cruz Mountains; the hills and banks of the San Lorenzo River, whose headwaters originate in the Santa Cruz Mountains before emptying into Monterey Bay and the Pacific Ocean; and miles-long beaches as well as high rugged cliffs along the coastline. Today's Santa Cruz County spans from Davenport in the north, serenely carpeted with organic strawberry and artichoke fields, to Aptos and Seacliff State Beach in the south.

The life of the Awaswas was abundant with mountain animals and marine life all around. As one historian observed, there would have been scores of California sea lions playfully surfing on big waves, as well as a "carpet" of sea lions lying from one end of the beach to the other, so that one could literally walk on their backs without ever touching the sand; one could have heard the "roar" of annual salmon runs in San Lorenzo River from miles away and seen sea otters everywhere clinging to sea kelp forests near the beach and sea cliffs. In addition, boats were unable to sail in a straight line from Santa Cruz to the opposite side of the Monterey Bay because of the abundance of humpback whales, dolphins, porpoises, and an army of sea turtles that could have easily caused them to capsize. Santa Cruz Mountains would have contained majestic 300-foot redwoods where one could have seen grizzly bears, black-tailed deers, western gray squirrels, elks, antelopes, chipmunks, and raccoons, all of whom once roamed freely without human restraints (Jensen, 2007).

Following the establishment of the State of California and the federal system in the mid-nineteenth century, nearly all of these animals were either gone or brought into extinction. Spanish explorer Don Gaspar de Portola "discovered" the land area known as today's City of Santa Cruz in 1769. Father Fermin de Lasuen built Mission Santa Cruz in 1791, the twelfth mission to be established in California, along with Villa de Branciforte across the San Lorenzo River. Branciforte was one of three major Spanish settlements in California, in addition to San Jose in the north and Los Angeles in the south. One historian depicted the missions as "concentration camps where California's Indians were beaten, whipped, maimed, burned, tortured and virtually exterminated by the friars" (Castillo, 2004). In 1821, after Mexico won its war of independence against Spain, Mexico assumed control of the Spanish territories in California, including Santa Cruz. After the 1846–1848 Mexican–American War, the U.S. claimed ownership of California. Some twenty years later, in 1866, Santa Cruz was incorporated as a municipality under the laws of the State of California, and ten years later in 1876, received its first charter as a city.

After California had been incorporated into the U.S. in 1848, new European settlers began to carry out mass genocidal campaigns against indigenous populations, including the Awaswas, Mutsun, and other members of the Ohlone Nation (Lindsay, 2012). In 1851, California's first Governor, Peter H. Burnett, issued an executive order stipulating "that a war of extermination will continue to be waged between the races, until the Indian race becomes extinct, must be expected. While we cannot anticipate this result but with painful regret, the inevitable destiny of the race is beyond the power or wisdom of man to avert" (Burnett, 1851). A bounty was placed on every Indigenous body, with a total of $1.5 million being paid to those who participated in military expeditions for the purpose of exterminating California Indians. More than a quarter of a million dollars was spent on extermination efforts in Monterey County next to Santa Cruz, and in Mariposa County in the Central Valley (Nazaryan, 2016; Amah Mutsun Land Trust, 2020).

Meanwhile, ancient redwood forests in Santa Cruz had been appropriated and cleared, so as to create vast pastureland for agri-business for those Spanish and European settlers who had moved to Santa Cruz. On the "stolen land" of both pasturelands and ancient redwood forests, the University of California, Santa Cruz was later constructed, beginning its educational mission in 1965, and growing to become recognized as one of the ten most beautiful college campuses in the U.S. The curricula offered at UCSC rarely included or analyzed this colonial historical legacy of genocide, ecocide, ethnocide, and colonization, nor the destruction of the self-sustaining cultures and self-governing communities of the Awaswas and Mutsun people who had once lived in Santa Cruz for many centuries (Burns, 2010).

The struggles of the indigenous nation of the Awaswas and Ohlone people continue today against the state's occupation, exploitation, and destruction of their ancestral homeland. In order to restore the homeland and revive self-sustaining cultures and indigenous ecological knowledge, surviving descendants of the Awaswas helped organize, and became active members of, the Amah Mutsun Tribal Band. The Amah Mutsun Tribal Council and its Constitution were established in 1990, and in 2004, the California State Senate formally recognized the Tribal Government (Jones, 2019). The tribal government has been fighting for recognition of their history and the restoration of dignity, freedom, justice, and rights to self-determination. At a recent event, a Historic Mass of Reconciliation, Amah Mutsun Tribal Chairperson Valentin Lopez declared that his ancestors are "still here. ... this is an opportunity to tell our history in an honest way. There were Indians who lived here, and we're still here today and we're continuing." (Jones, 2019). In order to restore the land and preserve indigenous knowledge and cultural practices of the original nation and peoples in Santa Cruz, the Amah Mutsun Land Trust was established in 2013 and was incorporated into a non-profit organization in 2015.

The original nation's attempt to restore ancestral lands and to serve as stewards of Mother Earth has become one of the many strategies adopted by indigenous and original nations in North America and across the globe, as the Anthropocene accelerates such global threats as climate change, rising sea levels, air and water pollution, frequent forest fires, species extinction, loss of agricultural biodiversity, and soil erosion. There have been ever-increasing damages from annual bush fires in Australia, and for the last several years alone, Northern California has also suffered from numerous forest fires that have devastated multiple communities, including Indian reserved territories.

The Awaswas and Amah Mutsun people have long recognized that Mother Earth is an indivisible self-regulating community of interconnected and interdependent beings that sustain, contain, and reproduce all lives, including both human and non-human species. For many centuries, this indigenous knowledge and stewardship had supported and nurtured self-sustaining cultures and self-governing communities of the Ohlone Nation without consciously harming or destroying the surrounding environment. The Amah Mutsun Land Trust was designed to conserve and restore indigenous cultural and natural resources, and to steward the lands and waters. This land protection would combine "traditional resources and environmental management with contemporary approaches—ensuring a resilient future for all inhabitants of

Popeloutchom and fulfilling our obligation to Creator," and would also "research and teach the ways of nature—returning to the path of traditional ecological knowledge that our ancestors followed for thousands of years" (Amah Mutsun Land Trust, 2020). As part of this attempt to restore the ancestral homeland, the Awaswas and Amah Mutsun people have opposed numerous corporate development projects, including the Sargent Ranch mining development at "*Juristac*," their sacred site in the city of Gilroy, located east of Santa Cruz at the border of neighboring Santa Clara County. A private corporation, the Debt Acquisition Company of America (DACA), proposed a sand and gravel mining operation on an area of nearly 320 acres situated on the sacred ground and applied for permission to the Santa Clara Department of Planning and Development.

As observed in Chapter 6 of this volume, "Earth Jurisprudence, the Rights of Nature, and International Rights of Nature Tribunals," the corporation in the U.S. has been provided the constitutional instrument called the "commerce clause" which allows it to engage in the wanton exploitation and destruction of nature, environment, and ecosystems without regard for the desires of local residents, including indigenous populations. In order to protect the homeland and strategize for grassroots opposition, Tribal Chairperson Valentin Lopez participated in the 2017 National Bioneer Conference in San Rafael, California, sharing with them the exploitive corporate project proposed for their sacred land, and trying to develop strategies with indigenous peoples and environmental organizations, including the Community Environmental Legal Defense Fund (CELDF) and its executive officer Thomas Linzey. CELDF had pioneered the creation of the robust structure of law and legal strategies, often called "Earth Jurisprudence," to try to nullify the effect of the commerce clause, the right of "corporate personhood," and other legal measures weaponized to prioritize the interests of profit-driven private corporations over the rights of the original nation, peoples, and local residents. The struggle of the Awaswas and Amah Mutsun to preserve their ancestral homeland from corporate depredation and destruction continues today.

This book chronicles and analyzes the resilience and resistance of the original nation across the globe. It recounts the continued efforts to strategize, collaborate, and mobilize resources, so as to create a sure path toward the restoration of homeland and the reclamation of dignity, freedom, equity, and justice. The original inhabitants of Santa Cruz persist in a similar endeavor, despite enduring many years of discrimination, forceful dislocation, and even death. Why do the Awaswas, Amah Mutsun Ohlone people, and other original nations across the globe continue to fight for their land and freedom?

According to French philosopher Jean-Jacques Rousseau, the oppressed have been able to endure sacrifices and even death to attain their freedom and independence from tyrannical institutions because of innate human nature and character. He noted that Africans in European colonies had faced starvation, torture, and death in their struggle to attain independence and freedom despite the significant human toll involved (Rousseau, 1753). Using the genomic science terminology of today, this human desire to break free from an oppressive system may be a genetically endowed faculty built into human DNA (Harari, 2015). Rousseau's observation became reality once again several decades later, when hundreds of thousands of Africans took up arms and ignited the first slave-led revolution in 1791 on the island of Hispaniola in the Caribbean. Much earlier, by the beginning of the sixteenth century, most of the eight million Taino and other original inhabitants of Hispaniola had been exterminated, and Africans were imported to work on plantations as slaves (Horne, 2015). France once called the island of Hispaniola a "Jewel of the Caribbean" because of the enormous wealth produced by the harsh labor of the Africans. In the slave revolution, Africans fought formidable military expeditions of two French armies, Spanish imperial troopers, and heavily armed British Redcoats, and were successful in defeating them and declaring their independence and national sovereignty in 1804. They changed the name of the island—no longer using the colonial name of Saint-Domingue that had been given by the French masters, but calling it Haiti, "a land of high mountains" in the indigenous Taino language, thus honoring the sacrifices of the original inhabitants of the island. Haiti became the first free African republic in the world (Horne, 2015).

Our hope is that the Original Nation scholarship helps to generate radically different interpretations and narratives of geography, politics, and history in relation to the many ongoing struggles and conflicts in the world. We envision the Original Nation approach as an omnipresent genealogical intellectual tool that leads to critical interrogation of the predatory and ecocidal "state-building" and "nation-destroying" endeavors that continue to occur in multiple regions across the globe. The themes animating this book reflect our wish to help contribute to the fulfillment of the innate human desire for freedom of the original nation and peoples; to help provide both theoretical and methodological frameworks within which to examine the historical, political, and structural causes for the persistent, and multilayered tension and conflict that exists between the nation and the state; and ultimately to help in the search for dignity, justice, equity, and freedom for the original nation and peoples all across the world.

Santa Cruz, USA

Hiroshi Fukurai
Richard Krooth

Bibliography

Amah Mutsun Land Trust (2020) "Our Mission," (accessed 15 May 2020), available at https://www.amahmutsunlandtrust.org/our-mission.

Burnett, Peter H. (1851) "Executive Order, Peter Burnette, 1st Governor, Independent Democrat 1849–1851: State of the State Address," 6 January, available at https://governors.library.ca.gov/addresses/s_01-Burnett2.html.

Burns, Jim (2010) "'UC Santa Cruz Makes' Most Beautiful College Campuses' List," *UCSC Santa Cruz News Center*, 10, March.

Castillo, Elias (2004) "The Dark, Terrible Secret of California's Missions," *SF Chronicle*, 8 November.

Harari, Yuval Noah (2015) *Sapiens: A Brief History of Humankind*. NY: HarperCollins.

Horne, Gerald (2015) *Confronting Black Jacobins: The U.S., the Haitian Revolution, and the Origins of the Dominican Republic*. NY: NYU Press.

Jensen, Derrick (2007) *Thought to Exist in the Wild: Awakening from the Nightmare of Zoos*. Santa Cruz, CA: Novoice Unheard.

Jones, Donna (2019) "Healing Memories Recall California Mission Heritage," *Santa Cruz Sentinel*, 11 September.

Lindsay, Brendan C. (2012) *Murder State: California's Native American Genocide, 1846–1873*. Lincoln, NE: University of Nebraska Press.

Nazaryan, Alexander (2016) "California Slaughter: The State-Sactioned Genocide of Native Americans," *Newsweek Magazine*, 17 August.

Rousseau, Jean-Jacques (1753) "Against Arbitrary Authority," available at https://www.cooperative-individualism.org/rousseau-jean-jacques_against-arbitrary-authority-1753.htm.

ACKNOWLEDGMENTS

This book is the fruit of many years of discussion, exchange of ideas, and research collaboration with socio-legal scholars, indigenous activists, research groups, legal experts, and students all around the globe. We have been fortunate to come into contact with many dedicated people involved in indigenous struggles, racial and ethnic movements, grassroots organizing, and political activism in their local communities. We appreciate the great contributions made by specific individuals too numerous to mention, but we particularly wish to thank these professors from The University of Ryukyus, a national university of Japan in Okinawa: Ikue Kina, Yoko Fujita, Masa'aki Gabe, Tetsumi Takara, and Masahide Ishihara who have taught us about the history of the struggles of Okinawan people; Professor Akira Fujimoto of Nagoya University and Professor Setsuo Miyazawa of the University of California, Hastings Law School, who provided suggestions and critical comments on the Original Nation scholarship; Edgar W. Butler, Alfredo Mirande, Adalberto Aguirre, Jr., and late Maurice Jackson of the University of California, Riverside who shared their own struggles to fight social and racial inequities; Washington University Professor David Law and Nihon University Professor Ric Powell, who shared and exchanged ideas with us about indigenous rights for freedom and sovereignty; Indonesian legal scholar Yance Arizona, currently completing a doctoral program at Leiden University in The Netherlands, who participated in a number of indigenous panels and discussions at several international conferences in the past few years; former University of Colorado, Boulder Professor and prominent indigenous activist Ward Churchill who read the manuscript and provided valuable comments and suggestions; Georgia State University Distinguished Professor Natsu Taylor Saito who provided valuable assistance for the completion of the project; and Australian National University Professor Jonathan Liljeblad, who has examined multiple indigenous nations and their struggles in Myanmar and neighboring regions.

Many other scholars have also introduced us to the struggles of original nations throughout the world, including National Chiao Tung University Professor Chih-Chieh Carol Lin, who has explored indigenous struggles in Taiwan during the Japanese occupation of Formosa; Argentinean law professor and political activist Andres Harfuch and Argentina National Congress consultant Maria Sidonie Porterie, who helped to successfully install *El Jurado Indígena* (Indigenous Jury) in Neuquén, Argentina, in order to ensure the inclusion of indigenous people in criminal jury trials; California State Polytechnic University in Pomona Professor Jack Fong, who completed a doctoral program in sociology at UCSC some years ago and has critically examined ethnic conflicts in Thailand and Myanmar; Cornell University Professor Valerie Hans and Northwestern University Professor Shari Seidman Diamond, who collaborated with Andres Harfuch and his colleagues to establish the indigenous and gender equity jury model in Argentina; Dr. Julie Hazlewood of UCSC, who has been assisting Afro-Ecuadorian communities in the Pacific Northwestern rainforest in protecting their ancestral homeland from corporate exploitation; Amah Mutson Tribal Chairperson Valentin Lopez, who has educated us concerning the history of indigenous struggles in Santa Cruz; UCSC Professor Craig Haney, Wilfrid Laurier University Professor Nikolai Kovalev, University of Hawaii Professors David T. Johnson and Mark Levin, Law Professor and Temple University Japan President Matthew Wilson, K.U. Leuven University Professor Dimitri Vanoverbeke, and Professor Zhuoyu Wang of the Southwest University of Finance and Economics of China, who educated us about the importance of citizen participation in justice systems; and Kokugakuin University Professor Satoru Shinomiya, Toyo University Professor Emeritus Kaoru Kurosawa, Senshu University Professor Takayuki Ii, Aoyama

Gakuin University Professor Emeritus Osamu Niikura, Osaka Attorney Takeshi Nishimura, Patent Attorney Seiki Takita and other key members of the grassroots organization called the Research Group on Jury Trial (*Baishin Saiban o Kangaeru Kai* or RGJT) in Japan, who have worked tirelessly to examine the history of civil jury trials and socio-legal struggles of Ryukyuans and other indigenous peoples in the island of Okinawa in the 1960s and 1970s.

Great appreciation is also extended to Professors Chulwoo Lee of Yonsei University and Eva-Darian Smith of UC Irvine for their insistence on the importance of indigeneity in socio-legal discourse, and to UCSC Professors Karen Tei Yamashita, John Brown Childs, Boreth Ly, and David Anthony, as well as Professors Rostam J. Neuwirth, Denis de Castrol Halis, and Alexandr Svetilicinii of the University of Macau for their friendship and support over many years.

The first exploration of the Original Nation scholarship was presented at the inaugural Asian Law and Society Association (ALSA) Conference in 2016 at the National University of Singapore organized by NUS Professors Andrew Harding and Lynette Chua. More refined analyzes of the Original Nation scholarship, including the Original Nation Approaches to International Law (ONAIL), were presented at the 2017 Symposium on Populism and Globalization held at Indiana University Maurer School of Law. Many scholars who attended the symposium provided valuable suggestions and critical comments, including professors Alfred C. Aman, Yvonne Cripps, Carol Greenhouse, Susana Narotzky, Jayanth Krishnan, and others.

Our gratitude and appreciation are also extended to colleagues and staff in the Department of Sociology and the Department of Legal Studies at UCSC who have provided valuable support and assistance, including Wendy Martyna, Julie Bettie, Miriam Greenberg, Jessica Lawrence, Veronica Terriquez, Juhee Kang, Barbara Laurence, Meenoo Kohli, Tina Cossaboom, Colleen Stone, Leah Hanson, and Jerry Diaz, among others. We have had numerous important discussions of indigenous knowledge and feminist-indigenism with present and past UCSC students, including Yvonne Sherwood, Laura Harrison, Yvonne Kwan, Lindsay Tavaras-Sabido, Aldinette Lockett, Charlee Donovan, Xiaochen Liang, as well as other graduate and undergraduate scholars.

Lastly, we wish to thank Ann and Karl Krooth, as well as Chikako, Yuki, Mihoka, and Haruka Fukurai and Sachiko Hasegawa for their love and support. We also wish to thank Arun Kumar Anbalagan, Rebecca Roberts, and other editorial members of Palgrave Macmillan for their wonderful editorial assistance, as well as for their kind patience, as they awaited final completion of the manuscript. Needless to say, we accept full responsibility for the accuracy of the material we present in this book as we critically examine the relationship between the nation and the state and its ongoing implications for our world.

Hiroshi Fukurai
Richard Krooth

CONTENTS

CHAPTER 1

Introduction: The Original Nation Scholarship

Much of today's widespread violence and military aggression in various regions around the globe reflects the legacies of historical tension and conflict between the nation and the state. These current levels of human suffering and death have exposed persistent global patterns of genocide, ecocide, and ethnocide that have resulted from attempts by the state to occupy, oppress, exploit, and ultimately destroy the nation.[1] The collective efforts of the nation in resisting state encroachment and engaging in emancipatory struggles have displayed great resilience, aspiration, and dedication to building a vibrant alternative world across the globe.

In the last several decades, the state's promotion of globalization and neoliberal policies has accelerated the disfigurement and radical alteration of the nation's bioregional spheres. The persistent actions of the state in supporting dispossession, ecologically unsustainable projects, and agri-industrial development of the nation's homeland have led to the increasing rate of climate change and ecological disasters around the globe. Armed violence and ecological destruction have also been used to propel the forced eviction and displacement of already-marginalized

---

[1] Grey (2011, p. 22). Other acts of state violence included "terrorism (including state terrorism), racism, criminalization, slavery, political repression, economic marginalization (underdevelopment) and small arms proliferation."

© The Author(s), under exclusive license to Springer Nature Switzerland AG 2021
H. Fukurai and R. Krooth, *Original Nation Approaches to Inter-National Law*,
https://doi.org/10.1007/978-3-030-59273-8_1

1

nations, to eradicate biological diversity, and to destroy many self-sustaining cultures and self-governing communities.[2] In areas where there is significant resistance, the state has mobilized state troopers, private paramilitary forces, and counterterrorism intelligence units to quash the resistance. During the Cold War period, state-sponsored intelligence operations alone were responsible for the deaths of six million resisters.[3]

The state has also engaged in many illegal acts, including the arbitrary arrest, detention, interrogation, torture, extrajudicial killings, and other human rights violations directed against the nation and peoples. Studies have shown that wars and armed violence conducted by the state killed an average of 1–1.5 million people each year throughout the twentieth century.[4] Since the beginning of the twenty-first century, armed violence of the state has increased, leading to the worldwide dislocation of nearly 42 million people each year from the nation's territories.[5] The state's military violence has been justified through hegemonic rhetoric referring to the state's noble campaign, crackdown, and "war against terror," or under the pretext of national security concerns related to the allegation of communist or socialist infiltration or the threat of potential takeover of the state by national "terrorists," "insurgents," and armed rebels.[6] The state suppression of the nation has been exacerbated by the growing expansion and development of sophisticated technologies and transportation capacities which allow large shipment of ever more lethal arms and intelligence tools to every conflict area across the globe.

1   THE ORIGINAL NATION SCHOLARSHIP

When the perspective of the nation and peoples is placed at the "centric-core" of the geopolitical analysis of domestic and global affairs, a fundamentally different interpretation, de-centered perspective, and critical

---

[2] Institute for the Studies of Human Rights (2017, p. 119). The term, "the nation" or "the original nation" came from various sources. See Newcomb (2008), Ryser (2012), Starblanket (2018), and Watson (2018).

[3] For detailed accounts of CIA's global operation, see Blum (2014).

[4] Leitenberg (2006) and Garfield (2008).

[5] UNHCR (2009, p. 3).

[6] Ibid. See also Dekdeken, et al. (2013).

narrative of history, geography, politics, identity, citizenship, gender-dynamics, human and non-human relations, as well as of the role and efficacy of domestic and international laws, begins to emerge and predominate. Instead of focusing on the state and its relations with international organizations and transnational corporations as traditional geopolitical analyzes tend to do, the Original Nation approach produces diametrically opposed "on the ground," "bottom-up," and de-centered portraits of the significance of the nation and peoples in domestic and international affairs, conflicts, and possible remedies.

Dominant and traditional scholarship tends to interpret the world and analyze the intricacies of global affairs through a neatly enclosed canonical framework of a fixated, legal network, and political community of 193 United Nations (UN) member states, whose affairs are facilitated by internationally recognized organizations such as various UN agencies and affiliated institutions, as well as World Bank (WB), International Monetary Fund (IMF), and World Trade Organization (WTO). Supra-state unions and regional confederations also serve to strengthen the network of the state, such as European Union (EU), the Organization of American States (OAS), the African Union (AU), the Association of Southeast Asian Nations (ASEAN), and other state collaborations and global alliances. Transnational corporations are also recognized as crucial global actors in the operation of domestic and international laws, supported by the state and legitimized by international organizations. The global network of military alliances, such as the status of forces agreement (SOFA) and visiting forces agreement (VFA), allows the presence of armed forces and military outposts of dominant states in poor and peripheral states, under the rhetoric of a global security arrangement. It is significant to note that the construction of military bases and armed personnel deployment have been targeted in, near, or around the ancestral homeland and territories of the nation.[7]

The state-centric interpretation and canonical narratives of global affairs have routinely relegated nation peoples, who have defended

---

[7] For example, nearly three quarters of the American military bases and personnel in Japan are found in Okinawa, formerly an independent kingdom until Japan's forceful annexation in 1879. See Fukurai (2010).

their homeland against the encroachment of the state, to the vilified status of religious fundamentalists,[8] ethnic minorities,[9] indigenous people,[10] scheduled tribes,[11] tribal groups,[12] landless peasants,[13] socialists,[14] communists,[15] anarchists,[16] separatists,[17] independent nationalists,[18] ignoble savages,[19] indigenous rebels,[20] leftwing guerrillas,[21] revolutionaries,[22] subversives,[23] or even insurgent and "non-state-supported" terrorists,[24] depending upon the degree of perceived threat that the nation's resistance and opposition movement has posed to the state. The U.S. is no exception, given the application of such vilified rhetoric against indigenous nations in North America. In critiquing indigenous nations' resistance against the policy of "settler-state colonialism," the Founding Fathers, in the 1776 Declaration of Independence, characterized them as "the merciless Indian Savages whose known rule of warfare, is an undistinguished destruction of all ages, sexes and conditions."[25] Spanish *conquistadores* in the Americas similarly characterized indigenous

---

[8] Derichs and Fleschenberg (2010).

[9] "Reaching Indigenous Youth With Reproductive Health Information and Services" (1999).

[10] Ibid.

[11] Ibid.

[12] Rifkin (2009).

[13] Takaki (2008).

[14] Ward (2018).

[15] Parker (2009).

[16] Williams (2017).

[17] Manganyi et al. (2019).

[18] Suny (2001).

[19] Dippie (2020).

[20] Godelmann (2014).

[21] Watts (2017).

[22] Paige (2020).

[23] Garfield (2001, p. 192).

[24] Cheng (2013).

[25] U.S. Declaration of Independence (1776).

nations and peoples as native savages,[26] primitives,[27] the ignorant,[28] and uncivilized creatures.[29]

The process of the "state-building" project in North America brought with it the parallel project of "nation-dismantling" programs, which led to destruction of ecological diversity in the nation's homeland, where dynamic natural equilibrium and delicate balance between humans and non-human species had existed for millennia. As a result, the actions of the state have driven many species to near or complete extinction. As many as 15 million indigenous people had lived in North America prior to *Cristóbal Colón's* arrival in the late fifteenth century. By the end of the nineteenth century, that number had been reduced to only a quarter million, which represents nearly 98% liquidation of indigenous populations. Other species were also driven to extinction. Several billion passenger pigeons that "flew in flocks so large they darkened the sky for days"[30] were brought to complete extinction by the beginning of the twentieth century. Millions of American bison that once roamed the Great Prairie were also brought to near extinction, as well as much of the population of sea mink, Labrador heath hen, Eskimo curlew, pronghorn antelope, pollinators, prairie dogs, whales, seals, and salmon.[31] Outside North America today the state has continued to dominate, occupy, and destroy many of the remaining nations, peoples, and their land within state-delimited boundaries across the globe, forcing the extinction of a multitude of species and eliminating the ecological diversity that had existed in the nation's bioregion for many centuries.

The Original Nation scholarship, as critically analyzed in this volume, allows the systemic examination of how colonial empires and modern

---

[26] Buchan (2001, pp. 143–44).

[27] Ibid., p. 150.

[28] Ibid., p. 145.

[29] Canny (2012, p. 83). In a different historical context, a similar caricature of targeted groups may be found in Nazi Germany in the extermination of Jews, Slavs, Roma, and others as "less than human," "not-human," or "non-people," i.e., a set of demonized terminologies used in the extermination camps or during the era of Francisco Franco's suppression of anarchist resisters during the Spanish Civil War in late 1930s. See also Lang (2010, pp. 225–246), Smith (2011), and Sulish (2017).

[30] Jensen (2002, p. 15). See also Leonard (2002).

[31] See generally Leonard (2002), Dudley and Woodford (2002), Vermeij (1993), McCabe et al. (2010), and Lichatowich, et al. (1999).

states have invaded and occupied the nation's ancestral homelands and exploited and usurped their "natural resources."[32] The Original Nation approach focuses on the predatory behavior of the state-centric system of law and its authority in the state's destructive, expansive application around the globe. Original Nation Approaches to Inter-National Law (ONAIL), in particular, recognizes the application of international law as a predatory instrument employed by the tripartite alliance of the state, corporate actors, and multilateral organizations in exploiting the nation and people, dispossessing them of their ancestral territory, jeopardizing the viability of self-sustaining communities, destroying the nature and ecosystems, and eradicating biological and cultural diversity—all of which need to be preserved for present and future generations of human and non-human species in the global community.

The state-assisted catastrophe of the Anthropocene now threatens the survival of human and non-human species on the planet. Scientists attribute the arrival of the Anthropocene to several factors, including the last several centuries' ecological destruction and violence, which has been characterized by endless industrial expansion, pollution and radical disfigurement of Mother Earth; the legalized enslavement of the nation and ecosystems for corporate profit; and the instituting of massive extractive activities in multiple regions across the world, without recognizing such environmental externalities as climate change, rising sea levels, and other anthropogenic disasters.[33] This era has also involved the expansion and installation of the system of law that privileges private property at the expense of nature, ecosystems, and the equity of autonomous nations.[34] Exploitation by the state and corporate entities has relied on a worldview that ennobles humans above nature, thus facilitating the ongoing state destruction of self-governing nations and self-reliant cultures and traditions.

In protecting the rights of the nation, peoples, and the nature from encroachment by the state and from corporate exploitation, ONAIL

---

[32] The U.N. estimated in 2010 that there were 5,000 culturally distinct groups and communities in the world. See Press Release (2010). Richard Griggs and Peter Hocknell estimated that there were nearly 7,500 nations, and the majority of these were located in Asia and the Pacific. See Griggs and Hocknell (1995).

[33] Watanabe and Watanabe (2019), Wyk (2019), and DeLoughrey (2019).

[34] See Churchill (2002).

recognizes the significance of the following two sets of universal standards that have been developed internationally. First, the Original Nation scholarship supports the prescient vision of the nation and people embedded in the Universal Declaration of the Rights of Indigenous Peoples (UNDRIP). After many decades of dedicated work by the nation, indigenous activists, and environmental organizations, the Declaration that was adopted by the U.N. in 2007 finally established a universal framework to protect the rights of the nation and peoples. Specifically, UNDRIP stipulated that "indigenous peoples have the right to the full enjoyment, as a collective or as individuals, of all human rights and fundamental freedom as recognized in the Charter of the United Nations, the Universal Declaration of Human Rights and international human rights law."[35] At the U.N., 144 states voted in favor of the Declaration, eleven abstained, and four states opposed it, including the U.S., Canada, Australia, and New Zealand.[36]

In protecting the rights of nature and ecosystems, the Original Nation scholarship also supports the stipulation of nature and its well-being as the collective subject of common interests installed in the Universal Declaration of the Rights of Mother Earth (UDRME). This Declaration was adopted by representatives of 130 states at the World Conference on Climate Change and the Rights of Mother Earth in Bolivia in 2010. UDRME stipulated that "the inherent rights of Mother Earth are inalienable in that they arise from the same source as existence."[37] According to UDRME, Mother Earth has the following ten sets of inalienable and inherent rights: (1) the right to life and to exist; (2) the right to be respected; (3) the right to regenerate its biocapacity and to continue its vital cycles and processes free from human disruptions; (4) the right to maintain its identity and integrity as a distinct, self-regulating, and interrelated being; (5) the right to water as a source of life; (6) the right to clean air; (7) the right to integral health; (8) the right to be free from contamination, pollution and toxic or radioactive waste; (9) the right to not have its genetic structure modified or disrupted in a manner that threatens its integrity or vital and healthy functioning; and finally (10) the right to

---

[35] UN Universal Declaration of the Rights of Indigenous Peoples, Art. 1.

[36] These four states later adopted varied versions of the Declaration. See Gussen (2017).

[37] Universal Declaration of the Rights of Mother Earth, Art. 1 (4).

full and prompt restoration for violation of the rights recognized in this Declaration caused by human activities."[38]

The policies of the state with its "state-building" and "nation-destroying" agendas, together with the impending threats posed by the Anthropocene, have illuminated the state's persistent actions that display a disregard of the rights of the nation, peoples, and the nature, as well as an unceasing thirst for private profits and corporate wealth, resulting in endless industrial development, technological innovation, ecologically unsustainable projects, and the legalized enslavement of the nation and nature for profit maximization over the past several hundred years. The extent of the current and future power of the nation and people who are fighting in tenuous territories across the globe is still uncertain, due to such devastating powers of centralized states as expanding wars, targeting and killing indigenous resisters, extending and profiting from corporate empires, and dispossessing and destroying ancestral territories without restraint. Yet the collective aspirations animating the nation's resistance have conveyed the strong possibility of ultimately successful defiance against the centralized state and its corporate allies.

The inevitable irony of the state's destructive projects is that the general population has begun to experience some of the same negative impacts of predatory state policies and corporate exploitation that have long been felt by the nation and peoples. Prominent legal philosopher Felix S. Cohen once predicted that the indigenous nation in North America had served as the proverbial "Miner's Canary" in relation to state policies and corporate practice,[39] warning that the state depredation inflicted upon them would become a prototype for projects to be applied to the U.S. as a whole and even beyond. We have since seen that the state's neoliberal policies installed in the 1970s have resulted in many municipalities and towns increasingly having to face the threat of ecologically unsustainable projects in their communities, including shale gas hydraulic fracking, industrial factory farms, coal and uranium mining, oil pipeline, incinerators, power plants, chemical trespass, sewage sludge dumping, GMO farming, pesticide, and large-scale aquifer seizures, among many others.[40] Many of these unecological projects had already

---

[38] Ibid., Art. 2. (1).

[39] Cohen (1953).

[40] Valdmanis (2015) and Nobel (2018).

been imposed on the indigenous nations in North America,[41] resulting in cancers, respiratory diseases, high rates of miscarriage, kidney diseases, congenital anomalies, and other serious pollution-related ailments and diseases that have persisted in indigenous nations and peoples.[42] The "nation-destroying"—or today's equivalent, "municipality-decimating"—agendas have also ignited widespread support for grassroots environmental movements throughout the U.S. and across the world. Many municipalities supported by grassroots environmental organizations have begun to pass new environmental regulations, ordinances, and policies to protect their own residents, the nature, and ecosystems. Other countries also begun to amend their constitutions and strengthen environmental laws to protect the rights of the nation, nature, and Mother Earth. In 2008, Ecuador became the first state in the world to enshrine the rights of nature in its constitution, followed by Bolivia in 2010, which also passed its own historic Mother Earth law mandating a radical ecological transition of economy and society. Similar efforts to protect nature and ecosystems were then underway in substate communities across the globe. The nations in North America have also inscribed the rights of nature into their constitutions, including the Ho-Chunk Nation in Wisconsin, the Ponca Nation in Oklahoma, among others.

The Original Nation scholarship urges the establishment of global cooperation and "alliance-making" activities among the nation, peoples, grassroots environmental groups, and ecological conservation organizations, in order to secure and restore the rights of the nation, the land, ecosystems, and biodiversity. This book makes the strong claim that such intellectual and "on-the-ground" endeavors are desperately needed, and provides a theoretical tool designed to reconceptualize the existing cognitive perception with one that that places the nation and peoples, rather than the state, at the center of geopolitical analyses. Also proposed and examined are potential paths that could restore the dignity, freedom, and the rights to self-determination of the nation and peoples. The nation has persisted for hundreds, if not thousands, of years and has outlasted the state's predecessors, including powerful kingdoms, monarchies, oligarchies, and other predatory imperial entities. The Original

---

[41] Mazerolle-McGill (2020).
[42] Ibid.

Nation scholarship contends that the nation must persist in its contributions to the preservation of autonomy, nature, and life on earth, just as it has protected, nurtured, and embraced them for thousands of years.

2   OUTLINE OF CHAPTERS

To elucidate the basic tenets of the Original Nation scholarship, this book is structured as follows.[43] Chapter 2 provides a clear conceptualization of the nation and the state. The misuse and misrepresentation of these terms and related geopolitical concepts has gravely obscured, distorted, and misinterpreted issues of identity, geography, and history; reasons and causes related to wars and armed conflicts, regional tensions, refugee flows, genocide, and other acts of human rights violations; as well as issues related to rapidly degrading conditions of the nature and ecosystems. Terms such as the state, nation, nation-state, country, and republic and other varied geopolitical descriptions have been used interchangeably, despite the fact that their origins, geographies, histories, and relations to the rule of law are quite distinct and different. This chapter also explains why the neologism "Original Nation" is used in this book to delineate the nation, peoples, history, culture, identity, tradition, and memory, instead of the "Fourth World," a common and more accepted terminology that has been used in the analysis of geopolitical affairs. The neologism of the "Fourth World" was predicated on the scholarship of a three-tiered global system—the First, Second, and Third Worlds—arising from the state-centric, geopolitical model that the Original Nation scholarship criticizes, challenges, and tries to overcome.

Chapter 2 additionally presents the taxonomy of the nation and the state. The nation has been struggling to attain the right to self-determination in opposition to the oppressive state. However, some nations have recently been inspired to assert their independence without regard to the rights and welfare of other nations elsewhere. This self-serving political movement has been referred to as Original Nation Libertarianism (ONL) and has been seen in some prominent nations

---

[43] In the late 2010s, a new perspective rooted in the nation-centered scholarship emerged to explain the predatory practices of international law in relation to ethnocide and ecocide that resulted from the states' efforts to occupy, subordinate, and expropriate five thousand nations around the globe. Such a perspective came to be known as the Fourth World Approaches to International Law (FWAIL). See Fukurai (2018, p. 224).

in Europe that have sought independence from their respective states. And yet, these nations have continued to embrace the system of law that relies on neoliberal policies and persists in the exploitation of nations and peoples in the Global South for their own economic welfare and industrial progress. The Original Nation scholarship opposes such unilateral political movements by the nation, based on the self-centered aspiration for independence in pursuing Original Nation libertarian agendas.

Chapter 3 focuses on ongoing struggles of nations and peoples against the intrusion of states—such as state-sponsored terrorism and corporate exploitation—that have resulted in ethnocide and ecocide in the homeland of the nation and peoples. The U.S. government and intelligence communities had recognized as early as 1950 that the most imminent and pandemic crises of "nation-state conflicts," including an "indigenous nationalist revolution," would "arise in Asia."[44] Since then, major conflicts between the nation and the state have been largely concentrated in multiple regions of Asia, ranging from the central to the southeast, southern, and western regions, including the Middle East.

Today such conflicts continue to manifest in the struggles of the Moro and other Muslim communities in Mindanao, the Philippines; in Rakhine, Karen, Mon, Arakan and other substate autonomous communities in Myanmar; among Tibetans and Uighurs in the western region of the People's Republic of China (PRC); in hundreds of indigenous communities in more than 13,000 Indonesian islands, such as West Papua in New Guinea; in the principality of Kashmir at the cross-state border area of India, Pakistan, and China, and among Muslims of Assam in northeastern India; in Khalistan and Balochistan in multiple regions of India, Pakistan, and Iran in South Asia; in Kurdistan in the southwestern region of Asia; among the Ryukyuans (aka Okinawans) whose struggle for the right to self-governance continues in the southern-most island of Japan; and among others across various regions of Asia and beyond. These struggles stem from respective nations' resistance against states' denial of dignity, freedom, and the right to self-determination; the continuous usurpation and extraction of natural resources by industrial sectors protected and legitimized by the state's courts and government agencies; and the destruction of self-governing and self-sustaining culture and

---

[44] Central Intelligence Agency (1950).

biological diversity in the homeland of the nation in Asia and across the globe.

The analysis of the theoretical tenets of ONAIL is the focus of Chapter 4. It begins with a critique of the state's engagement in the simultaneous processes of "state-building" and "nation-destroying" projects, and the state's role in serving as a strong advocate for the promotion of international law, while also serving as an intermediary instrument of transnational corporations to violate the rights of nature and the nation that has been captured and occupied by the state within its delimited borders. It also critiques the predatory structures of international law, including the Investor State Dispute Settlement (ISDS) and supranational institutions of legal decision-making such as the International Center for Settlement of Investment Disputes (ICSID) of the World Bank in the U.S. and the Permanent Court of Arbitration in The Hague, the Netherlands, the rulings of which have commodified the environment and ecosystems as "property," prioritizing corporate profits over the rights and welfare of the nation, peoples, and nature; and the corporate practices of global clinical trials, involving "human experiments," to promote biopiracy and biocolonialism, which treat indigenous bodies and knowledge as a form of intellectual property rights owned and profited by multinational corporations. ONAIL's opposition to the military alliances used to promote ethnocide and ecocide is also explored, as the loss of cultural and biological diversity has been facilitated by a series of military incursions and acts of state violence against the nation and homeland. The state policy of pacifying the nation and peoples and eradicating their culture has been assisted by the Status of Forces Agreements (SOFA), which has been signed by states and international agencies, including the U.N. The presence of foreign armed personnel and military bases in the host state has led to the environmental destruction of cultural- and biodiversity of the nation in the host state.

Chapter 5 examines the nation's effort to attain legal recognition of the right to exist, flourish and be recognized under the existing system of international law. Currently international law does not recognize the nation in the same manner that it recognizes and legitimizes the state. In opposition to this, some nations have organized, strategized, and mobilized on the path toward formal recognition of the nation under international law. This chapter focuses on the recent actions of the Nation of Lakota in North America, which has declared their independence, and attempted to secede from the U.S. and obtain legal recognition from the international community of the right to self-determination. The "constitution-making" activity of the Lakota Nation, and other indigenous nations in North America and elsewhere, involves actions designed to incorporate the rights to self-determination into their constitutions. The legal strategies of the Lakota Nation and its newly declared "nation-state" known as the "Republic of Lakotah" are examined, including their efforts to nullify past treaties signed with the U.S. government, such as the 1851 and 1868 Fort Laramie treaties, both of which were ratified by the U.S. government. Also examined are the 1803 Louisiana Purchase Treaty (LPT), in which the Lakota Nation was a third-party beneficiary. The Nation of Lakota has long rejected the option to join the Union, arguing that Article III of the treaty guaranteed their sovereign status prior to the U.S. signing of the LPT treaty with the French state. This quest for sovereignty was augmented by the emancipatory doctrine of three international laws, including the 1960 U.N. Declaration on the Granting of Independence to Colonial Countries and Peoples; the 1969 Vienna Convention on the Law of Treaties (VCLT); and the 2007 U.N. Declaration of the Rights of Indigenous Peoples (UNDRIP). The chapter concludes with an exploration of the legal strategies of other nations seeking to create their own emancipatory constitutions, establish the right to self-determination, and create self-governing communities, including the Nation of Inuit in *Nunavut*, Canada; Ho-Chunk Nation in the states of Wisconsin, Nebraska, and Iowa, in the U.S.; West Papua in Indonesia; Iraqi Kurdistan in northern Iraq; and Catalonia in northern Spain, among others,

Chapter 6 explores ONAIL strategies employed to establish "the Rights of Nature" in law and to build a robust system of "Earth Jurisprudence" in order to prevent the further destruction of the environment and ecosystems. ONAIL contemplates the potential cultivation of close collaborations with the state's judicial and legislative forces, for while ONAIL proposes the eventual dissolution of coercive state structures, at this point the power of the state can be effectively instigated to deter predatory corporate actions and destructive state projects. In 2008, Ecuador became the first state to pass a constitutional amendment to establish the "Rights of Nature" in its constitution. In 2017, the Maori Nation in New Zealand used judicial activism to help establish robust jurisprudence to protect the rights of nature in their homeland. Other efforts to recognize the rights of nature and ecosystems have been proposed in multiple regions across the globe, including Nepal's proposal to incorporate "the Rights to Healthy Climate" into its constitution in order to alleviate climate change and its associated effects, such as the rapidly accelerating meltdown of Himalayan glaciers, leading to regional floods and mudslides; the adoption in 2017 of Mexico City's constitution to recognize the rights of nature; Colombia's recognition in 2019 of the Plata River as a "subject of rights" to exist and flourish on its own; Uganda's enactment of the 2019 National Environmental Act to establish the rights of nature and ecosystems, among many others. In these proliferating international efforts to institute the rights of nature in the state's legal system, the Philadelphia-based grassroots organization known as the Community Environmental Legal Defense Fund (CELDF) has played a prominent role, working with many indigenous nations and pro-nature governments to formulate constitutional amendments and legislative bills. CELDF also helped launch another powerful environmental organization, the Global Alliance for the Rights of Nature (GARN), which launched the International Rights of Nature Tribunal (IRNT) to adjudicate cases that resulted from the violation of the rights of nature across the world.

Chapter 7 shifts focus from the discussions of legal justifications for attaining sovereignty of the nation to the "on-the-ground" direct activism of the nation to organize and create an autonomous, self-governing community on their own. Such efforts have been organized as direct responses to the organized assaults of the state, the international corporate consortium, and the criminal cartels whose activities have been largely protected by the state and corporate interests. The political ideologies of direct action are derived from many sources: a multiple "cocktail" of such political philosophies as anarchism, participatory democracy, environmental justice, women's political activism, labor militancy, and other horizontal "bottom-up" philosophies that promote social–cultural, political, economic, and environmental transformations.

Similar to the origin of Spain's anarchist governments of Valencia, Aragon, Catalonia, and other self-governing communities in the 1930s, the rural poor of largely indigenous communities in southern Mexico began to engage in a bold experiment to create a new form of governance and to incorporate rights to self-determination based on the principles of direct action. They began to explore the creation of "another world" in establishing structures of law and culture that reflected and were directly responsive to the interests of the nation and people. One such group, dating back to 1994 in Mexico, is the Zapatista of the armed peasant communities, largely composed of indigenous Mayan people of the Tzeltal and Tzotzil Nations in the southern state of Chiapas;

another, dating back to 2011, is in the Municipio of Cherán in the heart of the P'urhépecha Nation in Michoacán, where indigenous people took over governmental functions and built a self-governing community. Following lengthy legal battles, the Mexican government finally recognized autonomous Cherán as a self-governing indigenous community.[45] The Zapatista has been effective in exploiting the international media and utilizing the internet cyberspace to help create global solidarity and alliances with indigenous communities, feminist organizations, environmental proponents, labor and trade unions, politically motivated grassroots organizations, and nucleated autonomous rural communities across the globe who have similarly adopted the strategies of "on-the-ground" direct action in establishing and maintaining their political autonomy and independence. The National Indigenous Congress of Mexico backed by the Zapatista has continued to explore the possibility of strong international alliance and collaboration with other nations, environmental organizations, indigenous communities, and political activists across the globe in order to facilitate much-needed nation- and people-centered, horizontal global political transformation.

The last section of Chapter 7 focuses on the direct judicial action of the nation to protect the rights of nature and the nation. Examined here is Argentina's recent adoption of the ancient jury model, "*Jury de Medietate Linguage* (Split Jury)" or "*Jurado Indigena* (Indigenous Jury)" in 2015. Prior to that, the state had overzealously prosecuted and criminalized hundreds of indigenous "land protectors" and sent them into prison. The affirmative jury model used in criminal trials, guaranteeing the inclusion of both indigenous members and women among its 12-members, has provided substantial fairness and justice for indigenous activists and their supporters who have fought against the corporate mining and extractive activities in the homeland. The last section also explores the possibilities for constructing a truly inter- "national" alliance among nations and their support organizations in order to resist the organized assault of the state and transnational corporations.

Chapter 8, the final chapter, studies the prospects for the further development of the Original Nation scholarship and explores the cognitive shift needed to develop a new paradigm for perceiving such fictitious entities

---

[45] Zabludovsky (2012) ("Cheran acquired a degree of autonomy from the Mexican government ... under a legal framework called 'uses and customs' that has been granted to some indigenous communities."); See also Espinosa (2015, p. 666).

as the state, corporations, and court-invented "corporate personalities." ONAIL proposes that this cognitive transformation related to perceptions of the state and the nation must be accompanied by a new robust rubric of the legal system, whose primary objective would be to protect the rights of the nation and nature through such prescient doctrines as those embedded in the UNDRIP and UDRME. Particular attention is given to: (1) the creation of an International Grand Jury (IGJ) to investigate allegations of human activities that have violated the rights of the nation and nature, and (2) the transformation of the International Rights of Nature Tribunal (IRNT) into an international jury court to adjudicate the charges filed by IGJ. Similar to Argentina's recent adoption of the affirmative jury model, it is also suggested that the panels of both the IGJ and the IRNT guarantee the expansive participation of jurors based on national identity and gender, so as to achieve broader inclusion of multiple voices, indigenous knowledge, varied perspectives, and lived experiences of the global community into the deliberative process. The final section offers suggestions for the further refinement of the Original Nation scholarship and reflects on its emancipatory vision for the construction of a self-sustaining and self-governing global community, one that properly acknowledges the importance of humanity's interconnectedness and interdependence in order to live in harmony with the natural world.

3   Conclusion

The state continues to target and commit violent acts against the nation throughout the world. Public discourses related to wars, armed violence, and human atrocities, however, have not included broader discussions of historical and enduring tensions between the nation and the state.[46] The Original Nation scholarship is proposed to offer a fundamentally differing interpretation of geography, history, politics, and the role of international law, one in which the identity of the nation is placed at the center of geopolitical analyses of global affairs. Rather than focusing on the state

---

[46] The term "the nation" is often conflated with the collective geopolitical entity of "the state" that exercises political control and sovereignty over a territorially delimited area. In the discussion by Ernest Gellner in the Warwick Debate on the issue of nationalism and its recent rise in Europe and the rest of the world, such a phenomenon should have been called the rise of "statism," not nationalism, so as to counter the myth of congruence between the two geopolitical entities of the state and the nation. See Fukurai (2019).

and international organizations, as traditional and mainstream analyses tend to do, the Original Nation scholarship adopts a "bottom-up" world view which includes the centrality of the nation and peoples in global affairs, regional conflicts, human struggles, and possible solutions.

In examining the history of the state—its origin, evolution, and development—it becomes clear that a great many states have either been broken up, or have broken down. The nation, in contrast, has persisted for many centuries. It may be safe to assume that the nation's ability to resist the state will outlast the state's efforts to oppress and destroy the aspirations and determination of the nation and peoples. The Original Nation scholarship hopes to provide a glimpse of the beginning of successful defiance by the nation, with its opposition to, and resilience in the face of, both the state-centric perspective embodied in analytic, academic, and scholarly orientations, and the specter of international law, which has served as a most powerful instrument of the "state-building" and "nation-destroying" projects that still continue to manifest in today's world.

Bibliography

Blum, William (2014) Killing Hope: U.S. Military and CIA Interventions Since World War II. London, UK: Zed Books.

Buchan, Bruce (2001) "Subjecting the Natives: Aborigines, Property and Possession Under Early Colonial Rule, 45 Social Analysis 143–162.

Canny, Nicholas (2012) "A Protestant or Catholic Atlantic World? Confessional Divisions and the Writing of Natural History," 181 Proceedings of the British Academy 83–121.

Central Intelligence Agency (1950) "CIA-RDP67, Review of the World Situation as it Relates to the Security of the United States," 16 January, available at https://www.cia.gov/library/readingroom/docs/CIA-RDP67-00059A000500100009-6.pdf.

Cheng, Sinkwan (2013) "Terrorism, Hegel, Honneth," 2 Las Torres de Lucca 47–67.

Churchill, Ward (2002) Struggle for the Land: Native North American Resistance to Genocide, Ecocide and Colonization. San Francisco, CA: City Lights Books.

Cohen, Felix S. (1953) "The Erosion of Indian Rights," Yale Law Journal 62: 348–390.

Dekdeken, Sarah K. Julius Caesar Daguitan and Abigail B. Anongos (2013) "Declaration: World Trade Organization (WTO) and Indigenous

People: Resisting Globalization, Asserting Self-Determination", available at https://www.wto.org/english/thewto_e/minist_e/mc9_e/indigenous_p eoples_declaration.pdf.

DeLoughrey, Elizabeth M. (2019) Allegories of the Anthropocene. Durham, NC: Duke University Press.

Derichs, Claudia & Andrea Fleschenberg (2010) Religious Fundamentalisms and Their Gendered Impacts in Asia. Berlin, Germany: Friedrich-Ebert-Stifung.

Dippie, Brian W. (2020)"American Indians: The Image of the Indian," National Humanity Center (accessed on 15 May 2020), available at https://nationalh umanitiescenter.org/tserve/nattrans/ntecoindian/essays/indimage.htm.

Dudley, J. P., & Woodford, M. H. (2002) "Bioweapons, Biodiversity, and Ecocide: Potential Effects of Biological Weapons on Biological Diversity," BioScience, 52(7): 583–592.

Espinosa, Nayeli E. Ramirez (2015) "Consulting the Indigenous Peoples in the Making of Laws in Mexico: The Zirahuen Ampara," Arizona Journal of International & Comparative Law 32: 647–670.

Fukurai, Hiroshi (2010) "People's Panels vs. Imperial Hegemony: Japan's Twin Lay Justice Systems and the Future of American Military Bases in Japan," Asian-Pacific Law & Policy Journal 12: 95–142.

Fukurai, Hiroshi (2018) "Fourth World Approaches to International Law (FWAIL) and Asia's Indigenous Struggles and Quests for Recognition under International Law," Asian Journal of Law and Society 5(1): 221–231.

Fukurai, Hiroshi (2019) "Original Nation Approaches to 'Inter-National' Law (ONAIL: Decoupling of the Nation and the State and the Search for New Legal Orders," Indiana Journal of Global Legal Studies 26: 199–261.

Garfield, Richard (2008) "The Epistemology of Law." In Barry S. Levy and Victor W. Sidel, eds., War and Public Health. Baltimore, MD: John Hopkins University Press, pp. 23–36.

Garfield, Seth (2001) Indigenous Struggle at the Heart of Brazil: State Policy, Frontier Expansion, and the Xavante Indians, 1937–1988. Durham, NC: Duke University Press.

Godelmann, Iker Reyes (2014) "The Zapatista Movement: The Fight for Indigenous Rights in Mexico," Australian Institute of International Affairs, 30 July.

Grey, Sam (2011) "Decolonisation as Peacemaking: Applying Just War Theory to the Canadian Context," International Journal of Critical Indigenous Studies 4(1): 21–29.

Griggs, Richard & Peter Hocknell (1995a) "Fourth World Faultlines and the Remaking of 'Inter-National' Boundaries," IBRU Boundary and Security Bulletin 3(3): 49–58.

Gussen, Benjamin Franklen (2017) "A Comparative Analysis of Constitutional Recognition of Aboriginal Peoples," 40 Melbourne University Law School 867–904.

Institute for the Study of Human Rights (2017) Indigenous people's Rights and Unreported Struggles: Conflict and Peace. NY: Columbia University.

Jensen, Derrick (2002) A Language Older than Words. White River Junction, VT: Chelsea Green Publishing.

Lang, Johannes (2010) "Questioning Dehumanization: Intersubjective Dimensions of Violence in the Nazi Concentration and Death Camps," Holocaust and Genocide Studies 24: 225–246.

Leitenberg, Milton (2006) "Deaths in Wars and Conflicts in the 20th Century," Cornell University Peace Studies Program Occasional Paper #29, available at https://www.clingendael.org/sites/default/files/pdfs/200 60800_cdsp_occ_leitenberg.pdf

Leonard, David L. (2002) "Extinct Birds by Errol Fuller: Hope is the Thing with Feathers: A Personal Chronicle of Vanished Birds by Christopher Cokinos," The Auk, 119: 574–577.

Lichatowich, J., L. Mobrand, & L. Lestelle (1999) "Depletion and Extinction of Pacific Salmon (Oncorhynchus spp.): A Different Perspective," 56(4): 467–472, available at https://doi.org/10.1006/jmsc.1999.0457

McCabe, Richard E., Henry M. Reeves, & Bart W. O'Gara (2010) Prairie Ghost: Pronghorn and human interaction in Early America. Boulder, CO: University Press of Colorado.

Manganyi, N. Chabani and Grahame Hayes, Garth Stevens, and N. Ndebele (2019) Being Black in the World. Johannesburg, South Africa: Wits University Press.

Mazerolle-McGill, Frederique (2020) "Indigenous People Bear The Brunt of Pollution," Futurity, 20, May.

Newcomb, Steven T. (2008) Pagans in the Promised Land: Decoding the Doctrine of Christian Discovery. Golden, CO: Fulcrum Publishing.

Nobel, Justin (2018) "The Rights of Nature Movement Goes on Trial," Rolling tone, 10, January.

Paige, Jeffrey M. (2020) Indigenous Revolution in Ecuador and Bolivia, 1990–2005. Tucson, AZ: University of Arizona press.

Parker, Jean (2009) "The History of the Communist Party's Support for Aboriginal Struggles," Solidarity, 21 April.

"Press Release, Dept. of Public Information, State of the World's Indigenous Peoples" (2010) U.N. Press Release DPI/2251, 14 January.

"Reaching Indigenous Youth With Reproductive Health Information and Services" (1999) In Focus, February, available at https://www2.pathfinder. org/pf/pubs/focus/IN%20FOCUS/Indigenous.htm.

Rifkin, Mark (2009) "Indigenizing Agamben: Rethinking Sovereignty in Light of the 'Peculiar' Status of Native People," 73 Cultural Critique 88–124.

Ryser, Rudolph C. (2012) Indigenous Nations and Modern States: The Political Emergence of Nations Challenging State Power. NY: Routledge.

Smith, David L. (2011) Less Than Human: Why We Demean, Enslave, and Exterminate Others. NY: St. Martin's Griffin.

Sulish, Clive (2017) "Bombing of Basque Town of Gernika Commemorated in Dublin," RebelBreeze, 2 May.

Suny, Ronald Grigor (2001) "Constructing Primordialism: Old Histories for New Nations," 73 Journal of Modern History 862–896.

Takaki, Ron (2008) A Difference Mirror: A History of Multicultural America. NY: Little, Brown and Company.

Starblanket, Tamara (2018) Suffer the Little Children: Genocide, Indigenous Nations and the Canadian State. Atlanta, GA: Clarity Press.

United Nations Declaration on the Rights of Indigenous Peoples (2007), available at https://www.un.org/esa/socdev/unpfii/documents/DRIPS_en.pdf.

United Nations Universal Declaration of the Rights of Mother Earth (2010), available at https://therightsofnature.org/universal-declaration/.

United Nations High Commissioner for Refugees (UNHCR) (2009) Global Trend: Refugees, Asylum-Seekers, Returnees, Internally Displaced ad Stateless Persons.

U.S. Declaration of Independence (1776), https://history.state.gov/milestones/1776-1783/declaration.

Valdmanis, Richard (2015) " Green Group's Unconventional Fight Against Fracking," Reuters, 28, June.

Vermeij, G. (1993) "Biogeography of Recently Extinct Marine Species: Implications for Conservation. Conservation Biology," 7(2): 391–397.

Ward, Brian (2018) "Socialism, Solidarity and the Indigenous Struggle," Socialist Worker, 12 September.

Watanabe, Toru & Chiho Watanabe (2019) Health in Ecological Perspectives in the Anthropocene. NY: Springer.

Watson, Irene (2018) Indigenous Peoples as Subjects of International Law: We Were Here First. NY: Routledge.

Watts, Jonathan (2017) "Battle for the Mother Land: Indigenous People of Colombia Fighting for Their Lands," Guardian, 28 October.

Williams, Dana M. (2017) Black Flags and Social Movements: A Sociological Analysis of Movement Anarchism. Manchester, UK: Manchester University Press.

Wyk, Gary van (2019) Our Anthropocene: Eco Crisis. NY: Center for Book Arts.

Zabludovsky, Karla (2012) "Reclaiming the Forests and the right to Feel Safe," NY Times, 3 August.

CHAPTER 2

The Nation and the State

The geopolitical analysis of global affairs has been burdened by the multiplicity of terminologies that have been used to represent varied forms and levels of political governance and geographical collective entities. Such terms as the state, nation, nation-state, city-state, state-nation, country, federation, republic, confederation, union, tribes, democracy, and other geopolitical formulations, have pre-empted discussion of the critical role that international law plays in relation to global politics, economic affairs, sovereignty, sustainability, war, and peace. Jeremy Bentham first coined the term "international law" to refer to a collection of rules, norms, and standards governing relations between states.[1] Prominent Danish legal scholar Alf Ross has defined international law as "the body of legal rules created by the common consent or mutual agreement of states,"[2] while the U.N. defines international law as "the legal responsibilities of States in their conduct with each other, and their treatment of individuals within State boundaries."[3]

---

[1] Janis (1984, p. 409) (Bentham "assumed international law was exclusively about the rights and obligations of states inter se and not about rights and obligation of individuals").

[2] Ross (2006, p. 21).

[3] United Nations Information Service (2020).

© The Author(s), under exclusive license to Springer Nature Switzerland AG 2021
H. Fukurai and R. Krooth, *Original Nation Approaches to Inter-National Law*,
https://doi.org/10.1007/978-3-030-59273-8_2

These definitions of international law exclude the use of such geopolitical entities as a nation, nation-state, or even state-nation, as well as other "collectivist" terminologies. The resulting confusion is exacerbated by the use of another misnomer, "inter-national" law, instead of "inter-state" law, referring to the system of law that binds the state, not "the nation," and its responsibilities and relations to other states and state-recognized institutions. The use of "nation" in place of "state" offers false assumptions that the state is somehow composed of people with a common culture, ethnicity, tradition, language, history, and memory. The conflation of the state and the nation is further manifested in the neologism of today's highest level of global management system, i.e., the United Nations, which is comprised of 193 "member states," not "member nations." Similarly, the League of Nations (LON), the U.N.'s precursor, was founded by a total of 44 "states." The appearance of "nation" in the official titles of such "state-centered" powerful organizations as the United Nations, the League of Nations, and such legal actors as "trans-national" corporations and "inter-national" institutions, has helped mitigate the violent history of the state against the original nation and people.

The first section of this chapter offers a clear conceptual differentiation of the nation and the state. Here, the "original nation," "indigenous nation," and the "nation" are used interchangeably in order to emphasize the notion that the nation has preexisted as the "original" community of people who shared a common tradition, culture, and territorially bound psychological bond and memory long before the advent of the state and its forceful imposition upon the original nation and peoples.[4] Similarly, the "state" and the "country" are used interchangeably, as the state tends to lack historically informed, and territorially rooted psychological commonality across multiple groups of populations who thus must be necessarily bound by law through the myriad of externally imposed lawful mechanisms and legal institutions. In other words, the state is, by definition, necessarily a legal construction, or in a legal term, a "legal fiction," and is maintained by force and violence justified by the "self-certified" and "self-serving" centralized government to serve their "national" interest.

---

[4] A "tribal nation" may also be used in the discussion of Native Indian nations in North America, as the indigenous nations have been referred as "tribes," "tribal communities," and "tribal confederation."

The differentiation of the nation and the state is crucial for understanding the Original Nation scholarship, for the nation has been the world's most enduring, persistent, and resilient organization of people and historically rooted community, thereby predating, and possibly outliving, the ephemeral lifecycle of the state, its generative laws, and predatory institutions.[5]

The second section of this chapter explains the use of the neologism "Original Nation" instead of the more commonly accepted term the "Fourth World" in international discourse involving indigenous nations and people. The "Fourth World" was first coined by North American indigenous activist George Manuel, used in reference to the collectives of indigenous societies that had been colonized and occupied through the waves of European imperial expansion in North America. The critique of the use of the "Fourth World" observes that it was a derivative of the three-tiered world system which relied on the analysis of global, geopolitical affairs from the "state-centric" perspective of the First, Second, and Third Worlds. This section also explains the importance of "nation-centered" rather "state-privileged" global analyzes.

1   THE NATION

The term *nation* refers to the culture-bound territory of a common people as well as the peoples themselves, not the political apex of the centralized government or its authoritarian bureaucracy. A nation is a cultural territory made up of the organic community of unconstrained, self-identifying individuals who are sufficiently conscious of their common ancestral value of history, tradition, ideology, language, religion, and memory, and who possess shared psychological bonds that are strongly attached to the historically interconnected, culture-bound territory and space.[6] In sharing this historical bond and deep-rooted mental affinity,

---

[5] Nietschmann (1994, p. 227).

[6] The nation has been defined by many scholars. See Knight (1983, p. 114), Nietschmann (1994), and Griggs and Hocknell (1995a, 1995b). For indigenous nations, see generally, Danver (2012, p. 749). For discussions of nation and nationalism in relation to state sovereignty, see Gottlieb (1993). For anthropological investigations of borders in relation to nation and state, see Wilson and Donnan (1998). For earlier works on the nation, nationalism, and nation-state in Europe, including definitions of nation by Abbe Sieyes, see Chiaramonte (2010, pp. 39–59). From the Frankfurt School perspective, Habermas, for example, defined the nation as a "political community shaped by common

nation peoples have held together on the basis of self-sustained tradition and self-reliant governance through ecologically adapted, centripetal cultures and economies, surviving ecological richness and variegated natural environments.[7] Today, 80% of all biodiversity that still remains on earth thrives in the 22% of global territories that are home to the original nations and peoples.[8] The original nation recognizes that the biodiversity does not belong to the state, who will only destroy it by industrial expansion and economic development in its "state-making" process and "state-building" project.

Since the state was largely formed by imposing itself upon unconsenting original nations and peoples, nation peoples who resisted the state encroachment have been referred to, and often vilified by the state, as rebels, landless peasants, tribal nationalists, clans people, savages, military insurgents, and communist terrorists, among many other demonized terms.[9] According to the most recent U.N. estimates, 370 million indigenous populations still exist in 5,000 culturally distinct nations, many of which also continue to practice a self-sustaining culture in a self-managed and self-governed society. The U.N. report also suggests that each of these nucleated nations may contain an average of approximately 70,000 people who intimately share a strong psychological bond and historically rooted, place-based self-sustaining culture.[10] The original nation recognizes that one of the best ways to protect, if not to possibly restore and revive, the Earth's remaining and surviving biological diversity is to

---

descent, or at least by a common language, culture, and history. A people becomes a 'nation' in this historical sense only in the concrete form of a particular form of life"). See Habermas (1999, p. 238).

[7] The U.N. Working Group on Indigenous Populations offered more generally accepted guidelines for defining the original nations and peoples, which this book largely follows. These working definitions included: (1) self-identification as indigenous peoples at the individual level and accepted by the community as their member; (2) historical continuity with pre-colonial and/or pre-settler societies; (3) strong link to territories and surrounding natural resources; (4) distinct social, economic, and political systems; (5) distinct language, culture, and beliefs; (6) non-dominant sector of society; and (7) resolve to maintain and reproduce their ancestral environments and systems as distinctive peoples and communities. See U.N. Department of Economic and Social Affairs (2004).

[8] U.N. Development Programme (2011, p. 54). See also Agarwal (2010).

[9] See also Chapter 1 for the multiplicity of vilified nomenclatures used against nation peoples and resisters.

[10] United Nations Permanent Forum on Indigenous Issues, Indigenous People, Indigenous Voices (2019).

support the original nation's rights, preserve their ancestral homeland, and ensure original nation's self-determination.

According to this definition, Japan is not considered a nation, despite hegemonic depictions of Japan in popular discourse or canonical historical literature.[11] Japan suffers from the continuing decline of self-sufficiency[12] and has never had culturally or ethnically homogeneous populations in its ever "shape-shifting" boundaries. The heterogeneity of Japan's populations and cultures spiked in the post-Meiji Restoration era, when Japan began to conquer, subjugate, and incorporate a multiplicity of culturally divergent and historically differentiated and colonized groups of communities—some indigenous and others "imported" as laborers into its homeland through forced annexation and colonization during Japan's imperial ventures in Asia and the Pacific in the late nineteenth and early twentieth centuries. Japan has also been a dynamic geopolitical entity that has shifted and changed its territorial boundaries on multiple occasions, each time encapsulating and incorporating multiplicities of nations and peoples into its imperial domain.[13] Japan's population today is made up of

---

[11] Burgess (1986), Laszlo (2002), Jandt (2012, p. 176), Yamamoto (2015), and Toyosaki and Eguchi (2017, p. 16).

[12] Japan also has one of the lowest food self-sufficiency rates among the developed countries. Further deteriorating its seed and food sovereignty, the Japanese government eliminated the "Main Crop Seeds Act" (hereinafter "the Seeds Act)" in 2018 to prohibit the traditional seed-saving custom by farmers and agricultural experimental stations managed by local governments, and decided to promulgate the so-called MONSANTO law to ensure the use of genetically modified seeds. The Seeds Act was originally created in 1952 to achieve food self-sufficiency by boosting the harvest of staple foods, including rice, wheat and soybeans. See "Abolition of Main Crops Seeds Law Puts Nation at Risk" (2018) and Yamada (2018).

[13] After the Meiji Restoration of 1868 reinstated imperial rule in Japan, the Japanese central government soon moved to annex the northeast island of Hokkaido that had been the homeland of the Ainu, who were the original inhabitants of Japanese islands and also lived in the Kurile Islands and Sakhalin in the Northern Sea of Okhotsk. In 1899, the Japanese government classified the Ainu "former aborigines," confiscated their lands, and declared them Japanese citizens in order to hasten their assimilation. The Japanese government also took over the southwestern islands of Ryukyu in the South China Sea, abolished the Ryukyu Kingdom, which had governed the region since the fifteenth century, claimed sovereignty, and established the Okinawa Prefecture in 1879. During this time, the people once called Ryukyuans became known as Okinawans, as the names Ryukyu and Okinawa have been used interchangeably. Japanese imperial ventures in East Asia continued, leading to the further annexation of the Kurile Islands in 1875; the Island of Formosa, today's Taiwan, as the homeland of Atayal and other indigenous communities in 1895; South Sakhalin with Russia's indigenous peoples of Evenki, Nivkhi,

distinct groups of multiple cultural and historical backgrounds, including indigenous populations of Ainu, *burakumin* (outcasts), Koreans, Chinese, Okinawans, and migrant workers from Indochina, Middle East, the Pacific, the Americas, and Africa, with each group continuing to maintain their tradition, identity, and distinct culture.[14] The Ainu, for instance, continue to engage in the revival of self-sustaining and self-reliant culture, native language, and ancestral tradition, with their intimate connections to multiple homelands, including Hokkaido, Japan's second largest northern island; Sakhalin island of the Russian Federation located to the north of Hokkaido; and other adjacent regions situated in the North Pacific Ocean. After many decades of grassroots activism by Ainu people and their supporters, the Japanese Diet was finally forced to recognize the Ainu as Japan's original native people by passing the Resolution Calling for the Recognition of the Ainu as an Indigenous People on June 6, 2008.[15]

Historically, the state has played a prominent role in shaping the discussion of national identity through the means of government recognition and criteria. Government definitions, however, do not necessarily reflect the experiences or understandings of nation, people, and history. The U.S. government, for instance, has devised its own policy regarding the use of the blood quantum to determine original nation identity. Today, while the nation may be free to devise their own rules in determining criteria for national identity and membership, approximately two-thirds of all federally recognized tribal nations have continued to rely on a blood quantum in their national membership criteria, with one-quarter blood degree being the most frequent minimum requirement.[16] The Office of Management and Budget (OMB) in the Executive Office of the President currently defines the identity of nations for American Indians or

---

and Uita in 1905; Korea, including the Korean kingdom and its domain in the Korean Peninsula in 1910; and Northern Mariana and South Pacific islands with indigenous inhabitants in 1918. The Japanese imperial government promoted forced migration of multiple groups to serve as members of Japanese military and to work in factories and mines in Japan and its colonies. Japan's WWII defeat in 1945 resulted in the loss of many of its newly acquired territories, leaving it only with the island of Hokkaido as part of Japanese national jurisdiction, while Okinawa was not reverted back to Japan until 1972. For detailed history of ethnic groups in Japan, see Weiner (2004).

[14] Danver (2012, p. 630).

[15] Winchester (2009).

[16] Garroutte (2001, p. 224).

Alaska Natives as follows: "a person having origins in any of the original people of North and South America (including Central America) and who maintains tribal nation affiliation or community attachment."[17] The U.S. Census Bureau has also required that, once American Indian or Alaska Native is chosen as a "racial" identity, the identity of the "enrolled or principal tribe" should also be provided.

Many Indian nations have criticized the use of governmental legal criteria in determining national identity, including the blood quantum and similar "eugenics codes" that have also been applied to Africans and their descendants. The blood quantum method, as used by the government, has been a double-edged sword in racial politics in the U.S. On one hand, it has historically ensured that any percentage of African blood automatically categorized an individual as black, thereby facilitating the system of perpetual enslavement and race-based segregation of all African descendants. Nazi Germany adopted the U.S. eugenics method to advance their political agendas in determining the identity of Jews and Jewish descendants, thus facilitating their extermination in the 1930s and 1940s. On the other hand, the continued use of blood quantum for the identity of American Indians could possibly lead to eliminating the significance of the tribal nation affiliation, as many generations of intermarriages and adoptions between Indian families and immigrant communities has led to the diminishing nature of Indian "blood." The nation's continued reliance on the blood quantum threshold will eventually guarantee the legal extinction of identity of the Indian nations, thereby undermining ultimate indigenous self-determination in North America.[18]

The U.N. estimates that nearly five thousand culturally distinct communities exist in the world, making up 15% of the world's poorest populations.[19] Another study has suggested that at least five thousand distinct nations exist in the world, spreading over nearly 95% of all states; many are partitioned, not properly counted in the official census, or forcefully integrated into respective state systems without their proper consent and thus remaining internationally unrecognized.[20] Political

---

[17] The U.S. Census Bureau (2010, p. 2).

[18] American Indian Movement (AIM) activist Ward Churchill once referred to the whole notion of blood quantum as "arithmetical genocide or statistical extermination." See Churchill (1994).

[19] United Nations (2010, p. 84).

[20] Nietschmann (1994).

geographers Richard Griggs and Peter Hocknell provide another estimate, noting that there are at least seven thousand nations that continue to endure as distinct political cultures within the boundaries of states.[21] Griggs adds that approximately 110 culturally and socially independent nations currently exist in Europe alone, many of which are not politically recognized by their own state government or by international organizations, including the U.N.[22] Currently, 160 countries in the world have multiethnic groups that make up at least 1% of the respective state population.[23] Many of them have been involved in resistance to the state, to preserve the territorial and political integrity of their nations and homelands.[24]

1.1   Taxonomy of the Nation

A multitude of nations exist in the world.[25] According to Nietchmann, the nations may be classified into the following groupings, depending upon the degree of their struggles, resistance to state domination, and historical opposition to coercive assimilation and accommodation policies of the state: (1) autonomous, self-governing nations that successfully resisted the state's forced cultural and territorial integration and whose autonomy is recognized by the state, such as Catalonia and Basque Country in Spain, Inuit in Canada, and Kuna Yala in Panama; (2) semi-autonomous nations that achieved a partial or limited political recognition of autonomy by the state, such as Saamiland in northern Europe and Yapti Tasba in Nicaragua; (3) revival nations whose desire for autonomy and political recognition has recently spiked, such as Scotland and Wales in the U.K.; and (4) phantom nations, i.e., nations whose desire for national independence was largely supported by diasporic populations and their organized activity, such as the island of Diego Garcia of the Chagos Archipelago in the Indian Ocean, and yet where almost all inhabitants of the island were forcefully removed to the U.K. and neighboring islands,

---

[21] See Griggs and Hocknell (1995b, p. 59).

[22] Griggs (1992).

[23] Fearon (2003, p. 195).

[24] Ibid.

[25] Nietschmann (1994, p. 233).

in order for the U.S. and U.K. to build military bases, highly advanced communication facilities and naval and airbase installations.[26]

Other groups of the original nation include: (5) hegemonic nations, i.e., nations whose sociopolitical and cultural domination began to hegemonize the formation of the "idealized" state, such as England in the U.K., Russia in the U.S.S.R., Castile in Spain, Java in Indonesia, and Han in China; (6) "irredentist" nations, in which part of hegemonic nations lost to other states by treaty, political claim, war, or powerful annexation, such as Northern Ireland in the U.K., South Tyrol in Italy,[27] Okinawa in Japan, and Karelia in Russia; (7) independent nations that endured the history of state occupation but won political independence, such as Latvia, Estonia, Lithuania, and many former Soviet republics; Eritrea in East Africa; and the Federation of Micronesia in the Western Pacific; (8) "shattered" nations that were partitioned into, and occupied by, two or more multiple states, which hindered the potentiality of political mobilization and territorial integration, such as Kurdistan in Southwestern Asia and Kashmir and Pashtun in South Asia; (9) militarily occupied nations, such as the Miskito Nation in Honduras, the Sahrawi Nation in northwest Africa, and Palestine in the Middle East; and (10) armed resistance nations, such as the Karin against Myanmar, the West Papua against Indonesia, the Moro against the Philippines, and many other nations in the Southwestern region of Asia.[28]

Another grouping of nations includes: (11) integrated nations with no internal or external sovereignty, participation, or sharing in political instruments of the state, and with full economic dependency, such as Kalaallit Nuaat in Greenland in the Arctic and North Atlantic Ocean; (12) associated nations that have exercised inherent powers of government with full internal sovereignty, such as the Lummi in western Washington State in the U.S.[29]; and, lastly, (13) internally colonized nations, including the majority of indigenous tribal nations in the Americas, and other distinct, yet politically unrecognized, nations and culturally distinct nucleated communities in Southeast Asia, South Asia, Africa, and many

---

[26] Evers and Kooy (2011).

[27] South Tyrol in Austria was taken by Italy following Austria's loss in the First World War. See Steininger (2003)

[28] Griggs and Hocknell (1995a, 1995b). See also Nietschmann (1994, p. 233).

[29] Seton (1999).

remote regions across the globe.[30] Some of these classifications or group-ings of nations may change or overlap, due to ever-shifting geopolitical conditions resulting from their struggles, state responses to conflicts, and policy changes of the state regarding the nation within its borders.

The Nation of Lakota in the U.S., one of the internally colonized nations in North America, declared national independence in 2007, immediately after the U.N. Declaration of the Rights of Indigenous Peoples (UNDRIP) was adopted on September 13, 2007. The Lakota Nation also declared that it would secede its national territory from the U.S. on the basis of the 1868 Treaty of Fort Laramie that the Lakota Nation had signed with the U.S. government, which had officially ratified the compact in 1869.[31] The Lakota Nation has been subjected to the greater settler-state colonial policy of the U.S. government ever since the U.S. signed the Louisiana Purchase Treaty with France on April 30, 1803, thereby forcefully encapsulating the Nation of Lakota within its state-claimed territory.[32] The Louisiana Territory included 84 million acres of lands that extended to the Mississippi River in the east, the Rocky Mountains in the west, the Gulf of Mexico in the south, and the Cana-dian border in the north.[33] As of today, neither the U.N. nor any of its member states has recognized the Lakota Nation as an independent and sovereign nation.

In 2017, the West Papua Nation in Indonesia, one of 250 Melane-sian nations in Southeast Asia and the Pacific, also submitted the petition for national independence to former Chilean President Michelle Bachelet, head of the Office of the U.N. High Commissioner for Human Rights (OHCHR), calling for West Papua to be put on the U.N. Decolonization Committee agenda. West Papua had been colonized by the Netherlands and was forcefully integrated into Indonesia in 1963. The brutal suppres-sion of the West Papuan nationalist movement led to a petition with 1.8 million signatures that was smuggled out of the island of New Guinea, the second largest island in the world, and delivered to the OHCHR.[34] The

[30] For many culturally distinct nations in Southeast Asia, see Scott (2010).

[31] Treaty of Fort Laramie (1868), Art. 1.

[32] For stateless nations and their aspiration for independence, see Minahan (2016).

[33] Rodriguez (2002).

[34] Doherty and Lamb (2017a, 2017b).

U.N. Decolonization Committee, however, refused to consider its peti-tion for independence.[35] These internally colonized nations continue to struggle for independence and the rights to self-determination around the world. The historical genealogy of struggles and potential paths toward independence are critically examined in later chapters; with Chapter 3 focusing on the West Papua Nation, and Chapter 5 on the Nation of Lakota.

Another taxonomy of the nation is informed by the historic formation of the fluid, nomadic communities of peoples who still continue to flee from and evade the state and its "state-building" and "nation-destroying" project. These culturally distinct nations and nucleated communities include so-called "hill tribes" of Southeast Asia across Himalayan trans-state corridors; communities in an upland, remote zone of West Africa, which remained "unmolested" by centuries-long slave-raiding and human trafficking; and multiple regions of Latin American highlands and rain forests.[36] Large collectives of state-less groups of peoples, who inhabited water regions, including "oceans," for centuries, such as Malays, Illanu, Bugis, Bajau, and other Austronesian peoples in Southeast Asia, have also fought and evaded the project of the state's colonial-encapsulation.[37] Mesopotamian marshlands and wetland areas in southern Iraq, south-western Iran, and Kuwait have been the homeland for culturally distinct indigenous Marsh Arabs for the last several thousand years.[38] In retal-iation for their opposition to the state and its efforts to develop their territories, the Iraqi government has engaged in efforts to drain the marshes. These activities increased during Saddam Hussein's presidency and lasted until the time of his fall in 2003.[39]

The taxonomy of the historical origin of the nation across the globe shows that the majority of territories of continents, major and small islands, and coastal waters and oceans have long been inhabited and claimed by original nations and peoples, and that the vast majority of these originated and persisted long before the invention of, and the forceful

---

[35] Ibid. See also Kluge (2020).

[36] Ibid. See also Scott (2010).

[37] Sopher (1965) and Langenheim (2010).

[38] Stevens (2007).

[39] Ibid.

invasion by, the state. This suggests that nations had in fact laid the original building blocks and socio-political foundations for the modern state that later emerged into dominance.

1.2   Original Nation Libertarianism (ONL) in Europe

The overwhelming majority of the people of the nations have long protected and respected the rights of nature and ecosystems by preserving the principles of self-sustaining tradition, self-reliant culture, and self-governance. They have also held the world view that humans were neither independent of, nor superior to, the nature and environment, but were instead an integral part of the larger natural world and ecosystems. The nation has fought against globalized neoliberal assaults by protecting their homeland from the state-assisted, ecologically unsustainable corporate projects across the globe. Recently, original nations in multiple states with highly developed economies and advanced industrial production began to assert their desire to liberate themselves from their respective states, after they had allowed the destruction and eradication of their own natural ecosystems. As a result, these states continue to engage in globalized, state-assisted neoliberal programs in order to exploit, usurp, and destroy the nature and environment of the ancestral homeland of other nations and peoples elsewhere.

In identifying different groups of original nations, another important means of classification is to demarcate whether or not the nation has committed itself to building a self-sustainable community by asserting the following two important sociocultural precepts: (1) to protect the rights of nature, environment, and ecosystems of the original nation in such a way that the nation will not depend on the exploitation, usurpation, and destruction of the ecosystems of other nations elsewhere, and (2) to respect the rights to self-governance and self-rule, and to protect nation peoples under liberal principles of equality and autonomy, without interference of the predatory state and its autocratic institutions and invasive projects. The respect for the rights of nature recognizes that "human activities and development must not interfere with the ability of ecosystems ... to thrive and evolve, and requires that those responsible for destruction ... be held fully accountable."[40] The rights of

---

[40] Movement Rights, Rights of Nature and Mother Earth: Rights-Based Law for Systemic Change (2017, p. 3).

nature also presuppose the preservation of fundamental human rights and non-human rights, as human beings remain an integral part of the nature and ecosystems. The respect for nature's rights further benefits the preservation of human rights because the destruction of the nature and ecosystems, i.e., Anthropogenic activities and the resultant effects of climate change, global warming, sea-level rising, deforestation, and other man-made environmental catastrophes, threatens the enjoyment of a wide range of human rights, including the rights to life, water and sanitation, health, food, education, culture, housing, and self-determination.[41]

Today, nations' struggle for independence and freedom continues across the globe. The nation's unilateral political aspiration for independence without regard to other nations' rights to self-governance, self-sustaining cultures, and the ecological health of the environment is referred as Original Nation Libertarianism (ONL). The ONL is dominated by new nation cultures and peoples characterized by dense and large populations, environmentally unsustainable centrifugal economies, biological impoverishment and depletion, and often, razed landscapes and battered scopes of nature. The nation that pursues the Original Nation Libertarian agenda thus relegates other original nations to the status of external "resource colonies" that supply them necessary natural resources and cheap labor because its own economy, ecosystems, and biological diversity are no longer able to sustain its own population, economy, and socio-political system. Many internally colonized nations across the globe, regardless of whether they were trapped in advanced Western states or less-developed countries in the Global South, can thus be targeted by ONL nations for further exploitation, usurpation, and destruction.

In recent years, Catalonia, Scotland, Northern Ireland, and other "autonomous" and "revival" nations in Europe have begun to seek the path of independence and national freedom from respective state systems. Other European nations also emerged with the strong development of nationalism and strong separatist movements, including Brittany in northwestern France[42]; Flanders in the borders of Belgium, France,

---

[41] Bachelet (2019).

[42] Pellan (2013), and Tran (2014), and Pereltsvaig (2015).

and the Netherlands[43]; and Bavaria in southeastern Germany[44] among many others.[45] However, these European nations have failed to practice or follow the tradition of the self-sustaining culture or to establish self-reliant economies. The national territory of these European nations had already suffered from the long history of destructive deforestation, large-scale depletion of fertile soil and freshwater, destruction of wildlife and fisheries, and significant reduction of genetic-biological diversity. Having failed to develop their own self-reliant economic system and self-sustaining culture, these nations have followed the ideology of centrifugal economic expansion to fuel their unchecked growth by relying on, and often actively participating in, the state-assisted colonial project to further exploit "natural resources," biological diversity and mineral wealth of the original nation in Africa, Asia, and the Americas.[46]

There was once an exception in Europe, however. In the 1930s, Catalonia and other sub-autonomous regions in Spain had attempted to construct a society of anarchistic self-sufficiency and "quasi-autarkic" political systems. This prescient anarchist vision, however, was violently crushed during the Spanish Civil War lasting from 1936 to 1939. A collaborative network of powerful imperial states, including the fascist autocracy of Adolf Hitler's Nazi Germany and Benito Mussolini's Italian National Fascist Party, as well as the direct and indirect intervention of the U.S. and Soviet governments, joined in support of dismantling the anarchist nation pursued by the Second Spanish Republic.[47] While these super-states had deep conflicts over their differing political philosophies and economic pursuits, they were united in their belief that the free,

---

[43] Stares (2009), Galinda (2019), and Moens (2020).

[44] Breitenbach (2014), "One in Three Bavarians Want Independence from Germany, Poll Shows" (2017), and Shen (2017)

[45] Similar separatist movements in Europe included Wales and Cornwell in the U.K.; Galicia, Aragon, and the Basque region in Spain; Silesia in Poland; Corsica in France; Faroe Islands in Denmark; Frisia in the borders of the Netherlands and Germany; Sardinia, South Tyrol and Veneto in Italy; Occitania, Alsace and Savoy in France; and Aland in Finland. See McGrath (2014) and Noack (2014).

[46] For instance, on Scottish participation in the colonization of the Americas, see Klieforth and Munro (2004), Landsman (2014), and Murdoch (2009). For the Irish colonization of the Americas, see McGee (1855), Ford (1915), O'Grady (1935), Miller (1976), Dobson (1997), Horning (2013), and Dunleavy (2019).

[47] Orwell (1938) and Preston (2007). For detailed analyses of the U.S. and Soviet interventions, see generally Chomsky (2013)

independent and self-governing, anarcho-syndicalist nation should not succeed in this effort to assert national sovereignty. These powerful states feared that the establishment of a successful independent anarchist nation in Europe could become an idealized model of national freedom elsewhere. The success of the Second Spanish Republic could have possibly suggested the contour of emancipatory paths toward attaining independence and the rights to self-determination to other struggling nations and nucleated communities across Africa, Asia, and the Americas.[48]

Historically, the culture and religion of many nations in Europe have demonized original nations and peoples outside the European continent and regions as "barbarous nations [to] be overthrown and brought to the [Catholic] faith itself."[49] These ideological perspectives gave some powerful European nations that later morphed into dominant states the moral rights and religious justifications to conquest, convert, evangelize, and ultimately "subjugate" non-European nations and peoples into their Christianized traditions.[50] With a few exceptions, these European states moved on to indoctrinate other original nations and peoples, working to instill in them a world view that saw nature and the environment as legalized "property" that could be transformed into "natural resources" to be privatized, exploited, and destroyed.

Today, many of these European nations seeking independence have also actively participated in European states' neoliberal policies and globalization projects across all areas of the world. The utilitarian notion of "human resources," similarly to "natural resources," had also hegemonized their culture by transforming people of other nations into "private property," exploiting them as chattel slaves, "factory girls,"[51] and wage slaves in order to maximize profit for the European nation, the state and corporate oligarchs.

It is important to recognize that some European nations have attempted to deviate from the Original Nation Libertarianism in order to explore new ecological policies of their own, in efforts to engage in the conservation and sustainable use of their biocultural diversity. Catalonia, for instance, has adopted the framework of the principles of

---

[48] Ibid.

[49] Phan and Ray (2014, p. 29).

[50] Ibid.

[51] Tsurumi (1990). See also Chomsky (1996, p. 85).

the 1993 U.N. Convention on Biological Diversity (CBD) in Rio de Janeiro, Brazil and the 2010 U.N. Biodiversity Summit held in Nagoya, Japan.[52] Basque Country in Spain has also followed Catalonia's example by adopting a program to conserve and sustain their own biodiversity in northern Spain.[53] Catalonia and Basque had been two strongholds of anarchist soldiers and supporters of the Second Spanish Republic during the Spanish Civil War, and the anarchist tradition and culture of self-governance still ran deep in their ideology and society. Scottish Canals in Great Britain, the public corporation of the Scottish national government which manages its waterways, also announced implementation of a biodiversity strategy, in 2015, declaring that "[H]uman societies and economies are fundamentally dependent on biodiversity for ... food provision, clean air, water and healthy soil and cultural aspiration."[54]

The adoption of CBD and its progeny in Europe, however, has been strongly criticized on the ground that these "ecological justice" legalities helped codify the dominant neoliberal narrative of nature as capital for profit maximization; reified biological diversity as generic material for exchange in a global market; and unfairly endowed the state with exclusive power and sovereign rights to determine access to biodiversity in its delimited territory.[55] Consequently, the CBD and protocols have failed to conserve biological diversity for sustainable use in Europe. In Catalonia in Spain, for instance, despite the long history of anarcho-syndicalist movements and the emphasis on self-governance, newly instituted policies of

---

[52] Generalitat de Catalunya (2012). The key objectives of the CBD and other protocols were to develop robust strategies for the conservation and sustainable use of biodiversity; establish Prior Informed Consent (PIC) of the party providing genetic resources and indigenous knowledge; share benefits arising from the use of genetic resources; and report the efforts to implement treaty commitment. See also Prestre (2003); Rosendal (2013). The limitations of the convention and protocols were known, including: (1) insufficient human and financial resources; lack of available environmental data; (3) weak institutional structures and lack of adequate intersectoral coordination; (4) inadequate resources to review and monitor impact assessment decisions; and (5) lack of meaningful public and stakeholder participation in planning and management. See Convention on Biological Diversity (2007).

[53] Biodiversity Strategy of the Basque Autonomous Community (2019).

[54] "09-Biodiversity Management" (2015).

[55] Sullivan (2005, 2006, 2009), Swanson (1999), Moran et al. (2001), Igoe and Brockington (2007), Brockington et al. (2008), Dressler and Buscher (2008), Brockington and Duffy (2010), MacDonald (2010a, 2010b), Arsel and Buscher (2012), Buscher (2012), Buscher et al. (2012), Roth and Dressler (2012), Death (2014), and Sjostedt (2020).

neoliberal biodiversity governance have enhanced the active participation of state and business sectors and legitimized the reframing of nature conservation as a profitable neoliberal business agenda.[56] Europe's failure of biodiversity conservation strategies has also been reported elsewhere,[57] and much effort is needed by European nations to create self-sustainable cultures, a reliable economy, and autonomous local communities. The Original Nation scholarship opposes Original Nation Libertarianism in Europe and self-proclaimed independent and unilateral emancipatory movements of European nations, who, for their survival, continued to rely on the predatory policies of state-supported neoliberal programs in the Global South in order together to usurp, exploit, and ultimately destroy the biological diversity and ecological health of the original nations elsewhere.

2   THE STATE

The "state" is distinctly different from the "nation." In its historical and territorial structure and single monolithic identity, the state is largely an outward manifestation of European kingdoms and regional power centers, mainly through overseas colonial and imperial ventures, forceful expansion, or the disintegration of large colonial empires into smaller pieces of neocolonial independent polity.[58] The birth of the state involves the dense history of colonialism and imperialism projected upon the multiplicity of nonconsenting nations across the globe. Unlike in the nation, there is little shared thread of cultural, historical, and traditional commonality to bind together the resulting multiplicity of "strangers," including fragmented, if not decimated, nations and peoples. As a result, the state is, by definition, a legal construction, or a "legal fiction," in which people are coercively held together by a forced network of legal mechanisms and authoritarian institutions bound in the imaginative collective community of the state.

---

[56] Maestre-Andres et al. (2018)

[57] Palacin and Alonso (2018), Huisman (2019), Lazard (2020), and Niranjan (2020).

[58] See, Nietschmann (1994) (provides an overview of idea of state vs. nation and growing dissonance); Griggs and Hocknell (1995a) (paints a picture of nation-state warring in Southeast Asia in a vision of Indonesia and Pilipino warfare). Spanish historian Bruno Aguilera-Barchet argue that the Greek Polis was the original precursor to the modern state in Europe, see Aguilera-Barchet (2013).

No nation and people have voluntarily given up their own territories, resources, languages, cultures, identities, or ultimately, sovereignty. The state has imposed itself upon the original nation by force and violence, acting as an "imaginary" geopolitical entity through war, colonial occupation, and genocide, in combination with heavy state propaganda efforts to perpetrate, manufacture, and legitimize its "fictitious existence" in relation to the nonconsenting, recalcitrant nations and peoples.[59] Other state-centric international organizations and actors, including the U.N., supranational unions, and even multinational corporations, are also a "legal fiction," i.e., powerful imaginary collectivist entities that gained their legitimacy and power by the international legal norms, mechanisms and institutions that the state had invented, supported, and maintained.[60]

The state lacks historically informed and territorially entrenched bonds and psychological commonality across multiple groups of its populations. As a result, the security and cohesiveness of a state is almost always maintained by legalized coercive force, and its centralized government must be justified through self-certifying political-judicial institutions and self-justifying legal pronouncements. In protecting and preserving its "imagined" sovereignty, the state's delineated borders and boundaries must also be militarily patrolled and secured by its centralized government and authoritarian bureaucracy.

The state is also a centralized political system that often demands a dedicated loyalty to a single dominant linguistic system, one economy, one currency, and typically one dominant religion. As part of the effort to create hegemonic propagandas to unite people and maintain its imaginative collectivist entity, the state creates new scripts of history, geography, map, and memory. The state also actively manufactures and

---

[59] Nock (1935, pp. 23–24). Nock uses Franz Oppenheimer's definition of the state as an institution "forced on a defeated group by a conquering group with a view only to systematizing the domination of the conquered by the conquerors and safeguarding itself against insurrection from within and attack from without. This domination had no other final purpose than the economic exploitation of the conquered group by the victorious group." See also Anderson (1983). Anderson devised the term "imagined communities" in analyzing the rise of "nationalism." Anderson's analysis also failed to decouple the geopolitical entities of the state and the nation. Relying on the definition of the state and the nation used in our analysis, the state may also be referred to as a geopolitical territorial entity with "imagined sovereignty and independence" rooted in the notion of "statism," not "nationalism."

[60] For the state and corporations as fictitious collectivist entities, see Harari (2020)

promotes cognitive illusions to justify that its birth, history, expansion, growth, construction, and its whole "artificial" existence have preexisted, predated, precluded, and, most importantly, prevented all nations' historical claims to the territory, culture, tradition, and rights to control their own ancestral homelands, resources, nationhood, livelihood, ecosystems, and knowledge of the lands. The state simultaneously attempts to eradicate the ancient histories, traditions, cultures, identities, languages, memories, knowledge, and geographies of nations and peoples they occupy; to invent new perceptual and cognitive symbols, identities, and neologisms for new state and nation peoples; to create new geographies, landscapes, and maps; and to invent new state-centric histories, traditions, cultures, and patriotic narratives. These new "self-serving" scripts and imaginations, along with such new common symbols, songs, and pictographs as a flag, national anthem, patriotic logos, and historical memories are introduced at educational institutions and disseminated by the mass media to create the necessary illusion that the nations are under state authority and people are indeed living under the one-state governmental system. Most states assert that people live in a single "nation" with a single common people who share the same history, as has been falsely "storied" in the cultural commonality and ethnic homogeneity imposed by the state's central government and educational institutions.[61]

The state also consciously conflates the meaning of nation in referring to its history and culture, thereby classifying and marginalizing the nation and people who resist the state indoctrination into a newly invented class of people with a vilified identity and degrading status. They have often been classified and morphed into ethnic people, religious minorities, poor *campesinos*, tribesmen, peasants, agriculturalists, indigenists, socialists, communists, anarchists, or even terrorists, rebels, insurgents, and radical separatists, especially if they take up arms against the state intrusion or occupation. Nowhere are states depicted as recent inventions whose authority derives from brute force, necessary illusion, and the hegemonic system of indoctrination and propaganda.

Despite the fact that most of the world's wars, including today's armed struggles, low-intensity warfare operations, targeted assassination programs, hybrid wars, and anti-terrorist drone campaigns, have resulted in the production of tens of millions of displaced populations, including

---

[61] See Horne (2014) (explaining how the script created by the newly independent state transformed the true history of the experience of African slaves in the U.S.).

nation-less and state-less refugees and asylum seekers, these atrocities and human suffering generally do not come under international laws, treaties, declarations, conventions, covenants, or agreements, unless scrutinized and exposed by investigative journalists, whistle-blowers, indigenous activists, and international human rights organizers and institutions.

The extraction and destruction of biological diversity is one of the salient features of the state and its "state-building" project. The "legal fiction" of the state largely began with a government without resources or environments of its own; it was the array of the preexisting original nations that possessed the land, forests, fresh water, fertile soil, species, genes, and ecosystems. Following the "state-building" ideology of centrifugal economic and territorial expansion to fuel its unchecked growth and development, the state utilized environmentally unsustainable projects and resource-destroying methods, often coupled with military invasions and armed repression, to extract the biological diversity, environmental wealth, and natural resources from the territories of the original nation and peoples. Among the so-called "Seventeen Megadiverse States" in the world that currently possess more than 70% of the planet's terrestrial biological diversity, the largest proportions of biodiversity were found in the homelands and territories of the original nations in these megadiverse states.[62] These states exercised their unilateral power to determine how best to use and exploit biodiversity for expansion and development, while relegating the original nation and peoples to the status of sub-state, ethnic minorities who may be solicited for tertiary opinions or assistance; however, nation peoples possessed no legally binding authority to alter the state decision.

Today, the state has largely succeeded in establishing legal rights, political authority, and economic hegemony over and above the interests of nations and peoples. International law became a hegemonized set of legal rules, lawful norms, and standards that apply between the states and the international institutions that they created and maintained,

---

[62] These countries include: Australia, Brazil, China, Colombia, Ecuador, the United States, Philippines, India, Indonesia, Madagascar, Malaysia, Mexico, Papua New Guinea, Peru, Democratic Republic of Congo, South Africa, and Venezuela. For the state's exploitation of biological diversity, see Lindenmayer et al. (2008), Pariona (2018), and Keong (2020). In the U.S., while the Indian nations have been confined to the reserved territories and remote Indian lands, they still contain as much as 50% of potential uranium reserves, nearly 30% of coal reserves, and up to 20% of known natural gas and oil reserves. See "Native American Lands and Natural Resource Development" (2011).

such as the World Bank (WB), International Monetary Fund (IMF), and World Trade Organization (WTO). While the state and internationally recognized organizations are primary architects of the multitude of international laws, the nation, with its rights, rules, and often its constitution, remains unrecognized under such law. Thus, the common terminology of "international" law should be replaced with the term "inter-state'" law, as the system of legal doctrine only recognizes the state and its progenies, not the nation. Similarly, the title of the U.N. should be replaced with the neologism the "U.S." as it principally recognizes and is composed of member states rather than "member nations." The common usage of such terms as international law, the United Nations, or even transnational corporations in legal discourse, academia, scholarship, and the mass media serves to obfuscate the distinction between the state and the nation, to effectively hide the colonial history and predatory policies and projects of states and international organizations against nations, to perpetuate the false history of the state as based on the common "national" origin, and to maintain the vilification of already oppressed and marginalized nations and peoples.

Lastly, it is important to revisit and recognize the ephemeral character of the life cycle of the state, which becomes apparent in an examination of the historical genealogy of many states that have experienced periods of breakdown and breakup in the past. In 1919, only forty-four states existed globally and they became member states of the first global management system called the League of Nations. The number grew to fifty-one by 1945 at the end of World War II.[63] By 2020, the total had reached 193, with many of these states largely originating in the breakdown of previous European colonial empires in Africa, South and Southeast Asia, the Pacific, and the Caribbean. Another group of states was also born from the breakup of "mega-states" or such "super-states" as the Soviet Union, Yugoslavia, Czechoslovakia, Ethiopia, and Sudan. The state system has been extremely fragile over time, and is necessarily held together by laws, brute force, and state propaganda, while its system of government continues to impose itself on the multiplicity of nonconsenting nations and associated peoples within its delimited border.

---

[63] See Grimal (2013, p. 21).

2.1   Taxonomy of the State

The state is a legally constructed imaginary community and does not embody a physical, objective reality.[64] The 1933 Montevideo Convention on the Rights and Duties of States, which was organized by the representatives of twenty states in the Western Hemisphere, including the U.S., laid out the major legal criteria to establish the statehood. The convention also served to set legal parameters on the definition of the state by equating it with the status of person, i.e., "legal personhood," thereby embracing the status of a natural person endowed with the entitlement to rights, privileges, protections, responsibilities, and legal liability.[65] Article 2 of the convention stipulated that the state "shall constitute a sole person in the eyes of international law."[66] Article 6 asserted that the state "signifies ... [and] accepts the personality of the other with all the rights and duties determined by international law."[67] In defining the state "as a person of international law,"[68] the convention also provided the following four qualifications of the state, including: (1) a permanent population; (2) a defined territory; (3) government; and (4) capacity to enter into relations with other states.[69]

These four criteria applied equally to the qualification of nationhood. For example, many indigenous nations in North America held the tribal membership, lived in the ancestral homeland for centuries, and maintained their tribal government with courts and legislative branches, with some nations having their own constitutions. The indigenous nations in North America had also signed treaties with the U.S. government, nearly 400 of which had been ratified by the U.S. government. The 1933 convention, however, failed to recognize the rights of nation and other semi-autonomous communities "within the limits of national territory."[70] Since the state's jurisdiction "applies to all the inhabitants,"[71]

---

[64] Anderson (1983).

[65] The Montevideo Convention (1933), Art 4.

[66] Art. 2.

[67] Art. 6.

[68] Art. 1.

[69] Ibid.

[70] Art. 9.

[71] Ibid.

Article 9 stipulated that "[N]ationals and foreigners are [equally placed] under the same protection of the law and national authorities," [72] and "foreigners may not claim rights other or more extensive than those of the nationals."[73]

Furthermore, the state, which is endowed with the hierarchical power of the centralized government, has the prerogative to assert internal sovereignty over all of its population, regardless of the nationality of its subjects. The state has the power to reign with external sovereignty, including military security over a spatially delimited, state territory. Using the convention's definitions of the state, Russia became the largest state, with over 6.6 million square miles, covering nine different time zones and sharing borders with fourteen neighboring states. Vatican City became the smallest state, with 0.2 square miles, landlocked by the state of Italy. China exercised the largest internal sovereignty, over a population of 1.4 billion, followed by India with 1.3 billion. Vatican City had a populace of only 800, the smallest state in the world.[74]

Variants of the state size and government structure also emerged, due largely to the distinct histories of "state-building" projects, the density of European imperial ventures and colonial projections, as well as the degree of resistance and opposition by the nation and people to the formation and imposition of state sovereignty. One rare instance of a successful "state-building" project through the resistance and militant opposition to the European colonial domination was found in the island of Hispaniola, resulting in the birth of the first African revolutionary republic, Haiti, located in the Caribbean. After millions of Taino and other original inhabitants of the island of Hispaniola had largely been exterminated through slavery and the policy of genocide, imported African slaves and free people of color launched the Haitian Revolution and emancipatory efforts.[75] After waging an anti-imperialist war against the French rule, starting in 1791, the newly freed black republic declared its sovereignty and independence in 1804.[76] Many states in the world have had their own

---

[72] Ibid.

[73] Ibid.

[74] See generally, U.N. Statistics Division (2019).

[75] James (1938) and Horne (2015).

[76] See generally Roy (1999).

varied histories of collective resistance against, and emancipatory trajectories from, colonial projections imposed by European and other powerful states.

Another geo-political taxonomy of the multiplicity of the state system is based on the "three-tiered model" of legally constructed geopolitical formation across the globe. In 1952, French scholar Alfred Sauvy first provided a systematic vision of geopolitical formation of the world system, introducing the term First World to refer to the multiple polar systems of capitalist states with an advanced market economy in Western Europe, the U.S., Japan, and Australia.[77] The Second World included the People's Republic of China, the USSR, Yugoslavia, and its socialist and communist allied states in Eastern Europe. The Second World was later extended to post-1959 revolutionary Cuba and post-Vietnam War socialist Vietnam and other states that followed socialist agendas and communist doctrines.[78] The Third World, according to Sauvy, included all the rest of the states that were not aligned with either side in the Cold War, plus the newly declared states that emerged out of the decolonization projects in the 1950s and 1960s, including those in Africa, the Middle East, the Americas, and Asia.

After the dissolution of the Soviet Union in 1991 and the breakup of Yugoslavia in the 1990s and early 2000s, the term "Second World" of socialist and communist states became almost obsolete. However, the Third World still remains as the commonly used nomenclature in the analysis of geopolitical relationship. Similarly, such terms as "developing countries," "low-income countries," and the "Global South" as opposed to the "Global North," have also been used to refer to the Third World states. Another state-centric analysis was provided by Immanuel Wallerstein, who developed the scholarship based on the theory of "world systems analysis" in the 1970s.[79] Similar to the three-tiered, state-centric model of the First to Third Worlds, Wallerstein's world systems theory was based on the tripartite classification of state systems into the core, peripheral, and semi-peripheral countries. Core states were characterized by an advanced capitalist and market system that exploits the peripheral

---

[77] Ibid.

[78] Ibid. Venezuela may also be classified as another pro-socialist state after the so-called Bolivarian Socialist Revolution sought by former Venezuelan President Hugo Chavez. See Marino (2018) and Marquina and Gilbert (2020).

[79] See generally Wallerstein (2004).

states for cheap labor and raw materials. Semi-peripheral states were less developed than core states, but more advanced in economy and technology than peripheral states. They represented the economic buffer between core and peripheral states, including such countries as South Korea, Taiwan, and India in Asia, Mexico, and Brazil in the Americas, and Nigeria and South Africa in Africa.[80] Semi-peripheral states have come into existence due to the developing peripheries and the declining influence of core states. The desire to join the group of powerful core states and their economic sphere of influence tends to generate the state policies supporting the state-initiated and state-sponsored corporate projects that have continued to destroy the nation and its people, as well as the nature, environment, and ecosystems. The self-sustaining cultures of original nations have been rapidly disappearing in these semi-peripheral states. However, the state-centric scholarship has consistently overlooked the historical struggles of the nation and its consistent opposition to the state encroachment and to state-sponsored, ecologically destructive corporate activities in the ancestral homeland of the nation all across the core, semi-peripheral, and peripheral state systems.

2.2   The State and Post-Colonial Narratives of the Third World Approaches to International Law (TWAIL)

One prominent theoretical approach that examined the predatory impact of international law on the "developing countries" of the Third World is called Third World Approaches to International Law (TWAIL). This innovative and dynamic socio-legal analytic framework was largely developed, debated, and advanced by critical scholars in the "developing" Third World states, and peripheral or semi-peripheral countries in the Global South, as well as progressive socio-legal scholars who have been concerned with the growing disparity and increasing polarization of political power, economic inequality in wealth accumulation, and inequities in human rights protection in the Third World.[81] The theoretical tenets of

---

[80] Ibid.

[81] Since a group of Harvard Law School graduate students initiated meetings to establish TWAIL in the spring of 1996, a rich and voluminous TWAIL literature has developed. See Gathii and Nyamu-Musembi (1996), Mutua and Anghie (2000), Mutua (2000), Rajagopal (2000a, 2000b, 2006, 2013), Koskenniemi (2001), Ngugi (2002a, 2002b), Anghie and Chimni (2003), Nesiah (2003, 2016), Anghie (2004), Okafor (2005, 2008, 2016),

TWAIL, as well as its deficiencies and strengths, will also be discussed in Chapter 4. It is sufficient to note here that the TWAIL scholarship, while offering a critical analytic lens on the predatory impacts of international law on economically poor and impoverished states and regions in the Third World, has unfailingly privileged the state-centric narratives and generative discussions by accepting the state as a monolithic, collective geopolitical actor that embodies more or less the homogenized culture, social norm, political system, and populace within its state-delimited boundaries.

TWAIL's focus on the predatory socio-legal system and international economic regime that reproduce and perpetuate the plunder and subordination of the Third World by the West has been significant and influential. Similarly, our analysis substantiated that the ecological devastation and human atrocities have also been taking place in the homeland of the original nation, not only in the core states of the "First World," but also in the peripheral, or semi-peripheral states of the "Third World," as well as non-state geopolitical autonomous regions all around the globe.[82] The state-sponsored, predatory corporate project by the West, for instance, would not "discriminate" based on whether or not the original nation existed in highly advanced and "democratic" First World states or economically impoverished, peripheral "Third World" states. The transnational corporate culture which works to reduce nature and humans to "raw materials" for plunder, and to monopolize profits and control, has refused to respect or recognize legally protected state borders or "inter-state" boundaries. For example, in the Lakota Nation, perhaps one of

Chimni (2006, 2007a, 2007b, 2011), Khosla (2009), Badaru (2008), Gathii (2008, 2011, 2019, 2020), Michelson (2008), Michelson et al. (2008), Odumosu (2008), Al Attar and Tava (2010), Seck (2011), Al Attar and Thomson (2011), Al Attar (2012), Eslava and Pahuja (2012), Natarajan (2012), Gathii et al. (2013), Haskell (2014), Achiume (2016, 2019), Kiyani (2016), Kiyani et al. (2016), Natarajan et al. (2016, 2019), Ugochukwu (2016), Ramina (2018a, 2018b), Murphy et al. (2019), Frisso (2019), Okafor et al. (2019), and Stone (2019).

[82] Non-state autonomous geopolitical units (GPU) include non-territorial entities (NTE) or non-state armed groups (NSA) that have no internationally defined territorial base. For the definitions and classifications of non-state geopolitical entities, see Ramadhan (2019). The disputed "non-state" territory of Western Sahara in North and West Africa, for example, has suffered from human rights violations, the depletion of biodiversity, and the destruction of vast areas of forests through ecologically unsustainable forestry practices. See Stephen and Mundy (2006), Zunes and Mundy (2010); Ojeda-Garcia et al. (2016), and "Western Sahara Environment: Current Issues" (2019).

the most impoverished original nations in North America, the century-old state-corporate ravages of indigenous territories, including its sacred homeland of the "Black Hills," had led to the extraction of gold since 1876 without interruption.[83] The industrial extraction of gold, silver, lead, zinc, tungsten, and other minerals has led to the massive contamination and pollution of fertile soils and fresh water in large territories with high concentrations of arsenic, mercury, and other pollutants, all of which have been manifested in significant health and socioeconomic inequities in the indigenous communities.[84] Today Lakota peoples have the U.S.'s lowest life expectancy of 44 years among men; a high tuberculosis rate which is 800% above the U.S. average; more than 90% of adults with alcoholism; an unemployment rate of more than 85%, and 90% of Lakota people living below the poverty line.[85]

These existing health and economic disparities made the Lakota Nation particularly vulnerable to the 2020 coronavirus pandemic, as were many indigenous nations in Utah, Montana, New Mexico, and Wyoming, where the death rate from COVID-19 was five times higher than in the general population.[86] These higher death rates from COVID-19 have been reported, not only in indigenous nations in North America,[87] but also in the nations in Brazil, Colombia, and other Amazonian regions in Latin America[88]; India, Bangladesh, Thailand, and the Philippines in

---

[83] Cerney and Sago (2010).

[84] "SD Mines Researchers Trace Pollution from Historic Northern Hills Mine Tailings Hundreds of Miles Downstream (2018).

[85] Means (2008). America's indigenous nations and peoples suffered from significant economic inequality, systemic absence of social services, disproportionate poverty, lower life expectancy, disproportionate diseases, and poor economic conditions. See Nebelkopf and Phillips (2004), Williams (2007), and Moss (2015)

[86] Campbell and Levine (2020).

[87] Mobie (2020); "Tribal Health Board: Native Americans Hit Hard by Covid-19 (2020). See also Rogin (2020). The origin of the coronavirus has been disputed. Spanish virologists, for example, found the trace of the novel coronavirus in a sample of Barcelona's sewage water in March 2019, nine months prior to the COVID-19 outbreak in China. See Allen and Landauro (2020).

[88] As of July 2020, the COVID-19 "has affected at least 38 indigenous nations in Amazonia." Fox (2020), Gamba (2020), Gonzalez (2020), and Hansen (2020).

Asia[89]; Australia and New Zealand in the Oceania[90] and beyond.[91] The Centers for Disease Control and Prevention (CDC) observed that indigenous nations and peoples have been disproportionately affected by the COVID-19 all around the world.[92] Anne Nuorgam, the Chair of the U.N. Permanent Forum on Indigenous Issues, made this plea to the members of the U.N., "[W]e urge Member States and the international community to include the specific needs and priorities of indigenous peoples in addressing the global outbreak of COVID 19."[93]

While the TWAIL scholarship provided critical portraits of environmental devastation and human rights violations in the Third World, the most significant destruction of the biological variety of species, genes, ecosystems, and environments, as well as the annihilation of the cultural variety of indigenous peoples, knowledge, and traditions have been taking place in the original nation and peoples within and across the First and Third World states. In Brazil, for example, the government policies led by President Jair Bolsonaro have been responsible for the efforts to suppress and exterminate Brazil's vast Amazonian indigenous nations and populations. Since taking office in 2018, his government has "drained power from the National Indian Foundation; sacked inspectors of the Brazilian Institute of the Environment and Renewable Natural Resources; and eroded both the Unified Health System and the National Policy for Attention to the Health of Indigenous Peoples."[94] As results, mining and logging activities have brought the COVID-19 to indigenous nations and peoples in the Amazon rainforest.[95] In Asia, President Rodrigo Duterte in the Philippines has also been waging war against indigenous nations and peoples on behalf of logging and extractive corporate projects in

---

[89] "Bearing the Brunt: The Impact of Government Responses to COVID-19 on Indigenous Peoples in India" (2020), Bociago (2020), Chakma (2020), Kamal et al. (2020), and Salva (2020).

[90] McLeod et al. (2020) and Yashadhana et al. (2020).

[91] Hatcher (2020).

[92] Ibid.

[93] The U.N. Department of Economic and Social Affairs (2020).

[94] Santos et al. (2020).

[95] Ibid.

multiple Philippine islands.[96] Similar atrocities among the indigenous nation and peoples have also been reported in North America. The Western Shoshone Nation in Nevada has been subjected to ecologically unsustainable corporate mining projects for many decades, while their ancestral homeland of *Newe Segobia* had been subjected to nearly one thousand nuclear detonation experiments by the U.S. government, making the Western Shoshone Nation the most "atom-bombed" nation in the world.[97]

The coronavirus pandemic and its predatory impact on the original nation has had infamous precedence in the Western Hemisphere. Since Cristóbal Colon's "discovery" of North America in 1492, the "biological warfare" waged by European settlers, intentionally or unintentionally, led to the destruction of the original nation and peoples, as the pandemics caused by such diseases as smallpox, measles, typhus, cholera, and other viruses wiped out millions of indigenous populations in the Western Hemisphere.[98] Today Brazilian President Jair Bolsonaro's politics invoked the past calamity, as he once famously asserted his anti-indigenous rhetoric by stating, "[T]here is no indigenous territory where there aren't minerals. Gold, tin and magnesium are in these lands, especially in the Amazon, the richest area in the world. I'm not getting into this nonsense of defending land for Indians." He further asserted, "it is [a] shame that the Brazilian cavalry hasn't been as efficient as the Americans, who exterminated the Indians."[99]

The theoretical analysis of TWAIL, the statist global network of the three-tiered world model, and the state-centric world system theory have failed to adequately address and shed a critical light on the intra-state, or "within- or across state" reality of subjugation, discrimination, suffering, as well as violence against the original nation and people who have long opposed the "state-building" and "nation-destroying" projects. The Original Nation scholarship provides the critical lens to cut across the façade of statist and state-centric analyzes by offering an "on-the-ground" and "bottom-up" perspective that reflects, and speaks to, the common

[96] Bevins, Vincent (2018) "Instead of Peace, Indigenous Filipinos Get the Duterte Treatment," *Washington Post*, 22 April.

[97] Woodard, Stephanie (2017) "Warnings from First Americans: Insidious Changes are Underway That Will Affect Us All," *In These Times*, 5 October.

[98] Watson (2018).

[99] Marques and Rocha (2015).

struggles, resilience, and perseverance of the original nation and people all across the First and Third World states around the globe.

3   THE "FOURTH WORLD" INTERNATIONAL ANALYTIC DISCOURSE

The neologism "the Original Nation" is introduced in the present analysis to refer to the nation and people, rescinding the use of the terminology of the "Fourth World," which has been commonly used to refer to the nation and people in international legal discourse and geopolitical analysis.[100] The term was originally coined by George Manuel, chief of the National Indian Brotherhood of Canada, in his 1974 work, *The Fourth World: An Indian Reality*. He stated, "the Fourth World is a vision of the future history of North America and of the Indian people."[101] Yet the original use of "Fourth" World was derived from the Euro-centric hierarchical model of the state-based world system. There are several compelling reasons for rejecting its use and urging its replacement with "Original Nation." The last section of this chapter provides the justification for this replacement through a discussion of the struggles, resistance, and perseverance of the original nation and people.

First, the term the Fourth World is based on the extension of the three-tiered global model of the First, Second, and Third Worlds as used in the "statist-privileged" discourse. As examined earlier, this triad model of the state-centric world system assumed that Euro-American states had the most advanced capitalist and free market economy of the First World, while the Second World embodied the states that pursued State-Party Socialist or Communist development and nonmarket economies, such as China, the former Soviet Union, and East European states. The Third World consisted of the rest of the state systems, whose market economies were either developing, or undeveloped and underdeveloped, and mostly located in the Global South. This numerically ordered hierarchical model of the world order has been primarily advanced by scholars, economists, and politicians of the First World. At the bottom of the economic and political hierarchical order, the Fourth World refers to "a

---

[100] For example, Fukurai first coined the term, "Fourth World Approaches to International Law (FWAIL)" at the Second Asian Law and Society Conference in Taiwan, 2017. See Fukurai (2018).

[101] Manuel and Posluns (1974, p. 291).

group of nations especially in Africa and Asia characterized by extremely low capita income and an absence of valuable natural resources."[102] The World Bank identified the Fourth World as the economically underdeveloped, most impoverished regions of the Third World countries in Africa and Asia, such as Tanzania and Bangladesh.[103] The canonical narrative of the Fourth World, including the World Bank's view of the state-centric global model, failed to recognize the existence of the multiplicity of original nations in the First World states themselves, including a large number of indigenous communities and peoples in the Global North.

Second, the Fourth World often refers to the assortment of original nations whose lands and inhabitants have been severed, partitioned, and fragmented by ongoing predatory policies of the First and Third Worlds. For example, the 1893 "Durand Line" imposed by the colonial power of Britain partitioned the nation of Pashtunistan into Afghanistan and Pakistan. The 1923 British and French mandate systems further divided the nation of Kurdistan, formerly in the Ottoman Empire, into the French-controlled Syria, the British-governed Iraq, the newly emerged independent state of Turkey, and Persia, or today's Iran. The 1947 British-imposed "Radcliffe Line" divided the nation of Kashmir into India, Pakistan, and the People's Republic of China. Other original nations in Asia, Africa, the Americas, and many regions of the globe similarly faced such colonial partitions and fragmentations in their national boundaries and histories. The fragmented original nations have been independently and/or co-jointly struggling to gain independence within and across their partitioned state borders. The use of "Original Nation" narrative forcefully decenters the geopolitical analysis from the state-centric perspectives and discourses, exposing the ways in which the Western power had purposely exploited the geopolitical boundary of the state to partition, deconstruct, and subordinate the severed nation and peoples into their respective, state-centralized polity. The refocusing on the original nation thus helps expose the history of colonialism and imperialism as an integral part of the state's ongoing "state-building" and "nation-destroying" projects.

Third, the use of the Fourth World mistakenly implies that its etymological root is somehow sequential to the advent of the First to Third

---

[102] Merriam-Webster Dictionary (2018).
[103] Kramarae and Spender (2000, p. 1942).

Worlds, suggesting that the geopolitical status of the Fourth World was produced by, or even became derivative of, state policies that the First, Second, and Third Worlds imposed on the original nations. Such an assumption certainly does not reflect the etiological history of the nations and peoples in the world. The nations and associated peoples had already been distributed over the majority of Earth's planetary surface long before the state was invented and imposed. The term Original Nation clearly provides a more accurate historical vision than that falsely implied by the term Fourth World.

Fourth, the notion of the Fourth World still depends on the Eurocentric view of privileging the state over the nation, as the state borders and boundaries continue to encapsulate, partition, fragment, and occupy the nations. The Declaration of Indigenous Peoples of the World, adopted at the Global Forum for Indigenous Peoples on June 7, 1992, emphasized the overbearing influence of the state-dominant global system upon the original nations. It states, "[T]he global community of colonial states has been meeting with each other as First, Second, and Third world powers. All are recognized members of the United Nations. The Indigenous Nations are primarily considered Fourth World and are excluded.... Our exclusion is colonial racism in all its institutional forms."[104] The primacy of the Original Nation places the nation and people at the "centric-core" of geopolitical analysis. It also offers a viable, visionary alternative strategy for resisting and opposing the state-dominated discourses and imaginations.

Lastly, a different reification of the Fourth World has been advanced by urban sociologist Manuel Castells. As the Original Nation analysis attempts to extrapolate new narratives, his vision of the Fourth World similarly breaks the confines of the three-tiered model of world systems, extending his Fourth World analysis to the community of subpopulations who have been excluded from the global society of highly advanced digital networks and technological communication. According to Castells, the Fourth World now includes socially marginalized groups in the ghettoized neighborhoods of inner cities in the U.S., the *banlieues* and the enclaves of jobless youth in European capitals in the First World, and the shantytowns of Asia's prosperous and newly emerged states in the Third

[104] Danver (2012, p. 870).

World.[105] The inhabitants of the Fourth World also include individuals excluded by a variety of factors, such as mental illness, homelessness, physical and mental disability, illiteracy, and other factors that have forced the disenfranchised groups into "drifting toward the outer regions of society, inhabited by the wreckage of failed humanity."[106] Castells' invention of the Fourth World is radically different from the prescient vision of indigenous activist George Manuel who originally coined the term in the 1970s, seeking the indigenous nation's sovereignty and the right to self-determination in North America. Another prominent indigenous scholar, Ward Churchill, equated the Fourth World with indigenous activists, scholars, and organizers, whom he calls *indigenists*, referring to those who descended from the aboriginal population and are today deprived of their own territory and environment instead of being seen simply as marginalized urban inhabitants.[107] The use of the term "Fourth World" thus conflates the meaning of nations and associated peoples with other groups, such as urban dwellers of subpopulations that have been disenfranchised by highly advanced networks of digital technology and communication.

4   THE PRIMACY OF THE ORIGINAL NATION IN GEOPOLITICAL ANALYZES

The term "Original Nation" is used to refer to the thousands of nations and associated peoples around the globe in the present and the past. Prominent indigenous scholar and political activist Winona LaDuke once introduced the neologism "the Host World" to depict the nations and peoples. Specifically, she called the original nation "the Host World upon which the First, Second, and Third Worlds all sit at the present time."[108] LaDuke's analysis suggests that the nation has long served as the organic community whose people originally encountered, greeted, and incorporated many groups of visitors, guests, foreigners, and strangers

---

[105] See Castells (2010, p. 169).

[106] Ibid., p. 73.

[107] Churchill (2002, pp. 367–402).

[108] LaDuke (1983, p. viii). By its definition, the "Orginal Nation" used in our analysis also includes original inhabitants of "First Nations" in Canada and neighboring regions in North America.

into their homeland. These outsiders later morphed into colonizers and invaders and organized the armed troops of empire to take over, expropriate, occupy, and destroy the ancestral homeland of "the Host World" of the original nation and people.

Cultural anthropologist Bernard Nietschmann provides a detailed account of the fifteen stages of the state-building project, which involved simultaneously destroying the multitudes of "the Host World" of the original nations and ultimately taking over the national territories and peoples through the historical-geographic sequence of colonial projects and imperial policies.[109] There is an analogue to be found in the biological sphere. The term "host" also refers to the original body of the collective biological organism in which a new parasite, commensal, or other harmful outside agent begins to cohabitate and proliferate, ultimately taking over the entire organic body and destroying the original world of the biological organism.

While the notion of "the Host World" signifies the spatial and territorial dimension of the ancestral homeland of the nation, the term Original Nation also signifies the space–time continuum of the ancestral homeland of the nation and peoples whose existence predates the invention and imposition of the state system. As noted earlier, a multitude of nations had already existed over nearly all territories of the Earth's surface prior to the advent of the state, which later gained a foothold and eventually expanded by taking over the lands and people of the Host World of the original nation, as LaDuke's assertion correctly pointed out. The Original Nation perspective further helps create a penetrating narrative diametrically contrasted to the narratives of the state, which continues to powerfully, unilaterally, and, most importantly, "legally" impose itself upon the nation and peoples. The Original Nation approach points toward the need to replace the neoliberal, state-centric, geopolitical analysis and imaginations with the alternative form of a "ground-up" and "bottom-up" portrait of reality, one more attuned to the natural ecology of inter-human and cross-species relationships that largely prevailed in the nation prior to the global projection of European colonialism. Finally, the Original Nation perspective helps examine the history, expansion, and justification of the states and how they were brought into being in the first place, thereby challenging the basis of the justification that lies beneath their formal structures.

---

[109] Nietschmann (1994, pp. 232–236).

5 Conclusions

This chapter began with the clear differentiation of two geopolitical collective entities: the state and the nation. The state can be seen as a legally constructed, recently invented, imaginary geopolitical entity, while the nation is defined as the organic community of people who have long shared a strong psychological bond tied to a specific, territorially defined space and place. Due to the density and history of colonial projections, varied groups and multiple forms of the original nation exist today across the globe—from the autonomous or self-governing nation to semi-autonomous, revived, as well as phantom nations, where almost all the inhabitants of the distinct national community have been forced to relocate to exterior geological locations, such as is the case with the original people who inhabited the island of Diego Garcia in the Indian Ocean. Many original nations in the world have also been internally colonized and forcefully subordinated within and/or across the state.

Some European nations have recently attempted to assert their independence through trying to secede from their respective states, including Catalonia from Spain and Scotland from the U.K., among others. Their aspiration for national sovereignty and freedom has been admired by many original nations in the world. These independent-minded nations in Europe, however, have failed to propose government policies or introduce effective national ecological programs essential to freeing themselves from the necessity to continuously usurp, exploit, deplete, and destroy the natural and human resources of other original nations in non-European regions for their survival. The exploitive aspiration of Europe's "self-serving" original nations has been called Original Nation Libertarianism (ONL). In order to avert the further exploitation and destruction of original nations elsewhere, the "libertarian" movement of European nations must be deterred. Instead, they should be encouraged to institute national ecological policies that ensure the preservation of their own natural environment and the restoration of whatever had been lost in their ecological world. The "libertarian" nations in Europe should also be encouraged to actively collaborate with other original nations throughout the world in order to cultivate, restore, and revive their own "ecological knowledge," develop their self-sustenance culture, and devise and manage, as much as possible, self-sustainable communities.

The last section of this chapter examined the rationale for the use of the term Original Nation instead of the Fourth World. While the

Fourth World has been used by indigenous activists, legal scholars, and progressive political proponents, this term still presupposes the state-centric, three-tiered model of the world system largely advanced by "Global North" scholars who have privileged the economic and industrial advancement of the First World, vis-à-vis the "backward," economically less-developed states in the Third World and the Global South. The conflation of the organic community of indigenous people with the digitally disenfranchised community of the Fourth World was another reason presented in support of the disuse of the Fourth World in geopolitical discourses.

The next chapter offers a critical examination of ongoing struggles and resistance among the original nation and people in various regions of Asia. In the midst of the global decolonization movement in the 1950s, the U.S. intelligence community had already predicted that multiple regions in Asia would become the next major epicenter of the major struggles and resistance of original nations against the "state-building" projects. The analysis of Asia's original nations' unceasing struggles against the state-sponsored corporate projects and further state encroachment provides an exemplar of the resistance, resilience, aspiration, and defiance of the original nation in the past and the present, as well as the contour of the potential emancipatory path toward national independence and rights for self-determination for the original nation and people in Asia and all other regions across the globe.

Bibliography

"09-Biodiversity Management" (2015) Scottish Canals, Theme 9: Biodiversity Management, available at https://www.scottishcanals.co.uk/wp-content/uploads/sites/2/2015/12/9-Biodiversity-Management.pdf.

1868 Treaty of Fort Laramie, Apr 29 (1868) article 1, https://www.republicoflakotah.com/2009/1868-treaty/ (accessed 15 March 2019).

"Abolition of Main Crop Seeds Law Puts Nation at Risk" (2018), *Japan Times*, 20 March.

Achiume, E. Tendayi (2016) "Syria, Cost-Sharing, and Responsibility to Protect Refugees," 100 *Minnesota Law Review* 687–761.

Achiume, E. Tendayi (2019) "Migration as Decolonization," 71 *Stanford Law Review* 1509–1574.

Agarwal, Bina (2010) *Gender and Green Governance: The Political Economy of Women's Presence Within and Beyond Community Forestry*. Oxford, U.K.: Oxford University Press.

Aguilera-Barchet, Bruno (2013) A History of Western Public Law: Between Nation and State. NY: Springer.

Al Attar, Mohsen (2012) "Third World Approaches to International Law and the Rethinking of International Legal Education in the 21st Century." York University, Ph.D. Dissertation.

.AL Attar, Mohsen & Vernon Tava (2010) "TWAIL Pedagogy: Legal Education for Emancipation," 15 Palestine Yearbook of international Law 7–39.

Al Attar, Mohsen & Rebekah Thompson (2011) " A Multi-Level Democratisation of International Law-Making: Popular Aspirations Towards Self-Determination," 3 Trade, Law and Development 65–102.

Allen, Nathan & Inti Landauro (2020) "Coronavirus Traces Found in March 2019 Sewage Sample, Spanish Study Shows," *Reuters*, 26 June.

Anderson, Benedict (1983) Imagined Communities: Reflections on the Origin and Spread of Nationalism. London, UK: VERSO.

Anghie, Antony (2004) Imperialism, Sovereignty and the Making of International Law. Cambridge, UK: Cambridge University Press.

Anghie, Anton & B.S. Chimni (2003) "Third World Approaches to International Law and Individual Responsibility in Internal Conflicts," Chinese Journal of International Law 2:77–103.

Arsel, Murat & Bram Buscher (2012) "Nature Inc.: Changes and Continuities in Neoliberal Conservation and Environmental Markets," 43 *Development and Change* 53–78.

Bachelet, Michelle (2019) "Human Rights and Climate Change," United Nations Human Rights Office of the High Commissioner, 9 September, available at https://www.ohchr.org/EN/Issues/HRAndClimateChange/Pages/HRClimateChangeIndex.aspx.

Badaru, O.A. (2008) "Examining the Utility of Third World Approaches to International Law for International Human Rights Law," 10 *International Community Law Review* 379–387.

"Bearing the Brunt: The Impact of Government Responses to COVID-19 on Indigenous Peoples in India" *International Working Group for Indigenous Affairs (IWGIA)*, 10 September, https://www.iwgia.org/en/news-ale rts/news-covid-19/3839-bearing-brunt-covid-19.html.

Bevins, Vincent (2018) "Instead of Peace, Indigenous Filipinos Get the Duterte Treatment," *Washington Post*, 22 April.

"Biodiversity Strategy of the Basque Autonomous Community: 2030 and First Action Plan 2020" (2019) Regions4, available at https://www.regions4.org/resources/biodiversity-strategy-for-the-basque-autonomous-community-2030-and-first-action-plan-2020/.

Bociago, Robert (2020) "For the Philippines' Mangyans, COVID-19 Extends a Long History of Discrimination," *Mongabay*, 7 August.

Breitenbach, Dagmar (2014) "A Free and Independent Free State of Bavaria?" *DW*, 19 September.

Brockington, Dan and Rosaleen Duffy (2010). "Capitalism and Conservation: The Production and Reproduction of Biodiversity Conservation," 3 *Antipode* 469–482.

Brockington, Dan, Rosaleen Duffy and Jim Igoe (2008) *Nature Unbound: Conservation, Capitalism, and the Future of Protected Areas*. London, UK: Earthscan.

Burgess, John (1986) "Japanese Proud of Their Homogeneous Society," Washington Post, 28 September.

Buscher, Bram (2012) "Payments for Ecosystem Services as Neoliberal Conservation: (Reinterpreting) Evidence from the Maloti-Drakensberg, South Africa," 10 *Conservation and Society* 29–41.

Buscher, Bram, Sian Sullivan, Katja Neves, Jim Igoe & Dan Brockington (2012) "Towards a Synthesized Critique of Neoliberal Biodiversity Conservation," 23 *Capitalism, Nature, Socialism* 4–30.

Campbell, Alexia Fernandez & Carrie Levine (2020) "Native Americans, Hit Hard by Covid-19, Faced Major Barriers to Vote," *The Center for Public Integrity*, 5 November.

Castells, Manuel (2010) End of Millennium, in The Information Age: Economy Society, and Culture. Oxford, UK: Blackwell.

Cerney, Jan & Roberta Sago (2010) *Images of America: Black Hills Gold Rush Towns*. Chicago, IL: Arcadia Publishing.

Chakma, Trimita (2020) "A Rapid Assessment Report: The Impact of COVID-19 on Indigenous and Tribal Peoples in Bangladesh," *International Working Group on Indigenous Affairs (IWGIA)*, 10 August.

Chiaramonte, Jose (2010) Carlos Nation & State in Latin America: Political Language During Independence. NY: Routledge.

Chimni, B.S. (2006) "Third World Approaches to International Law: A Manifesto," *International Community Law Review* 8: 3–27.

Chimni, B.S. (2007a) "A Just World Under Law: A View From the South," 22 *American University International Law Review* 199–220.

Chimni, B.S. (2007b) "The Past, Present and Future of International Law: A Critical Third World Approach," 8 *Melbourne Journal of International Law* 499–515.

Chimni, B.S. (2011) "Asian Civilizations and International Law: Some Reflections," 1 *Asian Journal of International Law* 39–42.

Chomsky, Noam (1996) Powers and Prospects: Reflections on Human Nature and the Social Order. Boston, MA: South End Press.

Chomsky, Noam (2013) On Anarchism. NY: The New Press.

Chomsky, Noam & Michel Foucault (2006) The Chomsky-Foucault Debate: On Human Nature. NY: New Press.

Churchill, Ward (1994) Indians Are Us? Culture and Genocide in Native North America. Monroe, ME: Common Courage Press.

Churchill, Ward (2002) Struggle for the Land: Native North American Resistance to Genocide, Ecocide and Colonization. San Francisco, CA: City Lights Books.

Convention on Biological Diversity (2007) "What's the Problem?" (accessed 22 October 2020), https://www.cbd.int/impact/problem.shtml.

Danver, Steven (2012) The Native Peoples of the World: An Encyclopedia of Groups, Cultures, and Contemporary Issues. Armonk, NY: Sharpe Reference.

Death, Carl (2014) Critical Environmental Politics. NY: Routledge.

Dobson, David (1997) Irish Emigrants in North America. Baltimore, MD: Cleacrfield Publishing Company.

Doherty, Ben & Kate Lamb (2017a) "Banned West Papua Independence Petition Handed to UN," Guardian, 27 September.

Doherty, Ben & Kate Lamb (2017b) "West Papua Independence Petition is Rebuffed at UN," Guardian, 29 September.

Dressler, Wolfram and Bram Buscher (2008) "Market Triumphalism and the So-Called CBNRM 'Crisis' at the South African Section of the Great Limpopo Transfrontier Park," 39 Geoforum 452–465.

Dunleavy, Harry (2019) Irish Immigration to Latin America. Red Bank, NJ: Newman Springs Publishing.

Eslava Luis & Sundhya Pahuja (2012) "Beyond the (Post) Colonial: TWAIL and the Everyday Life of International Law," Journal of Law and Politics in Africa, Asia and Latin America 45: 195–221.

Evers, Sandra J.T.M. and Mary Kooy (2011) Eviction from the Chagos Islands: Displacement and Struggle for Identity Against Two World Powers. Netherlands: Brill Publishers.

Fearon, James D. (2003) "Ethnic and Cultural Diversity by Country," 8 Journal of Economic Growth 8(2): 195–222.

Ford, Henry Jones (1915) The Scotch-Irish in America. Princeton, NJ: Princeton University Press.

Fox, Michael (2020) "Brazil's Indigenous Peoples Fight COVID-19 in Their Territories Amid Government Neglect," The World, 4 September.

Frisso, Giovanna Maria (2019) "Third World Approaches to International Law: 'Feminists" Engagement with International Law and Decolonial Theory," in Research Handbook on Feminist Engagement with International Law, eds. Susan Harris Rimmer & Kate Ogg (Northampton, MA: Edward Elgar Publishing), pp. 479–498

Fukurai, Hiroshi (2018) "Fourth World Approaches to International Law (FWAIL) and Asia's Indigenous Struggles and Quests for Recognition under International Law," Asian Journal of Law and Society 5(1): 221–231.

Galinda, Gabriela (2019) "Nearly 40% of Flemish Would Vote for Independence," *The Brussels Times*, 17 December.

Gamba, Laura (2020) "Coronavirus Hitting Indigenous Tribes Hard in Brazil," *AA*, 24 July, https://www.aa.com.tr/en/americas/coronavirus-hitting-indigenous-tribes-hard-in-brazil-/1920595.

Garroutte, Eva Marie (2001) "The Racial Formation of American Indians: Negotiating Legitimate Identities Within Tribal and Federal Law," American Indian Quarterly 25(2): 224–239.

Gathii, James Thuo (2008) "Third World Approaches to International Economic Governance," in *International Law and the Third World: Reshaping Justice*, eds. By Richard Falk, Balakrishman Rajagopal & Jacquelin Stevens (NY: Routledge), pp. 255–268.

Gathii, James Thuo (2011) "TWAIL: A Brief History of Its Origin, Its Decentralized Network, and a Tentative Bibliography," Trade Law. & Development 3(1): 26–48.

Gathii, James Thuo (2019) "The Agenda of Third World Approaches to International Law (TWAIL)," forthcoming in Jeffrey Dunoff & Mark Pollack, eds. *International Legal Theory: Foundations and Frontiers*. Cambridge, MA: Cambridge University Press, https://papers.ssrn.com/sol3/papers.cfm?abstract_id=3304767 (accessed 22 October 2020).

Gathii, James Thuo (2020) "The Promise of International Law: A Third World View," https://uichr.uiowa.edu/assets/Documents/GathiiGrotiusLecture2020.pdf (accessed 22 October 2020).

Gathii, James & Celestine Nyamu (1996) "Reflections on United States-Based Human Rights NGO's Work on Africa," 9 *Harvard Human Rights Journal* 285–296.

Gathii, James, Antony Anghie & Obiora Okafor (2013) "Africa and TWAIL," *African Yearbook of International Law* 9–13.

Generalitat de Catalunya (2012) Biodiversity in Catalonia: The Challenge of Conservation, available at https://www.qlf.org/wp-content/uploads/2016/10/biodiversity-in-catalonia.pdf.

Gonzalez, Luisa (2020) "Coronavirus Threatens the Survival of Colombia's Indigenous Wayuu," *NBC News*, 13 August.

Gottlieb, Gidon (1993) Nation Against State: A New Approach to Ethnic Conflicts and the Decline of Sovereignty. NY: Council of Foreign Relations Press.

Griggs, Richard (1992) "The Meaning of 'Nation' and 'State' in the Fourth World," CWIS Occasional Paper #18.

Griggs, Richard & Peter Hocknell (1995a) "Fourth World Faultlines and the Remaking of 'Inter-National' Boundaries," IBRU Boundary and Security Bulletin 3(3): 49–58.

Griggs, Richard & Peter Hocknell (1995b) "The Geography and Geopolitics of Europe's Fourth World," IBRU Boundary and Security Bulletin, Winter 3(4): 59–67, available at https://citeseerx.ist.psu.edu/viewdoc/download?doi=10.1.1.177.155&rep=rep1&type=pdf.

Grimal, Francis (2013) Threats of Force: International Law and Strategy. NY: Routledge.

Habermas, Jurgen (1999) "The European Nation-State: On the Past and Future of Sovereignty and Citizenship." In Ciaran Cronin & Pablo De Greiff, eds.,The Inclusion of the Other: Studies in Political Theory. Cambridge, UK: Polity Press, pp. 237–245.

Hansen, Terri (2020) "How Covid-19 Could Destroy Indigenous Communities," BBC, 27 July.

Harari, Yuval Noah (2020) "Yuval Noah Harari: The World After Coronavirus," Financial Times, 19 March.

Haskell, John D. (2014) "TRAIL-ing TWAIL: Arguments and Blind Spots in Third World Approaches to International Law Scholarship," 27 Canadian Journal of Law and Jurisprudence 383–415.

Hatcher, Sarah M. et al. (2020) "COVID-19 Among American Indians and Alaska Native Persons – 23 States, January 31-July 3, 2020: Morbidity and Mortality Weekly Report," CDC, 28 August.

Horne, Gerald (2014) The Counter Revolution of 1776: Slave Resistance and the Origin of the United States of America. NY: NYU Press.

Horne, Gerald (2015) Confronting Black Jacobins: The U.S., the Haitian Revolution, and the Origins of the Dominican Republic. NY: NYU Press.

Horning, Audrey J. (2013) Irish in the Virginia Sea: Colonialism in the Britain. Chapel Hill, NC: The University of North Carolina Press.

Huisman, Nick (2019) "EU Fails to Meet 2020 Targets Against Biodiversity Loss," European Wilderness Society, https://wilderness-society.org/eu-fails-to-meet-2020-targets-against-biodiversity-loss/ (accessed 22 October 2020).

Igoe, J. & D. Brockington (2007) "Neoliberal Conservation: A Brief Introduction," 5 Conservation and Society 432–449.

James, C.L.R. (1938) The Black Jacobins: Toussaint L'ouverture and the San Domingo Revolution. U.K.: Secker & Warburg Ltd.

Jandt, Fred E. (2012) An Introduction to Intercultural Communication: Identities in a Global Community. LA, CA: Sage.

Janis, M.W. (1984) "Jeremy Bentham and the Fashioning of 'International Law'," American Journal of International Law 78: 405–418.

Kamal, Sultano, Elsa Stamatopoulou & Myrna Cunningham Kain (2020) "International Chittagong Hill Tracts Commission: Indigenous Peoples in Chittagong Hill Tracts Experiencing Human Rights Violations," International Working Group on Indigenous Affairs (IWGIA), 26 June.

Keong, Choy Yee (2020) *Global Environmental Sustainability: Case Studies and Analysis of the United Nations' Journey Toward Sustainable Development.* Cambridge, MA: Elsevier Inc.

Khosla, Madhav (2009) "TWAIL Discourse: The Emergence of a New Phase," 9 *International Community Law Review* 291–304.

Kiyani, Asad G. (2016) "Third World Approaches to International Law," 109 *American Journal of International Law Unbound* 255–259.

Kiyani, Asad G., John Reynolds & Sujith Xavier (2016) "Foreward, Symposium The Third World Approaches to International Law, Cairo, Egypt," 14 *Journal of International Criminal Justice* 915–920.

Klieforth, Alexander Leslie & Robert John Munro (2004) *The Scottish Invention of America, Democracy and Human Rights: The History of Liberty and Freedom from the Ancient Celts to the New Millennium.* NY: University Press of America.

Kluge, Emma (2020) "How the World Failed West Papua in Its Campaign for Independence," The Jakarta Post, 24 January.

Knight, David B. (1983) "The Dilemma of Nations in a Rigid State Structured World." In Nurit Kliot & Stanley Waterman, eds., *Pluralism and Political Geography: People, Territory and State.* NY: Routledge, pp. 114–137.

Koskenniemi, Martti (2001) The Gentle Civilizer of Nations: The Rise and Fall of International Law. Cambridge, UK: Cambridge University Press.

Kramarae, Cheris & Dale Spender, (2000) Routledge International Encyclopedia of Women: Global Women's Issues and Knowledge. NY: Routledge.

Kropotkin, Peter (1902) Mutual Aid: A Factor of Evolution. Manchester, NH: Extending Horizons Books.

LaDuke, Winona (1983) "Preface." In Marxism and Native Americans (Ward Churchill), pp. viii.

Landsman, Ned C. (2014) *Scotland and Its First American Colony, 1683–1765.* Princeton, NJ: Princeton University Press.

Langenheim, Johnny (2010) "The Last of the Sea Nomads," Guardian, 9 September.

Laszlo, Tony (2002) "Japan's Homogeneous Diversity," *Japan Times*, 20 January.

Lazard, Olivia (2020) "The EU Must Fight the Collapse of Biodiversity," Carnegie Europe, https://carnegieeurope.eu/2020/10/19/eu-must-fight-collapse-of-biodiversity-pub-82986 (accessed 22 October 2020).

Lindenmayer, David, Stephen Dovers, & Molly Harriss Olson (2008) Ten Commitments: Reshaping the Lucky Country's Environment. Collingwood, Canada: CSIRO Publishing.

MacDonald, Kenneth (2010a) "Business, Biodiversity, and the New 'Fields' of Conservation: The World Conservation Congress and the Renegotiation of Organizational Order," 8 *Conservation and Society* 256–275.

MacDonald, Kenneth (2010b) "The Devil is in the (Bio)Diversity: Private Sector "Engagement and Restructuring of Biodiversity Conservation," 42 *Antipode* 159–184.

Maestre-Andres, Sara, Laura Calvet-Mir, & Evangelia Apostolopoulou (2018) "Unravelling Stakeholder Participation on Conditions of Neoliberal Biodiversity Governance in Catalonia, Spain," 36 *Politics & Space* 1299–1318.

Manuel, George & Michael Posluns (1974) The Fourth World: An Indian Reality. Toronto, Canada: Collier-Macmillan Canada, Ltd.

Marino, Angela (2018) *Populism and Performance in the Bolivarian Revolution of Venezuela.* Evanston, IL: Northwestern University Press.

Marques, Anatonio & Leonardo Rocha (2015) "Bolsonaro diz que OAB so defende bandido e resera indigena e un crime [Bolsonaro Says OAB Only Defends Bandit and Indigenous Reservation and a Crime]," *Campo Grande News,* 22 April

Marquina, Cira Pascual & Chris Gilbert (2020) *Venezuela the Present as Struggle: Voices from Bolivarian Revolution.* NY: Monthly Review Press.

McGee. Thomas D'Arcy (1855) *A History of the Irish Settlers in North America: From the Earliest Period to the Census of 1850.* Boston, MA: Horart & Robbins.

McGrath, Timothy (2014) "This Map Shows What Europe Will Look Like if Every Separatist Movement Gets Its Own Country," *The World,* 17 September.

McLeod, Melissa, Jason Gurney, Ricci Harris, Donna Cormack & Paula King (2020) "COVID-19: We Must Not Forget About Indigenous Health and Equity," 10 *Australia and New Zealand Journal of Public Health* 253–256.

Means, Russell (2008) Petition for Recognition of Lakotah Sovereignty. 8 February, https://danco.org/amer/Petition.pdf.

Merriam-Wester Dictionary (2018), available at https://www.merriam-webster.com/dictionary/fourth%20world.

Michelson, Karin (2008) "Taking Stock of TWAIL Histories," 10 *International Community Law Review* 355–362.

Michelson, Karin, Ibironke Odumosu, & Pooja Parmar (2008) "Foreword, Situating Third World Approaches to International Law (TWAIL): Inspirations, Challenges and Possibilities," 10 *International Community Law Review* 351–353.

Miller, Kerby Alonzo (1976) *Emigrants and Exiles: The Irish Exodus to North America From Colonial Times to the First World War.* NY: Oxford University Press.

Minahan, James B. (2016) Encyclopedia of Stateless Nations: Ethnic and National Groups Around the World. Santa Barbara, CA: ABC-CLIO "More Than 92% of Voters in Iraqi Kurdistan Back Independence" (2017) Guardian, 28 September.

Mobie, Nora (2020) "Native American Tribes Have Been Hit Harder by COVID-19. Here is Why," *Great Falls Tribune*, 5 August.

Moens, Barbara (2020) "The Flemish Nationalist Exist Strategy," *Politico*, 11 May.

Montenegro, Raul A. & Carolyn Stephens (2006) "Indigenous Health in Latin America and the Caribbean," 367 *The Lancet* 1859–1869.

Moran, Katy, Steven King & Thomas Carlson (2001) "Biodiversity Prospecting: Lessons and Prospects," 30 *Annual Review of Anthropology* 505–526.

Moss, Margaret P. (2015) *American Indian Health and Nursing*. NY: Springer Publishing Company.

"Movement Rights, Rights of Nature and Mother Earth: Rights-Based Law for Systemic Change" (2017), available at https://www.ienearth.org/wp-con tent/uploads/2017/11/RONME-RightsBasedLaw-final-1.pdf.

Murdoch, Alexander (2009) *Scotland and America, c.1600–c.1800*. NY: Palgrave Macmillan.

Murphy, Sean D. et al. (2019) "Closing Plenary: International Law as an Instrument for Development: Remarks," 113 *American Society of International Law Proceedings* 389–400.

Mutua, Makau (2000) "What is TWAIL?" 94 *The American Society of International Law Proceedings* 31–40.

Mutua, Makau & Anton Anghie (2000) "What is TWAIL?" *Proceedings of the ASIL Annual Meeting*, 94: 31–38.

Natarajan, Usha (2012) "TWAIL and the Environment: The State of Nature, The Nature of the State, and Arab Spring," 14 *Oregon Review of International Law* 177–201.

Natarajan, Usha, John Reynolds, Amar Bhatia & Sujith Xavier (2016) "Introduction: TWAIL-On Praxis and the Intellectual," 37 *Third World Quarterly* 1946–1956.

Natarajan, Usha, John Reynolds, Amar Bhatia & Sujith Xavier (2019) *Third World Approaches to International Law: On Praxis and the Intellectual*. London, UK: Routledge.

"Native American Lands and Natural Resource Development" (2011) *Natural Resource Governance Institute*, 15 June.

Nebelkopf, Ethan & Mary Phillips (2004) *Healing and Mental Health for Native Americans: Speaking in Red*. Long Beach, CA: Native Nations Law and Policy Center.

Nesiah, Vasuki (2003) "The Ground Beneath Her Feet: 'Third World' Feminism," 4 *Journal of International Women's Studies* 30–38.

Nesiah, Vasuki (2016) "Local Ownership of Global Governance," 44 *Journal of International Criminal Justice* 985–1009.

Ngugi, Joel (2002a) "The Decolonization-Mobilization Interface and the Plight of Indigenous Peoples in Post-Colonial Development Discourse in Africa," 20 *Wisconsin International Law Review* 297–351.

Ngugi, Joel (2002b) "Making New Wine for Old Wineskins: Can the Reform of International Law Emancipate the Third World in the Age of Globalization," 8 *UC Davis Journal of International Law and Policy* 73–106.

Nietschmann, Bernard (1994) "The Fourth World: Nations Versus States." In George J. Demko & William B. Wood, eds., Reordering the World: Geopolitical Perspectives on the Twenty-First Century. Boulder, CO: Westview Press, pp. 227–242.

Niranjan, Ajit (2020) "Countries Pledge to Reverse Destruction of Nature After Missing Biodiversity Targets," *DW*, 28 September.

Noack, Rick (2014) "These 8 Places in Europe Could be the Next to Try for Independence," *Washington Post*, 18 September.

Nock, Albert J. (1935) Our Enemy, the State. Scotts Valley, CA: Createspace Independent Publisher, available at https://famguardian.org/Publications/OurEnemyTheState/OurEnemyTheState-byAlbertJKnock.pdf.

Odumosu, I (2008) "Challenges for the (Present/) Future of Third World Approaches to International Law," 10 *International Community Law Journal* 467–477.

O'Grady, John (1935) "Irish Colonization in the United States," 19 *Studies: An Irish Quarterly Review* 387–407.

Ojeda-Garcia, Raquel, Irene Fernandez-Molina & Victoria Veguilla (2016) *Global, Regional and Local Dimensions of Western Sahara's Protected Decolonization: When a Conflict Gets Old.* Granada, Spain: Palgrave Macmillan.

Okafor, Obiora Chinedu (2005) "Newness, Imperialism, and International Legal Reform in Our Time: A TWAIL Perspective," 43 *Osgoode Hall Law Journal* 171–191.

Okafor, Obiora Chinedu (2008) "Critical Third World Approaches to International Law (TWAIL): Theory, Methodology, or Both?" 10 *International Community Law Review* 371–378.

Okafor, Obiora Chinedu (2016) "Praxis and the International (Human Rights) Law Scholar: Toward the Intensification of TWAILian Dramaturgy," 33 *Windsor Yearbook Access to Justice* 1–35.

Okafor, Obiora Chinedu, T. Adebola & Basema Al-Alami (2019) "Viewing the International Labour Organization's Social Justice Praxis Through a Third World Approaches to Internatonal Law Lens: Some Preliminary Insights," in *ILO 100: Law for Social Justice*, eds. By George P. Politakis, Tomi Kohiyama & Thomas Lieby (Geneva: International Labour Organization), pp. 101–122.

"One in Three Bavarians Want Independence from Germany, Poll Shows" (2017), *The Local*, 17 July.

Orwell, George (1938) Homage to Catalonia. London, UK: Secker & Warburg.

Palacin, Carlos and Juan Carlos Alonso (2018) "Failure of EU Biodiversity Strategy in Mediterranean Farmland Protected Areas," 42 Journal of Nature Conservation 62–66.

Pariona, Amber (2018) "The World's 17 Megadiverse Countries," WorldAtlas, 25 July.

Pellan, Mael (2013) "Independence of Brittany and Why Bretons Will Never be French: Their Values and Ours," 7 Seizh, 17 October.

Pereltsvaig, Asya (2015) "Brittany, Another Independence-Seeking European Region," Languages of the World, 18 November.

Preston, Paul (2007) The Spanish Civil War: Reaction, Revolution and Revenge. NY: W.W. Norton & Company.

Prestre, Philippe G. Le (2003) Governing Global Biodiversity: The Evolution and Implementation of the Convention on Biological Diversity. London, UK: Routledge.

Phan, Peter C. & Jonathan Ray (2014) Understanding Religious Pluralism: Perspectives from Religious Studies and Theology. Eugene, OR: Pickwick Press.

Rajagopal, Balakrishnan (2000a) "From Resistance to Renewal: The Third World, Social Movements, and the Expansion of International Institutions," 41 Harvard International Law Journal 529–578.

Rajagopal, Balakrishnan (2000b) "Postdevelopment as a Vision: From a Third World Approach to International Law," 94 Proceedings of the American Society of International Law 306–307

Rajagopal, Balakrishnan (2006) "Reshaping Justice: International Law and the Third world: An Introduction," 27 Third World Quarterly 711–712.

Rajagopal, Balakrishnan (2013) International Law from Below: Development, Social Movements and Resistance. NY: Cambridge University Press.

Ramadhan, G.A. (2019) "The Development of Concept of Territory in International Relations," 20 Global: Jurnal Politik International 120–135.

Ramina, Larissa (2018a) "Framing the Concept of TWAIL: Third World Approaches to International Law," 32 Justica Do Direito 5–26.

Ramina, Larissa (2018b) "Third World Approaches to International Law and Human Rights: Some Considerations," 5 Revista de Investigacoes Constitucionais 261–272.

Rodriguez, Junius (2002) P. The Louisiana Purchase: A Historical and Geographical Encyclopedia. Santa Barbara, CA: ABC-CLIO.

Rogin, Josh (2020) "State Department Cables Warned of Safety Issues at Wuhan Lab Studying Bat Coronavirus," Washington Post, 14 April.

Rosendal, G. Kristin (2013) The Convention on Biological Diversity and Developing Countries. London, UK: Kluwer Academic Publishers.

Ross, Alf (2006) A Textbook of International Law. Clar, NJ: The Lawbook Exchange, Ltd.

Roth, Robin and Wolfram Dressler (2012) "Market-Oriented Conservation Governance: The Peculiarities of Place," 43 *Geoforum* 363–366.

Roy, Ash Narain (1999) The Third World in the Age of Globalisation: Requiem or New Agenda? London, UK: Zed Books.

Salva, Ana (2020) "The Coronavirus Pandemic Has Put Asia's Indigenous Communities Under Serious Pressure," *Equal Times*, 9 October.

Santos, Renato Antunes Dos, Denis Osorio Severo & Maria da Graca Luderitz Hoefel (2020) "Bolsonaro's Hostility Has Driven Indigenous Peoples to the Brink," *Nature*, 19 August.

Seck, Sara L. (2011) "Global Ecological Integrity and Third World Approaches to International Law," in *Globalisation and Ecological Integrity in Science and International Law*, eds. Laura Westra & Klaus Bosselmann & Colin Soskolne. Newcastle, UK: Cambridge Scholars Publishing, pp. 165–187.

Scott, James (2010) The Art of Not Being Governed: Ab Anarchist History of Upland Southeast Asia. New Haven, CT: Yale University Press.

"SD Mines Researchers Trace Pollution from Historic Northern Hills Mine Tailings Hundreds of Miles Downstream (2018) *South Dakota Mines*, 20 July.

Seton, Kathy (1999) "Fourth World Nations in the Era of Globalisation: An Introduction to Contemporary Theorizing Posed by Indigenous Nations," The Fourth World Journal 4(1): 49–69.

Shen, Simon (2017) "Is Bavaria Likely to Break Off From Germany?" *Ejinsight*, 3 August.

Sjostedt, Matilda Eriksson (2020) "The Role of Environmental Institutions in Producing and Reproducing Conditions for Neoliberal Biodiversity Conservation," 2 *Journal of International & Public Affairs*, https://www.jipasg. org/posts/2020/9/6/the-role-of-environmental-institutions-in-producing-and-reproducing-conditions-for-neoliberal-biodiversity-conservation (accessed 22 October 2020).

Sopher, David E. (1965) The Sea Nomads: A Study Based on the Literature of the Maritime Boat People of Southeast Asia. Singapore: Lim Bian Han.

Stares, Justin (2009) "Flanders Encouraged to Seek Independence from Belgium by EU's Growing Power," *The Telegraph*, 28 June.

Steininger, Rolf (2003) South Tyrol: A Minority Conflict of the Twentieth Century. NY: Routledge.

Stephan, Maria & Jacob Mundy (2006) " A Battlefield Transformed: From Guerilla Resistance to Mass Nonviolent Struggle in the Western Sahara," 8 *Journal of Military and Strategic Studies* 1–32.

Stevens, Michelle L. (2007) "Iraq and Iran in Ecological Perspective: The Mesopotamian Marshes and the Hawizeh-Azim Peace Park." In Peace Parks: Conservation and Conflict Resolution (Saleem H. Ali, ed.), pp. 313–331.

Stone, Ashley M. (2019) "Introduction to Third World Approaches to International Law," 20 *Oregon Review of International Law* 333–334.

Sullivan, Sian (2005) "Reflection on 'New' (Neoliberal) Conservation (With Case Material from Namibia, Southern Africa," 2 *Africa e Orienti* 102–115.

Sullivan, Sian (2006) "The Elephant in the Room? Problematizing 'New' (Neoliberal) Biodiversity Conservation," 33 *Forum for Development Studies* 105–135.

Sullivan, Sian (2009) "Green Capitalism and the Cultural Poverty of Constructing Nature as Service-Provider," 3 *Rural Anthropology* 18–27.

Swanson, Timothy (1999)"Why is There a Biodiversity Convention? The International Interest in Centralized Development Planning," 75 *International Affairs* 307–331.

The Montevideo Convention on Rights and Duties of States Adopted by the Seventh International Conference of American States, Montevideo (1933), available at https://treaties.un.org/doc/Publication/UNTS/LON/Volume%20165/v165.pdf.

Toyosaki, Satoshi & Shinsuke Eguchi (2017) *Intercultural Communication in Japan: Theorizing Homogenizing Discourse*. NY: Routledge.

Tran, Hugo (2014) "Fighting for Brittany: Autonomy in a Centralised State," *Open Democracy*, 5 December.

"Tribal Health Board: Native Americans Hit Hard by COVID-19" (2020) *AP*, 26 June, https://apnews.com/article/0f44f46abf994293acded741ff0dd403.

Tsurumi, E. Patricia, (1990) Factory Girls: Women in the Thread Mills of Meiji Japan. Princeton: Princeton University Press.

Ugochukwu, Basil (2016) "Global Governance in All Its Discrete Forms: The Game, FIFA, and the Third World," 33 *Windsor Yearbook of Access to Justice* 199–228.

United Nations (2010) "State of the World's Indigenous Peoples (SOWIP)," 14 January.

United Nations Department of Economics & Social Affairs (2004) "Workshop on Data Collection and Disaggregation for Indigenous Peoples: The Concept of Indigenous Peoples: Background Paper Prepared by the Secretariat of the Permanent Forum on Indigenous Issues," 19–21 January.

United Nations Department of Economics & Social Affairs (2020) "COVID-19 and Indigenous Peoples," https://www.un.org/development/desa/indigenouspeoples/covid-19.html (accessed 22 October 2020).

United Nations Development Programme (2011) Human Development Report 2011. NY: Palgrave Macmillan.

United Nations Information Service (UNIS) (2020) International Law, available at https://www.unis.unvienna.org/unis/en/topics/international-law.html.

United Nations Permanent Forum on Indigenous Issues (2019) Indigenous People, Indigenous Voices, Factsheet (accessed 15 May 2020), available at https://www.un.org/esa/socdev/unpfii/documents/5session_factsheet1.pdf.

United Nations Statistics Division, Methodology: Standard Country or Area Codes for Statistical Use (M49) (accessed 14 November 2019), available at https://unstats.un.org/unsd/methodology/m49/.

U.S. Census Bureau (2010) The American Indian and Alaska Native Population.

Wallerstein, Immanuel (2004) World-Systems Analysis: An Introduction. Durham, NC: Duke University Press.

Watson, Fiona (2018) "Bolsonaro's Election is Catastrophic News for Brazil's Indigenous Tribes," *Guardian*, 31 October.

Weiner, Michael (2004) Race, Ethnicity and Migration in Modern Japan: Imagined and Imaginary Minorities. London, UK: Routledge.

"Western Sahara Environment: Current Issues" (2019) *Indexmundi*, 7 December, available at https://www.indexmundi.com/western_sahara/enviro nment_current_issues.html#google_vignette.

Williams, Richard Allen (2007) *Eliminating Healthcare Disparities in America: Beyond the IOM Report*. Totowa, NJ: Humana Press.

Wilson, Thomas M. & Hastings Donnan (1998) Border Identities: Nation and State at International Frontiers. NY: Cambridge University Press.

Winchester, Mark (2009) "On the Dawn of a New National Ainu Policy: The 'Ainu' As a Situation Today," Asian-Pacific Journal 7(41):1–19.

Woodard, Stephanie (2017) "Warnings from First Americans: Insidious Changes are Underway That Will Affect Us All," *In These Times*, 5 October.

Yamada, Masahiko (2018) *Tane wa Donaru? Shushi-ho Haishi to Shubyo-ho Unyo de [What Happens to Seeds? The Abolition of the Main Crop Seeds Act and the Promulgation of the Seedling Act]*. Tokyo, Japan: Saizo.

Yamamoto, Kana (2015) "The Myth of 'Nihonjinron', Homogeneity of Japan and Its Influence on the Society," CERS Working Paper 2015.

Yashadhana, Aryati, Mellie Pollard-Wharton, Anthony B. Zwi & Brett Biles (2020) "Indigenous Australians at Increased Risk of COVID-19 Due to Existing Health and Socioeconomic Inequities," 1 *The Lancet Regional Health: Western Pacific*, 1 August, https://www.thelancet.com/journals/lan wpc/article/PIIS2666-6065(20)30007-9/fulltext.

Zunes, Stephen & Jacob Mundy (2010) *Western Sahara: War, Nationalism, and Conflict Irresolution*. Syracuse, NY: Syracuse University Press.

CHAPTER 3

The Conflict Between the Nation and the State

The Original Nation perspective recognizes the inherent tension between the state and the nation, seeing them as representing two seemingly irrepressible forces destined for collision. There have been 280 distinct armed conflicts in the post-WWII era, according to The Uppsala Conflict Data Program (UCDP), one of the world's leading data providers related to political violence,[1] The Center for Security Studies at the Swiss Federal Institute of Technology in Zurich reported in 2017 that 47 of the 49 major armed conflicts in the prior year had been fought within the boundaries of states over the government and/or territory of nations and peoples.[2] Another study reported that in 1993, nearly eighty percent of the 122 armed conflicts occurring at the time were being fought between the nation and the state, which had tried to claim political authority to dominate the nation and to appropriate its land and natural resources.[3]

This chapter begins with a critical examination of the original nation's struggles in Asia, pointing to ongoing conflicts between the state and

---

[1] Dupuy et al. (2017).

[2] Ibid., p. 4 ("Since 2013, we have seen a rise in both the number of conflicts and in battle casualties. Nationalism and religious extremism lie behind much of this uptick").

[3] See generally Nietschmann (1994) (eighty percent of the conflicts reported in 1993 were fought between the nation and the state).

© The Author(s), under exclusive license to Springer Nature Switzerland AG 2021
H. Fukurai and R. Krooth, *Original Nation Approaches to Inter-National Law*,
https://doi.org/10.1007/978-3-030-59273-8_3

the nation over territories and resources. Multiple states in Asia had adopted "Law and Development" policies which were first promoted by the WB, IMF, USAID, and other international organizations in the 1960s. There was a second wave of this in the 1980s[4] that led to such unsustainable development projects as mining, oil drilling, hydro-projects, and other environmentally destructive energy projects in the homeland of the nation.[5] Trade and investment liberalization have led to even greater corporate aggression, exploitation, and plunder of lands and resources. As already noted, the U.S. government had recognized as early as 1950 that the most immediate crises of the state-nation conflict would "arise in Asia."[6] Even though many nations in the east, south-east, south, and southwest regions of Asia have opposed predatory state and corporate behaviors and have defended their inherent and collective rights to self-determination, the nations have continued to suffer from increased militarization of state police, criminalization of community resistance, human rights violations, and international vilification by the state and corporate media through the use of labels such as terrorists, insurgents, rebels, and communists.[7] The original nation's resistance and opposition to predatory policies and projects continues across multiple regions of Asia. The following section critically examines the ongoing state-nation struggles and conflicts in the Philippines, Indonesia, India, Pakistan, Afghanistan, Iraq, and Japan.

1   The Philippines and Moro People

On April 17, 2018, Jerome Aladdin Succor Aba, a prominent Moro activist from Mindanao (the Philippines' second largest island) was being held by U.S. immigration authorities at San Francisco International Airport.[8] Aba, a twenty-five-year-old Filipino Muslim, was seized in customs, held for twenty-eight hours, and subjected to interrogation

---

[4] See generally Ohnesorge (2007) (discussing law and development theory in states throughout Asia).

[5] For specific applications of law and development policies by the WB, IMF, and USAID in Asia, see generally Upham (2018).

[6] Central Intelligence Agency (1950).

[7] Scott (2010).

[8] "Filipino Activist Claims He Was Given Weapons, Tortured At SFO" (2018).

concerning his personal political beliefs and views on the Philippine's President Rodrigo Duterte's controversial drug war. During this time, he was forced to strip naked; was offered no food other than a ham sandwich; was not allowed to sleep after a transcontinental flight, and was soon deported back to the Philippines. As the National Chair of Suara Bangsamoro (Voice of the Moro People) and Co-Chair of Sandugo Movement of Moro and Indigenous Peoples of Self-Determination, Aba had been invited to speak in the U.S. on the Moro Nation's quest for self-determination and independence in the Philippines.[9] This invitation had come from prominent church institutions, including the U.S. Conference of Catholic Bishops, the Sisters of Mercy, and the General Board of Global Ministries.[10] Aba's visit to the U.S. and speech about indigenous struggles in Mindanao was important for the Moro Nation in the Philippines. In the previous year, in May 2017, Philippine President Rodrigo Duterte had declared martial law in Mindanao, dispatching his state security forces to quell radical Muslim elements of the Moro peoples who have been fighting in decolonial struggles for independence for nearly four centuries.[11]

Islam first reached the shores of Mindanao in 1475 and spread throughout the island by trade and marriage rather than colonialism and conquest. Later to be known as "Moro," Philippine Muslims claimed and celebrated a hereditary line extending back to the Prophet Mohammad.[12] After WWII, the state government of the Philippines in Manila expanded the policy of Christian migration and multinational corporate presence in Mindanao, thus dislocating Muslim farmers and marginalizing voices of Muslim Filipinos.[13] The mounting tension between the state government and the Muslim minority eventually culminated in the 1968 Jabidah Massacre of Moro soldiers by members of the Armed Forces of the Philippines (AFP). This incident led to the formation of the militant Moro National Liberation Front (MNLF), an armed guerilla organization with

---

[9] Lee et al. (2018).

[10] Aba (2018).

[11] See Villamor (2017). See also Amnesty International (2017a, pp. 295–297).

[12] See generally McKenna (1998) (discussing Islamic solidarity and social disparity in the Muslim Philippines).

[13] Ibid., pp. 136–137.

the intent to liberate the Moro homeland. In 1972, then-President Ferdinand Marcos declared martial law, and by 1977, the conflict had displaced nearly one million people.[14] Finally, in March 2014, the Comprehensive Agreement on Bangsamoro (CAB) was signed between the state government of the Philippines and the MNLF, allowing the creation of an autonomous region for the Muslim population in the Southern Mindanao region. This involved a power-sharing agreement with the state government, with its own leadership to control most of its own natural resources and revenues.[15] Meanwhile, diplomatic documents appeared on Wikileaks showing that the U.S. government made a particular reference to untapped, rich mineral resources of Liguasan Marsh in the Cotabato Basin in Mindanao, spanning 288,000 hectares. This is among the areas controlled by MNLF.[16] In 2013, the U.S. Department of Energy had announced that huge deposits of oil and natural gas had been discovered in Mindanao, and a Philippine Supreme Court decision subsequently allowed the entry of international investors in mining.[17]

The struggles in the Philippines have an even deeper historical root, dating back to the 1898 Spanish-American War and the subsequent American occupation of the Philippines. In that year, the Treaty of Paris ended hostilities between the U.S. and Spain, which was to cede sovereignty over the Philippines to the U.S. for $20 million.[18] The previous cooperation between the Filipino nationalists and the U.S. abruptly ceased as the U.S. sent 120,000 troops to subdue the rebels that it previously aided, killing hundreds of thousands of Filipinos. The U.S. approach to the Filipino peoples had been modeled on its policies toward American Indians, as most U.S. generals had also fought during the Indian Wars of the nineteenth century. In the 1906 Battle of Bud Dajo, known as the Moro Crater Massacre, American troops slaughtered as many as one thousand Moro people.[19] David Prescott Barrows, an American anthropologist specialized in American Indian cultures, was appointed to the post of Chief of the Bureau of Non-Christian Tribes of the Philippine Islands. He

---

[14] Ibid., p. 156.

[15] "Philippines Signs Historic Peace Agreement With Muslim Group" (2014).

[16] Bayani (2011).

[17] Sebua (2012).

[18] Cochran and Chiu (1979).

[19] Hawkins (2011).

reconnoitered many islands and regions in the Philippines, an archipelago which now encompasses 71,000 islands and islets stretching 1,159 miles from north to south. More than 160 indigenous nations, including the Moro, have long inhabited these islands in the Pacific Ocean, situated approximately 500 miles off the coast of Vietnam. During this period, American companies such as Dole Food Company, Inc. seized tribal lands for plantations.[20]

After Japan's brief occupation of the Philippines during WWII, President Harry S. Truman proclaimed the independence of the Republic of the Philippines on July 4, 1946 and secured a rent-free lease on several military bases for 99 years, lasting through 2045.[21] The Military Base Agreement (MBA) in 1947 granted the U.S. the right to exercise jurisdiction over its military personnel, and in 1965, the signing of the Status of Forces of Agreement (SOFA) solidified the U.S. military presence in the Philippines. In 1992, after the Philippine Senate rejected the renewal of SOFA and closed the U.S. bases, the U.S. moved toward signing the Visiting Forces Agreement (VFA) in 1998. The U.S.-Philippine alliance was further bolstered by the signing of the Enhanced Defense Cooperation Agreement (EDCA) in 2014, allowing U.S. forces and contractors to operate on "agreed locations," including "facilities and areas that are provided by the Government of the Philippines through the Armed Forces of the Philippines (AFP) and that the United States Forces, United States contractors, and others as mutually agreed."[22] Four of five EDCA sites are on Philippine Air Force Bases, including the Lumbia Air Force Base in restive Mindanao, serving to boost counterterror cooperation by constructing housing for troops, improving the runway, and building additional storage facilities for equipment.[23]

In service of the further persecution of Moro Muslims in Mindanao, a five-month military battle in the Islamic city of Marawi in 2017 led to the killing of more than 1,000 soldiers, including 100 government troops; displaced nearly 600,000 people; and leveled this historic Islamic city long

---

[20] Danver (2012, p. 664).

[21] Cochran and Chiu (1979, p. 9).

[22] Official Gazette (2014).

[23] Poling and Cronin (2018).

inhabited by Moro people.[24] The U.S. supported counterterrorism activities through technical assistance, including intelligence logistics via drones and surveillance planes above the city, as well as joint training exercises.[25] This military conflict was the biggest and longest battle in the Philippines since WWII. In the following year, 2018, U.S. Ambassador to the Philippines Sung Y. Kim announced the Marawi Response Project of $25 million administered through the U.S. Agency for International Development (USAID) program, designed to improve social conditions of communities directly affected by the Marawi Siege.[26] The Moro Nation's struggle for the right to self-determination continues today, and the Moro Nation's claim for its territories represents a microcosm of a variety of armed struggles and military conflicts engaged in by the original nation in other regions of Asia.

2   MYANMAR AND ROHINGYA

Since the beginning of 2015, nearly 800,000 Rohingya people in the Rakhine State, one of Myanmar's poorest areas, have fled to Bangladesh in order to avoid the ethnic cleansing and genocide being carried out by Burmese State military forces.[27] Although the Rohingya people had been classified as Burmese citizens under the 1948 Constitution, the 1982 Citizenship Act led to the denial of citizenship to most Rohingya and other Muslim people.[28] In the nineteenth century, the first ethnic conflicts in the region had originated in the Arakan State in British-controlled Bengal, when British colonial policies led to long-term religious animosity between the Rakhine Buddhist majority and the Rohingya Muslim minority—whose fights for independence have repeatedly been crushed by the Burmese government.[29]

In recent times, many transnational corporations have begun to make substantial investments in Burma. Union Oil Company of California

---

[24] Heydarian (2017).

[25] Lagsa (2017).

[26] USAID (2018).

[27] Ibrahim (2017).

[28] Ibid.

[29] Ibrahim (2016) (discussing the plight of the Rohingyas of Myanmar, one of the most persecuted minorities in the world).

(UNOCAL), one of the largest foreign investors, was accused in 1996 of assisting the Burmese military junta in human rights violations against indigenous people. Such human rights organizations as EarthRights International, the Center for Constitutional Rights, and International Labour Rights Fund filed a lawsuit on behalf of indigenous people, decrying the torture, murder, and rape of villagers during the pipeline construction in 1992. Soon after the 2005 successful settlement between UNOCAL and victims of human rights abuses, Chevron bought UNOCAL, and began to build a natural gas pipeline from Myanmar to Thailand with the help of the Burmese military government.[30] The Burmese military provided security for this project, as Chevron poured millions of dollars into the coffers of the Burmese military junta.[31]

As was true for many other neighboring states, Burma had a long history of autocratic and brutal military dictatorship. From 1962 to 1988, Military General Ne Win controlled the country with an iron fist. The 1988 Nationwide Pro-Democracy Protests led by university students, monks, and civic activists finally forced his resignation, with the promise that he would hold a multiparty election. However, the military coup of September 1988 led to violent suppression of pro-democracy demonstrators. In 1990, although the National League for Democracy (NLD), led by Aung San Suu Kyi, had won eighty percent of the seats in Parliament, the military government annulled the election results, refusing to hand over power. Many NLD members were arrested, and Aung San Suu Kyi was placed under house arrest, where she remained for fifteen of the next twenty-one years until November 2010.[32]

In 2011, the government of Myanmar instituted economic and political reforms designed to open the country to renewed foreign investments. Shortly afterward, violent attacks escalated against the Rohingya people in the Rakhine State and against the Karen, Chin, Burman, and Mon peoples in marginalized territories.[33] Although the government of Myanmar currently grants official recognition to 135 distinct nations within the state, the Rohingya Muslims have been rendered stateless and

---

[30] Campbell (2004).

[31] "Oil Giant Chevron Urged to Cut Ties with Burmese Military Junta" (2007).

[32] Fong (2008) (exploring the Karen struggle for self-determination).

[33] Hill (2013).

stripped of citizenship.[34] Development projects have forcibly displaced many indigenous nations and peoples both internally and across the borders of Bangladesh, India, and Thailand, thus compelling them to set out by sea to Indonesia, Malaysia, and Australia.[35] In the northern state of Kachin, the military confiscated more than 500 acres of land to support extensive gold mining.[36] Nearly 100,000 indigenous people have been displaced in Kachin and northern Shan states, with fiercely violent conflicts occurring between the Myanmar Armed Forces and the indigenous nations and peoples in the region, including the Ta'ang National Liberation Army (TNLA), the Kachin Independence Army (KIA), the Arakan Army (AA), and the Myanmar National Democratic Alliance Army (MNDAA).[37]

In the Rakhine State, a transnational pipeline construction was financed by China National Petroleum Company (CNPC), which connected Sittwe, the capital of Rakhine State, to Kunming, China, in order to transport Myanmar's oil and gas from the Shwe gas field off the Rakhine State coastal region. International fossil fuel and energy companies from France, Indonesia, India, Russia, Singapore, Thailand, Malaysia, and Hong Kong have also begun to invest in offshore projects, while firms from South Korea, France, Malaysia, China, India, Thailand, and Vietnam have been involved in the exploration of natural resources in Rakhine and adjacent regions.[38] Significant industrial development investment in their homeland has been led by multinational corporate consortiums, and the Rohingyas in the Rakhine State have suffered human rights violations at the hands of Myanmar's security forces and state-sponsored terrorism. Myanmar's national government, led by Aung San Suu Kyi, Nobel Peace Prize Laureate, has staked its legacy on terminating armed conflicts with Myanmar's indigenous nations, and yet such conflicts have persisted in multiple regions. In particular, state-nation conflicts in Kachin, the northern Shan states, and the western Rakhine State have continued to intensify, and violations of human rights and international humanitarian

---

[34] Tantikanangkul and Pritchard (2016).

[35] Forino et al. (2017).

[36] Ibid.

[37] Amnesty International (2017b, pp. 11–12).

[38] Rai and Tun (2017).

laws against Rohingya, Karin, and other indigenous nations could worsen in coming years.

3 INDONESIA AND WEST PAPUA

In September 2017, the indigenous Papuan people's petition for independence, which contained 1.8 million signatures and had been officially banned by the Indonesian government, was "smuggled" out of West Papua, located on the western portion of the island of New Guinea, the world's second largest island. The petition was soon submitted to the U.N.'s decolonization committee that served to monitor the progress of former colonies toward independence.[39] In the early 1960s, the Netherlands had tried to create the independent Papuan state, but U.S. opposition to the independence effort led to the 1962 New York Agreement, forcing West Papua to become part of Indonesia.[40] West Papua makes up the western half of New Guinea; the division between West Papua and the independent state of Papua New Guinea (PNG) is an artificial border imposed by the Netherlands, which controlled the western half, Germany, which controlled the northeastern portion, and Britain, which controlled the southeastern region of New Guinea around the turn of the twentieth century. After West Papua became part of Indonesia in 1963, it was militarily occupied by Indonesian state security forces that were accused of gross human rights violations and violent suppression of the Free Papua Movement (*Organisasi Papua Merdeka* or OPM).[41] Some scholars have called the treatment of West Papuan people by the Indonesian military forces a genocide.[42] The independence petition asked the U.N. to appoint a special representative to investigate human rights abuses, and to put West Papua back on the decolonization committee agenda so as to ensure and recognize its right to self-determination.[43] However, the U.N.'s decolonization committee decided not to accept the

---

[39] Doherty and Lamb (2017a, 2017b).

[40] Heidbuchel (2007) (covering the root causes of the West Papua conflict, its evolution to the current situation, and possible solutions).

[41] Ibid. See also Human Rights Watch (2017, pp. 327–228).

[42] Wing and King (2005) (detailing concerns that pose serious threats to the survival of indigenous people of Papua and providing urgent recommendations).

[43] Doherty and Lamb (2017b).

petition, citing that West Papua's desire for independence was outside the committee's mandate.[44]

West Papua is the most geographically and culturally diverse of Indonesia's provinces, with more than 250 Melanesian nations comprising nearly half of its 2.7 million inhabitants.[45] Since 1963, the Indonesian state troops have countered the nations' attempts to create an independent state and have continued their repression, leading to the deaths of hundreds of thousands of West Papuans. In 1983, Indonesia's military action and appropriation of traditionally owned land for transmigration sites forced tens of thousands of West Papuans across the border to seek refuge in the neighboring state of Papua New Guinea, which had established its sovereignty in 1975. Indonesia's 1984–1989 transmigration plan called for five million indigenous people from Java, Madura, and Bali to be moved to other provinces. The indigenous nations in West Papua, East Timor, Kalimantan, South Molucca, Sulawesi, and Sumatra continued to resist the state military occupation of their homelands.

West Papua and both sides of the international border on the island of New Guinea possess great wealth in terms of easily exploitable minerals, forests, and other valuable resources.[46] The destruction of the environment in the ancestral homeland of nations has been led by international corporate consortiums and their investment on the island. In West Papua, for instance, an international consortium of logging companies from Canada, Australia, Malaysia, and Japan joined in the race to exploit New Guinea's massive tropical forests.[47] The extraction of natural resources and the destruction of the homelands continue in West Papua, further displacing refugees into Papua New Guinea.

On the other side of the island, in the state of Papua New Guinea, a similar exploitation of homelands continues. The state is composed of multiple nations and peoples who speak more than 800 distinct languages, each with its own unique culture, history, and tradition.[48] This extremely rich diversity of languages represents twelve percent of the world's total

---

[44] Ibid.

[45] Vaughn (2010, p. 14).

[46] Tebay (2005) (describing injustices in West Papua and providing recommendations to remedy them).

[47] Sands (1991).

[48] Danver (2012, p. 656).

languages.[49] In December 2016, the Papua New Guinea state government announced that it was deploying its military to quell violence in Hela Province, home to the country's largest oil and gas project. The original nations' opposition to the development in the area sparked debates about possible violations of human rights and public safety issues as well as potential impacts on the operation of Papua New Guinea liquefied natural gas (LNG) projects that were managed by ExxonMobil Corporation.[50] In January 2018, ExxonMobil revealed the high-quality, hydrocarbon-bearing reservoirs offshore in the Western Province of Papua New Guinea.[51] The Papua New Guinea Investment Promotion Authority had been earlier established, by an act of Parliament in 1992, and was supported by the International Finance Corporation, which is a member of the World Bank Group, headquartered in Washington, D.C.

The entire island of New Guinea has been subjected to neoliberal policies of international investment and to development projects that have led to the displacement and depopulation of indigenous nations and peoples, the usurpation of natural resources, and the destruction of ancestral homelands. The independent nationalist movement has been violently suppressed by the joint forces of the state police, the army, and the paramilitary troops called the "Mobile Brigade Corps," which is also known as "Brimob." As the specially trained counterinsurgency troop, the Mobile Brigade Corps was originally created in 1965 by the Central Intelligence Agency (CIA) in an attempt to overthrow then-Socialist President Achmed Sukarno, who had threatened to expropriate U.S.-owned rubber plantations and oil companies.[52] This counterinsurgency paramilitary group was also responsible for the systematic ethnic cleansing" of indigenous populations in East Timor from 1970 to 1990s.[53] While the United Liberation Movement for West Papua (ULMWP) finally united the factions of the various political movements in multiple nations seeking independence in 2014, both domestic and international development projects financed by transnational investment consortiums and protected by state military forces on the island have continued to hinder the nations'

[49] Nakatani (2017).

[50] Lynas (1998).

[51] "ExxonMobil Reports Papua New Guinea Discovery" (2018).

[52] Kuzmarov (2017).

[53] Carey (1995).

aspirations for independence and the right to self-determination in West Papua.

4   India and Kashmir

In April 2018, an Indian military operation killed at least twelve Muslim militants in Kashmir. They were caught up in a territorial dispute between Hindu-majority India and Muslim-majority Pakistan.[54] Kashmiris' national struggle for independence continues today despite the extreme violence of the Indian state police and paramilitary forces in the northwest Kashmir Valley of Jammu and Kashmir. The 1947 British-imposed border, called the "Radcliffe Line," divided Kashmir into India and Pakistan, thus igniting the beginning of the nation's struggles for the right to self-determination, struggles which continue to this date.[55] The Radcliffe Line also divided Bengal into India-held West Bengal and independent East Bengal in the east of India. East Bengal, which was later renamed as East Pakistan, attained its sovereignty in 1971, becoming the independent state of Bangladesh. The territorial dispute and conflict between India and Pakistan over Kashmir led to the establishment of the Line of Control (LOC), which partitioned Kashmir into the Indian- and Pakistani-controlled areas of the former princely state of Jammu and Kashmir. The line was not recognized as constituting a legally mandated international border, but still remains as a de facto boundary shared by the two states of India and Pakistan. In addition to the Indian-controlled state of Jammu and Kashmir, British colonial rule also partitioned the Kashmiris, native to the Kashmir Valley, into two separate regions: the Pakistani-controlled regions of Gilgit-Baltistan in the north and Azad Kashmir in the south and Chinese-controlled Aksai Chin in the east of Kashmir Valley.[56]

India and Pakistan fought several major wars over Kashmir, including the Indo-Pakistani Wars of 1947, 1955, and 1971 and the Kargil War of 1999.[57] A widespread, popular, and armed struggle by Muslim militant

---

[54] Fareed (2018).

[55] Mackey (2009).

[56] Krishan (2002) (historical overview of warring nation-states across much-sought-after Kashmir territory).

[57] Ganguly (2002) (analyzing why conflict persists between India and Pakistan as well as their prospects of war and peace).

groups for secession from India and for the right to self-determination began in India-administered Kashmir in 1989. The Indian government countered the independent nationalist movement by dispatching the state military and paramilitary troops, making India-controlled Kashmir one of the most militarized zones of the world, affected by Pakistan-backed militancy and India's military occupation. In 2011, The Human Rights Commission reported that it had evidence that 2,156 bodies had been buried in forty grave sites over the last twenty years.[58] The Indian government has claimed that the insurgents were Islamic terrorist groups from Pakistan-administered Kashmir and Afghanistan, who were fighting to make the state of Jammu and Kashmir a part of Pakistan. India further claimed that the terrorists had killed many peaceful civilians in Kashmir and committed other human rights violations, and denied that its own police and security forces were responsible for human rights abuses.[59] Today Kashmir's struggle for independence and right to self-determination continues in the India-Pakistan border areas. Human Rights Watch reported in 2018 that in the first ten months of 2017, forty-two reported attacks occurred in the Indian state of Jammu and Kashmir, leading to the deaths of 184 people and forty-four security force personnel.[60] Impunity for human rights abuses by the state military persists in Jammu and Kashmir. In 2017, the Supreme Court of India refused to reopen 215 cases, involving the deaths of over 700 members of the Kashmiri Pandit community in 1989. An appellate military court also suspended the life sentences of five army personnel convicted by a court martial of extrajudicial execution of activists in 2010.[61] Abdul Basit, Pakistan High Commissioner to India, declared on Pakistan's Independence Day in 2016, "Struggle for independence will continue until Kashmir gets freedom; sacrifice of the people of Kashmir will not go in vain."[62] The struggle continues: in early April 2018, at least twenty people died and seventy others were wounded as violent clashes erupted when Indian government forces opened fire on pro-independence militias

---

[58] "Kashmir Graves: Human Rights Watch Calls for Inquiry" (2011).

[59] Haqqani (2018). See also "Systematic Rights Violations Taking Place in Indian Held Kashmir: Human Right Bodies" (2012).

[60] Human Rights Watch (2018, p. 261).

[61] Ibid., p. 262.

[62] DNA Web Team (2016).

in Kashmir.[63] Kashmir's effort to gain independence and militant resistance to the occupation of Indian-administered Kashmir will no doubt continue on into the future.

5   IRAQ AND THE KURDISH HOMELAND

On what would become the historic day of September 25, 2017, more than 90% of Iraqi Kurds voted in favor of the independent Iraqi Kurdistan state, trying to secede from the Republic of Iraq, which had long been exercising genocidal policies against Kurds, including the Anfal genocidal campaign in northern Iraq during the final years of the Iraq-Iran War between 1986 and 1988, killing tens of thousands of Kurds.[64] During the war, the Kurds of northern Iraq sided with Iran. Saddam Hussein thus ordered Operation Al-Anfal (Arabic for "the spoils"), a series of military campaigns that included direct attacks on Kurdish militants and civilian populations, the assembly of Kurds at collection points for transit to prison campus in the desert, the separation of the Kurdish population by gender, the execution of fighting-age males, and the razing of villages over a large swath of Kurdish-dominant northern Iraqi regions. The U.S. intelligence communities, including the Defense Intelligence Agency (DIA), supplied Iraq with satellite imagery and maps of Iranian troop movements in and around the Kurdish city of Halabja, as well as Iranian logistics facilities and details about Iranian air defenses. Iraqi troops then used a variety of chemical weapons against Kurds and Iranian troops, including mustard gas and the deadly nerve agent sarin.[65] The gassing of Halabja in May 1988 was considered the most horrific incident during the war, killing 5,000 people, including women and children, mostly from nerve gas.[66] Iraqi forces also used aerial bombs and artillery shells filled with sarin against Iranian troop concentrations, helping the Iraqi forces win a major victory.[67]

The ancestral homeland of the Kurds was first partitioned after the First World War by the British- and French-led Mandate System, under the

---

[63] "Kashmir: Indian Forces Open Fire on Pro-Independence Protesters" (2018).

[64] Zucchino (2017).

[65] Hiltermann (2008).

[66] Ibid., p. 6.

[67] Harris and Aid (2013).

League of Nations sanction over the territories of the Ottoman Empire, which had been defeated by the Allied Powers in 1918. The secret Sykes-Picot Agreement between Great Britain and France in 1916 during WWI partitioned the Ottoman Empire into smaller administrative units. Immediately after WWI, the Mandate System of the League of Nations was created to manage the administrated units, in which Iraq, Palestine, and East Jordan were placed under British Mandate rule and Syria and later Lebanon under French rule. These mandated units later gained their independence and became sovereign states. As a result, the Kurdish homeland that had historically encompassed the northwestern Zagros Mountain and the eastern Taurus mountain ranges was divided into the present-day state borders of Iraq, Iran, Syria, and Turkey.[68]

Today's Iraq encompasses a multitude of distinct groups and religious sects. The 2005 Iraqi Constitution declared Iraq as an Arab nation, while also recognizing other indigenous groups, such as Assyrians, Chaldeans, Kurds, and Turkmen, as well as smaller religious and ethnic minorities, including Armenians, Mandaeans, Shabaks, and Yazidis.[69] Arabs, who constitute three-quarters of the Iraqi population, live mainly in central and southern Iraq, while the Kurds, who make up nearly twenty percent of the Iraqi population, live in the north.[70] The U.S. and Iraq signed the Status of Forces Agreement (SOFA) in 2008, making Iraq one of more than 115 countries in the world to sign this treaty with the U.S., which contractually prescribed terms for stationing U.S. troops and for applying laws to U.S. military personnel and contractors in a host country. The U.S. military soon built five new permanent bases in Iraq's Kurdish region.[71] The U.S.-Iraq SOFA also prevented Iraq from exerting its criminal jurisdiction over U.S. personnel who violate Iraqi citizens' rights, granting immunity to U.S. troops and private contractors for acts constituting criminal or civil violation under Iraqi law, thereby ensuring that statutory framework would be unlikely to permit Iraq from exercising jurisdiction over foreign troops.[72]

---

[68] Anghie (2004, pp. 120–121).

[69] Danver (2012, p. 628).

[70] Ibid.

[71] Rice and Gates (2008).

[72] Bassiouni (2010, p. 8).

The objective of U.S. military outposts in the Kurdish region was to "perpetuate its occupation of the conflict-ridden Arab country indefinitely … [and] help Americans to monitor movements in a vast expanse of land, which stretches from the western bank of the Tigris river to Tal Afar city [in northern Iraq],"[73] The military bases were also used to provide training, weapons, and intelligence for the Kurdish forces, including the Peshmerga and its security subsidiaries, in order to fight against the Islamic State of Iraq and Syria (ISIS) in Tal Afar and other neighboring areas.[74] Turkey has opposed the U.S. military assistance to Kurdish troops, as Turkey has also been fighting against the Kurdistan Workers' Party (PKK) that has long called for an independent Kurdish state in Turkey.[75]

Despite the fact that the 2017 pro-independent referendum by the Kurdish Regional Government (KRG) was supported by the overwhelming majority of Iraqi Kurds, the ultimate sovereignty of the Iraqi Kurdistan state has been opposed by every government of the partitioned states of Iraq, Iran, Syria, and Turkey.[76] U.S. Senator Chuck Schumer became the first political figure to openly support Kurdish independence, asking the U.S. government to aid "a political process that addresses the aspirations of the Kurds for an independent state."[77] The U.S. government, however, announced that it refused to recognize the unilateral referendum because the vote and results lacked legitimacy.[78]

Kurdish nationalism remains strong and has been supported by Kurds in each of the partitioned states as well as by the worldwide Kurdish diaspora. Nonetheless, the aspiration for an independent Kurdistan has been crushed by the military forces of each of the partitioned states, including the Kurdish–Turkish conflict led by Kurdish armed groups to challenge Turkish authority over the southeastern Kurdish region. This region has been referred to as "Northern Kurdistan" as it is located in the north of the original Kurdistan homeland. Many Syrian Kurds sought political autonomy within Syria and considered the Kurdish-majority region

---

[73] "US Military Constructing New Base in Iraq's Kurdish Region: Report" (2017).

[74] Goran (2018).

[75] "Turkey Balks at Arming Kurds Against ISIS" (2014).

[76] Dadouch (2017). See also Salim et al. (2017) and Srivastava and Bozorgmehr (2017).

[77] Bacon (2017).

[78] Zargham (2017).

of northern and northeastern Syria to be "Western Kurdistan," as it was in the western region of the original Kurdistan homeland. After the 1991 uprisings in Iraq, the Kurdish opposition to Iraqi President Saddam Hussein established the Kurdish Autonomous Republic in northern Iraq, which later became the Kurdistan Region of Iraq. It has also been referred to as "Southern Kurdistan" as it is located in the south of the original Kurdistan homeland. "Eastern Kurdistan" is an official term for the Kurdish-dominant northwestern area of Iran which borders Iraq and Turkey. While the entire population of nearly twenty-five million Kurds is spread across four states, the independent state of Iraqi Kurdistan could possibly lead to the creation of an independent Kurdish state by integrating the four partitioned regions of Kurdistan.

Iraq has the world's second largest oil reserves as a whole, but the Kurdistan Region of Iraq alone holds the world's seventh largest oil reserves and has been targeted for investment by global oil and fossil fuel multinational corporations.[79] Starting in 2011, a number of international energy companies began to invest in the oil-rich Kurdish region, starting with ExxonMobil and followed by Chevron, Talisman Energy of Canada, Gazprom of Russia, Addax Petroleum of China, Reliance Industries of India, and Korea National Oil Company of South Korea, among many others.[80] If Iraqi Kurdistan becomes an independent state, these oil companies must have separate terms of negotiation with the government of the newly established state, not the Iraqi government. With its enormous oil and natural gas resources, the Iraqi government has already decided to further integrate its economy into the international system of finance, trade, and investment. In December 2015, the Iraq government agreed to sign the International Center for Settlement of Investment Dispute (ICSID) Convention to help protect the rights of foreign investors in Iraq.[81] Iraq also resumed its membership in the World Trade Organization (WTO) in November 2017 after nine years of dormancy and acceded to the WTO provisions, including the Trade-Related Aspects of Intellectual Property Rights (TRIPS).[82]

---

[79] Foreign Investment in Iraqi Kurdistan (2017).

[80] For the names of international energy firms granted a license by the Kurdistan Regional Government, see *List of International Oil Companies in Iraqi Kurdistan* (2018).

[81] "The ICSID Convention Enters into Force in Iraq" (2016).

[82] World Trade Organization (2017).

In response to Iraqi Kurdistan independence and its potential ramifications for its own Kurdish populations in neighboring states, the presidents of both Iran and Turkey vowed to impose severe economic sanctions on Iraqi Kurdistan and launched joint military exercises with Iraqi troops on their borders with the separatist region.[83] However, the Kurdistan Workers' Party (PKK) in Turkey supported the referendum, stating that it was "a democratic right, no one should stand against it."[84] The PKK, which was founded on Kurdish nationalism in 1978 and based in Turkey and Iraq, has been fighting to achieve an independent Kurdish state. Immediately after the Iraqi Kurdish referendum was approved on September 25, 2017, Turkish jets hit northern Iraq and killed thirteen suspected Kurdish PKK fighters, silencing potential efforts for political activity to achieve the further reunification of Kurdish people in Iraq, Turkey, and beyond. Meanwhile, the U.N. Security Council opposed the referendum because it would have a potentially destabilizing effect in the region, hinder efforts to help refugees return home, and weaken the military campaign against the Islamic State (IS) group.[85] Furthermore, U.N. Secretary-General Antonio Guterres said that the referendum was opposed not only by "Iraqi authorities" but also by "the global community" and expressed concerns about potentially destabilizing effects of the nationalist referendum in the Kurdistan region of Iraq.[86]

6   JAPAN AND OKINAWA

Similar predatory behavior of the state and foreign actors against the nation is observed in other First World states, such as the U.S., Canada, Australia, New Zealand, and those in Europe.[87] Japan is also one of the highly industrialized states in the world, and the inhabitants of Okinawa have opposed colonial rule and egregious development projects that have been facilitated by the use of both domestic and international laws. For

---

[83] "Iran, Turkey Pledge to Stop Iraqi Kurdistan Independence from Taking Hold" (2017).

[84] Ali (2017).

[85] "UN Security Council Opposes Kurdish Independence Vote" (2017).

[86] "The Latest: UN Regrets Iraq's Kurds Went Ahead With Vote" (2017).

[87] For the colonial history and exploitation of indigenous population in former English colonies, including Canada, Australia, and New Zealand, see generally Miller et al. (2010). For indigenous people in the world, including Europe, see generally Danver (2012).

example, the Japanese government has been trying to construct a new U.S. Marine airfield in the northern village of Okinawa despite the strong pushback of nonviolent groups of Okinawans, environmental activists, and U.S. base opponents.[88]

Okinawa, or "Ryukyu" in an indigenous pronunciation and as spelled in the Chinese language, had been a sovereign and independent kingdom in the middle of the East China Sea for centuries. In 1372, the Ryukyu Kingdom accepted the supremacy of China, developed a formal trading relationship, and became a tributary state of the Chinese Empire.[89] The Ryukyu kingdom had hundreds of islands in a chain over one thousand kilometers long. While there are eight major islands in the archipelago, the largest is the island of Okinawa, where the Shuri Castle of the Ryukyu Kingdom was built. In 1609, the kingdom was attacked and invaded by the Shimazu clan of the Satsuma-Han (a feudal government) from the southern tip of Kyushu Island (Japan's third largest island), and this feudal clan then transformed the kingdom into its vassal nation. The Shimazu clan then became Japan's only feudal government to trade with the Ryukyu kingdom.[90]

Since the islands are located at the eastern perimeter of the East China Sea, close to Taiwan, China, Vietnam, Thailand, the Philippines, Indonesia, and other regions in Southeast Asia and the Pacific islands to the South, the Ryukyu Kingdom became a prosperous trading post for neighboring islands, regional lords, and kingdoms. Because of its strategic location, in the nineteenth century the Ryukyu Kingdom began to serve as an important supply station for Western powers, especially during their effort to colonize the region and expand their imperial outreach in Asia. For example, before American Commodore Matthew C. Perry and his black-hulled steam frigates traveled to Uraga Harbor in the Tokyo Bay near Edo (today's Tokyo), on July 8, 1853, and demanded the opening of its market to the U.S., Perry and his fleets had arrived in "the neighborhood of the Lew Chew [Ryukyu]"[91] on May 26, 1853. They entered its main city of Naha and paid a loyal visit to the Shuri Castle of the Ryukyu

---

[88] Ito and Yamashita (2018).

[89] Kerr (2000, p. 66).

[90] Turnbull (2009, p. 1610).

[91] Perry (1968, p. 61).

Kingdom.[92] When the new government of Japan declared its independence in 1868 and disclosed its intention to annex the Ryukyu Kingdom, China's Qing Empire asserted its sovereignty over the Ryukyu Kingdom. The U.S. government had signed the Treaty of Amity with the Ryukyu Kingdom in 1854.[93] When the negotiation with China finally broke down, Japan forcefully integrated the entire Ryukyu archipelago into its state project. The Japanese government thus abolished the kingdom and replaced it with the new Okinawa prefectural government in 1879.

Following Japan's surrender at the end of WWII, the first U.S. military base was established in Okinawa in 1945.[94] The 1951 Peace Treaty of San Francisco, signed by Japan and the Allied Powers, including the U.S., also made Okinawa a virtual U.S. military colony and facilitated the further installation of U.S. military bases, ports, and facilities in Okinawa.[95]

Today, nearly three-quarters of all U.S. military bases and facilities in Japan are found on the island of Okinawa, despite the fact that Okinawa accounts only for 0.6% of Japanese territory. Okinawa also has a high concentration of U.S. military troops and personnel, civil contractors, and base workers.[96] Under the Japanese-U.S. plan, the Futenma Marine Airfield was scheduled to be relocated from the dense, residential area of Ginowan to the coastal area of Nago and its coral-rich Henoko Bay, adjacent to the Marine Camp Schwab. The projected airfield would be funded by the Japanese government and equipped with two 3,000-m runways, a military port, and an integrated ammunition bunker capable of storing nuclear weapons. This original plan was secretly formulated by Chairman of the Joint Chiefs of Staff Earle Wheeler and approved by Defense Secretary Robert McNamara in 1968 during the U.S. military occupation of the island.[97] Local opposition to the facility has so far hindered efforts to continue this construction plan. In October 2015, the Japanese government began building the base, and both the Japanese government and the

---

[92] Ibid., p. 71.

[93] "US Shows a Copy of the Ryukyu-US Treaties and Letters by Commodore Perry" (2018).

[94] For the U.S. military occupation of Okinawa, see generally Fukurai (2010).

[95] For Okinawa's colonial history, see generally Fukurai (2011).

[96] Ibid.

[97] "Plan to Build Base Off Nago in 1960s Got OK by U.S. Top Brass, Document Reveals" (2016).

opposition group took the base issue to court the same year. The Japanese government sued Okinawa Governor Takeshi Onaga, who revoked his predecessor's permission for landfill work at Henoko Bay in 2016, and the Japanese Supreme Court ruled that it would let the judgment stand, thereby opening the door to the airfield construction. In April 2018, nearly 800 protesters staged a demonstration at the Henoko construction site, and a few hundred more demonstrated in front of a gate at Camp Schwab in order to assert Okinawans' opposition to, and independence from, U.S. imperialism and predatory Japanese occupation.[98]

Additionally, ever since the 1999 crash of a U.S. military helicopter near an elementary school, Takae citizens' sit-in protests have continued to prevent the construction and operation of helipads in the small village of Takae in the hills of northern Okinawa. In 2006, the U.S. military began to build six new helipads as part of a 1996 bilateral deal between the Japanese and U.S. governments. Despite the residents' complaints to the prefectural and state governments, the voices of Okinawans were ignored.[99] The bilateral agreement stipulated that the U.S. military would return fifteen square miles of its training grounds in exchange for the new helipads.[100] Since then, over 10,000 Okinawans, mainland Japanese, and foreign nationals have participated in the nonstop sit-in outside the planned helipad sites. In 2008, the Japanese government filed an injunction against fifteen of the protesters, including an eight-year-old child, so as to intimidate potential participants in the continuous sit-in demonstration.[101] Takae villagers were no strangers to U.S. imperial projects and military ventures. During the Vietnam War, Takae residents, including children, had been recruited to play the role of South Vietnamese soldiers and civilians during training exercises in the Northern Training Area, which had become a mock village for soldiers training in anti-guerrilla operations.[102] Takae had also been sprayed by the defoliant "Agent Orange" to test its chemical toxicity.[103]

---

[98] "Protesters Rally One Year After Start of Henoko Coastal Work" (2018).

[99] Mitchell (2010).

[100] Torio (2016).

[101] Mitchell (2010).

[102] Torio (2016).

[103] Ibid.

In December 2017, Okinawans' independence movement was reignited after a former U.S. Marine was sentenced to life in prison for raping and killing a twenty-year-old Okinawa woman.[104] Sexual victimization of Okinawan women and children at the hands of U.S. service members has a long history, dating back to 1945, when the U.S. military forcefully occupied the island following the "Battle of Okinawa," which killed more than one-quarter of the Okinawan population.[105] The 1960 Treaty of Mutual Cooperation and Security Between the U.S. and Japan (i.e., Japan-U.S. Security Treaty) was signed by both the U.S. and Japanese governments, requiring both states to act to meet the common danger and to support the continued presence of U.S. military bases in Japan to satisfy that requirement.

Article 6 of the Japan-U.S. Security Treaty also incorporated the Status of Forces Agreement (SOFA) that allowed the use of U.S. military bases for combat purposes other than the defense of Japan. SOFA granted special, extraterritorial rights to U.S. military personnel and imposed a limited jurisdiction on the local government's ability to prosecute the crimes committed by U.S. military personnel, dependents, and civilian contractors. SOFA also allows the U.S. military to retain custody of suspects inside a base until they are formally indicted by local prosecutors. Since the bilateral treaty also exempts military personnel from Japanese visa and passport laws, suspected criminals were often transferred back to the U.S. before facing criminal charges in Japanese courts. As a result, many Okinawans, including women and children, have long been victimized at the hands of soldiers and military contractors who enjoyed a relative climate of impunity in Okinawa. Two weeks after the life sentence was handed down to a former U.S. soldier for raping and murdering an Okinawan woman, a window from a U.S. Marine helicopter fell off and crashed onto a school playground at Futenma Daini Elementary School, injuring a child.[106] Three months prior to this incident, another U.S. helicopter had crashed into Takae in Higashi Village, following yet another crash of an MV-22 Osprey in Nago City in December 2016.[107]

---

[104] "Ex-U.S. Base Worker Appeals Life Sentence for Killing Okinawa Woman" (2017).

[105] Vine (2015, p. 260) ("Between 100,000 and 140,000 Okinawans—one quarter to one third of Okinawa's population—likely died during the fighting.").

[106] Yamaguchi (2017).

[107] "Japan Wants U.S. Choppers Grounded as Accident in Okinawa Leaves LDP Reeling Ahead of Election" (2017).

Okinawa remains America's key strategic outpost in Asia, one that has served an important imperial function in multiple U.S. military ventures in the region, including the Korean War in the 1950s, the Vietnam War throughout the 1960s and early 1970s, the first Gulf War in the early 1990s, and the Afghanistan and Iraq Invasions and subsequent occupation from the first decade of the twenty-first century to the present. Today, Okinawa's role in terms of U.S. global security in the region has become even more significant due to the increasing threats posed by China, Russia, and a nuclearizing North Korea. Multiple international treaties that the U.S. has signed with the Japanese government have continued to deter the nationalist aspiration of the Okinawan people and their efforts to attain independence and the right to self-determination on the island. The selective prosecution of Okinawan activists by the Japanese government and the favorable court rulings on military base constructions in Okinawa have continued to serve the interests of both the Japanese and U.S. governments. The construction projects of Marine airfield and helipads in northern Okinawa have been protected and facilitated by both domestic and international laws—state court decisions and bilateral treaties signed between states—that, for now, take precedence over the welfare and wishes of the Okinawan people.

7   OTHER CONFLICTS AND STRUGGLES IN OTHER REGIONS OF ASIA

There are other ongoing struggles and conflicts taking place in Asia, such as those of a Sikh separatist movement in Khalistan in the Punjab region of eastern Pakistan and northern India; a guerrilla warfare waged by Baloch nationalists in Balochistan against the governments of Pakistan and Iran; and insurgency movements in Assam, India's resource-rich Islamic region located at the borders of Bangladesh, where the Indian government decided in 2019 to strip the citizenship of nearly two million Muslims in the region, thereby facilitating their possible relocation to the neighboring state of Bangladesh.[108] The Indian government found Assam to be rich in crude oil, natural gas, coal, quartzite, and other precious minerals and made Assam the largest producer of onshore natural gas in India.[109]

---

[108] Eyre (2019).

[109] National Investment Promotion Facilitation Agency (2020).

During 2016 and 2017, pharmaceutical corporations also started production by capitalizing 952 species of plants used in medical practices.[110] Assam's Global Investors' Summit was held in February 2018, soliciting the participation of industrialists and business leaders of India and other countries around the globe.[111] The purging of Muslim populations has been a factor in helping to quell local resistance against unpopular and unsustainable corporate projects in the region.

Two autonomous regions in China have witnessed the struggles of two religious populations for their sovereignty and independence from China—the Buddhist majority in Tibet and the Uyghur Muslims in western China. Huge reserves of lithium, gold, silver, and copper have been discovered in Tibet. While the Tibetan religion does not promote the practice of disturbing the "Mother Earth," Chinese firms have begun mining in the region, thus contaminating adjacent regions.[112] In continuing protest against Chinese rule, more than 140 Tibetans have self-immolated.[113] The Xinjian Uyghur Autonomous Region was found to hold huge reserves of natural gas, oil, gold, uranium, coal, and other precious minerals, and the province has become a strategic center for energy production in China. Uyghurs have been fighting against colonization, ethnic and religious discrimination, political inequality, and the lack of political autonomy.[114] To stifle regional unrest, as many as one million Uyghur Muslims have been detained in western Xinjian to undergo reeducation programs.[115]

Other indigenous nations have been facing similar oppression by their own governments, including Arakan, Karen, Karenni, Chin, and Kachin, to name only a few of these, in Myanmar. In Indonesia, besides the indigenous people's struggles in West Papua, multiple nations such as Minahasa, Kalimantan, South Moluccas, Riau and many others have also been fighting for the right to self-determination. In the multiethnic state of Nepal, in the high altitude of the Himalayan plateau which shares

[110] Ibid.
[111] "About the Summit" (2020).
[112] Denyer (2016).
[113] Wong (2016).
[114] Castets (2019).
[115] Hughes (2018).

international borders with India and China, indigenous Madhesis of Indo-Aryan origin have been struggling for the right to self-determination, demanding the creation of ethnic-based federalism. After the promulgation of the new constitution in 2015, Madhesis launched a blockade of transporting goods at the India-Nepal border, leading to conflicts with the Nepalese national military.[116] In the island state of Sri Lanka, which is located in the Indian Ocean, Tamils and their Liberation Tigers of Tamil Ealam (LTTE) had been fighting for independence. In 2009, the Sri Lankan military finally defeated the Tamil Tigers, bringing nearly three decades of civil war to an end. Tamils' history goes back over two-thousand years, with origins traced back to their ancestry to Southern India and northeastern regions of Sri Lanka. Their struggle for the right to self-determination still continues today. Another significant example of the effort to gain the right to self-determination is the Palestinians' struggle against the military state of Israel, which began when the Jewish Agency issued the declaration of independence and proclaimed the establishment of the State of Israel in Palestine in 1948.

8 Conclusions

This chapter has examined multiple "state-nation" conflicts, from the northeastern region to the southwestern corner of Asia, including the Middle East. The original nation and people have long been fighting against the state domination and the impact of the system of law that privileges the rights of the state and corporations over the rights and welfare of the original nation, people, the nature, and ecosystems. While similar geopolitical conflicts have manifested in many regions across the globe, Asia has been the epicenter of such struggles and conflicts, especially since the 1950s, as was predicted by the U.S. government and its intelligence community. These conflicts in Asia have continued into the twenty-first century.[117] Soon after 9/11, the U.S. Office of the Secretary of Defense observed that further conflict would be seen in Iraq, Syria, Lebanon, and

---

[116] Asia Foundation (2017). See also Amnesty International (2019).
[117] Clark (2007).

Iran, along with the eastern African states of Libya,[118] Somalia,[119] and Sudan,[120] all of which stand at the crossroads between Asia and Africa.[121]

The original nation's struggle against the state has also been persistent in the industrially advanced states of Japan and Israel, as well as in the less industrialized states of Indonesia, Myanmar, India, the Philippines, and other neighboring regions in Southeast and South Asia. The state-nation conflict has been observed in the most populated states, China and India, as well as the lesser populated states, Nepal and Sri Lanka. The original nation and people have been targeted by state-sponsored corporate projects that promote neoliberal policies sought by domestic firms, overseas investors such as banks and financiers, and corporate consortiums organized by multiple countries. These state-assisted corporate projects have facilitated the exploitation of natural resources through mining and mineral extraction, leading to massive contamination and destruction of the nature, environment, and ecosystems of the national homeland. When strong protests have been mounted, the nation and people have been faced with even greater state persecution and prosecution.

The analysis of sub-state and across multiple state struggles and conflicts has revealed the deficiency of state-delimited, geopolitical discourses, and narratives which exclude consideration of the history of resistance by the original nation and people within and across the state-defined borders. The state-centric, legal analytic approach, such as Third World Approaches to International Law (TWAIL), has failed to account for the state exploitation of the nation and people, not only in the Third World states, but also in the First World states, as well as nearly every state in the Global North and Global South. The next chapter examines the theoretical tenets and utility of Original Nation Approaches to "Inter-National" Law (ONAIL), so as to understand the origin and historical genealogy of struggles of the original nation and people across

---

[118] Berbers or Amazighs, i.e., indigenous people of North Africa who were suppressed under Gaddafi, became crucial supporters of the rebellion seeking to topple Gaddafi. See also Graff (2011).

[119] For the clan and sub-clan ethnic enclaves and their impacts on Somali struggles, see Osman (2007).

[120] Ruey (2017). See also Council on Foreign Relations (2020).

[121] Some of these regional conflicts have also been supported by Russia. See for example, Dixon (2020) and Ignatius (2020).

the globe, to analyze the role of international law that serves as a "perfect instrument of empire"[122] in the engagement of "state-building" and "nation-destroying" projects, and to propose the path for the building of inter- "national" global alliance and solidarity among the original nations and their supporters, in order to mount effective resistance against the predatory state and corporate projects and thus to attain and assert the rights of self-determination in the foreseeable future.

BIBLIOGRAPHY

Aba, Jerome Succor (2018) "First Person Account: I Am Jerome Succor Aba. I Am a Muslim Human Rights Worker from Mindanao, NOT a Terrorist," MindaNews, 25 April, available at https://www.mindanews.com/mindaviews/2018/04/first-person-account-i-am-jerome-succor-aba-i-am-a-muslim-human-rights-worker-from-mindanao-not-a-terrorist/.

"About the Summit" (2020) Advantage Assam (accessed 15 May 2020), available at https://advantageassam.com/about-the-summit.

Ali, Sangar P. (2017) "KK Leader: Referendum a Democratic Right, No One Should Stand Against it," Kurdistan24, 13 June, available at https://www.kurdistan24.net/en/news/1ba4d164-3e06-431d-9a14-e83370cb869a.

Amnesty International (2017a) "Amnesty International Report 2016/17: The State of the World's Human Rights," available at https://www.amnesty.org/download/Documents/POL1048002017ENGLISH.PDF.

Amnesty International (2017b) "All the Civilians Suffer": Conflict, Displacement, and Abuse in Northern Myanmar," available at https://www.amnesty.org/en/documents/asa16/6429/2017/en/.

Amnesty International (2019) "Nepal 2017/2018," available at https://www.amnesty.org/en/countries/asia-and-the-pacific/nepal/report-nepal/.

Anghie, Anton (2004) Imperialism, Sovereignty and the Making of International Law. Cambridge, UK: Cambridge University Press.

Asia Foundation (2017) Nepal at a Glance, available at https://asiafoundation.org/wp-content/uploads/2017/10/Nepal-StateofConflictandViolence.pdf.

Bacon, John (2017) "Kurds Vote for Independence Amid U.S. Concerns," USA Today, 27 September.

Bassiouni, M. Cherif (2010) "Legal Status of US Forces in Iraq from 2003–2008," Chicago Journal of International Law 11: 1–38.

---

[122] Nebrija (1492). He declared that "Language has always the perfect instrument of empire," in which law was a declarative, written form of human relations written on the binding document.

Bayani, Makisig (2011) "Wikileaks: US Says Island Mindanao Has $1-Trillion Dollar Untapped Mineral Resources," Peso Reserve News, August, available at https://www.pesoreserve.com/2011/08/wikileaks-us-says-island-min danao-has-1.html.

Campbell, Duncan (2004) "Energy Giant Agrees Settlement with Burmese Villagers," Guardian, 14 December.

Carey, Peter (1995) "Letter: State Terrorism in East Timor," Indep., 2 October, available at https://www.independent.co.uk/life-style/letter-state-terrorism-in-east-timor-1575579.html.

Castets, Remi (2019) "What's Really Happening to Uighurs in Xinjiang?" Nation, 19 March.

Central Intelligence Agency (1950) "CIA-RDP67, Review of the World Situation as It Relates to the Security of the United States," 16 January, available at https://www.cia.gov/library/readingroom/docs/CIA-RDP67-00059A000500100009-6.pdf.

Clark, Wesley (2007) A Time to Lead: For Duty, Honor and Country. NY: Palgrave Macmillan.

Cochran, Charles L. & Hungdah Chiu (1979) "U.S. Status of Forces Agreements with Asian Countries: Selected Studies," 7 Occasional Papers/Reprints Series in Contemporary Asian Studies 1–144.

Council on Foreign Relations (2020) "Civil War in South Sudan," 18 June, available at https://www.cfr.org/global-conflict-tracker/conflict/civil-war-south-sudan.

Dadouch, Sarah (2017) "Damascus Rejects Iraqi Kurdish Independence Referendum," Reuters, 25 September.

Danver, Steven (2012) The Native Peoples of the World: An Encyclopedia of Groups, Cultures, and Contemporary Issues. Armonk, NY: Sharpe Reference.

Denyer, Simon (2016) "Tibetans in Anguish as Chinese Mines Pollute Their Sacred Grasslands," Washington Post, 26 December.

Dixon, Robyn (2020) "Russia Stands to Benefit as Middle East Tensions Spike After Soleimani Killing," Washington Post, 6 January.

DNA Web Team (2016) "Struggle for Independence Will Continue Till Kashmir Gets Freedom, Says Pakistan High Commissioner Abdul Basit," DNA INDIA, 14 August, available at https://www.dnaindia.com/india/rep ort-pakistan-s-independence-day-dedicated-to-kashmir-s-azadi-this-year-says-high-commissioner-abdul-basit-2244894.

Doherty, Ben & Kate Lamb (2017a) "Banned West Papua Independence Petition Handed to UN," Guardian, 27 September.

Doherty, Ben & Kate Lamb (2017b) "West Papua Independence Petition is Rebuffed at UN," Guardian, 29 September.

Dupuy, Kendra, Scott Gates, Havard M. Nygard, Ida Rudolfsen, Siri Aas Rustad, Havard Strand, & Henrik Urdal (2017) "Trends in Armed Conflict, 1946–2016," EthZurich: Center for Security Studies, 22 June, available at https://www.prio.org/utility/DownloadFile.ashx?id=1373&type=publicationfile.

"Ex-U.S. Base Worker Appeals Life Sentence for Killing Okinawa Woman" (2017) Japan Times, 12 December.

"ExxonMobil Reports Papua New Guinea Discovery" (2018) Rigzone, 16 January, available at https://www.rigzone.com/news/exxonmobil_reports_papua_new_guinea_discovery-16-jan-2018-153157-article/.

Eyre, Makana (2019) "Why India Just Stripped 1.9 Million People of Citizenship," Nation, 10 September.

Fareed, Rifat (2018) "Kashmir Tension Persists After Shopian Killings," Aljazeera, 2 April, available at https://www.aljazeera.com/news/2018/04/kashmir-tension-persists-shopian-killings-180402145339013.html.

"Filipino Activist Claims He Was Given Weapons, Tortured at SFO" (2018) CBS SF Bay Area, 24 April, available at https://sanfrancisco.cbslocal.com/2018/04/24/filipino-activist-claims-he-was-given-weapons-tortured-at-sfo/.

Fong, Jack (2008) Revolution as Development: The Karen Self-Determination Struggle Against Ethnocracy. Boca Raton, FL: BrownWalker Press.

Foreign Investment in Iraqi Kurdistan (2017) Aleph Policy Initiative, 4 February, available at https://alephpolicy.org/foreign-investment-in-iraqi-kurdistan/.

Forino, Giuseppe Jason von Meding, & Thomas Johnson (2017) "Religion Is Not the Only Reason Rohingyas Are Being Forced Out of Myanmar," The Conversation, 11 September, available at https://theconversation.com/religion-is-not-the-only-reason-rohingyas-are-being-forced-out-of-myanmar-83726.

Fukurai, Hiroshi (2010) "People's Panels vs. Imperial Hegemony: Japan's Twin Lay Justice Systems and the Future of American Military Bases in Japan," Asian-Pacific Law & Policy Journal 12: 95–142.

Fukurai, Hiroshi (2011) "Japan's Quasi-Jury and Grand Jury Systems as Deliberative Agents of Social Change: De-Colonial Strategies and Deliberative Participatory Democracy," Chicago-Kent Law Review 86: 789–829.

Ganguly, Sumit (2002) Conflict Unending: India-Pakistan Tensions Since 1947. NY: Columbia University Press.

Goran, Baxtiyar (2018) "US Continues Military Assistance for Kudistan's Peshmerga Forces," Kurdistan24, 14 February.

Graff, Peter (2011) "Berber Culture Reborn in Libya Revolt," Reuters, 11 July.

Haqqani, Husain (2018) "Aggressive Indian Posture, Kashmir Human Rights Violations Feed Extremism: Husain Haqqani," South Asian Media Journal, 13 April, available at https://southasiajournal.net/aggressive-indian-posture-kashmir-human-rights-violations-feed-extremism-husain-haqqani/.

Harris, Shane & Matthew W. Aid (2013) "Exclusive: CIA Files Prove America Helped Saddam as He Gassed Iran," Foreign Policy, 26 August.

Hawkins, Michael C. (2011) "Managing a Massacre: Savagery, Civility, and Gender in Moro Province in the Wake of Bud Dajo," Philippine Studies 59: 83–105.

Heidbuchel, Esther (2007) The West Papua Conflict in Indonesia: Actors, Issues and Approaches. Berlin, Germany: Die Deutsche Bibliothek.

Heydarian, Richard Javad (2017) "'Marawi Duterte: Liberated' from ISIL-Linked Fighters," Al Jazeera, 18 October, available at https://www.aljazeera.com/news/2017/10/duterte-marawi-liberated-isil-linked-fighters-171017071213300.html.

Hill, Cameron (2013) "Myanmar: Sectarian Violence in Rakhine—Issues, Humanitarian Consequences, and Regional Responses," Parliamentary Library, 24 July, available at https://parlinfo.aph.gov.au/parlInfo/download/library/prspub/2613925/upload_binary/2613925.pdf;fileType=application/pdf.

Hiltermann, Joost R. (2008) "The 1988 Anfal Campaign in Iraqi Kurdistan," SciencesPo, 3 February.

Hughes, Roland (2018) China's Uighurs: All You Need to Know on Muslim 'Crackdown," BBC News, 8 November.

Human Rights Watch (2017) World Report 2017: Events of 2016, available at https://www.hrw.org/sites/default/files/world_report_download/wr2017-web.pdf.

Human Rights Watch (2018) World Report 2018: Events of 2017, available at https://www.hrw.org/world-report/2018.

Ibrahim, Azeem (2016) The Rohingyas: Inside Myanmar's Hidden Genocide. London, UK: Hurst & Co Ltd.

Ibrahim, Azeem (2017) "Why the Rohingya Can't Yet Return to Myanmar," NY Times, 6 December.

Ignatius, David (2020) "Russia's Scavenger Diplomacy is in Full Effect in the Middle East: It's Approach is a taunt at the United States, as Opposed a Grand Strategy," Washington Post, 7 May

"Iran, Turkey Pledge to Stop Iraqi Kurdistan Independence from Taking Hold" (2017) CBC News, 4 October, available at https://www.cbc.ca/news/world/iraq-rouhani-turkey-erdogan-meeting-1.4327874.

Ito, Kazuyuki & Ryuichi Yamashita (2018) "Tempers Flare Between Police and Protesters to Henoko Move," Asahi Shimbun, 23 April.

"Japan Wants U.S. Choppers Grounded as Accident in Okinawa Leaves LDP Reeling Ahead of Election," (2017) Japan Times, 13 October.

"Kashmir Graves: Human Rights Watch Calls for Inquiry" (2011) BBC News, 25 August, available at https://www.bbc.com/news/world-south-asia-14660253.

"Kashmir: Indian Forces Open Fire on Pro-Independence Protesters" (2018) Democracy Now!, 2 April, available at https://www.democracynow.org/2018/4/2/headlines/kashmir_indian_forces_open_fire_on_pro_independence_protesters.

Kerr, George H. (2000) Okinawa: The History of an Island People. Tokyo, Japan: Tuttle Publishing.

Krishan, Yuvraj (2002) Understanding Partition: Separation, Not Liquidation. Mumbai, India: Bharatiya Vidya Bhawan.

Kuzmarov, Jeremy (2017) "American Complicity in Indonesian Killings Runs Deep," Huffington Post 18 October, available at https://www.huffingtonpost.com/entry/american-complicity-in-indonesian-killings-runs-deep_us_59e81584e4b0153c4c3ec537.

Lagsa, Bobby (2017) "Liberated and Angry: Months of Fighting Drove the Oslamic State from the Philippine City of Marawi But Left Behind Distrust and Destruction," Washington Post, 9 December.

Lee, Pam Tau, Terry Valen, & Rhonda Ramiro (2018) "Allow Jerome Succor Aba Entry to the US Now!" New York Committee for Human Rights in the Philippines (NYCHRP), 18, April.

"List of International Oil Companies in Iraqi Kurdistan" (2018) Iraq-Business News (accessed 8 May 2018), available at https://www.iraq-businessnews.com/list-of-international-oil-companies-in-iraqi-kurdistan/.

Lynas, Victor (1998) "Papua New Guinea Seen as 'Last Frontier,'" Oil & Gas Journal, 17 August, available at https://www.ogj.com/articles/print/volume-96/issue-33/in-this-issue/exploration/papua-new-guinea-seen-as-391ast-frontier39.html.

Mackey, Robert (2009) "Pakistan's British-Drawn Borders," N.Y. Times, 5 May.

McKenna, Thomas M. (1998) Muslim Rulers and Rebels: Everyday Politics and Armed Separatism in the Southern Philippines. Berkeley, CA: University of California Press.

Miller, Robert J. et al. (2010) Discovering Indigenous Lands: The Doctrine of Discovery in the English Colonies. Oxford, UK: Oxford University Press.

Mitchell, Jon (2010) "Postcard From ... Takae: In the Jungles of Northern Okinawa, Protests Against Planned U.S. Helipads Reach a Crisis Point," Foreign Policy In Focus, 5 October, available at https://fpif.org/postcard_fromtakae/.

Nakatani, Ryota (2017) "External Adjustment in a Resource-Rich Economy: The Case of Papua New Guinea," International Monetary Fund, Working Paper No. 17/267.

National Investment Promotion Facilitation Agency (2020) "Highest Recoverable Reserves of Crude Oil and Natural Gas in India" (accessed 15 May 2020), available at https://www.investindia.gov.in/state/assam.

Nebrija, Antonio de (1492) Gramatica de la lengua castellana [Castilian Grammar], available at https://www.ensayistas.org/antologia/XV/nebrija/.

Nietschmann, Bernard (1994) "The Fourth World: Nations Versus States." In George J. Demko & William B. Wood, eds., Reordering the World: Geopolitical Perspectives on the Twenty-First Century. Boulder, CO: Westview Press, pp. 227–242.

Official Gazette (2014) Document: Enhanced Defense Cooperation Agreement Between the Philippines and the United States, Article II (4), available at https://www.officialgazette.gov.ph/downloads/2014/04apr/20140428-EDCA.pdf.

Ohnesorge, John K.M. (2007) "Developing Development Theory: Law and Development Orthodoxies and the Northeast Asian Experience," University of Pacific Journal of International Economics Law 28(2): 219–308.

"Oil Giant Chevron Urged to Cut Ties with Burmese Military Junta" (2007) Democracy Now!, 12 October, available at https://www.democracynow.org/2007/10/12/oil_giant_chevron_urged_to_cut.

Osman, Abdullahi (2007) "Cultural Diversity and the Somali Conflict: Myth or Reality," African Journal on Conflict Resolution 7: 93–133.

Perry, Matthew C. (1968) The Japan Expedition 1852–1854: The Personal Journal of Commodore Matthew Perry. Washington, D.C.: Smithsonian Institution Press.

"Philippines Signs Historic Peace Agreement With Muslim Group" (2014) DW, 27 March, available at https://www.dw.com/en/philippines-signs-historic-peace-agreement-with-muslim-group/a-17523091.

"Plan to Build Base Off Nago in 1960s Got OK by U.S. Top Brass, Document Reveals" (2016) Japan Times, 4 April.

Poling, Gregory and Conor Cronin (2018) "The Dangers of Allowing U.S.-Philippine Defense Cooperation to Languish," War on the Rocks, 17 May.

"Protesters Rally One Year After Start of Henoko Coastal Work" (2018) Daily Manila Shimbun, 26 April.

Rai, Nay & Zayar Tun (2017) "Ministry to Drill for Rakhine Fuel," Eleven, 14, available at https://elevenmyanmar.com/local/7417.

Rice, Condoleezza & Robert Gates (2008) "What We Need Next in Iraq," Washington Post, 13 February.

Ruey, Tethloach (2017) The South Sudanese Conflict Analysis: Conflict Profile, Causes, Acors and Dynamics. Munich, Germany: GRIN Verlag.

Salim, Mustafa et al. (2017) "Tillerson Says Kurdish Independence Referendum is Illegitimate," Washington Post, 29 September.

Sands, Susan (1991) "West Papua: Forgotten War, Unwanted People," Cultural Survival. June, available at https://www.culturalsurvival.org/publications/cultural-survival-quarterly/west-papua-forgotten-war-unwanted-people.

Scott, James (2010) The Art of Not Being Governed: Ab Anarchist History of Upland Southeast Asia. New Haven, CT: Yale University Press.

Sebua, Melvin C. (2012) "Philippines Discover Deposits of Oil and Gas in Mindanao," RHSSS Foreign Ministry, 31 January, available at https://therhsssnews.wordpress.com/2012/01/31/philippines-discover-deposits-of-oil-and-gas-in-mindanao/.

"Systematic Rights Violations Taking Place in Indian Held Kashmir: Human Right Bodies" (2012) Pakistan News Releases, 24 May.

Tantikanangkul, Walaiporn and Ashley Pritchard (2016) Politics of Autonomy and Sustainability in Myanmar. NY: Springer.

Tebay, Neles (2005) "West Papua: The Struggle for Peace with Justice," CIIR, available at https://www.progressio.org.uk/sites/default/files/West_Papua_2005.pdf.

"The ICSID Convention Enters into Force in Iraq" (2016) Herbert Smith Freehills: Public International Law Notes, 7 January, available at https://hsfnotes.com/publicinternationallaw/2016/01/07/the-icsid-convention-enters-into-force-in-iraq/.

"The Latest: UN Regrets Iraq's Kurds Went Ahead With Vote" (2017) U.S. News, 25 September, available at https://www.usnews.com/news/world/articles/2017-09-25/the-latest-turkey-says-it-rejects-iraWqi-kurds-referendum.

Torio, Lisa (2016) "Can Indigenous Okinawans Protect Their Land and Water from the US Military?" The Nation, 20 December.

Turnbull, Stephen (2009) The Samurai Capture a King: Okinawa 1609. Oxford, UK: Osprey Publishing.

"Turkey Balks at Arming Kurds Against ISIS" (2014) Associated Press, 19 October.

"UN Security Council Opposes Kurdish Independence Vote" (2017) FRANCE24, 22 (September, available at https://www.france24.com/en/20170922-united-nations-security-council-says-opposes-kurdistan-iraq-independence-vote.

Upham, Frank K. (2018) The Great Property Fallacy: Theory, Reality, and Growth in Developing Countries. London, UK: Cambridge University Press.

"US Military Constructing New Base in Iraq's Kurdish Region: Report" (2017) PressTV, 22 August.

"US Shows a Copy of the Ryukyu-US Treaties and Letters by Commodore Perry" (2018) Ryukyu Shimpo, 20 November, available at https://english.ryukyushimpo.jp/2015/04/04/17747/.

USAID (2018) "Ambassador Kim Announces PHP 1.35 Billion Marawi Response Project: For Immediate Release," 16 October, available at https://www.usaid.gov/philippines/press-releases/oct-16-2018-ambassador-kim-announces-php135-billion-marawi-response-project.

Vaughn, Bruce (2010) Indonesia: Domestic Politics, Strategic Dynamics, and U.S. Interests, 31 January, available at https://heinonline.org/HOL/P?h=hein.crs/crsmthaatep0001&i=1.

Villamor, Felipe (2017) "Philippines Extends Martial Law in South for Another Year," N.Y. Times 13 December.

Vine, David (2015) Base Nation: How U.S. Military Bases Abroad Harm America and the World. Dallas, TX: Metropolitan Press.

Wing, John & Peter King (2005) "Genocide in West Papua? The Role of the Indonesian State Apparatus and a Current Needs Assessment of the Papuan People" available at https://sydney.edu.au/arts/peace_conflict/docs/WestPapuaGenocideRpt05.pdf.

Wong, Edward (2016) "Tibetan Monk, 18, Dies After Self-Immolation to Protest Chinese Rule," NY Times, 3 March.

World Trade Organization (2017) "Members Welcome Iraq's Firm Intention to Resume Formal WTO Accession Negotiations," 17 November, available at https://www.wto.org/english/news_e/news17_e/acc_irq_17nov17_e.htm.

Yamaguchi, Mari (2017) "Okinawa Boy Injured After Window Falls Off U.S. Marine Helicopter," USA Today, 13 December.

Zargham, Mohammad (2017) "U.S. Does Not Recognize Kurdish Independence Vote in Iraq: Tillerson," Reuters, 29 September.

Zucchino, David (2017) "After the Vote, Does the Kurdish Dream of Independence Have a Chance?", NY Times, 30 September.

Original Nation Approaches to Inter-National Law (ONAIL)

The Original Nation scholarship was proposed to critically interrogate the root causes of many of today's geopolitical tensions and conflicts between the nation and the state in various regions across the globe, which have often involved armed battles and violent struggles. Today, many states continue to expand low-intensity warfare, signature drone strikes, extra-judicial killings, secret assassination campaigns, counterinsurgency operations, "foreign internal defense" actions, and other hybrid warfare strategies.[1] These predatory operations have largely targeted recalcitrant nation peoples who have been vilified and often targeted as religious minorities, ethnic separatists, anti-assimilationists, indigenous rebels, savages, terrorists, insurgents, independent nationalists, and others, all of whom, according to the state's hegemonic narrative, have failed to display sufficient humility in submitting to civil rules and policies of the state and international organizations.[2] In noting the history

---

[1] Hoffman (2014) and Pindjak (2014). For the elaboration of hybrid wars fought all across the globe, including Military Operations Other Than War (MOOTW) tactics and strategies, see U.S. Department of the Air Force (1996) and Bonn and Baker (2000).

[2] McCuen (2008) and Wither (2016). McCuen further indicated that hybrid wars were battles involving "both physical and conceptual dimensions [including] a wide struggle for control … [of] the combat zone's indigenous populations" (pp. 107–108) and that "our desired end" would be achieved by "[C]learing, controlling, and counter-organizing

© The Author(s), under exclusive license to Springer Nature Switzerland AG 2021
H. Fukurai and R. Krooth, *Original Nation Approaches to Inter-National Law*,
https://doi.org/10.1007/978-3-030-59273-8_4

of canonical conflicts between the state and the nation throughout the world, recently retired U.S. Army Colonel John J. McCuen once declared that the enemies have been "the conflict zone's indigenous populations," and that "All [global] wars were and are being fought within the indigenous, home front, and international populations at least as much as on the physical battlefields."[3]

On the nonphysical battlegrounds, international law has played a prominent role as the state's primary means of oppression, persecution, and prosecution of the nonconsenting nation and peoples. Besides military hostility toward and violent attacks against the nation, the exploitive market-oriented neoliberal policies as well as the state-assisted ecologically unsustainable projects have been indiscriminately unleashed in assaults on the welfare of the nation, peoples, and their homeland. In order to examine the specificity of the predatory nature and egregious application of international law against the original nation and peoples, Original Nation Approaches to Inter-National Law (ONAIL) has been explored and proposed. There is truly no legal body called "international" law in its etiological origin or applicable form, as the corpus of international law has been created by the state and has largely applied to the state and its recognized institutions. The current system of "international" law does not recognize the legal rights or national status of the original nation and people who have been entrapped and internally colonized within, and across, the state-delimited borders. The term "inter-national" was devised to make clear the distinction from the "inter-state" law that currently governs the relationship among the state, state-recognized institutions, and other state-centric collective organizations.[4] Thus, "inter-national" law represents the symbolic corpus of rules, agreements, and principles that govern the intimate relations and collaborations among the alliance

the indigenous population through a values-oriented approach that fosters legitimacy" (p. 111).

[3] McCuen (2008, p. 112).

[4] Delbruck (2002). To explicate contradictions between general and customary dimensions of international law, as well as grave influences of Europe-dictated assortments of international law as stipulated in the statute of the International Court of Justice (ICJ) Article 38, see Onuma (2000, 2003, 2017). For greater elaborations of Onuma's nuanced transcivilizational approaches to international law, see also Barrow (2010), Keun-Gwan (2018), Neuwirth (2018), Gozzi (2019), and Li (2019).

and democratic network of the original nation and people across the globe.

The ONAIL scholarship posits that international law as devised and unleashed by the state has facilitated and justified a multitude of colonial policies and predatory programs against the nation and peoples, including: (1) the ongoing, colonial occupation of their land and natural environment; (2) the denial of the nation's political right to self-determination, independence, and self-governance; (3) the conscious devaluation of the history, tradition, language, knowledge, and ideology of the nation and peoples in contrast to the conscious elevation of the civilized and superior culture, history, and "benevolence" imposed by the state upon nation people[5]; (4) the deterioration of the quality of basic social, educational, and health services through privatization, government neglect, and discrimination against the nation and peoples; (5) the usurpation of knowledge of the nation and peoples through intellectual property by the forceful, if not deceitful, extraction through bio-piracy and bio-colonialism of indigenous bodies and knowledge; and (6) the destruction of the natural environment and biological diversity, resulting in detriment to the welfare and livelihood of the nation and peoples and their inter-human and cross-species relationships in ancestral lands and territories. By centering the nation in approaches to the understanding of struggles for the right to self-determination and the rights of territories, ONAIL seeks to create a socio-legal framework that recognizes the political rights and legal equity of the nation, in order that it may participate in the formulation of national and genuinely inter-"national" policies that affect the nation, peoples, culture, knowledge, tradition, community, ecosystems, and natural environment.

ONAIL first offers a strong critique of ongoing geopolitical processes involved in "state-building" and "nation-destroying" endeavors, tracing back to the state-making projects in Europe and their global projection in the late fifteenth century. Second, ONAIL investigates the role of the state in acting as an intermediary agency that seeks to serve the predatory objectives of international institutions, ones which the powerful states themselves helped to create and control, such as the World Trade Organization (WTO), World Bank (WB), and International Monetary Fund

---

[5] See generally Thiongo (1986) (discussing the conscious devaluation of indigenous languages and cultures as opposed to the conscious status elevation of languages of external imposition).

(IMF), among others. Third, ONAIL elaborates genuine inter-"national" alliance building in reaction to the predatory international organizations.

Fourth, the ONAIL scholarship investigates the predatory effect of the international legal mechanism known as the investor state dispute settlement (ISDS), which prioritizes economic growth, private profits, and corporate exploitation of natural resources despite strong opposition from the original nation and peoples. Today's Free Trade Agreements (FTA), including the 1994 North American Free Trade Agreement (NAFTA) signed by the U.S., Mexico, and Canada, have incorporated this specific legal mechanism. The ISDS provision allows private investors to gain access to supra-state adjudicative institutions, including the International Center for Settlement of Investment Dispute (ICSID) in the World Bank, whose decisions supersede the ruling of the state's own domestic court, in an effort to protect the rights of transnational investors, international financiers, and multinational corporations. The supranational dispute resolution mechanism also allows multinational corporations to sue the states on policy changes in order to open up the scope for wholesale liberalization of the state's domestic economies and markets, including the appropriation of indigenous genetic materials, indigenous knowledge, and traditional medicinal remedies shared and protected by indigenous nations and peoples. ONAIL's opposition thus extends to corporate practices of bio-piracy and bio-colonialism and the privatization of indigenous knowledge, bodies, and traditional genetic materials, as the FTA with ISDS provisions helped redefine rights and privileges for transnational corporations with respect to commercial control over biodiversity through intellectual property rights (IPR). Pharmaceutical and medical industries have targeted the original nation and people for the expropriation and commercialization of genetic and biological resources and indigenous forms of knowledge, leading to the creation of an exclusive monopoly through the patenting and legal "branding" of biological materials and genetic "discoveries" as intellectual property, so as to maximize corporate profits.

Fifth, ONAIL elaborates its opposition to another "inter-state" legal arrangement that allows the military presence of international organizations or powerful states, such as the U.N. "peacekeeping" troops and the U.S. military, in the multiplicity of "host states" across the globe. These international legal agreements, such as the Visiting Forces Agreement (VFA), Status of Forces Agreement (SOFA), and other "inter-state" military and armed arrangements, have allowed the exercise of military operations and the establishment of military bases and armed installations of ports, flexible "lily pad" facilities and "cooperative security locations" near or inside the original nation's homeland of the host states.[6] Additionally, under the U.N. and U.S. SOFA provisions which allow the presence of U.N. peacekeeping troops and U.S. military personnel, there have been multiple acts of rape and sexual assaults against girls, women, children, and other vulnerable populations of original nations in their homelands and neighboring conflict zones. These conflict areas are most likely to involve multiple groups of original nations' resisters who have been fighting to protect their indigenous homeland against the state and state-sponsored extractive activities and ecologically unsustainable corporate projects. Furthermore, the SOFA and VFA provided "extraterritorial" privileges and immunity to foreign military personnel from prosecution under a criminal justice system of the host states, thereby fostering the culture of impunity and violence shared among foreign soldiers and private contractors who continued to terrorize and victimize indigenous communities and peoples in the host states. The U.S. has already signed the SOFA, VFA and other military-related agreements with more than one hundred states around the globe, building more than 1,400 military bases and armed installations over 120 states. The U.S. has also successfully placed military personnel and civilian contractors in more than 150 states around the globe. This section focuses on the U.S. military bases in the islands of Okinawa, Japan and the island of Jeju, South Korea, both of which were prosperous international ports governed by independent indigenous kingdoms before they were forcefully integrated into the powerful governments of Japan and Korea, respectively. Both independent kingdoms in these two islands, which lie in the middle of the East China Sea and the Korea Strait, respectively, have played an important role in U.S. geo-strategic policies, while their traditional culture, biological diversity, and ecological health of ancestral homelands have largely been destroyed.

In the last section, ONAIL examines the development of counterinsurgency intelligence operations as an integral part of the "state-making" project. The powerful state has used oversea colonies to develop, refine, and "perfect" counterinsurgency intelligence operations to pacify,

---

[6] For the exploitation of "lily pad" operations in the U.S.'s hybrid wars, see Robinson (2008) and Rodrigues and Glebov (2009). For more elaborate analyses of lily pad bases, see Johnson (2004).

neutralize, and eventually destroy potential enemies, resisters, and political opponents against the state project. The U.S.-Spanish war in 1898 and the subsequent U.S.-Philippine War in 1899 helped set the stage for the U.S. military's use of the Philippines as a laboratory to develop the counterinsurgency intelligence techniques and "foreign internal defense" strategies used to crush Filipino indigenous resisters and their revolutionary movements. In order to satisfy, if not "pacify," military personnel overseas that have been dispatched as "shock troops of empire," the powerful state has also developed the Military-Sexual Complex (MSC) and managed the military-run brothel and institutionalized prostitution where military doctors policed and monitored a large group of prostitutes and sex workers, including indigenous women and girls who had been procured to serve the oversea troopers and civilian contractors. Today, the sprawl of MSC has been concentrated around multiple locations of oversea U.S. military bases and facilities around the globe, many of which have been established near and on the homeland of indigenous nations and communities. The conclusion to this chapter summarizes the ONAIL scholarship's prescient approach to protecting the rights of the original nation, their dignity, sovereignty, self-sustaining culture, biodiversity, the natural environment, and ecosystems, all of which are necessary for the survival of both human and nonhuman species in the coming years throughout the world.

1   Critiques of "State-Building" and "Nation-Destroying" Projects

ONAIL proposes a fundamentally different starting point for analysis by addressing and configuring geography, history, and politics based on the nation's perspectives, rather than, as traditional analyses do, focusing on the state as a principal unit of analysis and a primary agency of international law. Long before the artificial structure of the state system was invented, hundreds of thousands of nations had already been distributed over nearly every sphere of the planetary surface. Given that most territories on earth had already been inhabited by the original nation, the state had to be first implanted and then come to eventually incorporate the reluctant and unconsenting nations and peoples into its sphere of influence. In Europe, the Holy Roman Empire was one of the major contributors to the emergence of the state and its eventual proliferation around the world.[7] In 800 AD, Frankish King Charlemagne, or Charles the Great, was crowned by Pope Leo III and received the title of Emperor of the Holy Roman Empire in the western region of Europe. His grandsons Charles the Bald and Louis the German, and their successors, conquered and colonized many of the non-Christian nations in central and western Europe and created a powerful imperial domain based on Christianity as the dominant religion.[8] The imperial construction involved a number of colonial endeavors to subjugate the multiplicity of dissenting European nations and thus force them into the empire: (1) obliterate the nation's capacity to physically resist subordination; (2) eradicate their traditional understanding of relations, culture, history, religion, and memory of the nation; (3) Christianize the nation and people; and (4) create imperial troopers out of newly conquered and colonized subjects and dispatch them to other nations for further conquest and colonization.[9]

The Holy Roman Empire of Europe was thus created as a result of internal colonial construction, by integrating unconsenting European nations through the forceful, simultaneous process of occupation, conquest, Christian conversion, expansion, and further colonization. These imperial projects lasted largely until the mid-seventeenth century, when the infighting of monarchical powers of the Holy Roman Empire and the feudalistic aspirations of many regional powers within and around the imperial domain led to the death and immiserization of millions of people in Europe. Religious wars and conflicts also contributed to the further destabilization of Western Europe.[10] The Peace Treaties of Westphalia in 1648 finally ended the Thirty Years' War between the Habsburgs and their Catholic allies and the Protestant powers, such as Sweden, Denmark, Dutch, Holy Roman principalities, and their Anti-Habsburg allies. The peace agreements also ended the Eighty Years' War between

---

[7] For the history of Europe in 800 A.D., see Wolf (2010, pp. 101–125).

[8] *See generally* Hodges and Whitehouse (1983) (testing the Pirenne thesis using new archaeological data). See Tilly (1975) (analyzing the history of Europe through an anthropological lens).

[9] *See generally* Lopez (1966) (describing the development of European states and imperialism).

[10] See generally Nolan (2006).

the Dutch Republic and Spain, which soon recognized the independence of the Dutch Republic as a sovereign state.[11] The Westphalian
peace agreements effectively established a new system of political order in
Europe, one based on the concept of "state sovereignty" as a principal
cornerstone of international order. The peace treaties also recognized
the multitude of powerful kingdoms and collective oligarchs that shared
the characteristics of the modern state as separated by borders and the
delineation of territories.

Europe's imperial venture to colonize other nations went beyond the
continent of Europe into the "New World" of the Western Hemisphere
in the late fifteenth century and beyond, including the conquering of
the nations in the African continent, Asian peripheries, and the rest
of the planetary surface. The Berlin Conference of 1884–1885, for
example, involved thirteen European states and the U.S. partitioning
the entire continent of Africa's original nations and peoples, creating
their own imperial domains of resource colonies without the participation of a single conferee from the original nations of the African
continent. This international agreement among Euro-American powers
overrode existing orders of power relations that had existed among
African nations and peoples.[12] A number of African colonies were forcefully constructed with externally imposed borders and boundaries, often
severing and partitioning influential African original nations into multiple
European colonial compartments. During the de-colonial movement to
independence in the twentieth century, these European colonies in Africa
relied on externally imposed borders to delineate the geography of their
sovereignty and to claim statehood. As European colonialism had been
imposed across the globe, the concept of sovereign states born out of
the Westphalian principles became central to the formation of international law and to the prevailing legal norm of the international community
composed of the multitude of sovereign states, without the recognition
of the rights of the original nation and peoples.

The state-building project thus took place simultaneously with the
nation-destruction or nation-decimation endeavors which systemically
suppressed the sovereignty, dignity, and aspiration of the nation and its

---

[11] Ibid.

[12] See *generally* Forster et al. (1988) (describing the history and consequences of the
Berlin Conference).

peoples. The state's sovereignty also gave it the right and freedom to engage in genocide against the nation and its people without interference by other states. For instance, once the U.S. had declared and gained independence and achieved the status of "treaty-worthy" statehood, it proceeded to rid itself of the original nation and peoples, while further expanding the extreme system of chattel slavery based on the importation of Africans.[13] The presumed population of up to fifteen million original nation people in North America in the pre-Columbus era was reduced to a mere one-quarter million, with the extermination of nearly ninety-eight percent of the original population by the time that the first U.S. census was taken in 1880.[14] The destruction of the nation's homelands in North America also followed. The ancestral homeland to the Western Shoshone nation, called *Newe Segobia*, which covers two-thirds of the State of Nevada, became the site of nearly one thousand nuclear detonations as part of state-initiated national security programs. The nation's sacred Yucca Mountain also remains the largest nuclear waste repository in North America.[15] Consequently, it was the Western Shoshone nation, not Japan, that became the most "nuclear-bombed" nation in the world, and indigenous people have been exposed to, and adversely affected by, the toxicity of radiation and contamination for decades.

International law thus helped the new state to establish the legal rights of sovereignty, in which the state simultaneously gained rightful diplomatic recognition by other sovereign states and the freedom to act at home without interference from abroad.[16] ONAIL argues that the origin of international law and the concept of the modern state and its sovereignty was predicated on the colonial legacy of centuries-long "state-building" and "nation-destroying" projects that first started in Europe through invasion, annexation, subjugation, Christian conversion, occupation, subordination of the nations, and recruitment of nation peoples into state armies and shock troops of the empire for further invasion and colonization. State-building endeavors were soon projected globally,

---

[13] *See generally* Kuper (1981) (arguing that the state's sovereignty gave it the right to engage in genocide against the nation and its peoples within the border of the state because of the non-interference agreement from other states).

[14] Churchill (1996, p. 21).

[15] Churchill (1993, pp. 261–328) and Amaline et al. (2011, pp. 108–112) (examining the nations' struggles in North America). See also Ali (2001).

[16] For analyses of "treaty-worthy nations," see Gould (2014).

progressing with the simultaneous processes of nation-destruction and the systemic subjugation and obliteration of nation peoples without regard for their aspiration for self-determination.

2 THE STATE AS AN INTERMEDIARY AGENCY OF INTERNATIONAL LAW

ONAIL posits that the state acts as the effective intermediary agency of international law in the exploitation of the nation and peoples. The state-nation conflicts in Asia demonstrated that multiple nations in Asia have been forcefully subjugated by the state through its coercive military force, judicial decisions, and enforcement and execution of international agreements signed with powerful states and multilateral institutions in the West. Today, the predatory behavior of the state against the nation may be best illustrated by the impact of the structural adjustment program (SAP) of the International Monetary Fund (IMF) and the World Bank (WB) upon the states in the Global South that have experienced economic disasters and financial crises. SAP has been known to contribute to the deep structural causes of poverty by advancing reforms designed to weaken the state's role in social programs, to deregulate labor, to weaken environmental laws, and to promote the rapid privatization and foreign takeover of state enterprises and assets. This ultimately allows foreign investors, powerful banks, international financiers, and a small sector of well-connected domestic government and ruling corporate elites to reap the financial spoils. SAP's economic objectives have often been grounded in unsustainable natural resource extraction and exploitation of cheap labor, thereby perpetuating poverty in the poor state.[17] SAP has often been negotiated in secret with a small circle of state elites and corporate officials, rather than the civil society, including the nation and peoples, and this has prompted large civic protests against the implementation of undemocratic and nontransparent policies and programs. Given this background, former WB Chief Economist Joseph Stiglitz concluded in 2000, "[T]he IMF likes to go about its business without outsiders asking too many questions. In theory, the [IMF] fund supports democratic institutions in the nations it assists. In practice, it undermines the democratic

---

[17] *See generally* Reed (2013). See also Chang (2000) (examining the detrimental effects developed countries have on developing countries' economies by recommending policies and institutions that are incompatible with successful development).

process by imposing policies."[18] It is important to note that the term "nations" is used here in its current sense, not in the sense used in the ONAIL approach, which contrasts states and nations. In 1999, strong criticism had led the IMF and WB to create new Poverty Reduction Strategy Papers (PRSP), with the goal of eradicating poverty in Heavily Indebted Poor Countries (HIPC) and other low-income states.[19]

A review of fourteen PRSPs undertaken by the International Labor Organization (ILO), however, revealed that the program further excluded the meaningful participation of the nation and peoples from negotiation with the state sectors. Specifically, "indigenous and tribal peoples have not been involved in consultations leading to formulation of the PRSPs ... [largely due to] the 'invisibility' of indigenous and tribal issues in domestic development agendas ... and political circumstances that may introduce restrictive and exclusionary eligibility requirements for participation in consultation processes."[20] Even after ten years of applying PRSPs, the program failed to move the poor state out of poverty and further ignored the plight of the nation and peoples who often lack information about state government procedures and do not possess the resources necessary to participate in such processes. Exclusion from participatory processes has led to significant institutional discrimination and social marginalization of the nation and peoples in Latin America and Southeast Asia, where they have had no access to PRSP processes.[21]

Minority Rights Group International (MRG), an international human rights organization founded in the 1960s with the objective of securing the rights of the nation and peoples, made the following suggestions and recommendations to rectify PRSP failures: (1) at the international level, foreign policy experts on development must reexamine the macroeconomic prescriptions for all "concessional lending and debt relief"; (2) the state must develop policies that address the root causes of poverty and marginalization of nations and peoples; (3) the state must reduce internal corruption and curb the ability of economic and corporate elites to undermine these processes; (4) governmental consultation processes must include all marginalized groups, including the nation and peoples,

---

[18] Stiglitz (2000).

[19] Khan (2010, p. 4).

[20] Tomei (2005, p. 62).

[21] Khan (2010, p. 14).

in deliberations over government policies and strategies; and (5) the state needs to ensure that all poverty assessments are gendered through properly disaggregated data to reflect the reality of the nation and peoples, especially indigenous women, as key dimensions of designing appropriate development programs.[22] The report also substantiated the fact that SAPs and PRSPs of the WB and IMF have led to state policies that accelerated exposure of domestic markets to foreign investments, resulting in an increase in poverty and gender inequality, as well as a reduction in government social spending, and increased environmental harms through unsustainable development projects in the nation's homeland.[23]

Because of its strong criticism of "state-centric" approaches, ONAIL extends its critical voice to the theoretical assumptions of the now-familiar Third World Approaches to International Law (TWAIL). TWAIL scholarship was originally offered by Makau Mutua, B. S. Chimni, Antonio Anghie, and other critical legal scholars who specialized in Asia, Africa, the Americas, and other regions, and examined the predatory and racialized role of international law as it worked against the interests and aspirations of the Third World countries.[24] TWAIL scholars argued that international law promoted political subservience and facilitated further economic exploitation of the Third World by Euro-American powers through the predatory legal mechanisms and international institutions they had helped to create and control. This predatory international law and its implementation were thus considered one of the significant causes of the continuing exploitation of the Third World through systemic subordination to the West. While it also tried to explain the growing internal conflicts in the Third World, TWAIL failed to adequately elaborate the growing economic polarization, health disparity, and sociopolitical inequities among the multiplicity of sub-state communities and nation people, not only in the Third World countries but also in the

---

[22] Ibid., p. 4.

[23] Ibid., p. 14.

[24] Anghie (2004), Koskenniemi (2001), Natarajan et al. (2017), Anghie and Chimni (2003), Mutua and Anghie (2000), Chimni (2006), Eslava and Pahuja (2012), Gathii (2011), and Okafor (2005). See Chapter 2 for more comprehensive TWAIL references and bibliographies.

First World states in the Global North.[25] The nations and peoples suffer from today's statist predatory system that has continued to forcefully impose the partition, encapsulation, and occupation of their homeland within and across the procrustean borders from the First to Third Worlds. For instance, nearly four hundred "legally" recognized Indian nations have been trapped within and around the forty-eight contiguous U.S. state borders in North America despite the fact that their "international" treaties had been fully ratified by the U.S. government.

Neither TWAIL nor even Critical Race Theory (CRT) has effectively analyzed the impact of international law on the indigenous nation and peoples. TWAIL, in particular, largely focused on the "post-colonial" narratives of the continuing impoverishment, exploitation, and subordination of the Third World to Western powers.[26] ONAIL affirmatively asserts that there is nothing "post" or "post-colonial" about the unceasing imperial reality and colonial projects against the original nation and peoples who have continued to undergo the ravages of colonial subjugation. It is rhetorically impossible, if not improbable, to engage in a struggle for decolonization, while depicting the context of the struggle as "post-colonial" at the same time. As the latter invariably forecloses the former, the analytic use of "post-colonialism" in indigenous struggles only facilitates further perpetuation of the existing order of colonialism and imperialism. As TWAIL had largely formed its goals and advocacy

---

[25] See Gordon (2014, p. 404). ("an international institution from a TWAIL perspective] fails to adequately effectuate indigenous people's rights because ... the traditional international legal vocabulary places states and sovereign rights at the forefront of all international discourse ... and thus nullify such [indigenous] rights".) Seth Gordon tried to recognize the rights of the nation and peoples and their historical plights under international law, using the International Labor Organization's Convention No. 169, "Concerning Indigenous and Tribal Peoples in Independent countries" in 1989 as a case study. See also Bhatia (2012) (incorporating the distinct history and perspective of indigenous nations and peoples into the TWAIL scholarship); Phillips (2007) (arguing that that neither TWAIL nor Critical Race Theory (CRT) has effectively analyzed the impact of indigenous nations' concerns about international law). European biases, patriarchy, and state-centric views of the TWAIL scholarship were also criticized. See, for example, Rajagopal (2003, p. 23). (Academics in international law were unwilling to free their mind from the fetters of being "too western, elitist, male-centered, and imperial".)

[26] For TWAIL's post-colonial analyses of the Third World and international law, see Iglesias (1999), Aginam (2003), Anghie (2006), Mahmud (2007), Desierto (2008), Grahn-Farley (2008), Lim (2008), Chimni (2010), Singh (2010), Singh and Mayer (2014), Iskandar (2016), Martineau (2016), Sinclair (2018), Bhatt (2019), Tzouvala (2019), and Maluwa (2020).

during the decolonization movements in the 1950s and new age movements in the 1990s, during the so-called "post-colonial" era, TWAIL's analysis of indigenous nations and peoples had a tendency to lump their historical struggles into part of domestic social movements, thus implying that their resistance and demands for rights to self-determination could not be clearly distinguished from the struggles of the general mass of civil society in the Third World.[27] TWAIL's post-colonial posture in its theorization has seriously misinterpreted and misrepresented the continuing reality of colonialism and the struggle for decolonization against genocidal policies and mass violence directed against them by the governments of both First and Third World states.[28]

ONAIL argues that the political and economic subordination of the nation has been facilitated not only by international law but also by the law of the state that, in many instances, has played an even more sinister role in the exploitation, marginalization, and extermination of the nation and peoples with the assistance of international law and legal norm developed by the West. TWAIL often overlooked the oppressive role played by the states and their policies in opposing the interests of the welfare of the nation and peoples within and across state boundaries. Both ONAIL and TWAIL remain critical of the predatory role of the international organizations, including multinational corporations, the WTO, WB, IMF, and other supranational entities that impose neoliberal policies on the Third World and maintain hegemonic Euro-American domination. TWAIL, however, has failed to recognize that these neoliberal policies have not only been imposed unequally and inequitably across race, ethnicity, gender, region, or culture within the First and Third World states, but have also been concentrated in the most marginalized sectors

---

[27] See Lam (2000). Lam argued that the "on the ground" approaches taken by Maori scholars in New Zealand, for example, were much better suited to the task of analyzing the relationships among the state, international law surrounding traditional and indigenous knowledge, and the rights of indigenous nation and peoples. Gathii also recognized TWAIL's inability to adequately develop the "on the ground" approaches. See Gathii (2019). Some TWAIL scholars called for the radical incorporation of structural Marxism approaches such as Post-Marxist Anthropological perspectives in order to transform its scholarly focus from great state politics and international relations to an emphasis on biography and cultural practices on the ground. See Skouteris (2012) and Huskell (2014a).

[28] See generally Churchill (2002) (examining the multiplicity of nations and peoples in the U.S. and Canada).

of the nations and peoples within their borders. TWAIL's state-centric scholarship also fails to explain how neoliberal policies imposed by international organizations influence the ways in which domestic policies have been formulated and most often carried out by the state government with detriment to the social, political, economic, and ecological welfare of the nation and peoples.[29] For example, while uranium can be found nearly everywhere on earth, approximately seventy percent of uranium resources and thus extractive mining activities have been located in the lands inhabited by indigenous nations and peoples in Asia, Australia, and North and South America, regardless of the level of the state's economic development.[30] As a result, these original nations have suffered devastating, multigenerational impacts of environmental toxins and deadly contaminants in their communities.[31]

Lastly, ONAIL is critical of the TWAIL scholarship that is based on the forced and "assumed" homogeneity of political voices across domestic groups, including the original nation, in order to develop a common language of unified opposition and collaborative resistance to First World hegemony. Consequently, the call for close cooperation and alliance building among Third World states has been characterized by the possibility of silencing dissident histories, perspectives, and voices of

---

[29] For TWAIL's lack of indigenous analytic lenses, see Mutua (2000). Mutua further called for the necessity to incorporate subaltern and indigenous conceptions of governance, in which the issue of sovereignty should not remain exclusive to the state, but needs to incorporate new political units conducive to diverse cultural organizations, including indigenous communities. See Mutua (2009). Other critiques of TWAIL included its failure to explain international economic governance (IEG). While TWAIL offered sharp criticisms of international law, especially the new international economic order (NIEO), some critics argued that it failed to offer solutions to the problems in international economic inequities. See Hippolyte (2016). Other criticisms include: (1) its argumentative logic that ultimately relied on the same underlying Euro-centric assumptions of the system that it sought to transcend (Huskell 2014b); (2) its scholarship has still been committed to the ideal of an international normative regime largely based on existing inequal institutional structures that it sought to criticize (Eslava and Pahuja 2012); and (3) its lack of engagement with ethics and morality as a center of theoretical agendas to give a voice to the marginalized communities, including indigenous peoples (see Appiagyei 2015). This is despite the fact that Okafor once asserted that "TWAIL scholars are solidly united by a shared ethical commitment to the intellectual and practical struggles" (Okafor 2005, p. 178).

[30] Sovacool et al. (2013, p. 69).

[31] Gocke (2014).

marginalized original nations and peoples. For instance, the 1955 Anti-Colonial Bandung Conference in Indonesia was organized by Burma (today's Myanmar), Pakistan, Ceylon (today's Sri Lanka), Indonesia, and India in order to form the first large-scale Asian-African alliance among twenty-nine governments of Asia and Africa. The conference's main objective was to promote the Afro-Asian economic, political, and cultural cooperation between two continents and to oppose colonialism or neocolonialism by Western imperial powers. While these countries contained a multitude of original nations within their state borders, the Conference's Ten-Point Declaration failed to reflect or recognize the rights and interests of the indigenous nations and peoples in their respective state systems. The rhetoric of a united consensus and inter-state cooperation among the governments of the Third World states effectively eradicated the original nations' histories of struggles, resistance, and opposition to colonial policies imposed by European imperial powers, as well as "post-colonial" policies adopted by newly emerged state governments of the Third World.

3   INTER-NATIONAL ALLIANCE BUILDING AGAINST THE STATE AND PREDATORY INTERNATIONAL ORGANIZATIONS

ONAIL recognizes the importance of building a genuine inter-national alliance and global solidarity among the multiplicity of nations to resist predatory "accomplice" states and international organizations. The first major attempt to build such a truly inter-"national" alliance took place in 1974, when George Manuel, president of the National Indigenous Brotherhood and member of the Shuswap Nation Tribal Council, and other indigenous leaders of the nations from North America, Colombia, Greenland, Scandinavia, Australia, and New Zealand gathered at a conference in Guyana that promoted the World Council of Indigenous Peoples (WCIP). The WCIP became one of the first indigenous nongovernmental organizations (NGO) to attain official U.N. observer status, and currently represents over sixty million members from nations across the globe.[32]

Another foundational conference having significant impact was the International NGO Conference on Discrimination Against Indigenous

---

[32] Taber (2014).

Peoples in Americas, held in Geneva, Switzerland, in 1977.[33] The conference was initiated by the International Indian Treaty Council and organized by the NGO Sub-Committee on Racism, Racial Discrimination, Apartheid, and Colonialism, which was part of the Special NGO Committee on Human Rights, based in Geneva. More than fifty NGOs with U.N. consultative status were registered for the conference, which declared that the twelfth of October (the day of "Cristóbal Colón" or Christopher Columbus, for popular name dissemination) was designated as the International Day of Solidarity and Mourning with Indigenous Peoples of the Americas. The conference later served as an important platform for the recognition of indigenous nations and peoples under international law by adopting the document, "Draft Declaration of Principles for the Defense of Indigenous Nations and Peoples of the Western Hemisphere," which established an important basis for subsequent U.N. negotiations regarding the rights of indigenous nations and peoples around the globe.[34] The declaration contained unequivocal statements in thirteen areas of indigenous rights: (1) recognition of indigenous nations, in which "indigenous people shall be accorded recognition as nations"; (2) subjects of international law; (3) guarantee of rights; (4) accordance of independence; (5) treaties and agreements recognized and applied as other international laws; (6) treaties and other rights not subject to unilateral abrogation; (7) sovereignty, in which "No state shall assert or claim to exercise any right of jurisdiction over any indigenous nation or group"; (8) claims to territory; (9) settlement of disputes "through negotiations or other appropriate means ... for the binding [resolution]"; (10) natural and cultural integrity; (11) environmental protection; (12) indigenous membership, in which "No state, through legislation, regulation, or other means, shall take actions that interfere with the sovereign power of an indigenous nation or group to determine its own membership"; and a final declaration, (13) "All of the rights and obligations declared herein shall be in addition to all rights and obligations existing under international law."[35]

---

[33] Kronowitz et al. (1987, pp. 613–614).

[34] Ibid.; see also UN Comm. on Human Rights (1982, pp. 35–36) and Dunbar-Ortiz (2006).

[35] Dunbar-Ortiz (2006).

The Inuit Circumpolar Conference (ICC) in Alaska[36] was also held in 1977, later developing into a major international organization which held U.N. consultative status,[37] representing 150,000 Inuit from multiple polar regions in the Northern Hemisphere, such as Alaska, Canada, Greenland, and the former Soviet Union. In 1992, the World Conference of Indigenous Peoples on Territory, Environment, and Development was held in Brazil, serving to solidify advocacy positions on the use of nuclear material on indigenous lands, the destruction of indigenous ecosystems and natural resources, and the elimination of the principle of *terra nullius* (a Latin term for "vacant" lands or territories with "no rightful owners")—the European legal concept used to colonize Australia, New Zealand, and other indigenous nations around the world.[38]

Other NGOs were also created to contribute advocacy efforts and activism to indigenous identity building and human rights formulation. NGOs which held U.N. consultative status with the U.N. Economic and Social Council (ECOSOC) also participated in international and intergovernmental conferences that potentially involved human rights issues of indigenous nations and peoples,[39] and served to contribute to the U.N. Permanent Forum on Indigenous Issues (Permanent Forum) and other specialized working groups on indigenous affairs. The International Working Group for Indigenous Affairs (IWGIA) was first established in 1968 as an advocacy NGO organization to endorse indigenous rights to self-determination and self-governance, cultural integrity, and "development" based on indigenous needs and values in international conferences and regional forums.[40] *El Consejo Indio de Sud America* (CISA or "the Indian Council of South America") was founded in 1980 to promote respect for indigenous peoples' rights to life, justice, development, autonomy, and the peace of indigenous nations, and to coordinate activities for the exchange of knowledge, experiences, and projects among indigenous nations and peoples.[41]

---

[36] See ICC Canada (2012).

[37] Ibid.

[38] Washinawatok (1998, p. 50).

[39] United Nation Department of Economics and Social Affairs (2018).

[40] See generally IWGIA Mission Statement (2018).

[41] El Consejo Indio de Sud America (2018).

The effort to create the international indigenous alliance was assisted by advocacy NGO activism that helped raise awareness of a variety of indigenous issues, such as the systematic suppression of indigenous rights to self-determination and the environmental destruction of their homeland by neoliberal projects around the globe. Another wave of the indigenous movement also arose to fight economic globalization and the destruction of biodiversity and natural environment. The now-familiar "Alternative Globalization" (Alter-Globalization or Alter-Mundialization) movement was first derived from a popular slogan of the World Social Forum (WSF): "Another World is Possible." The WSF was formed in 2001 and was headquartered in Porto Alegre, Brazil, which had witnessed the presidential electoral victory of progressive-minded, former labor leader Luis Inacio Lula de Silva. Porto Alegre also became the first city in South America to adopt so-called participatory budgeting (PB), a process of democratic deliberation and decision-making in which municipal residents participated directly in determining how to allocate city budgets—a kind of civic involvement in government affairs based on the concept of direct and participatory democracy first developed and adopted in Ancient Athens of Greece some 2,500 years ago.[42] The WSF's purpose was aimed at energizing the political participation of underrepresented groups in international political discourses, including nations and peoples; women's groups, such as feminist advocacy activists demanding women's access to education, health care, and political participation; labor organizers working to abolish slavish servitudes, such as child labor; and environmental groups working to preserve ecosystems so that "on the ground" organizers and institutions could form a strong North-South, "red-green" global alliance. Approximately four hundred representatives of one hundred indigenous nations participated in the "Paxurim of Indigenous Arts and Knowledge," which was organized by the Coordinating Body of the Indigenous Organizations of the Amazon Basin (COICA) to build an effective indigenous national alliance to draw attention to the neglected issues of environmental and climate protection, economic justice, peace, civil liberties, and preservation of indigenous knowledge, cultures, and traditions. The term "Paxurim" meant "a joining of efforts for a common goal" in the local Tupi-Guarani language.[43]

---

[42] Santos (1998, p. 464).

[43] "Brazil: Indigenous Peoples Participate in World Social Forum" (2018).

These efforts represented strong attempts by the nations, feminist organizations, labor organizers, environmental organizations, and grassroots activists to create a strong advocacy alliance among themselves, with active participation of various "bottom-up" civic organizations as well as close collaborations and working relationships with U.N. committees and other agencies. However, the globalization and neoliberal movement supported by the symbiotic alliance of the state, transnational corporations, and multilateral international institutions still continues to dominate international activities. To accelerate the Anti- and Alter-Globalization activism in 2013, the international indigenous nation alliance called the Indigenous Peoples Movement for Self-Determination and Liberation (IPMSDL) submitted a declaration to the WTO Director General with "the intent of bringing to the WTO the urgent matter of globalization impacts to indigenous peoples of the world, whose historical political and economic marginalization was worsened by the globalization and policies."[44] The global meeting of the nations and peoples culminated that year in parallel with the WTO's ministerial meetings in Bali, Indonesia, including the Cordillera People's Alliance (CPA), Asia Pacific Indigenous Youth Network (APIYN), Center for Research and Advocacy-Manipur, Committee on the Protection of Natural Resources in Manipur, Land is Life (LIL), and the Archipelago Indigenous Youth Front-Indonesia (BPAN) under Aliansi Masyarakat Adat Nusantara (AMAN or Indigenous People's Alliance of the Archipelago in Indonesia).[45] Further alliance building and global solidarity among the nation and peoples must be sought in order to mount strong opposition to the policies and programs of the WTO, "accomplice" states, and other predatory organizations to "protect and defend the lands, water, territories, national resources, culture, and traditional knowledge, all of which are vital to the survival of all humanities and for future generations ... [including] the well-being of Mother Earth."[46]

---

[44] "Declaration of the World Trade Organization (WTO) and Indigenous Peoples: Resisting Globalizations, Asserting Self-Determination (hereinafter "Declaration)" (Dec. 6, 2013). See Aman and Greenhouse (2017, pp. 260–261). (Discussing Alter-Globalization activism, including indigenous and peasants movements against WTO and their insistence for the rights to self-determination.)

[45] Declaration (2013).

[46] Ibid.

4   INVESTOR STATE DISPUTE SETTLEMENT (ISDS) AND THE PRIVATIZATION OF NATURE AS "PROPERTY" FOR CORPORATE PROFIT

ONAIL recognizes that the nation includes land- and local-resource-based communities of people who have long relied on intimate knowledge of their surroundings and natural environment to shape their ecosystems and to provide sustainable substances, such as food, medicines, and other important materials for survival. With the spread of the Western idea that there can be private ownership of nature, much of the ancestral land originally held by the nations and peoples has been taken over by the state or leased or sold to multinational corporations and state-supported institutions. The nation has a unique relationship with its lands that cannot be easily reduced to the form of commodities, property, or resources to be exploited for private gain or profit by the state or transnational corporations. The land exists for the nation and peoples as a collective material and spiritual benefit and must be preserved for future generations.[47]

ONAIL thus proposes to eliminate, if not perpetually end, the practices of privatization, commodification, and other enslavement legalizations of nature and humans, and to prevent the private accumulation of extreme wealth and power that has privileged private property holders at the expense of community, ecology, and equity of the nation and peoples. Although the massive privatization of nature and ecosystems has led to horrifying consequences, it has had the full blessing of both domestic and international laws. ONAIL proposes to eliminate the matrix of legal mechanisms and the structure of law that have prioritized economic growth and privileged private profit, while protecting corporate control and acquisition of resources and property to the detriment of the interests and rights of the original nations and peoples.

The key international law that unequivocally prioritizes private profits above all else is the system of the Investor State Dispute Settlement (ISDS). This international legal mechanism allows private investors and

---

[47] Fabricant (2012) (explaining the encroachment of private capital upon indigenous lands in Bolivia, thereby threatening their sustainability); Miranda (2010) (discussing indigenous people's movement and activism beyond human rights discourse to address the proper and just allocation of scarce resources such as land and natural resources and their protection from state privatization projects); Goyes (2016) (discussing legal frameworks to privately appropriate lands and biological and genetic products in Colombia and their impact on the inversion of justice and the erosion of environmental sustainability).

transnational financiers to gain access to an "undemocratic" arbitration process outside of the state's own courts, one in which expert trade and corporate lawyers are allowed to make decisions on the complaint in question behind closed doors. The 1994 North American Free Trade Agreement (NAFTA) signed by the U.S., Canada, and Mexico became the first trade agreement in North America to include the ISDS provision. As a result, both Canada and Mexico became two of the most sued states in the world. Canada has paid over two hundred million dollars of punitive fines for environmental standards that the U.S. and other foreign corporations have claimed in lost investment incurred by Canada's bans on fracking, pesticide, and use of dangerous chemicals.[48] The Canadian state courts, supported and urged by the nation, peoples, and environmental activists, have slowly begun to enact strong environmental standards to protect the ecosystems and the natural environment that the nation has depended upon for their sustenance and survival. For example, in 2011, the Government of Quebec passed the environmental protection bill and revoked all permits for extractive activities. In 2013, Lone Pine Resources Inc (LPRC), through its U.S. affiliate, filed a $250 million NAFTA lawsuit against Canada over Quebec's moratorium on fracking for oil and gas. This NAFTA lawsuit is currently being adjudicated at the International Center for Settlement of Investment Dispute (ICSID), which is part of, and funded by, the WB, and located in Washington, D.C. ICSID was first established in 1966 by the World Bank Group (WBG) as an international arbitration institution for legal dispute resolution between international investors. More than 150 states have agreed to enforce and uphold arbitral awards in accordance with the ICSID Convention.[49] The ICSID arbitration court is more powerful than any state courts because its decisions can easily supersede those made by any domestic state court or government.

Another area in which ISDS cases have been brought before ICSID is that of biotechnology. Many pharmaceutical firms have brought ISDS lawsuits to protect their intellectual property rights (IPR). Ever since the 1980 U.S. Supreme Court in *Diamond v. Chakrabarty*[50] ruled that live,

---

[48] "Movement Rights, Rights of Nature and Mother Earth: Rights-Based Law and Systemic Change" (2017).

[49] Broadman (2019).

[50] *Diamond v. Chakrabarty*, 447 U.S. 303 (1980).

human-made genetically engineered organisms could become patentable subjects, pharmaceutical and drug industries began to apply for patents on a variety of genetically modified organisms. They soon began to engage in the systematic exploitation and monopolization of genetic or biological substances such as medicinal plant extracts in developing countries, without proper consent of, or monetary compensation to, the indigenous people from which the plants, substances, materials, and even knowledge were obtained.[51] Such a corporate practice is called "bio-piracy," a term first coined by environmental activist Pat Mooney, who was also a member of the Canada-based NGO Rural Advancement Foundation International (RAFI).[52] The term reflected the growing frustration of the original nation, people, and environmental activists over the privatization and corporate monopolization of medical and agricultural knowledge held by indigenous people around the globe. The practice of collecting rare plants and animals has been exercised by private enterprises for many years. But the emergence of "bio-piracy," through the application of bio-engineering technology in plants, animals, and humans, together with a variety of product patents held by powerful pharmaceutical industries, have exposed emerging inequities in the creation of new global intellectual property rights and led to a new platform of ICSID for the arbitration of intellectual property disputes. While there was a negligible number of ISDS cases in the early 1980s, there were 194 known and published ISDS cases as of January 1, 2019, and the majority of these were brought by powerful corporations against developing states.[53] In 2018, for instance, most of the 72 ISDS cases were filed by corporations in the Global North against the states in the Global South. From 1987 to 2018, the most "sued" states included Argentina, Venezuela, Egypt, India, Ecuador, Ukraine, among others.[54] The corporate investors in U.S. had filed 174 ISDS cases, trailed only by the Netherlands with 108 cases and the U.K. with 78 cases.[55]

---

[51] Haley (2005).

[52] Mgbeoji (2006).

[53] UNCTAD (2020).

[54] Ibid. Other countries also included Spain, Czechia, Mexico, Canada, and Russia. A large number of ISDS cases for Mexico and Canada were NAFTA-related claims.

[55] Ibid.

4.1   Bio-Piracy and Bio-Colonialism

Pharmaceutical and medical industries have also conducted a great number of human experiments and genetic extractions from indigenous people, the poor, rural women, and other vulnerable groups in many developing countries across the globe. This egregious form of human rights violation is called biological colonialism or bio-colonialism, a term coined by Debra Harry, who was the Executive Director of the Indigenous Peoples Council on Biocolonialism (IPCB).[56] She termed it "the new frontier of colonialism," arguing that "the indigenous people's struggle for self-determination has shifted from the battlefield [on the ground] and into the laboratory, as they assert the right to protect their own resources and lives against corporate commodification."[57] Harry warned about the immoral acts of bio-prospecting for the corporate theft of "DNA of indigenous people without their knowledge or consent."[58] Pharmaceutical companies have also relied on global clinical experiments and trials recruiting the poor and destitute in the Global South for drug testing.[59] Since the Nuremberg trials were held in the 1940s, the ethics of scientific research on human beings has been an increasing source of concern as well as controversy. Some scholars have claimed that the bio-piracy and the profit-driven experimentation on the poor and vulnerable, including indigenous people, women, and other marginalized populations in developing countries, may amount to crimes against humanity under international criminal law.[60]

The illegal act of "piracy" has a long history in the international community as a threat to both national and international security and has been defined as the first international crime.[61] The multiple forms of piracy and methods to combat them were recognized by the 1982 United Nations Convention on the Law of the Sea (UNCLOS), which stipulated that resources in the common area of high seas and deep ocean

---

[56] Suzara (2004).

[57] Ibid.

[58] Ibid.

[59] Kelly (2013).

[60] Negri (2017). For the U.S.'s Tuskegee syphilis medical experiment conducted upon African American residents in Alabama for four decades by the U.S. Public Health Service, see Jones (1993), Gray (1998), and Reverby (2012).

[61] Kelly (2013) and Dutton (2010).

bed were part of the "Global Commons."[62] Using the principles from the 1993 U.N. Convention on Biological Diversity (CBD) and the Nagoya protocol, as well as the rules set out in UNCLOS, the exploration of the global oceanic commons must take into account the need for fairness in equally sharing scientific, monetary and technological benefits.[63] The same principles were applied to, and broadly extended for, the protection of the global commons and the earth's shared eco-diversity and natural resources, many of which have been preserved in the ancestral homeland of original nations and peoples around the globe. Since the acts of bio-piracy and bio-colonialism have violated the essence of the international protocols and agreements, it has been suggested that indictable criminal charges should be brought by the International Criminal Court (ICC) against the following groups and organizations: (1) pubic officials of host and sponsoring states who sought to exploit resources for private gain; (2) researchers, clinicians, and scholars acting in their private capacity; and finally, (3) CEOs, field officers and project directors of pharmaceutical and medical corporations that relied on the use of the intellectual property rights (IPR) for the furtherance of private profit and the maximization of corporate gains.[64]

Given the egregious acts of the state and state-supported private entrepreneurial ventures, there is a significant historical parallel between the two kinds of state-initiated colonial projects against the indigenous nation and people. On one level, in biotechnology and medical fields, there has been systematic exploitation and expropriation of indigenous bodies, genetic materials, and indigenous knowledge through the global experiments and clinical trials supported by the state and pharmaceutical corporations that have led to new scientific innovation and genetic "discoveries" in the form of new intellectual property rights (IPR). The free trade agreement (FTA) and ISDS provisions further

---

[62] U.N. (2012). The UNCLOS established that "the seabed and ocean floor beyond the limits of national jurisdiction are the 'common heritage of mankind' whose use and protection are the right and responsibility of all." For discussions of the Global Commons and Oceanic Commons, see Wijkman (1982), Ostrom (1990), Nordhaus (1994), Baslar (1998), Buck (1998), Goldman (1998), Stern (2011), Carson and MacDonald (2012), Shaffer (2012), Vogler (2012), Epstein et al. (2013), Martin (2014), Bosselmann (2015), Cumbers (2015), and Creutzig (2017). For historical discussions of the Commons, see Hardin (1968) and Neeson (1996).

[63] Bird (2018).

[64] Negri (2017).

helped solidify legal rights and privileges of pharmaceutical transnational corporations and biochemical conglomerates to strengthen the commercial control and legal appropriation of unique genetic and genomic "markers" of indigenous bodies, biological diversity, traditional medicine, medicinal resources, and indigenous knowledge of original nations and peoples through the establishment of the Western intellectual property rights (IPR) regime.[65] Vandana Shiva, a renowned environmental activist and food sovereignty advocate, once declared that the bio-piracy and patenting of indigenous knowledge is "a double theft because first it allows theft of creativity and innovation, and secondly, the exclusive rights established by patents on stolen knowledge steal economic options of everyday survival on the basis of our indigenous biodiversity and indigenous knowledge."[66]

On another level, the state has also historically relied on "biological warfare" as one of the methods used in the colonization and expropriation of the ancestral territories of the original nation to create the "building-block" of the state and its socio-economic foundation. In the Americas and the Caribbean, for example, the indigenous nation and people had experienced germ warfare, military violence, slave labor, and genocide for centuries. Recent research has shown that tens of millions of indigenous peoples in the Western Hemisphere had been largely exterminated by numerous diseases, plagues, and sicknesses brought by European settlers into indigenous nations and nucleated communities that had no immunity protection against foreign germs and diseases.[67] The widespread biological warfare was also employed purposefully to germinate and spread disease pandemics to liquidate indigenous nations and peoples. Lord Jeffrey Amherst, who was the Commander in Chief of the British forces in the early 1760s, had advocated the use of the smallpox blanket as a goodwill gift to indigenous nations in order to weaponize the smallpox pandemic to systematically exterminate indigenous populations in North America.[68] The diseases brought by European settlers, such as smallpox, measles, influenza, whooping cough, and malaria also liquidated

---

[65] Shiva (2000, 2003, 2005).

[66] Shiva (2003).

[67] Diamond (1997) and Smith (2019).

[68] "Jeffrey Amherst and Smallpox Blankets" (2020). See also Durrhelm (2010) and Fernandez and Herzog (2014). For the original journal of Jeffrey Amherst, see Webster (1931).

indigenous nations and thus acquired their lands for private possession in the Caribbean.[69] The bio-colonial warfare in the form of the spread of smallpox, measles, and other deadly diseases in the New World further led to the systematic extermination of the multiplicity of original nations, thereby eradicating their indigenous knowledge, self-sustaining cultures, and self-governed society in the greater regions of the Western Hemisphere.[70] IPCB's Debra Harry has warned of the continuation of biochemical warfare in the name of neoliberal policies and globalization practices, arguing that "the problem [of bio-colonialism] stems from international policies, such as that espoused at the U.N. Conference on biological diversity, which refer only to recognized states, ignoring the contributions and validity of indigenous worldviews and rights [that had to be silenced and destroyed]."[71]

ONAIL supports the end to the unethical state-supported corporate practice of bio-piracy, bio-colonialism, and biological warfare against the original nation and peoples and urges that the International Criminal Court (ICC) instigate critical interrogation of human experimentation, corporate theft of indigenous bodies and knowledge, and other unethical medical practices as potential crimes against humanity under international law. Further, ONAIL opposes the ISDS claims and lawsuits filed by pharmaceutical and medical firms against the developing states in order to strengthen the commercial control and medical appropriation of indigenous bodies, cultural knowledge, and medicinal resources by solidifying their intellectual property rights regime in the Third World. The international alliance of the original nation and their supporters must be united in opposition to the further exploitation of the bodies and knowledge of the original nation and people.

---

[69] Fenn (2000), Nunn and Qian (2010), and Resendez (2016, p. 17).

[70] Calloway (1998), Harrison (2010), Herring and Swedlund (2010), Park (2012), Burnette (2013), and Dunbar-Ortiz (2014). See also Diamond (1997). One history scholar argued that "the biological warfare ... killed 23 million of indigenous population (95% of the U.S. area population in the 16th century) in general public arenas ... Censorship is a popular word for the conservative and liberal person with racial pathology and/or common sense deficiency syndrome." See Crawford (2005, p. 96).

[71] Suzara (2004).

4.2   Investor State Dispute Settlement (ISDS), Pipeline Projects, and the Original Nation in North America

ISDS has also had a devastating impact on the welfare of the nation and peoples and their struggles for independence in North America today. Multinational corporations have relied on ISDS to bring lawsuits against the state government to justify their environmentally unsustainable projects in the lands of the nation and peoples. The U.S. has witnessed liberation struggles and anti-colonial conflicts involving the indigenous nation and their activists taking action against predatory behaviors of the state and corporate sectors. For example, in the last several decades, the indigenous nations have engaged in the occupation of Alcatraz Island, from 1969 to 1971; the Bureau of Indian Affairs Building in Washington, D.C. in 1972; and Wounded Knee in South Dakota in 1973. The Nisqually, Suquamish, Lummi, and other northwestern Indian nations also battled over-fishing and hunting rights throughout the 1960s and 1970s, and other indigenous nations mounted robust armed resistance against state intrusion on the Pine Ridge Reservation in South Dakota in 1973.

More recently, the nations and their supporters stood in a coordinated alliance to oppose the construction of the $3.8 billion Dakota Access Pipeline (DAPL) Project by Energy Transfer Partners at the Standing Rock Sioux Indian Reservation in North Dakota. The opposition was organized to protect water against oil spills, pollution, and water contamination causing multiple health risks for Indians as well as the destruction of sacred and historic burial sites. A private security firm called TigerSwan was soon hired by Energy Transfer Partners, and their guards unleashed concussion grenades, sonic weapons, rubber bullets, water cannons, attack dogs, and other military-style counterterrorism measures against indigenous activists and international supporters who were gathered in North Dakota.[72] TigerSwan was founded in Dallas, Texas in 1995 as a U.S. Military and State Department contractor who helped to execute the global war on terror. This security firm, when hired by Energy Transfer Partners, has been used in the response to the indigenous opposition and resisters,

---

[72] "Private Mercenary Firm TigerSwan Compares Anti-DAPL Water Protectors to 'Jihadist Insurgency'" (2017).

who have been regarded as "jihadist fighters" and as "an ideologically driven insurgency with a strong religious component."[73]

Indigenous nations and their activists have also opposed the Keystone XL Pipeline (KXL) construction project that has been proposed by TransCanada Corp., a major North American energy company based in Calgary, Canada, in order to build a direct and shorter route between already-constructed pipelines in Hardisty, Alberta in Canada, and Steele City in Nebraska, going through South Dakota. The KXL was expected to transport 830,000 barrels of oil per day from the Athabasca tar sand in Alberta to Nebraska.[74] In anticipation of the eight billion-dollar KXL construction, the state legislature of South Dakota passed a law to prohibit groups of more than twenty people congregating on public land and allowed the Department of Transportation to prohibit stopping or parking in designated areas.[75] In May 2016, representatives of the Canadian first nations and Ponca tribe in the U.S., including the Blackfoot Confederacy in Canada and the Great Sioux Nation in the U.S., signed a declaration against the KXL construction in Calgary, Canada, where TransCanada's headquarter is based, asserting the use of whatever means necessary to block the pipeline construction in their homeland.[76] Once constructed, the existing Keystone pipeline networks would take the oil directly to Texas Gulf Coast refineries owned by ExxonMobil, Chevron, Koch Industries, Marathon Oil and Royal Dutch Shell Oil, all of which have invested in the exploitation of Canadian tar sands.[77]

The nations' oppositions and massive media campaigns finally forced the Obama Administration to cancel both projects in 2015. In response to the projects' cancellations, TransCanada filed a $15 billion lawsuit against the U.S. government under Chapter 11 of NAFTA that grants corporate investors the right to make claims against governments to recover costs and damages. Using the ISDS provision, TransCanada submitted the civil claim to the ICSID at the WB headquarter to recoup future monetary damages incurred by the U.S. government's decision to

---

[73] Brown et al. (2017).

[74] "Keystone XL Pipeline: Why Is It So Disputed?" (2017).

[75] Brown (2017).

[76] "First Nations Sign Anti-Pipeline Declaration in Calgary Wednesday" (2016). See also Nicholson (2016).

[77] Petroski (2013).

terminate the pipeline construction in the United States.[78] The company's lawsuit against the U.S. government, under NAFTA and ICSID's authority to make a ruling at the WB, illustrates the potential economic and political power that NAFTA and other international trade-related treaties yield to multinational corporations, at the expense of the nation, peoples, and natural environment. The company also sued the U.S. government separately in a federal court in Houston, Texas, over the KXL pipeline, asserting that President Obama's decision to deny the project exceeded his power under the U.S. Constitution.[79] TransCanada, however, suspended the lawsuit as soon as President Donald Trump was elected and later signed the orders to smooth the path for the pipeline construction in 2017.[80] Today, the nations' opposition to the pipeline construction continues in North America in reaction to at least five massive Keystone crude oil spills that were discovered in 2017, thereby threatening the further destruction of the nation's homeland, ecosystems, biodiversity, culture, food security, health, and sustainability.[81]

ONAIL recognizes that international law, especially FTAs, began to displace the state's domestic legal system by creating the supranational mechanism of decision-making institutions whose decisions override the law and policies made by a state government and its judiciary. International economic law, especially ISDS, became a highly exploitable instrument of multinational corporations, granting them the right to execute ISDS proceedings against the interests of the security of nations, peoples, and nonhuman species in their ancestral homeland.

---

[78] Lou (2017).

[79] Neuhauser (2016).

[80] Lou (2017).

[81] Brown (2018). See also "Keystone Pipeline Leak in South Dakota About Double Previous Estimate" (2018). While newly-elected US President Joe Biden has revoked a permit for the construction of the Keystone XL pipeline in January 2021, he has so far refused to shut down Dakota Access and other pipeline projects.

5 THE STATUS OF FORCES AGREEMENT (SOFA), VISITING FORCES AGREEMENT (VFA), AND THE ORIGINAL NATION

ONAIL examines another international legal instrument used to ensure the subservience of the original nation and peoples across the globe. The powerful state and international organizations have relied on military intelligence, armed forces, and other geopolitical armed operations to further promote the "state-building" and "nation-destroying" projects in the world.[82] Key international laws used in furtherance of these global projects are the Status of Forces Agreement (SOFA), Visiting Forces Agreement (VFA), and other bi- and multi-lateral military agreements and arrangements.[83] While the VFA allows the temporal military exercise and armed excursion of foreign soldiers and personnel in the host states, the SOFA is an agreement between host states and foreign states or international organizations, allowing the temporal or semi-permanent stationing of military forces and the establishment of armed bases in host states. Such military bases and facilities have included the installation of naval ports, air fields, drone stations, flexible "lily pad" facilities, command centers, and even military lodging and guesthouses that offered accommodation and recreational centers to military personnel and their guests. Members of these bases and facilities, such as U.N. peacekeeping troopers and U.S. military personnel have committed a series of rapes and sexual assaults against women, children, girls, and other vulnerable populations of the nation in their homeland and adjacent areas.[84]

SOFA, VFA, and other international military arrangements also provided special immunity from local prosecution to foreign military personnel, civilian contractors, intelligence operatives, and their dependents who continued to terrorize and victimize local residents of the

---

[82] Perkins (2016).

[83] See generally Fukurai (2010, 2012), Mason (2015), Fukurai and Wang (2014), Fleck (2018), Cochran and Chiu (2019), and Ministry of Foreign Affairs of Japan (2020).

[84] For UN peacekeepers' rape and sexual abuse of local women, girls, and children, see Larson and Dodds (2017), Hernandez (2020), and Wheeler (2020). For recent instances of US military personnel's rape and sexual abuse overseas, including their dependents who committed sexual assault abroad, see Institute for Policy Studies (1999), McNutt (2005), "U.S. Soldier Gets 100 Years for Iraq Rape, Killings" (2007), Bogota (2015), Brodzinsky (2015), Mitchell (2018), and Pritchard and Dunklin (2018).

host state, including those in indigenous nations and communities. Additionally, the conflict areas in the host states were more likely to involve multiple groups of original nations' resisters and armed opposition to protect their homeland from the state-corporate encroachment. International law of SOFA and VFA has provided the powerful states the ability to establish military outposts, "lily pad" operative facilities, and logistical support stations in host states in Latin America, Asia, and Africa, which helped in eradicating and destroying the original nation's opposition and resistance. During the period of the U.S.-backed Dirty Wars and the CIA-led Operation Condor in Latin America from the late 1960s to late 1980s, for example, the U.S. hybrid war was successful in imprisoning, torturing, and annihilating hundreds of thousands of indigenous resisters, political dissenters, and their sympathizers throughout Latin America, including in Argentina, Guatemala, Nicaragua, Paraguay, Bolivia, Brazil, Chile, Peru, Honduras, El Salvador, and other countries in the Western Hemisphere.[85]

Some researchers have proclaimed that, ever since its first founding in 1776, the U.S.'s "state-building" project has remained "unwaveringly" consistent in its engagement in genocidal wars against indigenous nations and peoples in North America and beyond.[86] Many of the five thousand U.S. "domestic" military bases, for example, have been established and concentrated in remote areas where Indian reservations were located. Thanks, in large part, to military facilities, industrial chemical and nuclear particle refineries, and the depository of industrial and nuclear wastes on and near the Indian reserved territories, a large swath of original nations' homelands have been permanently impaired by toxic runoffs, chemical poisons, nuclear wastes, and unexploded bombs and ordinances.[87] Today, the denial of indigenous rights, perpetual economic poverty, and the destruction of bio-ecological diversity have made these indigenous homelands into America's "national sacrifice zone," where indigenous peoples have suffered from significant economic divestment in the cleanup of

---

[85] For the genocide of indigenous populations in the 1980s in SOFA-sanctioned states in Latin America, see Tomuschat et al. (1999), Chomsky et al. (2010), Kohut and Vilella (2010), Salazar (2012), Cupples (2013, pp. 232–235), and Robins (2016). For the indigenous genocide in Guatemala, for example, see Nairn (1995, 2013, 2016). In Mexico, see Bornemann et al. (2007).

[86] See Churchill (1993, 1994, 1996), LaDuke and Cruz (2013), and Means (2020).

[87] Hooks and Smith (2004, 2005, 2012) and Hedges and Sacco (2012).

near-permanent environmental damages and pollutions in their home-land. Indigenous nations and people have long experienced calamity in North America. Following the U.S.-Mexican war and the signing of the Treaty of Guadalupe Hidalgo in 1848, the Pacific Northwest was force-fully annexed to the U.S., and first California Governor Peter Hardeman Burnett promptly issued the executive order in 1851 to exterminate California Indians by placing a bounty on every indigenous body and soul.[88] The California government also passed the "Act Concerning the Organization of the Militia" and the "Act Concerning Volunteer or Inde-pendent Companies," calling for a permanent militia of all free, white, and able-bodied citizens to exterminate indigenous populations in Cali-fornia.[89] Militia regiments were trained for this state-sponsored genocide, and between 1852 and 1857, the California legislature paid $1.5 million to settlers, soldiers, and bounty hunters who participated in twenty-four Indian-killing militias campaigns and armed expeditions to liquidate Cali-fornia's indigenous populations.[90] In 1856, a 25-cent bounty was paid for each Indian scalp, which was soon increased to $5 in 1860.[91] In 1866, the National Guard officially replaced the armed militias in California.[92] Today, the state of California retains the largest National Guard force, battalions, and brigade in the U.S., while it also became home to the largest number of "domestic" U.S. military bases in North America.[93]

In support of the powerful state's efforts to further expand impe-rial jurisdiction and establish oversea colonies, the special legal status of an "extraterritorial jurisdiction" outside the U.S. territory was carefully designed and developed. The concept of inter-state military agreements such as SOFA and its provision of "extraterritorial rights" to U.S. soldiers

[88] In his State of the State Address on January 6, 1851, Burnette proclaimed, "That a war of extermination will continue to be waged between the races until the Indian race becomes extinct must be expected. While we cannot anticipate this result but with painful regret, the inevitable destiny of the race is beyond the power or wisdom of man to avert." See Burnett (1851).

[89] Olson-Raymer (2014).

[90] Nazaryan (2016).

[91] Glaholt (2020).

[92] Olson-Raymer (2014).

[93] "California's National Guard Force, the largest and most frequently deployed nation-wide, includes more than 21,000 troops: 16,565 soldiers and 4,572 airmen." See Kovach (2013) and "California Military Bases" (2020).

overseas was advanced by U.S. War Secretary Elihu Root at the end of the nineteenth century, as the sprawl of U.S. military bases across the globe began. In 1898, the U.S. had invaded Cuba, Puerto Rico, Hawaii, and the Philippines and had begun to build U.S. military ports and base facilities in the North Atlantic and the Pacific Basins.[94] Under Root's leadership, the U.S. government also began to develop the legal framework of bilateral and multilateral military agreements in protecting U.S. armed forces from prosecution under domestic and international laws while stationed in foreign states. At present, the U.S. government has signed more than one hundred Status of Forces Agreement (SOFA) and successfully placed military personnel in more than 150 states and regions all across the globe.[95]

The SOFA also allows the construction of foreign military bases, including air force, army, marine, and naval facilities and installations in host states, and the locations of such bases have been concentrated in or near the original nations of host states. The U.S.-Japan SOFA, for example, allowed the construction of nearly three-quarters of Japan's U.S. military bases and facilities in the island of Okinawa, which had been a thriving independent nation until Japan's forceful annexation of the Ryukyu Kingdom in 1879. The U.S. military base construction in Okinawa began in 1945 soon after Japan's defeat in the Second World War. The U.S. began building its military bases in Korea at the onset of the Korean War in the early 1950s, including Camp Humphreys, Asia's busiest army airfield, in Pyeongtaek, as the U.S. converted a former military airfield that had been built during Japan's occupation of the Korea Peninsula from 1910 to 1945. The U.S. also built Camp McNabb in Jeju Island, which lies sixty miles south of the Korean peninsula in the Korea Strait near Japan. Jeju Island had been home to the independent kingdom of Tamna until it was taken over by the Korean Joseon Dynasty in the fifteenth century.[96]

Similar to the Ryukyu Kingdom in the island of Okinawa, the Tamna Kingdom in the volcanic island of Jeju had served as a vibrant international port in conducting active trades with the Han Dynasty of China,

---

[94] For the historical background on the U.S. development of extraterritorial rights, see Johnson (2004).

[95] Mason (2015, p. 2). ("The United States is currently party to more than 100 agreements that may be considered as SOFAs".) See also Defense Manpower Data Center (2019).

[96] Vovin (2013).

Yayoi Japan, and Southeast Asian nations.[97] Historically, in the ancient Jeju kingdom, women have been the head of the household and served as the main provider of the family by earning a living through diving in the sea. The Jeju tradition also maintained the matrilineal descendant system and family structure, in which every Jeju person was identified with their mother's lineage, including the inheritance of property and titles.[98] With a strong matriarchal social system, even after the annexation to the Korean dynasty, Jeju people have maintained the matriarchal tradition, distinct cultural identity, social autonomy, and political independence. Jeju people also resisted Japan's occupation of Korea in the beginning of the twentieth century by strategizing a strong resistance movement organized by women.[99] After Japan's WWII defeat in 1945, Jeju women and islanders who fought for the unification and independence of Korea were inspired by socialist visions articulated by Kim Il Sung of North Korea, rather than by the U.S. capitalist version of their future in Korea. In 1948, when a large group of Jeju women and the South Korean Labor Party called for Korean sovereignty and freedom from U.S. hegemony, a brutal suppression of Jeju people began. The "scorched earth strategy" was conducted by Korean troops with logistical support and armed assistance provided by the U.S. military, slaughtering anywhere from 14,000 to 30,000 Jeju women, men, elders, and children over the next 13 months. Nearly 70% of the island's 230 traditional villages were burned to the ground, while over 39,000 houses were destroyed.[100]

Meanwhile, the U.S. Army Military Government in Korea (USAMGIK) which was established in 1945 began constructing multiple military bases on Jeju island, including Camp McNabb, the Morale, Welfare and Recreation (MWR) Center, and other military facilities. The MWR center was established to provide free accommodation and discounted recreation to military personnel and their dependents. Dubbed the "Hawaii of Asia" for its scenic beauty, the Jeju island offered an ideal "Rest and Recreation" (R&R) site. U.S. military's Jeju vacation ads frequently included the visit to the ancient Tamnu Kingdom sites and the "Volcanic Island and Lava Tubes" that have been designated as a World Heritage Site. Jeju's scenic beauty also included the dramatic

---

[97] Alawi (2020) and Yang (2020).

[98] Changhoon (2007). Similar to Jeju's women-centered social system, many indigenous nations of North America also followed matriarchal traditions. See Means (2020).

[99] Kim (2016). For deeper analyses of Jeju Island, its history and geo-strategic significance in Cold War Asia, see Kil-Un (2007).

[100] Han and Kim (2003).

landscape of Mount Hallasan, the highest in Korea, with its waterfalls, multi-shaped rock formations, and lake-filled crater.[101] After the U.S. military decided to transfer the ownership of Camp McNabb to the Republic of Korea air force in 2005, a new plan was proposed in 2007 to build the Jeju-Civilian-Military Complex Port (JCMCP), a joint civil and Korean Navy base, in a tiny coastal village of Gengjeong in the south of the World Heritage site. Although the Jeju Provincial government had designated Gangjeong and surrounding areas as Absolute Conservation Area (ACA) in 1991, the JCMCP construction began, bringing the strong opposition of Gangjeong and Jeju people, environmental activists, and labor organizers.

JCMCP, constructed by the South Korean government, was projected to be used by the U.S. navy to provide a military foothold to oppose China's military presence in the region and to confront the communist government of North Korea. The construction had been halted on numerous occasions by Jeju and international protesters who saw it as a U.S.-driven project aimed at China, but the South Korean Supreme Court upheld the JCMCP construction in 2012, and the naval port officially opened in February 2016.[102] Today Jeju people continue to oppose the expansion and operation of the naval port, filing lawsuits to block its operation. A large group consisting of an international alliance of opposition has also been formed, including Korean resisters from Soseong-ri, Pyeongtaek, Gunsan, and Yongsan, as well as international activists and sympathizers from the U.S. and Japan, including those from Okinawa, Kanagawa, Yokosuka, and Sasebo, where U.S. military bases in Japan have been built.[103]

The SOFA also allowed foreign troops to pollute and destroy the nature, environment, and ecosystems of the nation where U.S. military bases are constructed and maintained. For instance, Camp McNabb in Jeju Island was said to be the "most oil-contaminated" military site among the U.S. military bases in Korea, where soils, groundwater, plants, and water supplies had been seriously polluted.[104] The U.S. military has also been accused of dumping Agent Orange at another military site in Jeju Island where not only Jeju people, but also U.S. military personnel,

---

[101] "MWR to Host a Trip to Jeju Island" (2017) and "Area 1 B.O.S.S. Jeju Island Trip" (2020). For the World Heritage Site information, see UNESCO (2020).

[102] Ogle and Ogle (2012), Kirk (2013), and Dickinson (2019).

[103] Ahae (2018) and "Moon Voices Regret Over Dispute Over Building of Naval Base" (2019).

[104] "A Returned US Base in Jeju, Proved to be 'Most Oil-Contaminated'" (2013).

began to suffer long-term health issues and problems.[105] In responding to civil complaints on pollution, contamination, the destruction of biological diversity, and significant alterations of landscape in Jeju island, the U.S.-Korea SOFA has ensured that the U.S. would remain immune to lawsuits pertaining to the cleanup of environmental contamination and the destruction of ecosystems. Specifically, Article 4 of the U.S.-Korea SOFA stipulates that the U.S. government has no obligation to restore the area to the original condition before its occupation, nor must it compensate Korea for the damages. Article 4 of the U.S.-Japan SOFA uses the same language in giving the U.S. military the immunity from lawsuits, specifically noting, "the United States is not obliged, when it returns facilities and areas to Japan on the expiration of this Agreement or at an earlier date, to restore the facilities and areas to the condition in which they were at the time they became available to the United States armed forces, or to compensate Japan in lieu of such restoration."[106]

Today, many U.S. military bases exist near or on the original nation in the Pacific, including those in Hawaii, once an independent kingdom whose monarchy had been overthrown in 1898, as well as in Guam, where the U.S. military had liberated indigenous people from the brief Japanese occupation in 1944, and has now constructed an air force base and two naval ports.[107] In North America, as examined earlier, many U.S. bases have also been built inside or near the Indian reserved territories, with indigenous peoples thus disproportionately exposed to toxic chemicals, radiation, and pollutants of hazardous commercial waste facilities.[108] Since the end of the nineteenth century, the rapid expansion of U.S. military bases has been concentrated in areas that are remote, unpopulated, and owned and controlled by the U.S. federal government, including Indian reserved lands and territories. U.S. military bases have also been constructed in remote islands that had long been inhabited by the original nation and people, including the Aleutian Islands near Alaska, Kwajalein Atoll in Marshall Islands, and the Naval Magazine Indian Island in the State of Washington.[109]

---

[105] Rowland et al. (2011).

[106] Ministry of Foreign Affairs of Japan (2020).

[107] See generally, Vine (2015a).

[108] Geranios (2004).

[109] Sweeney (2019).

Many of the nearly 1,400 overseas U.S. military bases and installations in over 120 states have also been built inside or near the homeland of the original nation.[110] Similar to the construction of the U.S. domestic military bases in the 48 continuous states and beyond, many U.S. oversea military bases have also been located in remote, unpopulated, and rural areas and islands, including Okinawa, Jeju, Diego Garcia, and even Cuba, as well as the Philippines and Greenland.[111]

5.1   The Immunity of Military Personnel in the Original Nation

The VFA, SOFA, and other military agreements have been made available by powerful states and international organizations to shield their troops, civilian contractors, and dependents from criminal prosecution in host states. By forcing foreign states to sign the SOFA and VFA, powerful international actors such as the U.N. and the U.S. have routinely violated customary provisions of international law and the sovereignty of the nation and the state by insulating the crimes committed by their personnel from prosecution under local criminal law. In particular, SOFA has been widely used to undermine the rights of crime victims and to keep their grievances from being incorporated in the adjudication process. Whether or not the granting of immunity for military personnel who commit crimes should be considered as a systemic violation of international norms and standards may be up for further debates and discussions. Regardless, it is important to recognize that the SOFA was originally designed to violate the sovereignty of the host state and its jurisdictional authority to punish foreign military personnel who commit crimes on their soils.[112]

In 2017, for instance, more than two thousand allegations of sexual abuse and sexual exploitation of children, women, and disabled or incapacitated civilians by U.N. peacekeepers have been reported around the world.[113] These personnel were not criminally charged or prosecuted because the U.N. SOFA that governs U.N. "peacekeeping" missions insulated their military troops from criminal jurisdiction of the host

---

[110] Barsocchini (2015).

[111] Sweeney (2019).

[112] Ibid.

[113] Gowrinathan and Cronin-Furman (2017).

country.[114] Rapes and sexual violence were committed by the Sri Lanka peacekeeping troops, for instance, who had previously combated the Liberation Tigers of Tamil Eelam (LTTE) and indigenous activists during its civil war, engaging in massive sexual violence against both women and men.[115]

On a similar note, in 2015, more than fifty Colombian girls and indigenous women had been sexually abused, with some sexual acts of violence videotaped and sold by U.S. soldiers and private contractors, but they have never been charged or prosecuted due to the immunity granted to U.S. military personnel in Colombia.[116] For example, a military contractor from DynCorp, a Virginia-based private military company, was implicated in sex scandals but was not prosecuted.[117] After President Bill Clinton had signed "Plan Colombia" in 2000 to strengthen U.S. military cooperation with Colombia, the signing of the 2009 U.S.-Colombia Defense Cooperation Agreement further strengthened the immunity by providing that "Colombia shall grant United States personnel and their dependents the privileges, exemptions, and immunities accorded to the administrative and technical staff of a diplomatic mission."[118] In 2009, the National Indigenous Organization of Colombia (ONIC) leader Karmen Ramirez Boscan, a member of the Wayuu Nation, had asked the U.N. Headquarter in Geneva, Switzerland to investigate multiple instances of sexual abuse and sexual violence against indigenous women by U.S. soldiers and military contractors.[119] Since U.S. military personnel were given immunity from the Colombian justice prosecution, Boscan urged the U.N. and international community to hold the Colombian state accountable for the sexual crimes committed by U.S. military personnel.[120]

The state of Colombia has been engulfed in a fifty-year internal conflict between the government forces and the guerrilla rebel organization called FARC (*Fuerzas Armadas Revolucionarias de Colombia* [The

---

[114] Ibid.

[115] Ibid.

[116] Brodzinsky (2015), Auken (2015), and Otis (2015).

[117] Grandin (2015).

[118] Art. 8, "U.S.-Colombia Defense Cooperation Agreement" (2009).

[119] Capdevila (2009).

[120] Ibid.

Revolutionary Armed Forces of Colombia]). FARC has its genealogical origin in the Colombian Communist Party, which organized peasant leagues in rural areas, including indigenous people, landless peasants, and Afro-Colombian farmers. The Communist Party also organized a popular alliance in urban areas under the common socialist objective of promoting radical agrarian reform and improving living standards, education, healthcare, and labor rights for working-class people.[121] FARC's strategies and political missions began to deviate from its original socialist objective in the 1990s, as the U.S. started to provide greater intelligence and logistical support to the Colombian military, including the training of their personnel at the infamous U.S. Army School of the Americas (SOA) at Fort Benning, Georgia.[122] In 1999, SOA instructed 555 Colombian soldiers, who represented more than half the total numbers of in-resident trainees that year.[123] Colombian soldiers were taught interrogation techniques such as torture, execution, blackmail, and arresting the relatives of rebels and others targeted for persecution and execution.[124] Plan Colombia has contributed more than $1 billion to engage in armed campaigns to subdue the insurgents, including the aerial fumigation campaign led by DynCorp, under the rhetoric of destroying coca fields grown and profited from by the rebels.[125] The fumigated toxin caused a massive environmental destruction of the natural habitats in the indigenous homeland of the Cofán Nation and other indigenous nations from northeast Ecuador to southern Colombia.[126]

The ancestral homeland of the indigenous nation in Colombia and Ecuador has also been contaminated and polluted since the late 1960s by the drilling activities of international petroleum industries, including a Texaco-Gulf consortium.[127] Such disasters as oil spills, gas flaring, and untreated wastes have destroyed the biodiversity of the environment

---

[121] See generally Chomsky (2000).

[122] Gill (2011).

[123] Ibid., p. 43.

[124] Ibid.

[125] See generally Buxton (2006, pp. 184–187).

[126] Cepek (2012).

[127] Ibid.

and compromised the self-sustaining culture of the Cofan Nation.[128] Ecologically destructive corporate projects also led to the deforestation of more than half of all Cofan territories.[129] While the Cofan Nation, other indigenous nations, and environmental activists began to oppose corporate activities in the Amazonian communities, Colombian soldiers and privately funded armed troops were mobilized to protect oil wells, extractive corporate facilities, and the 500-mile pipeline which transported 100,000 barrels of oil a day for Occidental Petroleum of Los Angeles, which has invested in Colombia for more than four decades.[130] DynCorp has also been responsible for spraying a toxic fumigant that led to the destruction of food crops, livestock deaths, infanticide, and serious health damages to Cofan people and other indigenous communities around the borders of Ecuador and Colombia.[131] The group of indigenous leaders and the Organization of Indigenous Peoples of the Colombian Amazon (OPIAC) filed an official complaint with the Colombian ombudsman, claiming that Monsanto-produced glyphosate spraying, known as "Roundup," has destroyed food supplies, contaminated water supplies, threatened their rights to self-subsistence, and harmed the physical and cultural integrity and dignity of families and their members.[132] DynCorp has supported nearly every U.S. military campaign since the Korean War, and its employees have been implicated in numerous allegations of rape, sexual assault, and sexual slavery.[133] In Colombia, however, none of the sexual predators, including U.S. armed personnel and private military contractors, have been prosecuted.

---

[128] Ibid.

[129] Danver (2012, p. 120).

[130] Forero (2002) and Ziegler-Otero (2004).

[131] Buxton (2006, p. 186). (The U.S. State Department has outsourced the responsibility for fumigation to "the US firm DynCorp Aerospace Technologies for $170 million".)

[132] Ibid.

[133] Isenberg (2010). See also Human Rights Watch (2002).

5.2   Prosecution of U.S. Military Personnel: Prosecution Review Commissions in Okinawa

Similar to the immunity given to U.S. soldiers and military contractors in Colombia, the signing of the U.S.-Japan SOFA has provided U.S. military personnel "extraterritorial" immunity from prosecution under Japanese jurisdiction. In Okinawa, the failure of local government to punish criminals had also created a culture of impunity among military personnel, dependents, and civic employees, thereby fermenting the false liberty of criminality that led to further victimization of Okinawan women, children, and local residents. From 1972 to 2015, military personnel have committed a total of 574 serious and violent crimes against local residents in Okinawa, including 394 robbery cases (n = 548 robbers[134]), 129 rapes (n = 147), 26 murders (n = 34), and 25 arson cases (n = 12).[135] For the five-year period from 1964 to 1968 alone, U.S. military personnel and their dependents in Okinawa committed a total of 5,376 crimes, including 504 serious and violent crimes.[136] Okinawa, an independent and prosperous kingdom until Japan's annexation in 1879, has suffered from the continued victimization of local residents and their communities, as a strong sense of impunity has been shared among U.S. military personnel for many decades.

While the SOFA effectively prevented the prosecution of U.S. soldiers under Japanese law, an exception occurred in Okinawa in 2011, when the criminal grand jury decided to prosecute U.S. military personnel, thus reversing the Japanese government decision's non-indictment decision. The grand jury's prosecution decision in Okinawa punctured a huge hole in the culture of impunity long enjoyed by U.S. armed forces personnel, dependents, and civilian contractors in the island.

Japan's criminal grand jury has the power to render an indictment decision, similar to the power endowed in the U.S. criminal grand jury. The Japanese grand jury is called the Prosecution Review Commission (PRC or *Kensatsu Shinsakai*) and is composed of eleven ordinary citizens who are randomly selected from local electoral rolls. PRC was first

---

[134]The numbers inside brackets show the actual number of people involved in crimes.

[135]"Fukkigo 574-Ken, Oinawa Beigunjin, Gunzoku Kyoaku Hanzai [Since the 1972 Reversion to Japan, 574 Criminal Cases by U.S. Military Personnel and Their Dependents]" (2016).

[136]Ibid.

created in 1948 in order to bring transparency to the Japanese prosecutorial decision-making process.[137] There are 165 PRCs in Japan's 50 district court jurisdictions. The term served is six months, and the panel of eleven citizens is requested to evaluate the propriety of non-indictment decisions rendered by the Japanese public prosecutors. If a prosecutor had decided not to indict, a victim or suitable proxy could request that the PRC review the non-prosecution, with an option of reversing its decision, should the evidence warrant. Since 99.9% of indicted cases by the Japanese prosecutors resulted in conviction, the possible abuse of prosecutorial power rests on the prosecution's decision not to indict the suspect.

The reversal of a non-indictment decision that took place against U.S. military personnel in Okinawa in 2011 meant that the PRC's decision to issue the indictment directly challenged the U.S.-Japan SOFA and its immunity clause. The defendant was eventually tried in the Japanese district court in Okinawa and sent to prison. A closer examination of this case is of significance, as it may present a potential model for the indigenous nation and people to create a structure of law enabling them to indict and prosecute serious and violent crimes committed by foreign military personal in their homeland. The rightful prosecution of serious criminal offenders would also eradicate the culture of immunity shared among military personnel and civil contractors. In Okinawa in January 2011, a twenty-three-year-old military civic employee, Rufus James Ramsey III, had consumed alcohol at the base party and was driving back to his apartment. His vehicle suddenly veered into an opposing lane and crashed into a compact car driven by a nineteen-year-old Okinawan youth Koki Yogi, killing him instantly.[138] Like many Okinawan youths, Yogi had decided to work in the main Japanese island and had found a job in Aichi Prefecture in central Japan.[139] He had just returned to his native island to attend the official "Coming of Age" event

---

[137] Fukurai and Wang (2014) and Johnson and Hirayama (2019). For further discussions of PRCs in relation to Japan's other citizen-led adjudication systems, see Johnson and Vanoverbeke (2020) and Johnson et al. (2020).

[138] "Japanese Man Died After Vehicle Collision with AAFES Employee on Okinawa (hereinafter AAFES)" (2011). See also "Beiheihanzai Fukiso ni Kogi [Protest against Non-Prosecutorial Decision]" (2011) and "Drinking at USF 'Official Event' is Regarded as Party of 'Official Duty'" (2011).

[139] "Indicted U.S. Base Worker Accepts an Involuntary Manslaughter Plea" (2012).

in January and to celebrate his transition into adulthood as he would turn twenty that year.

After the auto crash, the U.S. base employee was taken to U.S. Naval Hospital Okinawa on Camp Lester and shortly released. In March, the Japanese public prosecutors announced the decision not to indict Ramsey, since the traffic collision had taken place while he was still on official duty, according to U.S. military officials, citing SOFA's Article 17, in which the American military exercises primary jurisdiction over all accidents or crimes committed while on official duty.[140] His driving privilege was suspended for the next five years.[141] Ramsey was not tried in the U.S. military court, as he was not a member of U.S. armed forces.[142] It is important to note that in Okinawa, alcohol-related auto-accidents caused by U.S. base personnel have been common. Between 1981 and 2016, a total of 3,613 drunk-driving accidents were caused by U.S. military personnel, resulting in 82 deaths and 4,024 injuries. However, when a U.S. base worker injured or killed Okinawan residents, the punishment of drivers was almost nonexistent, thereby contributing to the culture of impunity and violence in Okinawa.[143]

Soon after the death of her son, the victim's mother, her friends, and concerned community members brought their grievances to prominent Okinawan attorney Toshio Ikemiyagi, who suggested that they might petition the Okinawa PRC to review the non-indictment decision rendered by the Japanese public prosecutors. Upon their request, Attorney Ikemiyagi also helped file a petition on behalf of a grieving mother, asking the PRC to review the non-indictment decision. In May 2011, the PRC deliberated on the case and announced that the indictment should have been issued in the first instance, reversing the Japanese prosecutors' non-indictment decision.[144]

According to the new 2009 PRC law, after the PRC issued the indictment decision, the local prosecutor's office was required to respond to

---

[140] AAFES (2011).

[141] "Beigunzoku, Kisosoto Chiikyotei ga Hikokusekini ["Indictment is Proper" for Military Employee: SOFA is on Defendant's Seat] (hereinafter Beigunzoku)" (2011).

[142] Ibid.

[143] Nihon Heiwa Iinkai [Japanese Peace Commission] (2017).

[144] Ibid.

the PRC's reversing decision within a three-month window. An unexpected event took place in this case. First, the local prosecutors did not make an announcement of the result of the reinvestigation of the case, as mandated by the new PRC law. Second, in November 2011, the U.S.-Japan Joint Committee, rather than the Japanese prosecutor's office, made a sudden announcement on this case. The U.S.-Japan Joint Committee is the powerful bilateral panel charged with administering the SOFA, largely in secret. Third, the Joint Committee stated that, in a period of peacetime, the U.S. military employee would not be protected by the SOFA provision.[145] That is, if a member of the armed forces or a military-linked civilian was apprehended by Japanese police while driving drunk, they would lose their "extraterritorial" status under SOFA, and Japan would have the right to exercise primary jurisdiction, whether they were on or off duty. Secondly, since civilian workers were not subject to the U.S. Uniform Code of Military Justice (UCMJ), i.e., military law that governs the conduct of U.S. military personnel, civilian employees could not be tried in a U.S. military court. U.S. base workers must then be tried in a civilian court and could be transferred to the U.S. for a criminal trial. Thirdly, if U.S. authorities decide that the transfer to the U.S. might be logistically impermissible or improbable, the U.S. authority might decide not to prosecute them. If the non-prosecution decision were rendered by the U.S. authority, Japan could formally request to try the case. In such an instance, the U.S. would be asked to grant a "sympathetic consideration" in handing the suspect over to the Japanese authorities.[146] Lastly, the Japanese government would be allowed to exercise jurisdiction over such a case. Two days after the Joint Committee's announcement, Okinawa's prosecutors' office indicted the military worker. He was soon arrested, prosecuted, tried, convicted in Okinawa's district court, and sentenced to prison for 18 months for vehicular manslaughter.[147]

This PRC's-forced prosecution was significant in effectively puncturing an unprecedented critical hole in the SOFA's immunity provision for U.S. base personnel and civilian contractors. It is equally important to recognize the importance of the PRC petition filed by the veteran Okinawan

---

[145] "Okinawa Prosecutors Indict U.S. Base Employee" (2011). See also "U.S. Civilian Worker in Okinawa Indicted for Fatality" (2011).

[146] Johnston (2012).

[147] Tritten and Sumida (2012).

attorney on behalf of the mother of the auto accident victim, for Ikemiyagi had enlisted key legal decisions and justifications in arguing that the military employee should be indicted and prosecuted in Okinawa.[148]

First, he indicated that the U.S. Supreme Court in 1960 handed down the decision that during a time of peace, the SOFA protection of military personnel would not be extended to civilian employees of American military bases overseas. He cited two rulings: (1) *McElroy v. Guagliardo* (1960), which specified that during peacetime, the Uniform Code of Military Justice (UCMJ) could not be applied to civilian employees of U.S. Armed Forces overseas in noncapital offenses,[149] and (2) *Grisham v. Hagan* (1960), which specified that, even in capital cases, different jurisdictional principles could be applied to civilian employees overseas.[150] Ikemiyagi's PRC petition had certainly influenced the PRC deliberation, for the PRC's Principal Statement (*giketsu no shushi*) issued by the Okinawa PRC on May 27, 2011, reversing the Japanese prosecutors' non-indictment decision, also cited these two U.S. Supreme Court decisions.[151]

Second, Ikegami's petition and the PRC Principal Statement had cited other exclusionary provisions of civil employees at U.S. military bases overseas. They cited that under the North Atlantic Treaty Organization (NATO) SOFA provision, civic employees and dependent families of military personnel were not considered to be protected under the NATO SOFA that had been signed by multiple European and North American countries.[152] Third, both Ikegami's petition and the PRC Principal Statement indicated that the Supreme Court of Korea had made a similar decision on the limited coverage of jurisdiction over the civilians employed in the U.S. military base in South Korea, in which the U.S. military had no right to exercise its jurisdiction over civilian workers of

---

[148] Personal interview of Attorney at his law office in Naha, Okinawa, conducted by the author on Nov. 30, 2016.

[149] *McElroy v. United States ex rel Guagliardo*, 361 U.S. 281 (1960).

[150] *Grisham v. Hagan*, 361 U.S. 278 (1960).

[151] The PRC Resolution Statement (2011) (on file with the author).

[152] Beigunzoku (2011). See also "Petition to Naha Prosecution Review Commission, Apr. 25, 2011" filed by Attorney Toshio Ikemiyagi (on file with the author). NATO countries also include non-European states such as Turkey, Georgia, Ukraine, among others.

American military bases in South Korea during peacetime, as related to the 1960 U.S. Supreme Court rulings.[153]

Lastly, Ikemiyagi indicated in his PRC petition (that was recited in the PRC Principal Statement) that civilian base workers are not U.S. military personnel, and their crimes were therefore not subjected to adjudication by the U.S. Court Marshal, since the Uniform Code of Military Procedure (UCMP) has no jurisdiction over civilian components. The PRC then suggested that civic employees should be properly subjected to the U.S.-Japan SOFA Article 17, section (1) (b), which states that "the authorities of Japan shall have jurisdiction over the members of USAF, the civilian component, and their dependents, with respect to offenses committed within the territory of Japan and punishable by the law of Japan."[154] The PRC Principal Statement thus concluded that Ramsey, a civilian employee at a U.S. base, should be properly indicted and tried in Japanese court. This whole process of turnaround—from the Okinawan youth's death to the PRC's prosecution decision—took place quickly, suggesting that the PRC had acted on the review of the petition expediently and enthusiastically. The PRC's indictment decision was also prompt and decisive: the Okinawan youth's death occurred on January 12, 2011; the petition to the Naha PRC was filed on April 25, 2011; and the PRC decision that supported the indictment of a civilian employee was announced on May 27, 2011.

The role that Ikemiyagi played in this case was significant. As an Okinawa native, he had witnessed great human suffering during the 1945 Battle of Okinawa, in which more than a quarter of Okinawan residents had been killed; observed the rapid expansion of U.S. military bases, installations, and facilities across the island of Okinawa; and witnessed the dramatic surge of U.S. armed personnel and military contractors during the U.S. wars in Korea, Vietnam, Persian Gulf, and the current U.S. campaign against terrorism in South Asia and the Middle East. U.S. military bases in Okinawa have played a prominent role in carrying out U.S. geopolitical functions, due largely to Okinawa's strategic location in the East China Sea. Similar to the strategic location of Jeju Island in the Korea Strait, Okinawa is located next to Taiwan, China, North Korea, and Russia, as well as Southeast Asian countries, including Indonesia, the

---

[153] Beigunzoku (2011).
[154] U.S.-Japan Status of Forces Agreement (2019).

Philippines, Thailand, Myanmar, and other "resource-rich" neighboring states. Attorney Ikemiyagi has also witnessed the morphing of Okinawa from being Japan's pre-war colony into a virtual U.S. military outpost following WWII, and has witnessed the significant increase in Okinawan people's victimization by U.S. military personnel since 1945, taking the form of murder, sexual assaults, rape, and traffic accidents resulting in injury or death.

Today, Ikemiyagi leads a group of lawyers representing more than 22,000 Okinawa people in an effort to stop the night-flight military exercises and noise pollution at Kadena Air Force Base, Asia's largest military airfield. The plaintiffs also include Ikemiyagi, who co-owned the land now being appropriated for the construction and expansion of the Kadena airfield. In 2017, the Okinawa District Court ruled to award the plaintiffs with 30.2 billion yen ($267 million) in compensation. But the request to ban nighttime and early morning flights was turned down because the Japanese court stated that Japanese government has no jurisdiction over the U.S. military bases and their activities in Okinawa.[155]

6   The "State-Building" Project, the Military-Sexual Complex, and Counterinsurgency Intelligence Operations

In the last section, ONAIL examines the recent establishment of the state security protocol and intelligence disciplines of the "state-making" project, including the counterinsurgency intelligence program, "gray zone warfare" protocols, "foreign internal defense" and other hybrid warfare strategies to quash and pacify indigenous resisters and their revolutionary movements.[156] ONAIL also interrogates the proliferation of the so-called "Military-Sexual Complex" to ensure the successful overseas dispatchment of state troopers and management of their imperial operations of counterinsurgency strategies and protocols. Specifically, ONAIL focuses on the intelligence techniques and security innovations that the U.S. military had developed in the Philippines after the 1898 U.S.-Spanish War, in which Philippine natives and indigenous populations

---

[155] "Court Awards Record Damages for U.S. Noise Pollution at Kadena Air Base" (2017).

[156] For hybrid warfare strategies, see Lovelace (2016) and Prashad (2020).

began to engage in significant resistance against U.S. colonialism after the U.S. successfully expelled the former Spanish colonial power from the Philippines. In response to the indigenous resistance and opposition, the U.S. military developed security techniques and intelligence strategies to neutralize the insurgent organizations and resistance movements with a lethal cocktail of violence, firepower, mass surveillance, strategic persecution and prosecution, targeted assassination, political collusions, disinformation campaigns, and incriminating fake-news dissemination. Counterinsurgency techniques developed in the Philippines were soon unleashed and applied domestically in the U.S. to achieve the successful suppression of numerous resistance groups and insurgent organizations, including labor unions, trade organizers, anarchists, and women's political organizations who opposed the U.S. involvement in the First World War in the late 1910s; war-resisters and other potential domestic enemies, including Japanese Americans who were interned during WWII; suspected communists, socialists, trade unionists, and political radicals who were blacklisted and expelled in the 1950s; the entirety of "New Left" sociopolitical groups and radical organizers who were targeted by FBI's illegal COINTELPRO program in the 1960s and 1970s; and, most recently, the entire U.S. population, through the National Security Agency's (NSA) "Prism project" of indiscriminate mass surveillance protocol that began after 9/11 in 2001 under the banner of insuring national security.[157]

As examined earlier, the state has been devised as a geopolitical "legal fiction" whose ephemeral existence has been legitimized by the state's own self-certifying judicial bodies, other "legally constituted" state entities abroad, transnational corporations, and international organizations and agencies that the state system has created and maintained in the world. The "state-building" project has also gone through a number of evolutions to refine its "nation-destroying" protocols and programs. For example, after the U.S. declared its state sovereignty in 1776, the state began to propagate the hegemony of "Manifest Destiny" campaigns to legitimize the further westward expansion and colonization of indigenous territories through multiple wars, treaties, and the imposition of economic policies and government programs designed to uproot, starve, and exterminate, as many as possible, the surviving original nations and peoples. When the U.S.'s "state-building" project finally reached the

---

[157] Churchill and Wall (2001), Hedges (2010), Sottek and Kopfstein (2013), and Gellman (2020).

Pacific Northwest, the U.S.'s colonial inquest and "Manifest Destiny" ambition soon extended beyond continental borders to further colonize and conquer the original nation and peoples in other continents, oversea islands, and territories. In 1898, the U.S. invaded former Spanish colonies in its infamous Spanish-American War and took over Cuba, Puerto Rico, Guam, Micronesia islands, and the Philippines.[158] The U.S. also annexed Hawaii in 1898, after it successfully overthrew the Hawaiian monarchy.[159] In December 1898, the Treaty of Paris had established the independence of Cuba, and ceded Puerto Rico and Guam to the U.S., which also acquired the Philippines in exchange for $20 million in compensation to Spain.[160]

The original inhabitants of the Philippines resisted the U.S. colonization, and in the 1899 Philippine-American War, the U.S. summoned the army infantry, cavalry regiments, and artillery units who had fought in the Indian War in North America, including the renowned Seventh ("Irish Wild Geese") Cavalry Regiment composed of Irish immigrants and their descendants, after their massacre of Lakota people at the Wounded Knee in 1890.[161] The U.S. extermination of Filipinos was so extensive that the U.S. forces ended up killing up to 1.2–1.5 million Filipinos, or nearly 12% of more than 9 million Filipinos from the last census taken during the Spanish colonial era.[162] U.S. Army and Marine troopers, for instance, turned the island of Samar, the third largest island of the Philippines, into a "howling wilderness," after killing all men above the age of ten, women, and young children.[163] The history of Irish immigrants acting as the "shock troops of empire," after many centuries of their own de-colonial struggles against the subjugation to English rules, exemplifies the ironic and sinister nature of European colonialism imposed on the original nation and peoples in Europe and elsewhere. In the U.S., similar

---

[158] Quesada (2014), Berner (2014). See also Gellately and Kiernan (2003) and Tucker (2011). For the significant reduction of indigenous populations in North America in the nineteenth century, see Olsen and Sheehy (1998, p. 78) and Churchill (1996, p. 21).

[159] See generally Van Dyke (2008) and Rosete (2016).

[160] Halili (2004) and Clinton (2016).

[161] Allen and Jensen (2001) and O'Keefe (2012).

[162] Nugrahanto (2018). E. Ahmed estimated that the number of total casualties reached 3 million Filipinos or about a third of the colonial Filipino population due to U.S. counterinsurgency strategies.

[163] Hurley (2011) and Ocampo (2018).

to Irish immigrants and descendants who participated in the U.S. imperial campaigns against the original nation, American Indians have served in the U.S. Armed Forces in greater numbers per capita than any other racial or ethnic group in U.S. military services.[164]

The U.S. colonization and occupation of the Philippines has also helped develop new and effective methods of "neutralizing" technologies and "psychological warfare" strategies to further legitimize the colonial policies and the subjugation of Philippine people, including numerous indigenous nations who lived in the islands for many centuries. The Philippines was one of the most diverse regions in the world, with more than 7,000 islands and islets stretching over 1,150 miles, while it also contained more than one hundred distinct indigenous communities, including the Bicolano, Chavacano, Ibanag, Ilocano, Ivatan, Kapampangan, Moro, Pangasinense, Sambal, Subanon, Tagalog, and Visayan. Other original groups in different islands and regions included the Palawan tribes, the Lumad, Igorot, Mangyan, and others, while the Tagalog remained the largest indigenous communities in the Philippines.[165] Through the brutal occupation of the Philippines and the effort to suppress peoples' resistance against the occupation, the U.S. devised the most modern police and intelligence units with sophisticated techniques of hybrid, psychological warfare strategies, including the systemic surveillance of oppositions and resisters, the dissemination of fake news and effective use of propagandas to discredit targets, political collusions, bribery, wrongful imprisonment, effective deployment of "snitches" and informants, politically measured threats against family and community members, targeted assassinations and persecutions, and other illegal counterintelligence techniques and imperial practices.[166]

---

[164] Gover (2017).

[165] Danver, supra 129, pp. 185, 664.

[166] See generally McCoy (2009). Similar techniques had been used to suppress anti-government, anti-war groups in the 1910s and beyond, including the FBI's CONTELPRO strategies used against communists, black liberation groups, Puerto Rican independence proponents, and women's liberation groups, among others, from the 1950s to 1970s. See Churchill and Wall (2001).

6.1   *The Military-Sexual Complex and the Counterinsurgency Against the Original Nation*

In order to solidify the U.S. presence in Southeast Asia and beyond, the U.S. took over the Subic Bay naval port which had been built by Spain in 1885 and expanded it further, with multiple military bases in its 262 square miles, eventually becoming the same size as the state of Singapore.[167] The "extraterritorial" privileges also afforded the occupying U.S. forces the capacity to terrorize and victimize local communities and residents with impunity.[168] The U.S. government constructed the "Military-Sexual Complex" in the Philippines that included U.S.-managed brothels, sex clubs, bars, and beach resorts, in which sex workers were routinely monitored by U.S. army doctors and medical inspectors for sexually transmitted diseases of syphilis and gonorrhea. In particular, militarized prostitution of native women and girls was so severe that " 'native women' [were targeted by military doctors] as the source of venereal diseases and the exclusive objects of inspection, treatment and isolation."[169] The Military-Sexual Complex also led to the proliferation of prostitution, sexual labor, disease control, and moral politics around the military base establishment, all of which became defining features of the U.S. colonial empire and U.S. military bases from Puerto Rico to Hawaii, and from Okinawa to South Korea, Thailand, and Vietnam, among other military facilities and installations around the globe.[170] The U.S. occupation of the Philippines by the turn of the twentieth century was so significant that renowned historian Alfred McCoy once asserted that the Philippines had become the laboratory petri dish for developing effective methodologies of counterinsurgency techniques, and rearming U.S.-supported local security forces for the repression of indigenous resisters, including Moro

---

[167] Whaley (2013).

[168] Kramer (2006).

[169] See generally Kramer (2011).

[170] Ibid. In South Korea, the medical surveillance of sex workers became so strict that U.S. military police could arrest sex workers without health inspection cards. U.S. military doctors then treated women who caught venereal diseases at the detention centers named as "the monkey house." See Vine (2015a, 2015b). For the sexual trafficking and labor exploitation of Korean women and children as war mascots by U.S. military personnel during the Korean War, see Hong (2020).

people in Mindanao and other separatist groups and political resisters in the Philippines.[171]

The Philippines also became one of a few states in the world to sign and ratify multiple SOFA and VFA agreements with the U.S. government. In 1947, one year after the Philippines gained independence from the U.S., the Philippine government signed SOFA with the U.S. government. The U.S. Naval Base Subic Bay became the largest naval facility in the world and facilitated the semi-permanent presence of U.S. armed forces in the Philippines until the Philippine Senate refused a SOFA renewal in 1991.[172] The Philippines later signed VFA in 1999 and resigned SOFA with the U.S. government in 2014. The Philippines also signed the Enhanced Defense Cooperation Agreement (EDCA) in 2014 in order to extend the U.S. troop's stay in the Philippines and build and operate joint-facilities on Philippine military bases to be used by both American and Philippine forces. The 2017 destruction of the Moro Nation and the Islamic City of Marawi in Mindanao and the torture and extrajudicial killing of Islamic resisters have been facilitated by the Philippine-U.S. military alliances.[173] More than 120,000 peoples were still displaced three years after the demolishment of Marawi and neighboring regions in Mindanao.[174]

U.S. military personnel, dependents, and civilian contractors had a long history of terrorizing and victimizing local communities, residents, women, and children, including indigenous peoples in the Philippines.[175] Through the joint military exercises and armed collaboration with U.S. military personnel, Philippine soldiers have also committed crimes against original nations and peoples throughout the Philippines. The most recent incident took place in Zambales Province, northwest of Manila, the Philippines' capital, where Philippine soldiers beat three indigenous residents, forcing one detainee to eat human feces.[176] Unlike Okinawa's

---

[171] McCoy (2009, pp. 440–445).

[172] Shenon (1991).

[173] Mogato and Lewis (2017).

[174] Westerman (2020).

[175] Morris (1996), Schirmer (1997), Chang (2001), Fukushima and Kirk (2013), and Hoyle (2014). As of 2013, "estimated 300,000 to 400,000 women and up to 100,000 children in the Philippines [continued to work in] commercial sex industry. See "United States: Address Role of U.S. Military in Fueling Global Sex Trafficking" (2013).

[176] Adams (2020).

strategic use of Japan's grand jury system called the Prosecution Review Commission (PRC) to prosecute crimes committed by foreign soldiers, thereby piercing the hole into SOFA's extraterritorial privilege granted to U.S. military personnel, the Philippines has had no history of lay participation in the adjudication of criminal trials. Numerous lawsuits called "Insular Cases" were filed in an attempt to introduce jury trials in the Philippines and other islands around the turn of the twentieth century.[177] The U.S. Supreme Court cases reviewed three appeals from the Supreme Court of the Philippine Islands, regarding whether or not the right to trial by jury should be extended to the Philippines.[178] Nonetheless, the Philippines' efforts have failed to establish the jury system and other lay adjudication institutions in the justice system.

Meanwhile, neoliberal policies had significantly weakened the Philippine economies and socio-political infrastructures. Unlike the counterparts of economically prosperous states in Southeast Asia, the Philippines has remained underdeveloped economically and industrially, perhaps largely due to the long-lasting residues of the counterintelligence gridlock devised and imposed by the U.S. to pacify and annihilate the Philippines' progressive elements from the turn of the twentieth century to the present.[179] The imposition of the structural adjustment program (SAP) by the WB and IMF had further retarded the Philippine economy so that its economic performance and industrial development continued to remain far behind its Asian neighbors.[180] FTA and ISDS further hampered the growth of so-called "resource-socialist" policies, while international extractive and logging activities in the indigenous territories in the Philippines have led to the eradication of the cultural and biological diversity, and the destruction of the ecological health of the environment and ancestral homelands of original nations and peoples in multiple islands

---

[177] For the review of the "Insular Cases," see Jones (2021).

[178] Wilfley (1904).

[179] See generally McCoy (2009).

[180] Danaher (1994). The first SAP in the Philippines was implemented between 1980 and 1983, in which a WB loan of $200 million was designed to promote exports, liberalize the tariff structure, simplify import procedures, and restructure export-oriented industries. The SAP policies, however "exacerbated the economic crisis of the mid-80s by supporting the disinvestment in agriculture and wrenching the unprepared Philippine manufacturing sector open to global trade" (p. 64). See Balisacan and Hill (2002).

of the Philippines.[181] Today, indigenous communities and peoples constitute only three percent of the Philippine population, and Moro peoples,
the Moro liberation army, Islamic progressives and separatist militants,
multiple indigenous nations, and anti-colonial resisters have continued to
fight for the rights to sovereignty and independence in the Philippines.[182]

7   CONCLUSIONS

This chapter examined the theoretical underpinnings of ONAIL, offering
strong critiques of ongoing "state-building" and "nation-destroying"
projects. The first section traced the history of the state-making project
in Europe and its global projection around the world. The critical role
of the state in the "nation-destroying" project was interrogated in the
second section of the chapter. The state has performed the role of an
intermediary agency of international law in the continuing exploitation of
the nation and peoples. For example, the structural adjustment program
(SAP) of the IMF and WB, in the states located for the most part in
the Global South, has had devastating impacts upon the nations, peoples,
their homeland and ecosystems. The third section explored the possibility
of the creation of a genuine inter-"national" alliance and global solidarity
among the nations, peoples, and global environmental organizations as
opposed to the predatory state and international organizations.

The international legal mechanism called the investor state dispute
settlement (ISDS) was the focus of the fourth section. The FTA and
its ISDS provision ensured that the investor's claim was not adjudicated in state courts, but in the "supranational" arbitration tribunal
called the International Center for Settlement of Investment Disputes
(ICSID), an element of the WB in which trade experts and corporate
lawyers are empowered to make the final decision. Research revealed that
ICSID rulings have privileged the economic interests of powerful transnational corporations over the rights and the welfare of the original nation,
people, and biodiverse populations of the ancestral territory. ONAIL also
examined the corporate practices of bio-piracy and bio-colonialism, as

---

[181] Bear (2020).

[182] Danver (2012). Another study indicated in 1993 that Philippine indigenous
people constituted nearly 10% of the population, suggesting the significant reduction
of indigenous communities in the Philippines. See Eder (1993).

implemented through the privatization and expropriation of indigenous bodies and knowledge.

ONAIL also examined the violation of state sovereignty in relation to the Visiting Forces Agreement (VFA), the Status of Forces Agreement (SOFA), and other bi- and multi-lateral military agreements, which allowed the presence of military personnel of foreign states on the domestic soil of the host states. In particular, SOFA was originally devised to violate the legal autonomy of the host state by providing immunity to foreign military personnel and civilian contractors from prosecution under a criminal justice system of a host state. It also allowed the construction of foreign military bases and the development of the "Military-Sexual Complex" in host states. The U.S. has signed more than 100 SOFAs and installed and maintained more than 1,400 military bases in over 120 states in the world.

The resiliency of two formal prosperous original nations in the islands of Jeju and Okinawa was examined, including their resistance against the construction of U.S. military bases in their ancestral homeland and Okinawans' use of a grand jury system called the Prosecution Review Commission (PRC) in order to challenge and eradicate the U.S. base employee's legal immunity that had been guaranteed under the bilateral Japan-U.S. SOFA agreement. The Okinawa PRC's prosecution decision ultimately led to the arrest, trial, and conviction of civilian military personnel under the Japanese legal system. In order to understand the simultaneous process of the "state-making" and "nation-destroying" programs, ONAIL also examined the ways in which a powerful state such as the U.S. has devised an innovative assortment of counterinsurgency intelligence programs and hybrid warfare strategies to combat, pacify, and eradicate the resistance movement of the original nation and peoples. The U.S. has used the Philippine conflicts to develop and sharpen its anti-terrorist protocols and intelligence strategies that have also been applied domestically against its own populations and nation peoples in North America throughout the twentieth century and in the beginning of the twenty-first century.

Bibliography

"A Returned US Base in Jeju, Proved to Be 'Most Oil-Contaminated,' Will Be Used Again to Militarize Jeju?"(2013) *Save Jeju Now*, 28 June, available at http://savejejunow.org/p7989/.

Adams, Brad (2020) "Philippines Soldiers Accused of Beating Indigenous People," _Human Rights Watch_, 4 September.

Aginam, Obijiofor (2003) "The Nineteenth Century Colonial Fingerprints on Public Health Diplomacy: A Postcolonial View," 2003 _Law, Social Justice and Global Development Journal_ 1–15.

Ahae, Jo (2018) "Symposium on the US Base in East Asia," _Gangjeong Village Story_, August/September.

Alawi, Hayla (2020) "Jeju Island, the Three Clans Myth, and Women Divers: Female Importance in Jeju's Cultural History," Pamela J. Mackintosh Undergraduate Research Award, https://deepblue.lib.umich.edu/bitstream/handle/2027.42/156011/haylaalawiresearchpaper.pdf?sequence=1&isAllowed=y (accessed 22 October 2020).

Ali, Saleem H. (2001) _Mining, the Environment, and Indigenous Development Conflicts_. Tucson, AZ: University of Arizona Press.

Allen, Charles W. & Richard E. Jensen (2001) _From Fort Laramie to Wounded Knee: In the West That Was_. Lincoln, NE: University of Nebraska Press.

Amaline, William T. et al. (2011) _Human Rights in Our Own Backyard: Injustice and Resistance in the United States_. Philadelphia, PA: University of Pennsylvania Press.

Aman, Alfred C. Jr. & Carol Greenhouse (2017) _Translational Law: Cases and Problems in an Interconnected World_. Durham, NC: Carolina Academic Press.

Anghie, Anton (2004) _Imperialism, Sovereignty and the Making of International Law_. Cambridge, UK: Cambridge University Press.

Anghie, Antony (2006) "Nationalism, Development and the Postcolonial State: The Legacies of the League of Nations," 41 _Texas International Law Journal_ 447–463.

Anghie, Anton & B.S. Chimni (2003) "Third World Approaches to International Law and Individual Responsibility in Internal Conflicts," _Chinese Journal of International Law_ 2:77–103.

Appiagyei-Atua, Kwadwo (2015) "Ethical Dimensions of Third-World Approaches to International Law (TWAIL): A Critical Review," 8 _African Journal of Legal Studies_ 209–235.

"Area 1. B.O.S.S. Jeju Island Trip" (2020) _MWR: Camp Casey_, https://casey.armymwr.com/calendar/jeju-island (accessed 22 October 2020).

Auken, Bill Van (2015) "US Troops Immune from Prosecution, Raped Dozens of Colombian Children," _World Socialist Web Site_, 28 March.

Balisacan, Arsenio M. & Hal Hill (2002) "The Philippine Development Puzzle," 2002 _Southeast Asian Affairs_ 237–252.

Barrow, Amy (2010) "History and Theory of International Law: A Transcivilizational Perspective on International Law," 3 _Asian Journal of International Law_ 192–193.

Barsocchini, Robert (2015) "US Now Has Over 1,400 Foreign Military Bases Spread Over 120 Countries: Assange," *Countercurrents*.org, 10 September, available at https://www.countercurrents.org/barsocchini100915.htm.

Baslar, Kemal (1998) *The Concept of the Common Heritage of Mankind in International Law*. Leiden, Netherlands: Martinus Nijhoff Pubs.

Bear, Sarah (2020) "Mining on Indigenous Territories in the Philippines: Geological Features, Environmental, Socioeconomic Impacts on the Indigenous Population of the Philppines," *Storymaps*, 16 August, https://storym aps.arcgis.com/stories/de2c08a0b1cd4d08a4f7e728adc0c22e (accessed 22 October 2020).

"Beigunzoku, Kisosoto Chiikyotei ga Hikokusekini ["Indictment is Proper" for Military Employee: SOFA is on Defendant's Seat] (hereinafter Beigunzoku)" (2011) *Okinawa Times*, 29 May.

"Beiheihanzai Fukiso ni Kogi [Protest against Non-Prosecutorial Decision] (2011) *Akahata Shimbun*, 19 April.

Berner, Brad K. (2014) *The Spanish-American War: A Documentary History with Commentaries*. Lanham, MD: Fairleigh Dickinson University Press.

Bhatia, Amar (2012) The South of the North: Building on Critical Approaches to International Law with Lessons from the Fourth World," *Oregon Review of International Law* 14: 131–176.

Bhatt, Kinnari (2019) "A Post-Colonial Legal Approaches to the Chagos Case and the (Dis)Application of Land Rights Norm," 15 *International Journal of Law in Context* 1–19.

Bird, John Samuel (2018) "Bio-Piracy on the High Sea? Benefit Sharing from Marine Genetic Resources Exploitation in Areas Beyond National Jurisdiction," 9 *Natural Resources* 413–428.

Bogota, John Otis (2015) "Colombians Accuse U.S. Soldiers and Officials of Sexual Assault and Rape," *Time*, 15 April.

Bonn, Keith E. & Anthony E. Baker (2000) *Guide to Military Operations Other War: Tactics, Techniques & Procedures for Stability & Support Operations: Domestic & International*. Mechanicsburg, PA: Stackpole Books.

Bornemann, Alberto Ulloa, Arthur Schmidt, and Aurora Camacho de Schmidt (2007) *Surviving Mexico's Dirty Wr: A Political Prisoner's Memoir*. Philadelphia, PA: Temple University Press.

Bosselmann, Klaus (2015) *Earth Governance: Trusteeship of the Global Commons*. Cheltenham, U.K.: Edward Elgar Publishing.

"Brazil: Indigenous Peoples Participate in World Social Forum" (2018) *Cultural Survivor*, (accessed 21 November 2018), available at https://www.culturals urvival.org/news/brazil-indigenous-peoples-participate-world-social-forum.

Broadman, Harry G. (2019) "Arbitration of International Investor-State Disputes Sorely Needs Reform," *Forbes*, 30 October.

Brodzinsky, Sibylla (2015) "US Army Investigates Reports That Soldiers Raped Dozens in Colombia," *Guardian*, 7 April.

Brown, Alleen (2017) "Approves Keystone XL Pipeline as Opponents Face Criminalization of Protests," *The Intercept*, 20 November, available at https://theintercept.com/2017/11/20/nebraska-approves-keystone-xl-pipeline-as-opponents-face-criminalization-of-protests/.

Brown, Alleen (2018) "Five Spills, Six Months in Operation: Dakota Access Track Record Highlights Unavoidable Reality: Pipelines Leak," *The Intercept*, 9 January, available at https://theintercept.com/2018/01/09/dakota-access-pipeline-leak-energy-transfer-partners/.

Brown, Alleen, Will Parrish & Alice Sper (2017) "Leaked Documents Reveal Counterterrorism Tactics Used at Standing Rock to 'Defeat Pipeline Insurgencies'," *The Intercept*, 27 May, available at https://theintercept.com/2017/05/27/leaked-documents-reveal-security-firms-counterterrorism-tactics-at-standing-rock-to-defeat-pipeline-insurgencies/.

Buck, Susan J. (1998) *The Global Commons: An Introduction*. Washington, DC: Island Press.

Burnett, Peter H. (1851) "Executive Order, Peter Burnette, 1st Governor, Independent Democrat 1849–1851: State of the State Address," 6 January, available at https://governors.library.ca.gov/addresses/s_01-Burnett2.html.

Burnette, Ryan (2013) *Biosecurity: Understanding, Assessing, and Preventing the Threat*. Hoboken, NJ: John Wiley & Sons, Inc.

Buxton, Julie (2006) *The Political Economy of Narcotics: Production, Consumption and Global Markets*. London, UK: Zed Books.

"California Military Bases" (2020) https://militarybases.com/california/#:~:text=California%20has%20more%20military%20bases,most%20heavily%20around%20San%20Diego (accessed 22 October 2020).

Calloway, Colin G. (1998) *New Worlds for All: Indians, Europeans, and the Remaking of Early America*. Baltimore, MD: The John Hopkins University Press.

Capdevila, Gustavo (2009) "Indigenous People Troubled by US Military Presence in Colombia," *TNI*, 14 August, available at https://www.tni.org/my/node/4501.

Carson, Catherine & Kenneth Iain McDonald (2012) "Enclosing the Global Commons: The Convention on Biological Diversity and Green Grabbing," 39 *Journal of Peasant Studies* 263–283.

Cepek, Michael (2012) *A Future for Amazonia: Randy Borman and Cofán Environmental Politics*. Austin, TX: University of Texas Press.

Chang, Emily Nyen (2001) "Engagement Abroad: Enlisted Men, U.S. Military Policy and the Sex Industry, 15 *Notre Dame Journal of Law, Ethics & Public Policy* 621–653.

Chang, Ha-Joon (2000) *Kicking Away the Ladder: Development Strategy in Historical Perspective.* London, UK: Anthem Press.

Changhoon, Ko (2007) "A New Look at Korean Gender Roles: Jeju (Cheju) Women Divers as a World Cultural Heritage," 23 *Asian Women* 31–54.

Chimni, B.S. (2006) "Third World Approaches to International Law: A Manifesto," *International Community Law Review* 8: 3–27.

Chimni, B.S. (2010) "International Law Scholarship in Post-Colonial India: Coping with Dualism," 23 *Leiden Journal of International Law* 23–51.

Chomsky, Noam (2000) *Rogue States: The Rule of Force in World Affairs.* London, UK: Plutobooks.

Chomsky, Noam, Lois Meyer, & Benjamin Maldonado (2010) *New World of Indigenous Resistance: Noam Chomsky and Voices from North, South, and Central America.* San Francisco, CA: City Lights Open Media.

Churchill, Ward (1993) *Struggle for the Land: Indigenous Resistance to Genocide, Ecocide, and Expropriation in Contemporary North America.* Monroe, ME: Common Courage Press.

Churchill, Ward (1994) *Indians Are Us? Culture and Genocide in Native North America.* Monroe, ME: Common Courage Press.

Churchill, Ward (1996) *From a Native Son: Selected Essays in Indigenism, 1985– 1995.* Boston, MA: South End Press.

Churchill, Ward (2002) *Struggle for the Land: Native North American Resistance to Genocide, Ecocide and Colonization.* San Francisco, CA: City Lights Books.

Churchill, Ward & Jim Vander Wall (2001) *COINTELRO Papers: Documents from the FBI's Wars Against Dissent in the United States.* Boston, MA: South End Press.

Clinton, Greg (2016) *Puerto Rico and the Spanish-American War.* New York: Cavendish Square Publishing, LLC.

Cochran, Charles L. & Hungdah Chiu (2019) "U.S. Status of Forces Agreements with Asian Countries: Selected Studies," *Occasional Papers/Reprints Series in Contemporary Asian Studies* 7:1.

"Court Awards Record Damages for U.S. Noise Pollution at Kadena Air Base" (2017) *Japan Times,* 23 February.

Crawford, Quinton Douglas (2005*) Knowledge for Tomorrow: A Summarized Commentary of World History, Nature, Health, Religion, Organized Crime, and Inspiration for the Youth.* New York: IUniverse.

Cruetzig, Felix (2017) "Govern Land as a Global Commons," *Nature,* 30 May.

Cumbers, Andrew (2015) "Constructing a Global Commons in, Against and Beyond the State," 19 *Space and Polity* 62–75.

Cupples, Julie (2013) *Latin American Development.* New York: Routledge.

Danaher, Kevin (1994) *50 Years is Enough: The Case Against the World Bank and the International Monetary Fund.* Boston, MA: South End Press.

Danver, Steven (2012) *The Native Peoples of the World: An Encyclopedia of Groups, Cultures, and Contemporary Issues*. Armonk, NY: Sharpe Reference.

"Declaration of the World Trade Organization (WTO) and Indigenous Peoples: Resisting Globalizations, Asserting Self-Determination" (2013) *IPMSDL*, 6 December, available at https://www.wto.org/english/thewto_e/minist_e/mc9_e/indigenous_peoples_declaration.pdf.

Defense Manpower Data Center (2019) *Number of Military and DoD Appropriated Fund (APF) Civilian Personnel Permanently Assigned by Duty Location and Service/Component* (accessed 22 October 2020).

Delbruck, Jost (2002) "Prospect for a 'World (International) Law?' Legal Developments in a Changing International System," *Indiana Journal of Global Legal Studies* 9:401–431.

Diamond v. Chakrabarty, 447 U.S. 303 (1980).

Diamond, Jared (1997) *Guns, Germs, and Steel: The Fates of Human Societies*. New York: W. W. Norton & Co.

"Drinking at USF 'Official Event' is Regarded as Party of 'Official Duty'" (2011) *Japan Press Weekly*, 14 April.

Desierto, D. A. (2008) "A Postcolonial International Law Discourses on Regional Developments in South and Southeast Asia," 36 *International Journal of Legal Information* 387–431.

Dickinson, Torry (2019) "Peace Activists Have Been Protesting Korea's Navy Base in Jeju for 12 Years!? *Friends Peace Teams*, 21 October.

Dunbar-Ortiz, Roxanne (2006) "What Brought Evo Morales to Power?" *Counterpunch*, 10 February, available at https://www.counterpunch.org/2006/02/10/what-brought-evo-morales-to-power/.

Dunbar-Ortiz, Roxanne (2014) *An Indigenous Peoples' History of the United States*. Boston, MA: Beacon Press.

Durrhelm, David N. (2010) "Bioterrorism: Being Prepared But Not Paralyzed," 90 *Issues* 15–17.

Dutton, Yvonne M. (2010) "Bringing Pirates to Justice: A Case for Including Piracy within the Jurisdiction of the International Criminal Court," 11 *Chicago Journal of International Law* 201–245.

Eder, James F. (1993) "Indigenous Peoples, Ancestral Lands and Human Rights in the Philippines," *Cultural Survival*, June.

El Consejo Indio de Sud America (2018) PUEBLO INDIO (accessed 21 November 2018), available at http://www.puebloindio.org/CISA/cisa.htm.

Eslava Luis & Sundhya Pahuja (2012) "Beyond the (Post) Colonial: TWAIL and the *Everyday Life of International Law*," *Journal* of Law and Politics in Africa, Asia and Latin America 45: 195–221.

Epstein Graham, et al. (2013) "Diagnosing Oceanic Commons ICCAT and the Atlantic Bluefin Tuna," Commoners and the Changing Commons:

Livelihoods, Environmental Security, and Shared Knowledge, the Fourteenth Biennial Conference of the International Association for the Study of the Commons, http://dlc.dlib.indiana.edu/dlc/bitstream/handle/10535/8879/EPSTEIN_1150.pdf?sequence=1&isAllowed=y (accessed 22 October 2020).

Fabricant, Nicole (2012) *Mobilizing Bolivia's Displaced: Indigenous Politics and the Struggle over Land*. Chapel Hill, NC: University of North Carolina Press.

Fenn, Elizabeth (2020) "Biological Warfare in Eighteen-Century North America: Beyond Jeffrey Amherst," 86 *The Journal of American History* 1552–1580.

Fernandez, James & John Herzog (2014) "Farewell Lord Jeffrey Amherst: Debate Over Amherst College's Institutional Anchorage in History," 30 *Anthropology Today* 7–9.

"First Nations Sign Anti-Pipeline Declaration in Calgary Wednesday" (2016) *Global News*, 17 May, available at https://globalnews.ca/news/3459305/first-nations-sign-anti-pipeline-declaration-in-calgary-wednesday/.

Fleck, Dieter (2018) *The Handbook of the Law of Visiting Forces*. Oxford, UK: Oxford University Press.

Forero, Juan (2002) "New Role for U.S. in Colombia: Protecting a Vital Oil Pipeline, *NY Times*, 4 October.

Forster, Stig., Wlfgang J. Mommsen, and Ronald Robinson (1988) *Bismarck, Europe and Africa: The Berlin Africa Conference 1884–1885 and the Onset of Partition*. Oxford, UK: Oxford University Press.

"Fukkigo 574-Ken, Oinawa Beigunjin, Gunzoku Kyoaku Hanzai [Since the 1972 Reversion to Japan, 574 Criminal Cases by U.S. Military Personnel and Their Dependents]" (2016) *Ryukyu Simpo*, 20 May.

Fukurai, Hiroshi (2010) "People's Panels vs. Imperial Hegemony: Japan's Twin Lay Justice Systems and the Future of American Military Bases in Japan," 12 *Asian-Pacific Law & Policy Journal* 95–142.

Fukurai, Hiroshi (2012) "Lay Prosecution of U.S. Military Crimes in Japan by Prosecutorial Review Commissions and the Saiban-in Trial." In Harry N. Scheiber & Tom Ginsburg, eds., *Japanese Legal System: An Era of Transition*. Berkeley, CA: Robbins Collection, pp. 131–160.

Fukurai, Hiroshi & Zhuoyu Wang (2014) "People's Grand Jury Panel and the State's Inquisitorial Institutions: Prosecution Review Commissions in Japan and People's Supervisors in China," *Fordham International Law Journal* 37: 929–971.

Fukushima, Annie Isabel & Gwyn Kirk (2013) "Military Sexual violence: From Frontline to Fenceline," Institute for Policy Studies, 17 June, https://ips-dc.org/military_sexual_violence_from_frontline_to_fenceline/ (accessed 22 October 2020).

Gathii, James Thuo (2011) "TWAIL: A Brief History of Its Origin, Its Decentralized Network, and a Tentative Bibliography," 3 *Trade Law. & Development* 26–48.

Gathii, James Thuo (2019) "The Agenda of Third World Approaches to International Law (TWAIL)," forthcoming in Jeffrey Dunoff & Mark Pollack, eds. *International Legal Theory: Foundations and Frontiers.* Cambridge, MA: Cambridge University Press, https://papers.ssrn.com/sol3/papers.cfm? abstract_id=3304767 (accessed 22 October 2020).

Gellately, Robert & Ben Kiernan (2003) *The Specter of Genocide: Mass Murder in Historical Perspective.* New York: Cambridge University Press.

Gellman, Barton (2020) *Dark Mirror: Edward Snowden and the American Surveillance State.* New York: Penguin Press.

Geranios, Nicholas K. (2004) "Study Finds Dangerous Waste Near Indian Reservations," *Sun Local,* 28 November.

Gill, Lesley (2011) *The School of the Americas: Military Training and Political Violence in the Americas.* Durham, NC: Duke University Press.

Glaholt, Eileen (2020) "California Indians and Genocide: Indian Genocide Is Not a Myth," *Sacramento Bee,* https://www.sacbee.com/opinion/letters-to-the-editor/article35247189.html (accessed 22 October 2020).

Gocke, Katja (2014) "Indigenous People in the Nuclear Age: Uranium Mining on Indigenous Lands." In Johnathan L. Black-Branch & Dieter Fleck, eds., *Nuclear Non-Proliferation in International Law.* New York: Springer, pp. 199–224.

Goldman, Michael (1998) *Privatizing Nature: Political Struggles for the Global Commons.* London, UK: Pluto Press.

Gordon, Seth (2014) "Indigenous Rights in Modern International Law From a Critical Third World Perspective," *American Indian Law Review* 31: 401.

Gould, Eliga H. (2014) *Among the Powers of the Earth: The American Revolution and the Making of a New World Empire.* Cambridge, MA: Harvard University Press.

Gover, Kevin (2017) "Greater Numbers Than Any Ethnic Group and Have Since the Revolution," *Huffington Post,* 6 December.

Gowrinathan, Nimmi & Kate Cronin-Furman (2017) "Rapists in Blue Helmets: The Crimes of UN Peacekeepers," *Environmentalists Against War,* 2 May.

Goyes, David Rodriguez(2016) "Land-Grabs, Biopiracy and Inversion of Justice in Colombia," 56 *British Journal of Criminology* 558–577.

Gozzi, Gustavo (2019) "Transcivilizational International Law Against the System of International Relations: Onuma Yasuaki's Normative Choice," 9 *Asian Journal of International Law* 170–176.

Grahn-Farley, Maria (2008) "Neutral Law and Eurocentric Lawmaking: A Postcolonial Analysis of the U.N. Convention on the Rights of Child," 34 *Brooklyn Journal of International Law* 1–32.

Grandin, Greg (2015) "What the Media Don't Cover When Colombian Women are Raped by Members of the US Military," *The Nation*, 7 April.

Gray, Fred D. (1998) *The Tuskegee Syphilis Study: An Insider's Account of the Shocking Medical Experiment Conducted by Government Doctors Against African American Men*. Montgomery, AL: New South Books.

Grisham v. Hagan, 361 U.S. 278 (1960).

Haley, Stein (2005) "Intellectual Property and Genetically Modified Seeds: The U.S., Trade, and the Developing World," *Northwestern Journal of Technology and Intellectual Property* 3:151–178.

Halili, Maria Christine (2004) *Philippine History*. Manila, Philippines: Rex Book Store.

Han, Rimwha & Soonhee Kim (2003) "Jeju Women's Lives in the Context of the Jeju April 3rd Uprising," 17 *Asian Women* 21–37.

Hardin, Garrett (1968) "The Tragedy of the Commons," 162 *Science* 1243–1248.

Harrison, Guy P. (2010) *Race and Reality: What Everyone Should Know About Our Biological Diversity*. New York: Prometheus Books.

Hedges, Chris (2010) *Death of the Liberal Class*. New York: Nation Books.

Hedges, Chris and Joe Sacco (2012) *Days of Destruction, Days of Revolt*. New York: Bold Type Books.

Hernandez, Brianna Nicole (2020) "Sexual Abuse in UN Peacekeeping: The Problem of Viewing Women as a 'Quick Fix,'" *E-International Relations*, 20 February.

Herring, D. Ann & Alan C. Swedlund (2010) *Plagues and Epidemics: Infected Spaces Past and Present*. New York: Berg.

Hippolyte, Antonius R. (2016) "Correcting TWAIL's Blind Spots: A Plea for a Pragmatic Approach to International Economic Governance," 18 *International Community Law Review* 34–52.

Hodges, Richard & David Whitehouse (1983) *Mohammed, Charlemagne and the Origin of Europe*. Ithaca, NY: Cornell University Press.

Hoffman, frank (2014) "On No-So-New Warfare: Political Warfare v. Hybrid Threats," *War on the Rocks*, 28 July.

Hong, Christine (2020) *A Violent Peace: Race, U.S. Militarism, and Cultures of Democratization in Cold War Asia and the Pacific*. Stanford, CA: Stanford University Press.

Hooks, Gregory & Chad L. Smith (2004) "Treadmills of Destruction: National Sacrifice Areas and Native Americans" 69 *American Sociological Review* 558–575.

Hooks, Gregory & Chad L. Smith (2005) "Treadmills of Production and Destruction: Threats to the Environmental Posed by Militarism," 18 *Organization & Environment* 19–37.

Hooks, Gregory & Chad L. Smith (2012) "Treadmills of Destruction Goes Global: Anticipating the Environmental Impact of Militarism in the 21st Century," in *The Marketing of War in the Age of Neo-Militarism*, eds. Kostas Gouliamos & Christos Kassimeris. New York: Routledge, pp. 60–83.

Hoyle, Lindsey (2014) "Command Responsibility: A Legal Obligation to Deter Sexual Violence in the Military," 37 *Boston College International & Comparative Law Review* 353–388.

Human Rights Watch (2002) The 2002 Report, available at https://www.hrw.org/legacy/reports/2002/bosnia/Bosnia1102-11.htm.

Hurley, Vic (2011) *Jungle Patrol, the Story of the Philippine Constabulary 1901–1936*. Salem, OR: Cerberus Books.

Huskell, John D. (2014a) "The Turn to History in International Legal Scholarship" in Jean D'Aspremont & Tarcisio Gazzini, Andre Nolkaemper & Wouter Werner, eds, *International Law as a Profession*. Cambridge, UK: Cambridge University Press.

Huskell, John D. (2014b) "TRAIL-ing TWAIL: Arguments and Blind Spots in Third World Approaches to International Law," 27 *Canadian Journal of Law and Jurisprudence* 383–414.

ICC Canada (2012) "ICC's Beginning, Inuit Circumpolar Council Canada," available at http://www.inuitcircumpolar.com/iccs-beginning.html.

Iglesias, Elizabeth M. (1999) "Mapping Intersections of Critical Race Theory, Postcolonial Studies and International Law," 93 *Proceedings of the Annual Meeting of the American Society of International Law*, 225–226.

"Indicted U.S. Base Worker Accepts an Involuntary Manslaughter Plea" (2012) *Weekly Japan Update*, 27 January.

Institute for Policy Studies (1999) "Women and the U.S. Military in East Asia," 1 March.

Isenberg, David (2010) "It's Déjà vu for DynCorp All Over Again," *Huffington Post*, 6 December.

Iskandar, Pranoto (2016) "Democracy and International Law in the Post-Colonial World," 3 *Indonesian Journal of International and Comparative Law* 799–806.

IWGIA Mission Statement (2018) "International Work Group for Indigenous" (accessed 21 November 2018), available at https://www.iwgia.org/en/.

"Japanese Man Died After Vehicle Collision with AAFES Employee on Okinawa" (2011) *Stars and Stripes*, 13 January.

"Jeffrey Amherst and Smallpox Blankets: Lord Jeffrey Amherst's Letters Discussing Germ Warfare Against American Indians" (2020), https://people.umass.edu/derrico/amherst/lord_jeff.html (accessed 22 October 2020).

Johnson, Chalmers (2004) *Sorrows of Empire: Militarism, Secrecy, and the End of the Republic*. New York: Metropolitan Books.

Johnson, David T. & Mari Hirayama (2019) "Japan's Reformed Prosecution Review Commission: Changes, Challenges and Lessons," 14 *Asian Journal of Criminology* 77–102.

Johnson, David T. & Dimitri Vanoverbeke (2020) "The Limit of Change in Japanese Criminal Justice," 49 *Journal of Japanese Law* 109–165.

Johnson, David T., Hiroshi Fukurai, & Mari Hirayama (2020) "Reflections on the TEPCO Trial: Prosecution and Acquittal after Japan's Nuclear Meltdown," 18 *The Asia-Pacific Journal: Japan Focus*, 15 January, https://apjjf.org/2020/2/Johnson.html (accessed 22 October 2020).

Johnston, Eric (2012) "SOFA: A Source of Sovereign Conflicts," *Japan Times*, 31 July.

Jones, Collin (2021) "the Island That Ate the Constitution," 42 *Liverpool Law Review* (forthcoming).

Jones, James H. (1993) *Bad Blood: The Tuskegee Syphilis Experiment: The Modern Classic of Race and Medicine Updated with an Additional Chapter on the Tuskegee Experiment's Legacy in the Age of AIDS*. New York: Simon & Schuster, Inc.

Kelly, Michael J. (2013) "The Pre-History of Piracy as a Crime & Its Definitional Odyssey," 46 *Case Western Reserve Journal of International Law* 26–42.

Kelly, Stephanie (2013) "Testing Drugs on the Developing World," *The Atlantic*, 27 February.

Keun-Gwan, Lee (2018) "International Law in a Transcivilized World: By Onuma Yasuaki," 87 *British Yearbook of International Law* 292–295.

"Keystone Pipeline Leak in South Dakota About Double Previous Estimate" (2018) *Reuters*, 7 April.

"Keystone XL Pipeline: Why Is It So Disputed?" (2017) *BBC News*, 24 January, available at http://www.bbc.com/news/world-us-canada-30103078.

Khan, Samia Liaqat Ali (2010) "Poverty Reduction Strategy Papers: Failing Minorities and Indigenous People," *Minority Rights Group International*, available at https://minorityrights.org/publications/poverty-reduction-strategy-papers-failing-minorities-and-indigenous-peoples-july-2010/.

Kil-Un, Hyun (2007) *Dead Silence and Other Stories of the Jeju Massacre*. Manchester, UK: EastBridge.

Kim, Soonhee (2016) "Jeju Island Women Divers' Association in South Korea: A Source of Social Capital," 9 *Asian Journal of Women's Studies* 37–59.

Kirk, Donald (2013) *Okinawa and Jeju: Bases of Discontent*. New York: Palgrave Macmillan.

Kohut, David R. & Olga Vilella (2010) *Historical Dictionary of Dirty Wars*. Toronto, Canada: The Scarecrow Press, Inc.

Koskenniemi, Martti (2001) *The Gentle Civilizer of Nations: The Rise and Fall of International Law*. Cambridge, UK: Cambridge University Press.

Kovach, Gretel C. (2013) "Cal Guard Soldiers Heading to Afghanistan," *San Diego Union-Tribune*, 17, January 2013.

Kramer, Paul A. (2006) *The Blood of Government: Race, Empire, and the United States and the Philippines*. Chapel Hill, NC: The University of North Carolina Press.

Kramer, Paul A. (2011) "The Military-Sexual Complex: Prostitution, Disease and the Boundaries of Empire During the Philippine-American War," *The Asia-Pacific Journal: Japan Focus*, 25 July, https://apjjf.org/2011/9/30/Paul-A.-Kramer/3574/article.html (accessed 22 October 2020).

Kronowitz, Rachel San et al. (1987) "Toward Consent and Cooperation: Reconsidering the Political Status of Indian Nations," *Harvard Civil Rights-Civil Liberties Law Review* 22: 507, 613–614.

Kuper, Leo (1981) *Genocide: Its Political Use in the Twentieth Century*. New Haven, CT: Yale University Press.

LaDuke, Winona & Sean Aaron Cruz (2013) *The Militarization of Indian County*. Callaway, MN: Lakwa Enewed.

Lam, Maivan Clech (2000) *At the Edge of the State: Indigenous Peoples and Self-Determination*. New York: Transnational Publishers, Inc.

Larson, Krista & Paisley Dodds (2017) "UN Peacekeepers in Congo Hold Record for Rape, Sex Abuse," *AP*, 23 September.

Li, Ming (2019) "Transcivilizational Perspective: A Legitimate and Feasible Approach to International Law," 9 *Asian Journal of International Law* 165–169.

Lim, Chin Leng (2008) "Neither Sheep Nor Peacocks: T.O. Elias and Postcolonial International Law," 21 *Leiden Journal of International Law* 295–315.

Lopez, Robert Sabatino (1966) *The Birth of Europe*. New York: M. Evans.

Lou, Ethan (2017) "TransCanada's $15 Billion U.S. Keystone XL NAFTA Suit Suspended," *Reuters*, 28 February.

Lovelace, Douglas (2016) *Hybrid Warfare and the Gray Zone Threat*. New York: Oxford University Press.

Mahmud, Tayyab (2007) "Geography and International Law: Towards a Postcolonial Mapping," 5 *Santa Clara Journal of International Law* 525–561.

Maluwa, Tiyanjana (2020) Reassessing Aspects of the Contribution of African States to be Development of International Law Through African Regional Multilateral Treaties," 41 *Michigan Journal of International Law* 327–416.

Martin, Summer Lynn (2014) *Ecosystem-Based Management for the Oceanic Commons: Applying the Concepts of Ecosystem Services, Indicators, and Trade-off to Make Informed Decisions*. Ph.D. Dissertation at the University of California, San Diego.

Martineau, Anne-Charlotte (2016) "Concerning Violence: A Post-Colonial Reading of the Debate on the Use of Force," 29 *Leiden Journal of International Law* 95–112.

Mason, R. Chuck (2015) Status of Forces Agreement (SOFA): What Is It, and How Has It Been Utilized?, available at https://fas.org/sgp/crs/natsec/RL3 4531.pdf.

McCoy, Alfred W. (2009) *Policing America's Empire: The United States, the Philippines, and the Rise of the Surveillance State.* Madison, WI: University of Wisconsin Press.

McCuen, John J. (2008) "Hybrid Wars," 88 *Military Review* 107–113.

McElroy v. United States ex rel Guagliardo, 361 U.S. 281 (1960).

McNutt, Kristen (2005) "Sexual Violence against Iraqi Women by US Occupying Forces," the UN Commission on Human Rights, March, Geneva, https://meaningfulworld.com/our-work/un/sexualized-violence-against-iraqi-women-by-us-occupying-forces (accessed 22 October 2020).

Means, Russell (2020) "For America to Live, Europe Must Die," https://archive.org/stream/ForAmericaToLiveEuropeMustDie/foramericatolive_read_djvu.txt (accessed 22 October 2020).

Mgbeoji, Ikechi (2006) *Biopiracy: Patents, Plants, and Indigenous Knowledge.* Vancouver, Canada: University of British Columbia.

Ministry of Foreign Affairs of Japan (2020) "Agreement Regarding the Status of Forces Agreement in Japan" (accessed 15 May 2020), available at https://www.mofa.go.jp/region/n-america/us/q&a/ref/2.html.

Michell, Jon (2018) "U.S. Marine Corps Sexual Violence on Okinawa," 16 *The Asia-Pacific Journal: Japan Focus,* 1–9, 1 February.

Miranda, Lillian Aponte(2010) "Indigenous Peoples as International Lawmakers," *University of Pacific Journal of International Law* 32: 203–263.

Mogato, Manuel & Simon Lewis (2017) "U.S. Forces Assist Philippines in Battle to End City Siege," *Reuters,* 6 June.

"Moon Voices Regret Over Dispute Over Building of Naval Base," (2019) *Korean Herald,* 11 October.

Morris, Madeling (1996) "By Force of Arms, Rape, War, and Military Culture," 45 *Duke Law Journal* 651–781.

"Movement Rights, Rights of Nature and Mother Earth: Rights-Based Law for Systemic Change" (2017), available at https://www.ienearth.org/wp-content/uploads/2017/11/RONME-RightsBasedLaw-final-1.pdf.

Mutua, Makau (2000) "What is TWAIL?" 94 *The American Society of International Law Proceedings* 31–40.

Mutua, Makau (2009) "The Transformation of Africa: A Critique of Rights Discourse," in Felipe Gomes Isa & oen de Feyter, eds, Hu*man Rights and Diversity: International Human Rights Law in a Global Context.* Bilbao: University of Deusto Press, pp. 899–901.

Mutua, Makau & Anton Anghie (2000) "What is TWAIL?" *Proceedings of the ASIL Annual Meeting* 94: 31–38.

"MWR to Host a Trip to Jeju Island" (2017) *Chinhae MWR*, 15 August, https://korea.stripes.com/community-news/mwr-host-trip-jeju-island.

Nairn, Allan (1995) "A Discussion of the Guatemalan and the CIA," Interview on Charlie Rose with Elliot Abrams, Robert Torricelli and Allan Nairin, 31 March, https://www.youtube.com/watch?v=1ig0YvJCh5w (accessed 22 October 2020).

Nairn, Allan (2013) "Exclusive: Allan Nairn Exposes Role of U.S. and New Guatemalan President in Indigenous Massacres," *Democracy Now*, 19 April.

Nairn, Allan (2016) "18 Ex-Military Guatemalan Leaders Arrested for Crimes against Humanity During U.S.-Backed Dirty War," *Democracy Now*, 8 January.

Natarajan, Usha, et al. (2017) *Third World Approaches to International Law: On Praxis and the Intellectual*. London, UK: Routledge.

Nazaryan, Alexander (2016) "California Slaughter: The State-Sactioned Genocide of Native Americans," *Newsweek Magazine*, 17 August.

Neeson, Jeanette M. (1996) *Commoners: Common Right, Enclosure and Social Change in England, 1700–1820*. New York: Cambridge University Press.

Negri, Stefania (2017) "Unethical Human Experimentation in Developing Countries and International Criminal Law: Old Wine in New Bottles?" *International Criminal Law Review* 17:1022–1048.

Neuhauser, Alan (2016) "TransCanada Sues White House for Rejecting Keystone XL," *US News*, 6 January.

Neuwirth, Rostam J. (2018) *Law in the Time of Oxymoron: A Synaesthesia of Language, Logic and Law*. New York: Routledge.

Nicholson, Blake (2016) "Keystone XL Pipeline Faces Opposition from 'Historic Union' of Canada, U.S. Indigenous Tribes," *CBC*, 17 May, available at http://www.cbc.ca/news/canada/calgary/keystone-xl-pipeline-indigenous-opposition-1.4117445.

Nihon Heiwa Iinkai [Japanese Peace Commission] (2017) "Okinawa deno Beikaiheitaiin ni yoru Inshuunten Shibojiko ni Kogisi, Beigunkichi no Tekkyo o Motomeru [The Elimination of U.S. Military Bases in Okinawa Due to Drunk-Driving Accidents Resulting in Deaths and Injuries by U.S. Marine Soldiers]," 20 November, available at http://j-peace.org/2011/statement/pdf/insyujiko_kougi171120.pdf.

Nolan, Cathal J. (2006) *The Age of Wars of Religion, 1000–1650: An Encyclopedia of Global Warfare and Civilization*. Westport, CT: Greenwood.

Nordhaus, William D. (1994) *Managing the Global Commons: The Economics of Climate Change*. Cambridge, MA: MIT Press.

Nugrahanto, Mohamad Radytio (2018) "Understanding American Genocide and Enslavement of Philippines," *World Bulletin*, https://www.worldbulletin.net/news-analysis/understating-american-genocide-and-enslavement-of-philippines-h203247.html (accessed 22 October 2020).

Nunn, Nathan & Nancy Qian (2010) "Columbian Exchange: A History of Disease, Food, and Ideas," 24 *Journal of Economic Perspectives* 163–188.

Ocampo, Ambeth R. (2018) "Samar, the 'Howling Wilderness'," *Inquirer.Net*, 19 December.

Odumosu, I (2008) "Challenges for the (Present/) Future of Third World Approaches to International."

Ogle, George & Dorothy Ogle (2012) *Our Lives in Korea and Korea in Our Lives*. Bloomington, IN: Xlibris Corporation.

Okafor, Obiora Chinedu (2005) "Newness, Imperialism, and International Legal Reform in Our Time: A TWAIL Perspective," *Osgoode Hall Law Journal* 43:171–191.

O'Keefe, Mike (2012) *Custer, the Seventh Cavalry, and the Little Big Horn: A Bibliography*. Norman, OK: The Arthur H. Clark Company.

"Okinawa Prosecutors Indict U.S. Base Employee" (2011) *House of Japan*, 25 November.

Olsen, Dale A. & Daniel E. Sheehy (1998) *South America, Mexico, Central America, and the Caribbean*. New York: Garland Publishing, Inc.

Olson-Raymer, Gayle (2014) "Americanization and the California Indians: A Case Study of Northern California," Humboldt State University's Department of History, http://gorhistory.com/hist383/CaliforniaIndians.html (accessed 22 October 2020).

Onuma, Yasuaki (1997) "Towards an Intercivilizational Approach to Human Rights: For Universalization of Human Rights Through Overcoming of a Westcentric Notion of Human Rights," 7 *Asian Yearbook of International Law* 21–81.

Onuma, Yasuaki (2000) "When was the Law of International Society Born? An Inquiry of the History of International Law from an Intercivilizational Perspective," 2 *Journal of the History of International Law* 1–66.

Onuma, Yasuaki (2003) "International Law in and with International Politics: The Functions of International Law in International Society," 14 *European Journal of International Law* 105–139.

Onuma, Yasuaki (2017) A *Transcivilizational Perspective on International Law: Questioning Prevalent Cognitive Frameworks in the Emerging Multi-Polar and Multi-Civilizational World of the Twenty-First Century*. Leiden, Belgium: Martinus Nijhoff Publishers.

Ostrom, Elinor (1990) *Governing the Commons: The Evolution of Institutions for Collective Action*. Cambridge, UK: Cambridge University Press.

Otis, John (2015) "Colombians Accuse US Soldiers and Officials of Sexual Assault and Rape," *Time*, 15 April.

Park, Young (2012) *The Dark Side: Immigrants, Racism, and the American Way*. Bloomington, IN: !Universe.

Perkins, John (2016) *The New Confessions of an Economic Hit Man*. Oakland, CA: Berrett-Koehler Publishers.

"Petition to Naha Prosecution Review Commission" (2011) 25 April, filed by Attorney Toshio Ikemiyagi (on file with the author).

Petroski, William (2013) "Debate Heats Up Over Keystone Pipeline's Gas Price Impact," *Consumer Watchdog*, 15 July.

Phillips, Valerie (2007) "Indigenous Rights, Traditional Knowledge, and Access to Genetic Resources: New Participants in Future International Law Making," *American Society of International Law*, Proc. 101: 319–323.

Pindjak, Peter (2014) "Deterring Hybrid Warfare: A Chance for NATO and the UE to Work Together," *NATO Review*, 18 November.

Prashad, Vijay (2020) *Washington Bullets*. New Delhi: LeftWord Books.

Pritchard, Justin & Reese Dunklin (2018) "U.S. Military Children Who Commit Sex Assault Abroad Rarely Prosecuted: Records," *Global News*, 30 December.

"Private Mercenary Firm TigerSwan Compares Anti-DAPL Water Protectors to "Jihadist Insurgency" (2017) *Democracy Now!*, 31 May, available at https://www.democracynow.org/2017/5/31/private_mercenary_firm_tigerswan_compares_anti.

Quesada, Alejandro de (2014) *The Spanish-American War and Philippine Insurrection: 1898–1902*. Oxford, UK: Osprey Publishing.

Rajagopal, Balakrishnan (2003) *International Law from Below: Development, Social Movement, and Third World Resistance*. Cambridge, UK: Cambridge University Press.

Reed, David (2013) *Structural Adjustment, the Environment and Sustainable Development*. New York: Routledge.

Resendez, Andres (2016) *The Other Story: The Untold Story of Indian Enslavement in America*. New York: Houghton Mifflin Harcourt.

Reverby, Susan M. (2012) *Tuskegee's Truth: Rethinking the Tuskegee Syphilis Study*. Chapel Hill, NC: University of North Carolina Press.

Robins, Simon (2016) *Dirty Wars: A Century of Counterinsurgency*. Gloucestershire, UK: The History Press.

Robinson, William I. (2008) *Latin America and Global Capitalism: A Critical Globalization Perspective*. Baltimore, MD: The Johns Hopkins University Press.

Rodriguez, Luis Nuno & Sergiy Glebov (2009) *Military Bases: Historical Perspectives, Contemporary Challenges*. Amsterdam, Netherlands: IOS Press.

Rosete, Maurice (2016) *Queen Liliuokalani: The Overthrow of the Hawaiian Kingdom*. Scotts Valley, CA: Createspace Independent Pub.

Rowland, Ashley Jon Rabiroff, and Yoo Kyong Chang (2011) "U.S. Bases Blamed for Oil-Tainted Groundwater in S. Korea," *Starts and Stripes*, 8 June.

Salazar, Egla Martinez (2012) *Global Coloniality of Power in Guatemala: Racism, Geocide, Citizenship.* New York: Lexington Books.

Santos, Boaventura de Sausa (1998) "Participatory Budgeting in Porto Alegre: Toward a Redistributive Democracy," *Politics & Society* 26(4): 461–510.

Schirmer, Daniel B. (1997) "Sexual Abuse and the U.S. Military Presence: The Philippines and Japan," *Monthly Review*, 1 February.

Shaffer, Gregory (2012) "International Law and Global Public Goods in a Legal Pluralist World," 23 *European Journal of International Law* 669–693.

Shenon, Philip (1991) "Philippine Senate Votes to Reject U.S. Base Renewal," *NY Times*, 16 September.

Shiva, Vandana (2000) "North-South Conflicts in Intellectual Property Rights," 12 *Peace Review* 501–508.

Shiva, Vandana (2003) "Biopiracy: Need to Change Western IPR Systems," World-Inforostructure, http://www.se.edu/nas/files/2018/08/A-NAS-2017-Proceedings-Smith.pdf (accessed 22 October 2020).

Shiva, Vandana (2005) *Earth Democracy: Justice, Sustainability, and Peace.* Cambridge, MA: South End Press.

Sinclair, Guy Fiti (2018) "Toward a Postcolonial Genealogy of International Organizations Law," 31 *Leiden Journal of International Law* 841–869.

Singh, Prabhakar (2010) "The Scandal of Enlightenment and the Birth of Discipline: Is Post-Colonial International Law a Science?" *International Community Law Review* 5–34.

Singh, Prabhakar & Benoit Mayer (2014) *Critical International Law: Postrealism, Postcolonialism and Transnationalism.* Oxford, UK: Oxford University Press.

Sovacool, Benjamin K. et al (2013) *Energy Security, Equality and Justice.* London, UK: Routledge.

Skouteris, Thomas (2012) "Engaging History in International Law" in David Kennedy & Jose Maria Beneyto, eds, *New Approaches to International Law: The European and American Experiences.* Hague, Netherlands: TMC Asser Press, pp. 99–122.

Smith, David Michael (2019) "Counting the Dead: Estimating the Loss of Life in the Indigenous Holocaust, 1492-Present," *Wayback Machine*, http://www.se.edu/nas/files/2018/08/A-NAS-2017-Proceedings-Smith.pdf (accessed 22 October 2020).

Smith, Gar (2009) "In Ecuador, Tree Now Have Rights," *Earth Island Journal* 23 (Winter 2009), available at https://www.earthisland.org/journal/index.php/magazine/entry/in_ecuador_trees_now_have_rights/.

Sottek, T.C. & Janus Kopfstein (2013) "Everything You Need to Know about PRISM," *The Verge*, 17 July.

Stern, Paul C. (2011) "Design Principles for Global Commons: Natural Resources and Emerging Technologies," 5 *International Journal of the Commons* 213–232.

Stiglitz, Joseph (2000) "The Insider: What I Learned at the World Economic Crisis," *New Republic*, 17 April.

Suzara, Aileen (2004) "Activist Debra Harry Speaks on Indigenous Peoples' Movement to Challenge Biocolonialism," *Indigenous Peoples Council on Biocolonialism*, 23 April, available at http://www.ipcb.org/publications/other_art/holyoke.html.

Sweeney, Chris (2019) "The World's 30 Strangest Military Bases," *Popular Mechanics*, 7 October.

Taber, Jay (2014) "Equals Not Subordinates, Intercontinental Cry," *IC*, 27 April, available at https://intercontinentalcry.org/equals-subordinates/.

The PRC Resolution Statement (2011) 27 May (on file with the author).

Thiongo, Ngugi wa (1986) *Decolonizing the Mind: The Politics of Language in African Literature*. London, UK: James Currey Ltd.

Tilly, Charles (1975) *Reflections on the History of European State Making, in The Formation of National States in Western Europe*. Princeton, NJ: Princeton University Press.

Tomei, Manuela (2005) *Indigenous and Tribal Peoples: An Ethnic Audit of Selected Poverty Reduction Strategy*. Geneva, Switzerland: International Labour Office.

Tomuschat, Christian, Atilia Lux de Coti & Alfredo Balsells Tojo. (1999) "Guatemala: Memory of Silence: Report of the Commission for Historical Clarification," *Guatemalan Commission for Historical Clarification*, February.

Tritten, Travis J. & Chiyomi Sumida (2012) "American on Okinawa Gets 18 Months in Prison for Vehicle Manslaughter," *Stars & Stripes*, 22 February.

Tucker, Arnold (2011) *The Encyclopedia of North American Indian Wars, 1607–1890*. Santa Barbara, CA: ABC-CLIO.

Tzouvala, Ntina (2019) "A False Promise? Regulating Land-Grabbing and the Post-Colonial State," 32 *Leiden Journal of International Law* 235–253.

UNCTAD (2020) "Fact Sheet on Investor-State Dispute Settlement Cases in 2018" (accessed 15 May 2020).

United Nations (2012) "Oceans: The Lifeline of Our Planet: Anniversary of the United Nations convention on the Law of the Sea: 20 Years of Law and Order on the Oceans and Seas (1982–2002)," https://www.un.org/depts/los/convention_agreements/convention_20years/oceansthelifeline.htm#%93Common+Heritage+of+Mankind%94+in+the+international+seabed+area (accessed 22 October 2020).

United Nations Commission on Human Rights (1982) "Report of the Sub-Commission on Prevention of Discrimination and Protection on Its 34th

Session: Study of the Problem of Discrimination Against Indigenous Populations," 10 March.

United Nation Department of Economics and Social Affairs (2018) "About Us,"
21 November, available at http://csonet.org/index.php?menu=77 (accessed
22 October 2020).

United Nations Educational, Scientific and Cultural Organization (UNESCO)
(2020) "Natural Sites in Madagascar, China and Korea Inscribed on
UNESCO World Heritage List," https://whc.unesco.org/en/news/358
(accessed 22 October 2020).

"United States: Address Role of U.S. Military in Fueling Global Sex Trafficking"
(2013) Equality Now, 2 March, https://www.equalitynow.org/united_states_
address_role_of_u_s_military_in_fueling_global_sex_trafficking (accessed 22
October 2020).

United States Department of the Air Force (1996) Military Operations Other
Than War. Secretary of the Air Force.

"U.S. Civilian Worker in Okinawa Indicted for Fatality" (2011) Asahi Shimbun,
25 November.

U.S.-Colombia Defense Cooperation Agreement (2009), 4 November, available at https://www.securityassistance.org/blog/us-colombia-defense-cooper
ation-agreement.

U.S.-Japan Status of Forces Agreement (2019) (last accessed 29 November),
available at https://www.nichibenren.or.jp/library/en/document/data/140
220_2_opinion.pdf.

"U.S. Soldier Gets 100 Years for Iraq Rape, Killings" (2007) KLTV, 23
February.

Van Dyke, Jon M. (2008) Who Owns the Crown Lands of Hawai'i? Oahu, HI:
University of Hawaii Press.

Vine, David (2015a) Base Nation: How U.S. Military Bases Abroad Harm
America and the World. Dallas, TX: Metropolitan Press.

Vine, David (2015b) "My Body Was Not Mine, but the US Military's: Inside
the Disturbing Sex Industry Thriving Around American Bases," Politico, 3
November.

Vogler, John (2012) "Global Commons Revisited," 3 Global Policy 61–71.

Vovin, Alexander (2013) "From Koguryo to T'amna: Slowly Riding South with
the Speakers of Proto-Korean," 15 Korean Linguistics 222–240.

Washinawatok, Ingrid (1998) "International Emergence: Twenty-One Years at
the United Nations," 3 New York city Law Review 41–57.

Webster, J. Clarence (1931) The Journal of Jeffrey Amherst. Toronto, Canada:
The Ryerson Press.

Westerman, Ashley (2020) "Over 120,000 People Remain Displaced 3 Years
After Philippines' Marawi Battle," NPR, 23 October.

Whaley, Floyd (2013) "Shadows of an Old Military Base," NY Times, 26 April.

Wheeler, Skye (2020) "UN Peacekeeper Has a Sexual Abuse Problem, *Human Rights Watch*, 11 January.

Wijkman, Magnus (1982) "Managing the Global Commons," 36 *International Organization* 511–536.

Wilfley, Lebbeus R. (1904) "Trial by Jury and 'Double Jeopardy' in the Philippines," 13 *Yale Law Journal* 421–429.

Wither, James K. (2016) "Making Sense of Hybrid Warfare," 15 *Connections* 73–87.

Wolf, Eric R. (2010) *Europe and the People Without History.* Berkeley, CA: University of California Press.

Yang, Changyong, et al. (2020) *Jejueo: The Language of Korea's Jeju Island.* Honolulu, HI: the University of Hawaii Press.

Ziegler-Otero, Lawrence (2004) *Resistance in an Amazonian Community: Huaorani Organizing Against the Global Economy.* New York: Berghahn Books.

CHAPTER 5

The Lakota Nation's Search for Independence: The Nation of Lakota Versus the State of "the United States of America" and the Constitutional Amendments for National Liberation

A constitution represents the corpus of fundamental legal principles by which the power of the state is established, limited, and defined. Aristotle envisioned the most desirable constitution as one that allows each and every citizen to attain a life of excellence and complete happiness. This conception has generated extensive philosophical reflection on varied forms of political governance, ranging from a small "City-Polis" such as ancient Athens, to today's "mega-states" such as the U.S., Russia, India, and the People's Republic of China (PRC), among others, in which hundreds of millions of peoples are incorporated into a single corpus of political and judicial order.[1]

The adoption of a constitution has been a topic of significant discussion among original nations of the world. While many of these have been historically "conquered" by, and internally colonized within, the powerful state, many have also decided to adopt their own constitutions, in parallel

---

[1] Ginsburg (2012, p. 11) ("Most societies of any scale have constitutions in the Aristotelian sense of *politeia*, defined as a set of fundamental legal and political norms and practices that are constitutive of the polity").

© The Author(s), under exclusive license to Springer Nature Switzerland AG 2021
H. Fukurai and R. Krooth, *Original Nation Approaches to Inter-National Law*,
https://doi.org/10.1007/978-3-030-59273-8_5

to the "over-arching" state constitution. Some notable examples include: (1) The "shattered" nations of Kashmir in India, Kurdistan in Iraq, and Palestine in Israel; (2) Catalonia in Spain, Bavaria in Germany, and other autonomous or semi-autonomous nations in Europe; and (3) The Lakota, Iroquois, Seminole, and other "internally colonized" nations in North America.[2] These sub-state nations have adopted what can be seen as "bifurcated" constitutions in an effort to protect their political autonomy, preserve human dignity, and maintain cultural and biological diversities in their ancestral homelands in the presence of state domination.

Despite the ongoing tensions arising from "duel" constitutional manifestations of the state and the nation, a revolutionary moment came on December 17, 2007, when the Nation of Lakota submitted a declaration of independence to the U.S. State Department in Washington, D.C. and officially proclaimed that it would "secede" its national territory from U.S. jurisdiction.[3] The Lakota Constitution was amended to substantiate the severance of the Lakota Nation, facilitate the nation's unilateral withdrawal from all treaty obligations with the U.S. government, and establish the independent nation of the Republic of Lakotah.[4] To assert its national independence and its free association with the U.S., the Republic of Lakotah subscribed to an array of renowned international laws and legal doctrines, including the 1803 Louisiana Purchase Treaty; the Lakota Nation's 1851 and 1868 treaties signed with the U.S.; the 1969 Vienna Convention on the Law of Treaties (VCLT); and finally the 2007 U.N. Declaration of the Rights of Indigenous Peoples (UNDRIP).

The territorial holding of the Lakota Nation has encompassed five U.S. states, including most of North and South Dakota, Nebraska, Wyoming, and Montana. Its geographical secession has created a huge "vacuum" in the middle of the U.S. federal system. In order to obtain international recognition of its independence, the Republic of Lakotah also sent

[2] See Vanhullebusch (2015). Western Sahara in Northern Africa and Kosovo in Southern Europe have also adopted their constitutions. They have been struggling to gain their independence.

[3] Harlan (2007). The Lakota delegation included Russell Means, the renowned co-founder of the American Indian Movement (AIM) and the prominent indigenous leader of the Oglala Sioux Tribe of the Pine Ridge Indian Reservation in South Dakota; Phyllis Young, the co-founder of Women of All Red Nations; Gary Rowland, a leader of the Chief Big Foot Riders in Wounded Knee, South Dakota; and Duane Martin Sr., the Rapid City Native activist, along with other distinct Indian members and supporters.

[4] See the Constitution of the Oglala Sioux Tribe of the Pine Ridge Reservation (2008).

copies of its declaration of independence to the embassies of Bolivia, Venezuela, Chile, South Africa, Ireland, East Timor, and other governments.[5] Despite their diplomatic efforts, however, no U.N. member state has yet recognized the Republic of Lakotah as an independent nation. Lakota's effort for sovereignty, however, has begun to encourage and ignite the original nation and other self-governing communities around the globe to seek the right to self-determination and political independence from their respective state systems.

In 2012, the government of Puerto Rico followed in the Republic of Lakotah's footsteps, holding a national referendum to gain independence from the U.S. Similar to the historical experience of the Lakota and other indigenous nations in North America, the people of Puerto Rico were militarily overwhelmed by the U.S. in 1898 and have been fighting for their political independence for more than one hundred years. Despite significant support for independence, coming from the ex-migrants and diasporic populations who had moved to the U.S. mainland and other territorial domains, the 2012 Puerto Rico Status Referendum failed.[6] Nevertheless, the U.N. Special Committee requested the U.S. government in 2016 to expedite the political process to allow "Puerto Rico people to take decisions in a sovereign manner, and to address their urgent economic and social needs."[7] Outside of North America, the regions of Donetsk and Lugansk have declared independence from Ukraine,[8] followed by Veneto in Italy in 2014.[9] The Kurdistan region of Iraq in the Middle East and the province of Catalonia in Spain each ran a referendum on independence in 2017, and both were overwhelmingly supported by the people.[10] In 2018, New Caledonia declared independence from France, although its popular decision was denied by the French government.[11] Many other nations and self-governing communities have also

---

[5] Harlan (2007).

[6] See generally Gonzalez, Juan, *Harvest of Empire* (2011).

[7] United Nations (2016).

[8] "Ukraine Separatists Declare Independence: Leaders of Eastern Donetsk and Luhansk Regions Declare Independence After Claiming Victory in Sunday's Self-Rule Vote" (2014).

[9] "89 % of Veneto Residents Vote for Independence from Rome" (2014).

[10] "More Than 92% of Voters in Iraqi Kurdistan Back Independence" (2017); "Catalan Referendum: Preliminary Results Show 90% in Favor of Independence" (2017).

[11] "New Caledonia's Independence Referendum: What You Need to Know" (2018).

adopted their own constitutions to assert their political independence and the right to self-determination.[12]

This chapter examines the historical path taken by the original nations who have relied on a constitution and political rights under international law to assert their independence from the state. The first section notes the clear differentiation of two contrasting geopolitical collectives in North America: the Nation of Lakota and the State of the "United States of America." The rhetorical conflation of these two entities has led to the misrepresentation and mischaracterization of the predatory policies of the state, as well as the state's coercive subjugation of the sub-state, yet culturally cohesive autonomous nations. It is important to emphasize that many nations, including indigenous communities, aboriginal societies, and nucleated autonomous regions, had existed for centuries prior to the domination by the modern state.[13] The interchangeable use of the terms "nation," "the state," and/or "the nation-state" has obfuscated the history of the nation and related struggles against the political, social, and military encroachment of the state.

The second section examines the historical evolution of the tension between the state constitution vis-à-vis the nation constitution, focusing on the Lakota Constitution and its 2008 amendment. The third section examines the legal rationales drawn on by the original nation for withdrawing all of its obligation from the state in order to achieve independence and assert the right to self-determination. The fourth section examines the constitutions adopted by other indigenous nations in North America, including the Iroquois Confederation and the Seminole Nation,

---

[12] The Constitution of the Commonwealth of Puerto Rico was ratified by Puerto Rico's electorate in a referendum on March 3, 1952. The Constitution of the Donetsk People's Republic was adopted by the Supreme Council of the Donetsk People's Republic on May 14, 2014. Iraq's 2005 Constitution recognizes an autonomous Kurdistan region in the north of the country, run by the Kurdistan Regional Government. For the Kurdish Regional Constitution, see Kelly (2010). The first constitutions of Catalonia were created in 1283. See Vargas (2018, p. 25). Other nations and self-governing territories that have their own constitutions include the Cayman Islands, Bermuda of Gibraltar in the UK; Greenland and Faroe Islands in Denmark; Aruba, Curacao, and Sint Maarten in the Netherlands; and Puerto Rico and the Virgin Islands in the U.S.

[13] The differing views of the evolution of the state and the nation were presented by anthropological scholars, including Pierre Clastres and James C. Scott. They argued that many nation peoples had originated in the state system and created their own independent communities in highlands and/or deep jungles in order to evade the state overreach. See Clastres (1989) and Scott (2010).

as well as original nations in Asia, such as Indonesia, Myanmar, India, and others, and delineates attempts to attain sovereignty in multiple regions of the world. The last section contemplates the future of nations and their constitutional activism around the globe, exploring the potential route leading toward the legal recognition of sovereignty for the nations and other self-governing communities.

1 THE NATION OF LAKOTA VERSUS THE STATE OF "THE UNITED STATES OF AMERICA"

The U.S. is often referred to as a nation, state, nation-state, country, or even empire,[14] while indigenous communities in North America such as the Lakota are characterized as a nation, tribe, or tribal society. The conflation and misrepresentation of varied "collectivist" groups and geopolitical entities has led to the misunderstanding of the concepts of the nation and the state, impacting the administrative and legal relationship between the Nation of Lakota and the State of "The United States of America."

1.1 The Nation of Lakota

As noted in Chapter 2, the nation represents the culture-bound territory of communities of unconstrained, self-identifying individuals who are sufficiently conscious of their common ancestral values of history, tradition, ideology, language, religion, and memory. According to this definition, Lakota people belong to the nation, as they share psychological bonds that are strongly attached to the historically interconnected, culture-bound territory and space. There are more than 170,000 Lakota people in North Dakota and South Dakota today, and 2,000 of them continue to speak a Sioux language.[15] The Iroquois and Seminoles, among others in North America, also represent indigenous nations and people who are bound by a strongly shared sense of cultural, historical, and ideological commonality. The U.S. Census Bureau has reported that 6.7 million people, or two percent of the total U.S. population, identify

---

[14] See Webb (2004), Bender (2006), and Agonito (2011, p. 101) ("Congress passed legislation permitting the army to recruit twenty-five hundred cavalry and build two new forts in Lakota country"); Sprague and Sprague (2015) and Andersson (2019).

[15] "Press Release: Lakota Language Now Critically Endangered" (2016).

as Native American or Alaska Native. As of May 2016, the U.S. recognized a total of 567 Indian nations; 326 of them with their own national homelands in the areas of Indian reservations, federal reservations, and off-reservation trust lands.[16]

Reaching beyond North America, the U.N. reported in 2010 that there were approximately 370 million indigenous people occupying 20 percent of the earth's planetary surface, and that there were 5,000 culturally distinct nations across the world.[17] While these original nations still retain legal title deeds to their homelands, the U.N. reported that these lands were often leased out by the state as mining or logging concessions for corporate profits without prior or sufficient consultation with original nations and peoples, leading to environmental degradation of the ancestral homeland and the destruction of self-sustaining cultures practiced by the original nation.[18] As a result, original nation peoples make up nearly 15 percent of the world's poorest populations.[19] While another research report estimated that there were nearly 7,500 nations, it also indicated that the majority of these are located in Asia and the Pacific.[20] While the original nation and peoples have gained increased recognition of their human and environmental rights at the international level,[21] especially after the passage of the UNDRIP in 2007, many decisions and directives enacted at the international level have not been respected or implemented at the state or international level. The nations' voices and grievances are often marginalized or suppressed, if they are heard at all, by their respective state governments or international organizations.

1.2   The State of "the United States of America"

The modern state has largely been created as Europe's outward manifestation of "state-building" ventures and imperial "nation-destroying"

---

[16] U.S. Census (2017).

[17] United Nations (2010).

[18] Ibid.

[19] Ibid.

[20] Griggs and Hocknell (1995).

[21] This is true, especially after the UN has adopted the UN Declaration of the Rights of Indigenous Peoples in 2007.

projects throughout the world.[22] In North America, the state has been unilaterally imposed upon a multiplicity of nonconsenting nations through war, conquest, slavery, germ warfare, genocide, and the scalp bounty.[23] For those who survived, the policies of state-enforced assimilation programs were imposed, with hegemonic forms of indoctrination justifying the state's "benevolent" policies toward those viewed as the benighted, uncivilized, and backward nations and their populace.[24] There was little or no degree of commonality of culture, identity, tradition, and history among assorted groups of immigrants, indentured servants, chattel slaves, decimated indigenous populations, and conquered Mexicans after the 1848 U.S.-Mexican War, in which the U.S. took over the northern half of Mesoamerica. As a result, the state of "the United States of America" became a legally constructed, imaginary collectivist entity, in which peoples were brought into the bondage of "multiethnic" or "multicultural" collectives by a network of coercive legal programs and authoritarian state agencies. By these definitions, the U.S. remains as the state, not the nation, as it has captured a multiplicity of migrant populations, internally colonized indigenous peoples, formerly Mexican nationals in the Southwest, as well as "kidnapped" Africans and more recent Asian imports and their descendants within its state-delimited borders.

As a geopolitical invention, the U.S. has created new scripts and invented stories of history, geography, map, and imagined memories in order to signify that its birth, history, expansion, and the growth of its artificial structure have preexisted, predated, precluded, and most importantly, precluded all nations' historical claims to their ancestral land, culture, tradition, resources, and knowledge of the land. The Marshall Trilogy—the decisions rendered by U.S. Supreme Court Chief Justice John Marshall—laid out the foundation of modern Indian law in the U.S. These cases included: (1) *Johnson v. M'Intosh* (1823); *Cherokee Nation v. Georgia* (1831); and *Worcester v. Georgia* (1832).[25] The socio-legal ramification of the trilogy will be examined in the later section of this chapter.

---

[22] See Scott (2010). The term, "state-building" or "state-making" has been used by Scott to designate the collectives of people who evaded the state encroachment in order to maintain their autonomy and freedom from the state-imposed taxation, conscription, and persecution.

[23] Churchill (1997).

[24] ibid.

[25] Abate and Kronk (2013, pp. 69–72).

It is sufficient here to note that *Johnson v. M'Intosh*, for example, gave legal justification to the state claim to land titles, using the discovery doctrine in North America, thereby invalidating the aboriginal claim to their ancestral homeland.

The U.S. has also relegated nation peoples to a vilified and marginalized status, such as that of ethnic minorities, savages, killers, rebels, or even groups of "terrorists" who took up arms and fought against the state intrusion and invasion of their homeland, including Geronimo, Black Hawk, Chief Joseph, Sitting Bull, and Tecumseh, to name just a few of the resisters among original nations in North America.[26] Given the numbers of "ethnic" and cultural minorities and autonomous nucleated communities, the U.S. also promoted the policy of multiculturalism, in which multiple "ethnic minorities" with different cultural practices and traditionally deviated backgrounds were forcibly integrated into the prevailing program of dominant cultural practices, institutional arrangements, and existing laws of adoption and forced assimilation.

Since the U.S. has been an "artificially constructed" legal entity from its inception with wars and violence, historical analysis has shown that the life cycle of state autonomy has often been brief, with many states that had been created through imperial construction disappearing into the dustbin of history. First emerging as a sovereign state in North America in 1776, the U.S. expanded its geopolitical territories by annexing the Republic of Texas in 1845; conquering and taking over the northern half of Mexico's Mesoamerica in 1848; and in 1898, invading and occupying the islands of Cuba and Puerto Rico in the Caribbean, and the islands of Hawaii and the Philippines in the Pacific Ocean. That year thus came to be called the year of "imperial thrust" in the making of the U.S. global empire.

2   THE HISTORY OF THE 1936 LAKOTA CONSTITUTION AND ITS AMENDMENT IN 2008

The nation has been historically bound together on the basis of common ancestry, ideology, language, tradition, society, institutions, territory, and

---

[26] See Dunbar-Ortiz (2018, p. 29). (The colonizers were met with resistance with "[indigenous] leaders such as Buckongeahelas of the Delaware; Alexander McGillivray of the Muskogee-Creak, Little Turtle and Blue Jacket of the Miami-Shawnee alliance; Joseph Brant of the Mohawk, and Cornplanter of the Seneca, as well as the great Tecumseh and the Shawnee-led confederation in the Ohio Valley".)

religion. The nation has rarely required a constitutional mandate, externally imposed judicial institutions, or European-style legal mechanisms in order to maintain its cultural integrity and territorially bound ideology and tradition. Nonetheless, in recent history it became increasingly common for the nation to produce its own "constitution" in order to assert its independence and insist on the right to self-determination, especially after the nation was forcefully incorporated into the state system. In North America, it is important to recognize that the constitution adopted by the nation did not arise from the nation's original initiative, but in response to changing and emerging socio-political contexts.

In 1934, the U.S. enacted the Indian Reorganization Act (IRA) to provide indigenous nations the opportunity to draft and ratify their constitutions in order to incorporate the nation into the political and legal matrix of the state system. The Office of Indian Affairs (OIA), a precursor to the Bureau of Indian Affairs (BIA), first promoted the adoption of the constitution of the nation and drafted the legal constitutional template in the 1930s. The OIA-drafted constitution had "standardized" narratives of preamble, articles, and sections, without the specificity of indigenous nations or territorial districts, so that the nation's identity and demographic information could be easily inserted into the model constitution.

On December 14, 1935, the OIA-drafted Constitution of the Lakota Nation was placed on the referendum, ratified, and put into effect on January 15, 1936.[27] The constitution was written in conformity with the OIA model of the Indian government, transferring the core of political power away from the traditional tribal council to the state agencies. Article IV, "Powers of the Council," for example, stipulated that the council power was "subject to any limitations imposed by the statutes of the Constitution of the United States and subject further to all express restrictions on such powers contained in this Constitution and the attached Bylaws."[28] Article IV (c) further required that the power of the tribal council be subject to the statutes of the federal law in order "to approve

---

[27] Lee (2013, p. 62). The tribal members of the Lakota Nation, such as the Oglala Sioux, Cheyenne River, Rosebud, Lower Brule, and Standing Rock had each adopted similar constitution. This chapter specifically focused on the Oglala Sioux Tribe of the Lakota Nation and their efforts to create the constitution and later amend to remove the constitutional compliance to the U.S. government.

[28] Constitution of the Oglala Sioux Tribe (1935).

or veto any sale, disposition, lease, or encumbrance of tribal lands, interest in lands, or other tribal assets which may be authorized or executed by the Secretary of the Interior, the Commissioner of Indian Affairs, or any other authorized official or agency of [the state] government, provided that no tribal lands shall ever be leased for a period exceeding five years, sold or encumbered except for governmental purposes."[29]

The model constitution thus ensured indigenous subservience and compliance with U.S. law, and any decisions on their property, economic transactions of land or resources, as well as any business activities within the indigenous territory had to seek approval from the state. The constitution further stipulated that the tribal council must "advise the Secretary of the Interior [of the U.S. government] with regard to all appropriation estimates or Federal projects ... prior to the submission of such estimates to the Bureau of the Budget and [the U.S.] Congress."[30] Its preamble also required that any decisions made by the Lakota Nation council must follow U.S. federal law, stating that "We ... promote the general welfare, conserve and develop our lands and resources, secure to ourselves and our prosperity the power to exercise certain rights of home rule not inconsistent with Federal law and our treaties, and in recognition of God Almighty and His Divine Province."[31]

In 2008, one year after the Lakota Nation submitted its declaration of independence to the U.S. government, the Lakota Constitution was amended to remove all of the constitutional provisions that required indigenous compliance with U.S. laws and federal agencies. For example, "Oaths of Office" for Article III was amended to eliminate the duty of an elected or appointed officer to pledge "himself to support and defend the Constitution of the United States and this [Lakota] constitution and by-laws."[32] The amendment also removed constitutional provisions requiring the Lakota's compliance with regulations of the U.S. Department of Interior, the Bureau of Indian Affairs, and other state agencies.[33]

---

[29] Ibid.
[30] Ibid.
[31] Ibid.
[32] Ibid.
[33] Ibid.

The amendment also strengthened constitutional compliance with renowned international law and pronouncements, such as the 1969 Vienna Convention on the Law of Treaties (VCLT), in order to ensure the rights of the indigenous nation and peoples under international law as required by the UNDRIP. Furthermore, the amendment ensured the rights of Lakota peoples to "support and defend this [Lakota] Constitution and ... the human rights of other peoples as recognized in international law and treaties."[34]

3   LEGAL FOUNDATIONS FOR NATIONAL INDEPENDENCE: THE CASE OF THE REPUBLIC OF LAKOTAH

Lakota has relied on an array of legal foundations to assert its sovereignty and independence, including: (1) the 1803 Louisiana Purchase Treaty signed by the U.S. and French governments[35]; (2) the 1969 Vienna Convention on the Law of Treaties (VCLT); (3) the 1960 U.N. Declaration on the Granting of Independence to Colonial Countries and Peoples; and (4) the 2007 U.N. Declaration on the Rights of Indigenous Peoples (UNDRIP). Lakota further cited additional legal instruments to solidify their assertion of autonomy, to ensure the nation people's human dignity, and to protect the biodiversities of the ancestral land from the state encroachment, including: (1) the 1776 U.S. Declaration of Independence; (2) the 1787 U.S. Constitution; and (3) U.S. Supreme Court decisions in the 1820s and 1830s.

3.1   The 1803 Louisiana Purchase Treaty

Lakota examined the U.S. signing of the Louisiana Purchase Treaty with France in order to restore its legal status as a sovereign nation. In 1803, the U.S. purchase of the Louisiana Territory, which stretched from the southern Louisiana border at the Gulf of Mexico to the northern border of Canada, doubled the U.S. territorial assets overnight.[36] The U.S.

---

[34] Ibid.

[35] Louisiana Purchase Treaty (1803), art. III.

[36] France was forced to sell its territorial holding, after the African revolutionary slave army led by General Henri Kristof had seen a decisive victory over French troops in 1803. In order to finance its imperial ventures in the remaining colonies in the Caribbean and Europe, France sold the Louisiana Territory to the U.S. government. See Horne (2015).

purchase of the Louisiana Territory, however, did not set forth that the U.S. purchased from France the legal title to Indian lands. The intergovernmental purchase agreement simply meant that France would not complete with the U.S. in making land treaties with the Indian nations that lay within the Louisiana Territory, including the homeland of the Lakota Nation.

Article III of the Louisiana Purchase Agreement stipulated that "the inhabitants of the ceded territory shall be incorporated into the Union of the United States ... and in the meantime they shall be maintained and protected in the free enjoyment of their liberty, property, and the religion which they profess."[37] Lakota argues that the requirement of the treaty to incorporate indigenous nations into the Union would be binding on the U.S. government, not the indigenous nation, such as the Lakota Nation, which was not a party to the treaty.

The treaty's requirement regarding the admission of nations into the Union had also been challenged by U.S. government officials in earlier times. For example, then-President Thomas Jefferson considered the treaty as unconstitutional, arguing that "the Constitution has made no provision for our holding foreign territory, still less for incorporating foreign [indigenous] nations into our Union. The Executive in seizing the fugitive occurrence which so much advances the good of their country, have done an act beyond the Constitution."[38] Prominent Massachusetts Senator Timothy Pickering questioned whether the indigenous nation would be incorporated into the Union and launched a campaign to sabotage the treaty. He stated, "it is declared in the third article [of the treaty] that the inhabitants of the ceded territory shall be incorporated into the Union of the United States. But neither the President and Senate, nor the President and Congress are competent to such an act of incorporation."[39] In addition to the question of the treaty's constitutionality, Lakota rejected the option to join the Union and declared the restoration of its original and "pre-treaty" rights. Furthermore, it was argued that since Lakota was not a direct party to the treaty, the nation could not be

---

[37] Louisiana Purchase Treaty (1803), art. III.

[38] Kloppe (2015) (citing the letter written by Jefferson to Kentucky Senator John Breckinridge, Aug 12, 1803).

[39] Geer (1904, p. 210).

bound by it against its will, even though it had agreed to obtain benefits from it. Specifically, Lakota people were "in a class of clearly intended third party beneficiaries of the Article III,"[40] so that Lakota "shall be maintained and protected in the free enjoyment of their liberty, property, and the religion which they profess," as stipulated in Article III of the treaty.[41]

3.2 The 1969 Vienna Convention on the Law of Treaties (VCLT)

Lakota also relied on the 1969 VCLT to withdraw all treaty obligations that they had signed with the U.S. government. The Nation of Lakota had signed the first treaty with the U.S. government in 1851 at Fort Laramie, Wyoming, which ensured that both the U.S. and the Lakota Nation "do hereby covenant and agree to abstain in future from all hostilities whatever against each other, to maintain good faith and friendship in all their mutual intercourse, and to make an effective and lasting peace."[42] The Nation of Lakota was formed from multiple indigenous communities, such as Brule, Oglala Sioux, Miniconjou, Yanktonai, Hunkpara, Blackfeet, Cuthead, Two Kettle, Sans Arcs, Santee, and Arapaho.[43] The U.S., however, failed to abide by their agreement and continued to violate the 1851 treaty through their continuous military excursions and invasions of indigenous territories. After the U.S. was defeated once more by indigenous warriors, the U.S. proceeded to sign the Treaty of Fort Laramie in April 28, 1868. The U.S. again promised that "from this day forward all war between the parties [of the U.S. and the Lakota Nation] to this agreement shall forever cease."[44] The U.S. Senate then moved to ratify the 1868 treaty on February 16, 1869.[45] The treaty officially recognized the Nation of Lakota with the status of protection guaranteed under Article VI of the U.S. Constitution.[46]

---

[40] Republic of Lakotah (2008).

[41] Louisiana Purchase Treaty (1803), art. III.

[42] 1851 Treaty of Fort Laramie (1851) article 1.

[43] Ibid.

[44] 1868 Treaty of Fort Laramie (1868) article 1.

[45] Ibid.

[46] U.S. Const. art. VI.

Soon after the U.S. Senate had ratified the treaty, in the 1870s, George Custer and his U.S. military cavalries led the violent invasion of the Lakota Nation, including the resource-rich Black Hills, the most sacred site in the Lakota territory. The U.S. invasion was assisted by hundreds of gold seekers and European settlers, provoking yet another war between the U.S. and the Lakota Nation. Today, the U.S. continues to ignore the treaty obligations, to illegally occupy the ancestral homeland, and to violate collective rights of ownership titles to ancestral homelands, cultural integrity, and the right to self-determination.[47]

In order to restore the original status of independent nation, Lakota cited Article 49 of the 1969 VCLT, which stipulates that "if a State has been induced to conclude a treaty by the fraudulent conduct of another negotiating State, the State may invoke the fraud as invalidating its consent to be bound by the treaty."[48] Article 60 (1) further specifies that "a material breach of a bilateral treaty by one of the parties entitles the other to invoke the breach as a ground for terminating the treaty or suspending its operation in whole or in part."[49] Lakota has thus argued that the U.S. government has materially and willingly breached its treaties with the Lakota Nation.

The U.S. has failed to respect the treaties and continued to disregard the Lakota Nation as a sovereign entity of an equal legal standing. Rather, the U.S. has misrepresented the Lakota Nation as a "domestic dependent nation," which was similar to the subordinate status of the Cherokee Nation, as declared by the U.S. Supreme Court in *Cherokee Nation v. Georgia*, 30 U.S. 1, 19 (1831), in which the court had characterized the Indian nations as internally colonized "dependent nations." With respect to the federal case involving the Sioux of the Lakota Nation, the U.S. Supreme Court further ruled in *United States v. Sioux Nation of Indians* (1980) that "a more ripe and rank case of dishonorable dealings will never, in all probability, be found in our [legal] history."[50] Such a characterization symbolized that the state party to a treaty could not unilaterally diminish the status of the indigenous nation, thereby constituting a fraud in the inducement, and giving Lakota the option to withdraw from the

---

[47] Mort (2018).

[48] United Nations (1969), VCTL, art. 49.

[49] United Nations (1969), VCLT, art. 60(1).

[50] *United States v. Sioux Nation of Indians*, 448 U.S. 371, 388 (1980).

treaties with the U.S. government. On the day of Lakota's declaration of independence in December 2007, Lakota announced that such a fraud had been committed by the U.S. and invalidated the Lakota treaties with the U.S. government.[51]

3.3   The 1960 U.N. Declaration on the Granting of Independence to Colonial Countries and Peoples

Lakota also invoked the 1960 U.N. Declaration on the Granting of Independence to Colonial Countries and Peoples in order to bring a speedy and unconditional end to all practices of colonial projects and coercive policies imposed by the U.S. Lakota has insisted on the restoration of fundamental human rights and human dignity to all indigenous nations large and small, in North America and beyond.[52]

Lakota has also insisted that their independence was long overdue because of the suffering of their people due to U.S. policies of forced assimilation programs, residential school requirements, forced sterilization, genocide, and economic devastation. These predatory policies have precipitated the devastation of the nation peoples, including: (1) a life expectancy of less than 44 years, the lowest of any country in the Western Hemisphere, including Haiti; (2) a 300% higher infant mortality rate than the U.S. average; (3) a 150% higher teenage suicide rate than the U.S. average; (4) over 90% of indigenous adults with drug and alcohol addiction; (5) a 500% higher rate of cervical cancer than the U.S. average; and (6) a 800% higher rate of diabetes than the U.S. average.[53] Other health-related devastations have also been observed, including a 800% higher tuberculosis rate than the U.S. average. The Federal Commodity Food Program, including the Food Distribution Program on Indian Reservations (FDPIR), is connected to higher sugar food intakes and continues to lead to the deaths of many Indian people through diabetes and heart diseases.[54]

Paralleling the devastation of indigenous lives, nation peoples have also been subjected to economic devastation, as reflected in these statistics: (1)

---

[51] Republic of Lakotah (2008).

[52] Ibid.

[53] Ibid.

[54] Ibid.

97% live below the poverty line; (2) the majority of families are without heating oil, wood, or running water; (3) the median income is approximately $2,600 to $3,500 per year; (4) one-third of homes are without sewage systems and basic clean water; (5) 40% of households are without electricity; (6) 60% of households are without a telephone; (7) there is an unemployment rate of 85%; and (8) an average of 17 people live in each family household, with up to 30 people living in a home which had been built for 6 to 8 people.[55]

Lakota's ancestral lands have also been targeted by state-supported corporate projects. Lakota's Oglala Sioux, for example, has been fighting against the National Regulatory Commission (NRC) that granted the uranium mining license to Canada's Azarga Uranium Corporation for the 10,000 acres Dewey Burdock project site, which was located on the unceded 1868 Ft. Laramie Treaty land adjacent to the Pine Ridge Indian Reservation.[56] The Standing Rock Sioux Indian reservation in North Dakota has also been fighting to prevent the $3.8 billion construction of the Dakota Access Pipeline (DAPL) by Energy Transfer Partners in their homeland. The group of indigenous "water protectors" and their supporters were met by scores of private security personnel of "Tiger-Swan," a private military firm founded in Dallas, Texas in 1995 as a U.S. Military and State Department contractor to assist them in fighting the global war on terror. In this case, TigerSwan security personnel unleashed concussion grenades, sonic weapons, rubber bullets, and water cannons in sub-zero winter weather, as well as other military-style counterterrorism measures against water protectors.[57] TigerSwan operatives also infiltrated an array of anti-pipeline groups and organizations for surveillance and provocation. [58] Specifically, internal infiltration by undercover TigerSwan employees was used in the camps to obtain evidence of potentially "illegal" activities, incite violence, harness a URL coding technique to discover hidden social media profiles, and gain access to private information of water protectors and demonstrators.[59]

[55] Ibid.

[56] Nauman (2019).

[57] "Private Mercenary Firm TigerSwan Compares Anti-DAPL Water Protectors to "Jihadist Insurgency"(2017).

[58] Brown (2018).

[59] Ibid.

Given the long history of social and economic policies that have devastated nation peoples and their lands, Lakota argues that "the subjection of people to alien subjugation, domination and exploitation [by the U.S.] constitutes a denial of fundamental human rights," echoing the language from the 1960 U.N. Declaration on the Granting of Independence.[60] Lakota has insisted on the development of self-sufficiency, the restoration of the right to self-determination, and the preservation of cultural and biological diversity of their ancestral homeland apart from state-assisted, ecologically unsustainable, corporate projects and exploitation.

3.4   *The 2007 U.N. Declaration of the Rights of the Indigenous Peoples (UNDRIP)*

After many decades of international advocacy and organizing movements in order to restore and establish the individual and collective rights of indigenous peoples and nations around the world, the U.N. finally adopted the UNDRIP, on September 13, 2007. Soon after the U.N.'s historical pronouncement, Lakota swiftly moved to strengthen their quest for national independence by adopting UNDRIP's language. Article 3, for example, stipulated that "Indigenous peoples have the right to self-determination. By virtue of that right they freely determine their political status and freely pursue their economic, social and cultural development."[61] Similarly, Article 8 specified that "indigenous people and individuals have the right not to be subjected to forced assimilation of destruction of their culture."[62] With respect to land rights, Article 8, Section 2 specified that the state shall provide effective mechanisms for prevention of, and redress for, "any action which has the aim or effect of dispossessing them of their lands, territories or resources."[63] Similarly, Article 26 stated that "indigenous peoples have the right to the land, territories and resources which they have traditionally owned, occupied or otherwise used or acquired."[64] Lastly, UNDRIP recognized the nation's right to reach a fair resolution of its disputes with the state. Article 40

---

[60] United Nations (1960).
[61] United Nations (2007).
[62] United Nations (2007), UNDRIP, art. 3.
[63] United Nations (2007), UNDRIP, art. 8, Section 2 (b).
[64] United Nations (2007), UNDRIP, art. 26.

specified that "indigenous peoples have the right to access to and prompt decision through just and fair procedures for the resolution of conflicts and disputes with States."[65]

The U.S. assimilation policy has had a devastating impact on the eradication of Lakota cultures, including the reduction of native speakers of Lakota language to a mere 14%, thereby bringing the peril of language extinction and cultural ways of life.[66] Similarly, the U.S. policy on the use of blood quantum to determine "tribal nation" identity has threatened the viable identity of indigenous nations, including the Lakota Nation. While each indigenous nation in North America may be free to define their own rules in determining the criteria for national identity and membership, two-thirds of all federally recognized tribal nations have relied on a blood quantum in their national membership criteria, with one-quarter blood degree being the most frequent minimum requirement. The blood quantum method used by the government has been at the core of racial politics in the U.S. As examined earlier, it has historically ensured that any percentage of African blood automatically categorized an African descent as black, thereby forever solidifying the race-based apartheid system in the U.S. However, the blood quantum mandate for the indigenous nation could possibly lead to the elimination of indigenous identity, as many generations of cross-racial, ethnic "marriages" have led to the "diminishing" trend of Indian "blood," thereby guaranteeing the eventual disappearance of the Indian identity and national affiliation. Today, the recognition of Lakota's right to self-determination in relation to its membership is crucial. UNDRIP stipulates the right of indigenous people to belong to an indigenous nation in accordance with the traditions and customs of the nation, not the blood lineage, thereby rejecting the history of the U.S.'s invasive policies in the determination of indigenous identity.[67]

---

[65] United Nations (2007), UNDRIP, art. 40.

[66] Republic of Lakotah (2008).

[67] United Nations (2007), UNDRIP, Art 9 ("Indigenous peoples and individuals have the right to belong to an indigenous community or nation, in accordance with the traditions and customs of the community or nation concerned. No discrimination of any kind may arise from the exercise of such a right").

3.5 Constitutions, the Declaration of Independence, and U.S. Supreme Court Rulings

Lakota also relied on U.S. domestic laws to rationalize its timely withdrawal from its treaty obligations with the U.S. government. The U.S. Constitution stipulates that all treaties between sovereign nations are "supreme Law of the Land."[68] Similarly, when the states of Montana, North Dakota, and South Dakota, within which the Lakota Nation lay, were admitted into the Union, the Enabling Act of 1889 Law allowed the state incorporation into the U.S., with the requirement that "the people inhabiting said proposed States do agree and declare that they forever disclaim all right and title ... to all lands lying within said limits owned or held by any Indian or Indian Tribes."[69] This "disclaimer" provision of the Act was repeated in other state constitutions, including Wyoming, in which the Lakota Nation also lay.[70] The Lakota Nation had never agreed that it would "forever disclaim all right and title," relinquish its sovereignty, or give up the rights to ancestral lands. Thus, the U.S. government has never had a legitimate claim to homelands held by the Lakota Nation.

Lakota also challenged the legacy of the U.S. government and its judiciary's pronouncement of their "self-proclaimed" plenary power over Indian affairs in North America. The jurisprudence rationalizing the violation of treaty obligations with indigenous nations emerged from the aforementioned trilogy of opinions authored by Justice John Marshall, whose decisions in *Johnson v. McIntosh* in 1823, *Cherokee Nation v. Georgia* in 1831, and *Worcester v. Georgia* in 1832 set important precedents for the U.S. government's handling of Indian affairs. Marshall's *Cherokee Nation* ruling asserted the indigenous nations as "domestic dependent nations" whose relation to the U.S. resembled that of a ward to his guardian, thereby justifying the U.S. assertion of its plenary power.[71] Subsequently, the U.S. government acted to forcibly move the

---

[68] U.S. Const. art. VI.

[69] The Enabling Act of Feb. 22, ch. 180. §4, 25 Stat. 676, 677 (1889); Mont. Const. ord. 1 (1889); Mont. Const. art.1 (1972).

[70] Wyo. Const. art. 21, §26 (1889).

[71] See Shevory (1994).

Cherokee and virtually all indigenous nations in the East Coast onto reservations West of the Mississippi River. Such government decisions were clear violations of its treaty obligations with indigenous nations.

As repeatedly asserted, Lakota has never relinquished its sovereignty and the right to its homeland despite the U.S.'s repeated attempts to diminish its sovereignty. Lakota has now legally and lawfully withdrawn from all treaties and agreement with the U.S., and Lakota's status shall remain the same as it was before the 1803, i.e., a sovereign nation with its people to be "predecessor sovereign" owner of traditional Lakota Territory that enjoyed "beneficially of all the protections," as the Louisiana Purchase Treaty had powerfully proclaimed.

Lastly, Lakota has cited the 1776 U.S. Declaration of Independence to finalize the severance of all of its political ties that had long connected Lakota to the U.S. The declaration stipulated that "when in the course of human events, it becomes necessary for one people to dissolve the political bands which have connected them with another ... [and] a decent respect to the opinions of mankind requires that they should declare the causes which impel them to the separation."[72] As specified above, Lakota has argued that they provided an array of international law and legal doctrines as compelling evidence and supporting documents spelling out all "the causes" as prescribed in the Declaration. Lakota has thus concluded that they have successfully impelled Lakota to the separation and finalized the complete and permanent dissolution of all "political bands" with the U.S.

3.6   Lakota's Impacts on Other Nationalist Movements in North America

Immediately after the declaration of independence, Lakota urged the U.S. to enter into bilateral diplomatic governmental negotiation.[73] Unless the U.S. entered into immediate diplomatic and peaceful negotiations, Lakota declared it would unilaterally impose liens on real estate transactions in the five-state area of the homeland.[74] Lakota's revolutionary action and its declared secession from the U.S. has ignited other secessionist movements in North America.

---

[72] U.S. Declaration of Independence (1776).

[73] Lakota Freedom Delegation (2007).

[74] Ibid.

The Alaskan Independent Party and its chair Lynette Clark have supported and congratulated Lakota for its secession from the U.S.[75] The Alaska Independence Party was originally founded with the goal of attaining the State of Alaska. After Alaska's 1958 admission to the union, the party objective shifted to the issue of secession, to the attainment of an internationally recognized sovereign statehood.[76] The Second Vermont Republic (SVR), another secessionist political group, also announced its support for the Republic of Lakotah. The SVR was founded by former Duke University economics professor Thomas Naylor in order to restore what was formerly known as "Vermont Republic," the independent nation which declared independence in 1777 from the British colony of Quebec and the American states of New York and New Hampshire. Vermont Republic had also drafted its own constitution that prohibited slavery, granted suffrage to non-landowning males, and established free public education, before its annexation to the U.S. in 1791. The SVR's Vermont Declaration of Independence stated that the secession of Vermont from the U.S. is of eminent importance, as "Vermont has been dragged into the quagmire of affluenza, technomania, megalomania, globalization, and imperialism by the U.S. government in collaboration with corporate America."[77]

4 THE CONSTITUTION OF THE STATE VERSUS THE CONSTITUTION OF THE NATION

The "constitution-making" efforts of Lakota and other indigenous nations in North America have differed greatly from those of the U.S. and modern states in Europe. The U.S. Bill of Rights, for example, was adopted to prevent excessive governmental intrusion into the individual lives of citizens. However, such a formal apex of the authoritarian institution and hierarchical government did not exist in the Lakota Nation, as

---

[75] Clark (2007).

[76] See Mackenzie (2005, p. 88) (in 1973, Joe Vogler, "the well-known contrarian who founded the Alaska Independence Party ... circulated a petition calling for Alaska's secession from the United States. He organized the Alaskans for Independence to actively pursue secession while he continued work with the Alaskan Independence Party to question the legitimacy of the 1958 Statehood Act").

[77] Vermont Declaration of Independence (1777).

its political decisions were made by consensus of the people who participated in culturally bound, collective activities. Private property was strictly
limited to horses, blankets, tools, and weapons, while the food was shared
by all, and the land was owned communally and preserved as hunting
grounds.[78]

One recent attempt to draft a declaration of independence of indigenous nations in North America was facilitated by prominent Indian
activist Russell Means and other members of the American Indian Movement (AIM) in June 1974. The purpose was to create an alliance of
indigenous nations and peoples in North America and beyond. They
had successfully organized an inter-national conference of 3,000 people
representing 97 nations, created the International Indian Treaty Council
(IITC), and adopted the "Declaration of Continuing Independence."[79]
Its declaration demanded that the U.S. respect Article VI of its constitution which "recognizes treaties as part of the Supreme Law of the United
States. We will peacefully pursue all legal political avenues to demand
United States recognition of its own Constitution in this regard, and
thus to honor its own treaties with Native Nations."[80] Furthermore, the
IITC charged the U.S. with "gross violation of our International Treaties
[including] the 'wrongfully taking' of the Black Hills from the Great
Sioux Nation in 1877 ... [and] the forced march of the Cherokee people
from their ancestral lands in the state of Georgia to the then-'Indian
Territory' of Oklahoma, ... The treaty violation, known as the 'Trail of
Tears,' brought death to two-thirds of the Cherokee Nation during the
forced march."[81] In 1977, the IITC became the first indigenous Non-
Governmental Organization (NGO) to be recognized by the U.N. with
consultative status with the U.N. Economic and Social Council.

Some of the IITC members had also once moved to create and ratify
their own constitutions in North America. The six nations of the Iroquois
Confederation decided to transform their oral tradition of the Great Law
of Peace into an English-transcribed written document with 117 separate articles and provisions in 1915, asserting the long powerful history

---

[78] See Fenelon (1998).

[79] International Indian Treaty Council (1974). Russell Means' fight for human rights
extended the U.S. borders to solidarity with Palestine, stating that "every policy now the
Palestinians are enduring was practiced on the American Indian." See Norrell (2012).

[80] Ibid.

[81] Ibid.

of their independence and autonomy in North America.[82] In 1924, the U.S. had passed the American Indian Citizen Act to force the naturalization of all Indians and incorporate them into the U.S. dominion. However, this "forced" assimilation policy was rejected by the indigenous nations, including the Iroquois Confederation, which immediately sent letters to the President and Congress, respectfully declining U.S. citizenship and insisting on its own constitutional independence and freedom.[83] In 1987, in what seemed to many an ironic gesture, the U.S. Senate finally recognized the significant contribution that the Iroquois Confederation had made in the early formation of the U.S. government, including the powerful impact of Iroquois' Great Law of Peace on the drafting of the U.S. Constitution.[84] In 2013, the Dutch government celebrated the 400th anniversary of the Two Row Wampum Treaty with the Iroquois Confederacy, which the two governments originally signed in 1613. The anniversary celebration with the Dutch government has also signified the Iroquois' right to native land rights, the conservation of environmental protection, and the preservation of self-sustaining culture and biological diversity of the ancestral homeland.[85] Besides the Iroquois Confederation, other indigenous nations have also approved new constitutions of their own to preserve their sovereignty and sanctity of their ancestral homelands, including the Seminole in 1969, Cherokee in 1976, Muscogee (Creek) in 1979, Chickasaw in 1983, and Choctaw in 1984.[86]

In order to preserve the biodiversity of indigenous homelands and protect the self-sustainable culture of indigenous nations and peoples, environmental groups and ecological activists began to work closely with indigenous nations and peoples. In 2016, the Ho-Chunk Nation of Wisconsin voted overwhelmingly to amend its own constitution to enshrine the Rights of Nature, and became the first nation in the U.S. to establish that "ecosystems and natural communities within the Ho-Chunk territory possess an inherent, fundamental, and inalienable right to exist and thrive."[87] With the input and support of environmental

---

[82] See Wolfe and Favor (2015).

[83] Heath (2018).

[84] Ibid.

[85] Gadoua (2013).

[86] Work (2010, p. 133).

[87] Ho-Chunk Nation Legislature (2015).

activists, its constitutional amendment contained provisions that prohibited "Frac sand" mining, fossil fuel extraction, and genetic engineering as violations of the Rights of Nature.[88] In 2017, environmental groups and the Ho-Chunk Nation filed a lawsuit against the Wisconsin Department of Natural Resources, challenging the agency's decision to allow frac sand mining in the nation's ancestral homeland.[89]

The Nation of Inuit in Northern Canada has also begun to collaborate with environmental groups and progressive politicians to preserve the sanctity of their homeland and protect it from state-sponsored corporate exploitation. Inuit people have lived in the territory of *Nunavut*, *Nunavik* in northern Quebec, and *Nunatsiavut* and *NunatuKavut* in Labrador. In 1993, the Nation of Inuit successfully reclaimed its ancestral homeland in the Eastern Arctic called *Nunavut* (which translates as "our land" in *Inuktitut*) from the Canadian government. In 1999, the official map of Canada was redrawn, and the Northwest Territories were divided into two territories to recognize the creation of the independent area of *Nunavut*, which now comprises the eastern half of the former Northwest Territories.[90] The Nation of the Inuit ratified their constitution in 2005. The constitution was first adopted in 2002 by the Inuit in Labrador, called the Labrador Inuit Association (LIA), and was put into effect in 2005.[91]

The independent movement to preserve the indigenous culture and sanctity of the ancestral lands also began to accelerate more rapidly in Asia, where the majority of indigenous nations in the world currently live and where many have long been struggling for their independence and sovereignty. Through many years of armed struggles and negotiations with the state, seven indigenous nations in Myanmar in 2017 finally earned the right to draft their own constitutions for equality and the right to self-determination. These nations include Kachin, Karen, Arakan, Mon, Shan, Chin, and Karenni.[92] In India, besides Kashmir, other nations also continue to struggle for independence and the right to self-determination,

---

[88] Ibid.

[89] Magnus (2017).

[90] Kulchyski (2017).

[91] See, for example, Borrows (2010).

[92] Zaw (2017).

including Nagaland, Punjab, and West Bengal.[93] Indonesia has multiple indigenous nations that are currently struggling to attain the right to self-determination, such as Aceh, Kalimantan, South Moluccas, Minahasa, Riau, and West Papua.[94]

In January 2019, West Papua submitted a petition signed by 1.8 million Papuans to the U.N. High Commissioner for Human Rights to assert their independence, secede from Indonesia, and attain the right to self-determination.[95] West Papua is rich with natural resources and has operated the world's largest gold mine and second largest copper mine.[96] State-supported, unsustainable corporate projects have led to mass deforestation of native trees in their homeland, and native people have been exploited for cheap labor. Despite they live in one of the most resource-rich areas in the world, they still remain one of the poorest peoples in Asia.[97] Similar to the exploitive history of Lakota in North America, the Republic of West Papua of Western New Guinea, which was formerly an independent nation, has been claimed by Indonesia since 1963. West Papua has also drafted a constitution to assert their independence and sovereignty, which consists of fifteen chapters, 54 sections, and 2 orders.[98] West Papuans' struggle to assert their human rights, human dignity, and the right to self-determination continues today in Asia.

5   CONCLUSIONS

In delivering the Republic of Lakotah's declaration of independence to the U.S. State Department, Lakota delegation leader Russell Means argued that "this is a historic day for our Lakota people. United States colonial rule is at its end."[99] Garry Rowland, a former indigenous representative to the U.N., also declared that "today is a historic day and our forefathers speak through us. Our forefathers made the treaties in good faith with the sacred *Canupa* and with the knowledge of the Great Spirit.

---

[93] See Kim (2019).

[94] See, Aveling and Kingsbury (2003).

[95] "West Papua: Petition Calling for Self-Determination Handed Over to UN" (2019).

[96] Sobel (2019).

[97] Ibid.

[98] Flassy (2019, p. 75).

[99] Lakota Freedom Delegation (2007).

They [the U.S. government] never honored the treaties, that's the reason we are here today."[100]

Even after substantial fanfare, accolades, and admiration from a wide spectrum of political organizations, however, the declaration of independence by the Republic of Lakotah in 2007 has been largely ignored by the U.S., as well as by the U.N. and its member states. In 2010, Russell Means stated that the Republic of Lakotah would submit the report of the instances of human rights violation by the U.S., "directly to the U.N. Human Rights Council, not to be filtered or sanitized by the [U.S.] State Department," arguing that "our report will indicate that the United States never intended to abide by the terms of the treaties, and has violated them consistently from the time of the signing to the present."[101] He also stated that "the Republic of Lakotah will report to the [Human Rights] Council and to the world, the exercise of its own rights under principles of international law … [which] allows the Lakotah to return to our status *quo ante* position prior to the signing of the treaties, … [and] the United States withdraw its presence from our homeland."[102] Even some members of the Nation of Lakota expressed skepticism about its independence and successful secession from the U.S.[103] Means, a long-time indigenous activist who helped form the American Indian Movement (AIM), passed away in 2012, before the Republic of Lakotah was formerly recognized in the international community.[104] Parallel to Lakota's historical struggles in North America, many original nations around the globe have also been struggling to assert indigenous title to the homeland and the right to self-determination.

In recent years, the efforts of nation peoples, environmental groups, and progressive activists have led to the creation of "rights-based" constitutions, referring to the "Rights of Nature and Mother Earth," in order to ensure the preservation of what little remains of unmolested environment and ecosystems. The next chapter explores the robust construction of "Earth Jurisprudence," incorporating the legal fortitude of the Rights of Nature and Mother Earth into the legislation and/or constitution of both

---

[100] Ibid.

[101] Means (2010).

[102] Ibid.

[103] Toensing (2008).

[104] McFadden (2012).

the original nation and the state. In 2008, Ecuador became the first state to amend its constitution to recognize the rights of nature, enshrining the inherent rights of ecosystems to protect them from human and corporate exploitation.[105] In 2016, the Ho-Chunk Nation of Wisconsin became the first original nation in the U.S. to incorporate the Rights of Nature into its constitution.[106]

ONAIL recognizes that indigenous rights are closely tied to the rights of ecosystems and the preservation of biological diversity. Many nations have begun to draft their own constitutions and to create constitutional amendments to suit their ecological objectives in protecting the ancestral environment. As a strategy to achieve that end, a "constitution-making" project has been observed in North America, Asia, and around the world, and the hope is that the original nation's constitutional activism will lead to the creation of more robust legal mechanisms to ensure the respect for human rights and human dignity of nation peoples, thus preserving cultural and biological diversities in the nation's ancestral homelands that future generations will surely require for their survival in coming decades and beyond.

BIBLIOGRAPHY

1852 Treaty of Fort Laramie, September 17 (1851) article 1, https://www.rep ublicoflakotah.com/2009/1851-treaty/ (accessed 15 March 2019).

1868 Treaty of Fort Laramie, Apr 29 (1868) article 1, https://www.republico flakotah.com/2009/1868-treaty/ (accessed 15 March 2019).

"89% of Veneto Residents Vote for Independence from Rome" (2014) Reuters, 23, March.

Abate, Randall Abate & Elizabeth Ann Kronk (2013) *Climate Change and Indigenous People: The Search for Legal Remedies.* Northampton, MA: Edward Elgar Publishing.

Agonito, Joseph (2011) *Lakota Portraits: Lives of the Legendary Plains People* 101. Guilford, CT: Atwodat Book.

Andersson, Rani-Henrik (2019) *A Whirlwind Passed Through Our Country: Lakota Voices of the Ghost Dance.* Norman: University of Oklahoma Press.

Aveling, Harry and Damien Kingsbury (2003) *Autonomy and Disintegration in Indonesia.* New York: Routledge.

---

[105] Biggs et al. (2017).

[106] Ho-Chunk Nation Legislature (2015).

Bender, Thomas (2006) *A Nation Among Nations: America's Place in World History*. New York: Hill and Wang.

Biggs, Shannon, Goldtooth, Tom B.K. and Lake, Osprey Orielle (2017) Rights of Nature and Mother Earth Rights-Based Law for Systemic Change, https://www.ienearth.org/wp-content/uploads/2017/11/RONME-Rights BasedLaw-final-1.pdf.

Borrows, John (2010) *Canada's Indigenous Constitution*. Toronto: University of Toronto Press.

Brown, Alleen (2018) "The Infiltrator: How an Undercover Oil Industry Mercenary Tricked Pipeline Opponents into Believing He Was One of Them," The Intercept, 30, December, available at https://theintercept.com/2018/12/30/tigerswan-infiltrator-dakota-access-pipeline-standing-rock/.

"Catalan Referendum: Preliminary Results Show 90% in Favor of Independence" (2017) *Guardian*, 1 October.

Chulov, Martin (2017) "More Than 92% of Voters in Iraqi Kurdistan Back Independence," *Guardian*, 27 September.

Churchill, Ward (1997) *A Little Matter of Genocide: Holocaust and Denial in the Americas 1492 to the Present*. San Francisco, CA: City Lights Publishers.

Clark, Lynette (2007) "To the Lakota Nation," Alaskan Independent Party: Alaska First- Alaska Always, 21 December.

Clastres, Pierre (1989) *Society Against the State: Essays in Political Anthropology*. Cambridge: Zone Books.

Constitution of the Oglala Sioux Tribe (1935), https://narf.org/nill/constitut ions/oglala_sioux/index.html (accessed 15 March 2019).

Constitution of the Oglala Sioux Tribe of the Pine Ridge Reservation (amended, 18 December 2008), https://narf.org/nill/constitutions/oglala_sioux/ogl alaconst.pdf.

Dunbar-Ortiz, Roxanne (2018) *Loaded: A Disarming History of the Second Amendment*. San Francisco: City Lights Books.

Fenelon, James V. (1998) *Cultricide, Resistance, and the Survival of the Lakota (Sioux Nation)*. New York: Routledge.

Flassy, Don A. L. (2019) "Constitution Vis-à-vis Constitution Indonesian 1945 Versus Papuan 1999," *Humanities and Social Science Research* 2: 53–94.

Gadoua, Renee K. (2013) "Anniversary Recalls Water as Sacred Source of Life," *Washington Post*, 31 July.

Geer, Curtis M. (1904) *The History of North America: The Louisiana Purchase and the Westward Movement*. Boston: Adamant Media Corporation.

Ginsburg, Tom (2012) "Constitutionalism: East Asian Antecedents," *Chicago-Kent Law Review* 88: 11–31.

Gonzalez, Juan (2011) *Harvest of Empire: A History of Latinos in America*. New York: Penguin Books.

Griggs, Richard & Peter Hocknell (1995) "Fourth World Faultlines and the Remaking of 'Inter-National' Boundaries," *IBRU Boundary and Security Bulletin* 3(3): 49–58.

Harlan, Bill (2007) "Lakota Sioux Secede from US, Declare Independence," Common Dreams, 21 December, https://www.commondreams.org/news/2007/12/21/lakota-sioux-secede-us-declare-independence.

Heath, Joseph (2018) "The Citizenship Act of 1924: An Integral Pillar of the Colonization and Forced Assimilation Policies of the United States in Violation of Treaties," Onondaga Nation, 7 June, https://www.onondaganation.org/news/2018/the-citizenship-act-of-1924/.

Ho-Chunk Nation Legislature (2015) "Acknowledgement of General Council Resolution 9/19/2015-09 and Legislative Action Regarding the Resolution to Amend the Constitution and Provide for the Rights of Nature," 20 October.

Horne, Gerald (2015) *Confronting Black Jacobins: The U.S., the Haitian Revolution, and the Origins of the Dominican Republic*. New York: NYU Press.

International Indian Treaty Council (1974), Declaration of Continuing Independence, available at https://history.hanover.edu/courses/excerpts/260continuing.html.

Kelly, Michael J. (2010) "The Kurdish Regional Constitution Within the Framework of the Iraqi Federal Constitution: A Struggle for Sovereignty, Oil, Ethnic Identity, and the Prospects for a Reverse Supremacy Clause," 114 *Penn State Law Review* 707–808.

Kim, Heewon (2019) *The Struggle for Equality: India's Muslims and Rethinking the UPA Experience*. Cambridge: Cambridge University Press.

Kloppe, Adam (2015) "The Louisiana Purchase and the Constitutionalism of Thomas Jefferson," Missouri Historical Society, 17 March.

Kulchyski, Peter (2017) "The Creation of Nunavut," Canada's History, 11 August, https://www.canadashistory.ca/explore/politics-law/the-creation-of-nunavut.

Lakota Freedom Delegation (2007) "A Declaration of Independence from the USA," *Counterpunch*, 21 December, https://www.counterpunch.org/2007/12/21/a-declaration-of-independence-from-the-usa/.

Lee, Patrick A. (2013) *Tribal Laws Treaties and Government: A Lakota Perspective*. Bloomington, IN: iUniverse.

Louisiana Purchase Treaty (1803), http://www.classzone.com/books/am_05_shared/pdf/psource/TAS03_6_201c_PS.pdf (accessed 15 March 2019).

Lyons, Kate (2018) "Catalan Referendum: New Caledonia's Independence Referendum: What You Need to Know," *Guardian*, 1 November.

Mackenzie, B.B. (2005) *Alaska Curiosities: Quirky Characters, Roadside Oddities and Other Offbeat Stuff*. Guilford, CT: Globe Pequot Press.

Magnus, Amanda (2017) "Environmental Groups and Ho-Chunk Nation Take Western Wisconsin Frac Sand Mine to Court," Wisconsin Public Radio, 21 June.

McFadden, Robert D. (2012) "Russell Means, Who Clashed With Law as He Fought for Indians, Is Dead at 72," *NY Times*, 22 October.

Means, Russell (2010) "UN Listening Session is US Smokescreen," 18 March, http://www.republicoflakotah.com/2010/russell-means-un-listening-session-is-us-smokescreen/.

Montana Constitution (1898), available at http://www.umt.edu/media/law/library/MontanaConstitution/Miscellaneous%20Documents/1889_const.pdf.

Montana Constitution (1972), available at https://leg.mt.gov/bills/mca_toc/Constitution.htm.

Mort, Terry (2018) *Thieves' Road: The Black Hills Betrayal and Custer's Path to Little Bighorn*. Amherst, NY: Prometheus Books.

Nauman, Talli (2019) "Oglala Sioux Tribe Keeps Up Fight Against Uranium Mine," Native Sun News Today, 8 February.

Norrell, Brenda (2012) "Russell Means: Warrior for the People," *Counterpunch*, 26 October.

"Press Release: Lakota Language Now Critically Endangered" (2016) *Wayback Machine*, 18 February, available at http://lakhota.org/lakota-language-critically-endangered/.

"Private Mercenary Firm TigerSwan Compares Anti-DAPL Water Protectors to "Jihadist Insurgency" (2017) Democracy Now!, 31 May, available at https://www.democracynow.org/2017/5/31/private_mercenary_firm_tigerswan_compares_anti.

Republic of Lakotah (2008) Petition for Recognition of Lakotah Sovereignty, https://web.archive.org/web/20080411181412/http://www.republicofla kotah.com/docs/Petition.pdf (accessed 15 March 2019).

Scott, James (2010) *The Art of Not Being Governed: Ab Anarchist History of Upland Southeast Asia*. New Haven, CT: Yale University Press.

Shevory, Thomas C. (1994) *John Marshall's Law: Interpretation, Ideology, and Interest*. Westport, CN: Greenwood Press.

Sobel, Alex (2019) "West Papua: The World's Forgotten Injustice," *Red Pepper*, 8 April.

Sprague, Donovin Arleigh and Rylan Sprague (2015) *Standing Rock: Lakota, Dakota, Nakota Nation*. Charleston, SC: Arcadia Publishing.

The Enabling Act of Feb. 22 (1889), available at http://leg.wa.gov/History/State/Pages/enabling.aspx.

Toensing, Gale Courey (2008) "Withdrawal from US Treaties Enjoys Little Support from Tribal Leaders," Indian Country Today, 4 January.

"Ukraine Separatists Declare Independence: Leaders of Eastern Donetsk and Luhansk Regions Declare Independence After Claiming Victory in Sunday's Self-Rule Vote" (2014) Al Jazeera, 12 May.

United Nations (1960) "Declaration on the Granting of Independence to Colonial Countries and Peoples, Adopted by General Assembly Resolution 1514 (XV) of 14 December 1960," https://www.un.org/en/decolonization/declaration.shtml (accessed 15 March 2019).

United Nations (1969) "Vienna Convention on the Law of Treaties," http://legal.un.org/ilc/texts/instruments/english/conventions/1_1_1969.pdf (accessed 15 March 2019).

United Nations (2007) United Nations Declaration on the Rights of Indigenous Peoples, available at http://www.un.org/esa/socdev/unpfii/documents/DRIPS_en.pdf.

United Nations (2010) "State of the World's Indigenous Peoples (SOWIP)," 14 January.

United Nations (2016) "Special Committee on Decolonization Approves Texts Calling Upon United States Government to Expedite Self-Determination Process for Puerto Rico," 20 June, https://www.un.org/press/en/2016/gacol3296.doc.htm(accessed 15 March 2019).

United States v. Sioux Nation of Indians, 448 U.S. 371, 388 (1980).

U.S. Census Bureau (2017) "American Indian and Alaska Native Heritage Month: November 2017," Newsroom, 6 October, https://www.census.gov/newsroom/facts-for-features/2017/aian-month.html.

U.S. Constitution (1787), available at https://constitutionus.com/.

U.S. Declaration of Independence (1776), https://history.state.gov/milestones/1776-1783/declaration.

Vanhullebusch, Matthias (2015) "The International Court of Justice's Advisory Jurisdiction on Self-Determination," 1 *Sri Lanka Journal of International & Comparative Law* 25–48.

Vargas, Michael A. (2018) *Constructing Catalan Identity: Memory, Imagination, and the Medieval*. London: Palgrave Macmillan.

Vermont Declaration of Independence, Second Vermont Republic (1777), http://vermontrepublic.org/vermont-declaration-of-independence/ (accessed 15 March, 2019).

Webb, Stephan H. (2004) *American Providence: A Nation With a Mission*. New York: Continuum.

"West Papua: Petition Calling for Self-Determination Handed Over to UN" (2019) UNPO, 30 January, https://unpo.org/article/21351.

Wolfe, James and Lesli J. Favor (2015) *Understanding the Iroquois Constitution*. Berkeley Heights, NJ: Enslow Publishers, Inc.

Work, L. Susan (2010) *The Seminole Nation of Oklahoma: A Legal History*. Norman, OK: University of Oklahoma Press.

Wyoming Constitution (1889), available at https://sos.wyo.gov/Forms/Public ations/WYConstitution.pdf.

Zaw, Htet Naing (2017) "Ethnic States Win right to Draft Constitutions," Irrawaddy, 12 May, https://www.irrawaddy.com/news/burma/ethnic-states-win-right-draft-constitutions.html.

CHAPTER 6

Earth Jurisprudence, the Rights of Nature, and International Rights of Nature Tribunals

ONAIL recognizes that globalization and neoliberal policies have accelerated the mass destruction of nature and ecosystems ("ecocide"), as well as the rapid cultural genocide of indigenous nations and peoples ("ethnocide"). Prominent Polish-Jewish legal scholar Raphael Lemkin coined the term "genocide" in 1944—a hybrid neologism of the Greek word "genos" ("race") and Latin suffix "cide" ("act of killing")—and defined it as "acts committed with intent to destroy, in whole or in part, a national, ethnic, racial or religious group."[1] Lemkin's identification of five definitive acts of genocide included: (1) killing members of the group; (2) causing serious bodily or mental harm to members of the group; (3) deliberately inflicting on the group conditions of life calculated to bring about its physical destruction in whole or in part; (4) imposing measures intended to prevent births within the group; and finally (5) forcibly transferring children of the group to another group.[2] Indigenous scholars have argued that the experience of indigenous nations and peoples in North America was indeed genocidal, for the indigenous population of nearly 15 million in 1492 was reduced to less than a quarter million by 1890, representing nearly a 98% liquidation of indigenous populations since the

---

[1] Lemkin (2011, p. 4).
[2] Ibid.

© The Author(s), under exclusive license to Springer Nature Switzerland AG 2021
H. Fukurai and R. Krooth, *Original Nation Approaches to Inter-National Law*,
https://doi.org/10.1007/978-3-030-59273-8_6

time of the Europeans' arrival.[3] Forced sterilization of indigenous women continued, and a military-style residential school was imposed on indigenous children as part of forced assimilation policies which did not end until 1996.[4]

After decades of organized international movements by the original nations and their allies, the U.N. Declaration of the Rights of Indigenous Peoples (UNDRIP) was finally adopted by the U.N. General Assembly in 2007. It paid much-deserved respect to and established the rights of the original nation and people, including the rights to cultural and traditional expression, language, historical memory, identity, and preservation of ecological diversity in the ancestral homeland.[5] Although the declaration was not a legally binding U.N. resolution, four developed states—the U.S., Canada, Australia, and New Zealand—opposed the adoption of the declaration in 2007.[6] Their opposition can be seen as reflecting centuries of genocidal policies and settler-state colonial programs imposed on indigenous nations and peoples, acts that have been replicated in other developing parts of the world.

Brazil, for example, has one of the largest rainforests and natural habitats in the world. Nearly 2,000 original nations existed in the Amazon when the Spaniards first reached America in 1498.[7] Today's ecological research has shown that the destruction of the indigenous nation, people, and their ancestral homeland in the Brazilian Amazon has been largely financed by transnational firms, large banks, and corporate investors in Europe and the U.S.[8] Brazil's newly elected President Jair Bolsonaro once declared that "it's a shame that the Brazilian cavalry hasn't been as efficient as the Americans, who exterminated the Indians [in North America],"[9] referring to his preference to have exterminated indigenous nations and peoples of Brazil.[10] Often referred to as "the lungs of the Planet Earth," the Amazon produces approximately 20% of the planet's

---

[3] Charny (1999, pp. 436–437).

[4] Churchill (2004).

[5] See Hall (2003); see also "American Indian in 1890" (2020).

[6] "Canada Votes 'No' as UN Native Rights Declaration Passes" (2007).

[7] Layton and Ucko (2000, p. 244) and Langevin (2016).

[8] Recinos (2019).

[9] Watson (2018).

[10] Andersen (2017).

oxygen.[11] Jair Bolsonaro, a retired military officer, in 2019 became the 28th Brazilian president, and since then, the Brazilian Amazon has seen more than 70,000 fires, up 84% from 2018, to open up the land for horticultural business interests and multinational mining corporations.[12]

The rapid deforestation and ecological breakdown in the Amazon was also facilitated by Brazil's legislature and judiciary. Until 2012, Brazil's "Forest Code" had required private landowners in the Amazon region to set aside 80% of their property with intact native vegetation as "legal reserve."[13] The 2012 law amended the Forest Code to allow any state in the Amazon region to reduce the "legal reserve" to 50%, if indigenous reservation and conservation units accounted for more than 65% of its territory.[14] Environmental organizations and conservation activists have challenged the 2012 law, but in 2018, Brazil's Supreme Federal Tribunal upheld the amendments, including the provision that also reduced penalties for past illegal deforestation and relaxed the requirement to restore the deforested areas.[15] Today, the forest fires continue to destroy the Amazon, which had already lost 19% of its original forests. The Atlantic Forest in the eastern coastal area of Brazil has also lost more than 80% of its original trees and natural habitats.[16]

To prevent the further destruction of the environment and to protect the rights of original nations and peoples to preserve their indigenous knowledge and self-sustaining culture, ONAIL examines the possibility of exploring an active collaboration of the original nation with state sectors to develop so-called "Earth Jurisprudence" in order to protect the ecosystems and biological and cultural diversity that is still preserved in original nations, not only in the Amazon, but in other original nations across the globe. While ONAIL contends that there should be an ultimate and eventual dissolution of the coercive state system, it also proposes to implement and instigate the power of the state, whenever possible, to help create structures of law and sets of legal frameworks that could tame and deter,

[11] Pagliarini (2019).

[12] Freeman (2019).

[13] "Revised Brazilian Forest Code May Lead to Increased Legal Deforestation in Amazon" (2019).

[14] Ibid.

[15] "Brazil 'Invites Deforestation' With Overhaul of Environmental Law" (2018).

[16] Calmon et al. (2019).

if not eliminate, egregious actions and projects of corporate sectors and predatory state institutions.

The first section of this chapter examines the efforts of the original nation, environmental activists, and grassroots organizations to work collaboratively with state sectors, namely the judiciary and legislature, in order to pass constitutional amendments and legislative bills necessary to establish the rights of nature and environment. The specific focus is on Ecuador and Bolivia, both of which successfully enshrined the rights of nature in their legal system.

The second section focuses on the nation's efforts to consider nature in terms of legal "personhood" and to establish the "personality" of nature so as to avert its destruction due to unwanted exploitation through pollution, contamination, and disfigurement. Such legal efforts have been underway in New Zealand, India, Nepal, and other states whose original nations are desperately trying to preserve nature's biological diversity from ecologically destructive projects. The U.S. jurisprudence, through the century-long judicial activism by corporate lawyers to obtain favorable court rulings, has finally established "corporate personhood," in which U.S. corporations are free to engage in their business as a legal "person" that is thereby guaranteed the rights of natural persons, such as free speech, due process protection, among many other constitutional rights afforded to individuals. While the state and corporations are a "legal fiction" without the presence of real objective or physical entities, nature—in the form of trees, rivers, lands, and other "sub-parts" of Mother Earth—is composed of objective, physical ecological realities. The original nation and grassroots environmental organizations have adopted similar strategies and legal tactics to transform nature from the status of "property" to that of "legal personhood." Such transformative legal arguments are necessary to ensure that nature would be endowed with its own rights and the legal power to protect itself. The Nepalese environmental organizations have gone one step further by giving the "healthy climate" the right to exist, flourish, and run its own natural course without human interventions.

The third section examines the grassroots environmental organization known as the Community Environmental Legal Defense Fund (CELDF), the world's leading environmental proponent that has been working closely with an array of original nations, rural municipalities, and grassroots environmental activists to transform nature into a subject having rights, rather than being mere property for exploitation and destruction.

The legal strategies being implemented to protect nature and ecosystems from the state and corporate sectors are examined, including a critical analysis of the following key legal concepts that have been used to give the state and corporate entities the right to privatize, exploit, and destroy nature: (1) the Commerce Clause; (2) corporate personhood; (3) Dillon's rules; and (4) the state's preemption rights. These four systems of law have privileged the rights of the state and corporate sectors by stripping away the legal sovereignty of the original nation, people, the nature, and ecosystems. The legal strategies that are relied upon in the fight to oppose the predation of state and corporate sectors are also examined in this section.

The limitation of the rights-based legal approach to protecting the original nation, people, nature, and ecosystems is discussed in the fourth section. Here, ONAIL attempts to strategize an effective opposition and collective resistance to the hegemony of the predatory state and corporation. In order to silence the original nation, nature protectors, and environmental organizations, the powerful states have relied on various supra-state arbitration institutions, such as the Permanent Court of Arbitration in The Hague, the Netherlands and the International Center for Settlement of Investment Disputes in Washington, DC in service of nullifying aspects of state constitutions, pro-nature amendments, environmental laws, and ecological regulations that were created and supported by the state court, government, the original nation, and environmental organizations in order to protect the nature and ecosystems. The last section looks at international tribunals, including the International Rights of Nature Tribunal (IRNT), organized by the nation, peoples, and grassroots environmental organizations to protect the land, resources, and ecosystems. This section also explores how the judgments and rulings of the tribunals have impacted the behaviors of the state, corporate actors, and multilateral international institutions.

1 EARTH JURISPRUDENCE: THE RIGHTS OF NATURE

The term "Earth Jurisprudence" was coined by cultural historian Thomas Berry in his groundbreaking work on the theory of Earth-centered law and jurisprudence.[17] As a strong critic of the "human-centered" view of

---

[17] Berry (1999).

the natural world, Berry called for the reconceptualization of humanity's place as being merely one of many interconnected members of the Earth community.[18] South African legal practitioner Cormac Cullinan has also argued for innovative legal and governance systems to support the Earth community and to reflect principles of Earth Jurisprudence based on the "Rights of Nature."[19]

Such an overarching effort to collaborate with the state sector first required the development of close working relations among the original nations within and across the state borders, actively seeking to gain the support of, and to collaborate with, advocacy groups, political institutions, environmental groups, and grassroots conservation organizations. These efforts led to "bottom-up," community-grounded movements and organizations, rather than the "pressure and influence" politics of top-down or "trickle-down" social transformation. The Earth Jurisprudence movement began in 1984, when Thomas Berry first asked the Gaia Foundation in England to work to protect biological and cultural diversity, preserve healthy ecosystems, and support indigenous nations and peoples in the Southern Hemisphere.[20] In 1996, the Gaia Foundation launched an Earth Jurisprudence initiative to promote the Rights of Nature and Mother Earth in order to protect the well-being of all components of the Earth community. This was followed by another conference in 2001, organized by the Gaia Foundation and the Center for Food Safety in Washington, DC.[21] This conference included legal specialists and indigenous activists from South Africa, Colombia, Britain, Canada, and the U.S., culminating in the 2002 publication of the conference declaration, "Wild Law: A Manifesto for Earth Justice." Also in 2002, the African Biodiversity Network was formed, through which Nobel Laureate Wangari Maathai, Ng'ang'a Thiong'o, and other prominent scholars and legal advisors helped incorporate an Earth Jurisprudence preamble into the new Kenyan Constitution in 2005.[22]

---

[18] Ibid., p. 280 (defining the Earth Community as "the interacting complexity of all of Earth's components, entities, and processes, including the atmosphere, hydrosphere, geosphere, biosphere, and mindshpere").

[19] Cullinan (2001, pp. 19–31).

[20] Tucker et al. (2019).

[21] Ibid.

[22] See generally Adam (2012).

In 2006, the Center for Earth Jurisprudence (CEJ) was established at the law schools of Barry University and St. Thomas University in Florida, following Thomas Berry's vision with the support of ecological philosophers, environmental activists, progressive lawyers, and eco-scientists. In 2007, another meeting was held in order to solidify the organizational and philosophical foundation for the establishment of Earth Jurisprudence. Cormac Cullinan of EnAct International in South Africa, Thomas Linzey of the Community Environmental Legal Defense Fund (CELDF) in the U.S., Liz Hosken of the Gaia Foundation in England, and other groups of lawyers and grassroots environmental activists met in Florida at the symposium, "Earth Jurisprudence: Defining the Field and Claiming the Promise."[23] Also in 2007, the U.N. Declaration of the Rights of Indigenous Peoples (UNDRIP) finally recognized the significant contribution of indigenous knowledge and self-sustaining cultural practices of the original nation and people, as well as their ecological governance and protection of ancestral homeland and environment. And in 2010, the Universal Declaration of the Rights of Mother Earth (UDRME) was developed and adopted at the World People's Conference on Climate Change and the Rights of Mother Earth hosted by the Bolivian government.[24] This event attracted thirty thousand participants from more than 100 countries. Since UDRME's preamble is significant in its articulation of the prescient vision of Earth Jurisprudence, it is included here in its entirety:

> We, the peoples and nations of Earth:
> considering that we are all part of Mother Earth, an indivisible, living community of interrelated and interdependent beings with a common destiny; gratefully acknowledging that Mother Earth is the source of life, nourishment and learning and provides everything we need to live well; recognizing that the capitalist system and all forms of depredation, exploitation, abuse and contamination have caused great destruction, degradation and disruption of Mother Earth, putting life as we know it today at risk through phenomena such as climate change; convinced that in an interdependent living community it is not possible to recognize the rights of only human beings without causing an imbalance within Mother Earth; affirming that to guarantee human rights it is necessary to recognize and defend the rights of Mother Earth and all beings in her and

---

[23] "History of Earth Jurisprudence" (2020).
[24] Schipani (2010).

that there are existing cultures, practices and laws that do so; conscious of the urgency of taking decisive, collective action to transform structures and systems that cause climate change and other threats to Mother Earth; proclaim this Universal Declaration of the Rights of Mother Earth, and call on the General Assembly of the United Nation to adopt it, as a common standard of achievement for all peoples and all nations of the world, and to the end that every individual and institution takes responsibility for promoting through teaching, education, and consciousness raising, respect for the rights recognized in this Declaration and ensure through prompt and progressive measures and mechanisms, national and international, their universal and effective recognition and observance among all peoples and States in the world.[25]

The Rights of Nature was first adopted by the government of Ecuador in its new constitution in 2008.[26] The nationwide referendum was drafted through the collaborative work of representatives of both the state government and the indigenous nation in Ecuador. After having been excluded from political participation for a long time, Ecuador's largest indigenous confederate group, CONAIE (*La Confederacion de Nacionalidades Indigenas del Ecuador* or National Confederation of Indigenous Nationalities of Ecuador), made up of fourteen Ecuadorian indigenous nations, began lobbying for a new constitution to incorporate the rightful recognition of Ecuador's original nations, history, languages, cultures, ancestral land rights, and an inherent concept of the "Law of Mother Earth."[27] Nearly two-thirds of Ecuadorian voters passed the constitutional referendum, and in 2008, Ecuador became the first state to grant constitutional rights to nature.[28]

Bolivia followed Ecuador's example, through legislative action in 2010 to enshrine the "Law of Mother Earth." This legislative reform was led by the Pact of Unity, a national alliance of grassroots organizations in support of indigenous rights, land reform, and indigenous transformations of the Bolivian state. The Pact of Unity was also led by the

---

[25] World People's Conference on Climate Change and the Rights of Mother Earth (2010).

[26] Barros (2015).

[27] Ibid. For greater discussions of the rights of nature in Ecuador, *see also* Smith (2009, p. 15) and Scanlan (2016, pp. 76–80). For general discussions on the rights of nature, *see* La Follette and Maser (2017).

[28] *See* Pietari (2016, p. 38).

Confederation of Indigenous Peoples of Bolivia (CIDOB), the Bartolina Sisa National Confederation of Campesino, Indigenous Native Women of Bolivia (*Confederacion Nacional de Mujeres Campesinas Indígenas Originarias de Bolivia: Bartolina Sisa* or CNMCIOS-BS), and other progressive civic and grassroots organizations. The Pact of Unity has completed the final version of the legislation in a collaboration with state sectors, including the Commission of the Plurinational Legislative Assembly, the Bolivian Vice-Ministry of Environment, and a legal team of constitutional development from the Bolivian Vice President's Office.[29]

The legislation also established new rights for nature that had previously been adopted in the UDRME, including: (1) the right to life and to exist; (2) the right to continue vital cycles and processes; (3) the right to be free from human alteration; (4) the right to pure water and clean air; (5) the right to equilibrium to complement the components of Mother Earth; (6) the right not to be polluted; and (7) the right not to have cellular structure modified or genetically altered.[30]

The indigenous nations in other states and regions took notice of these indigenous efforts at successful "law-making" to establish the rights of nature. In 2018, the Colombian Supreme Court extended the Rights of Nature to the Amazon ecosystems, including its river and forest territory, to be recognized as a legal subject, compelling the state to take action to prevent further deforestation, associated climate change, and the pollution of water in the Amazon region.[31] The Community Environmental Legal Defense Fund (CELDF) with its International Center for the Rights of Nature has been active in securing legal rights of nature, collaborating with indigenous groups, Afro-Colombian farmers, and progressive environmental activists in Colombia.[32]

As of today, more than a dozen countries have decided to adopt, or have substantially incorporated, environmental rights provisions into their constitutions. According to the U.N. report, these states include: Egypt,

---

[29] "Bolivia: Pacto de Unidad Exige al Gobierno la Aprobación de la Ley de la Madre Tierra [Bolivia: The Pact of Unity Requires the Government to Approve the Law of Mother Earth]" (2011).

[30] Vidal (2011). For greater discussions of the rights of Mother Earth in Bolivia, see Velasco (2013), McNeish (2013, p. 221), and Borie and Hulme (2015, p. 487).

[31] Macpherson and Ventura (2019).

[32] "Press Release: Colombia Supreme Court Rules That Amazon Region is 'Subject of Rights'" (2018).

Kenya, Madagascar, Morocco, Rwanda, Sudan, South Sudan, and Tunisia in Africa; France, Hungary, Montenegro, and Serbia in Europe; Jamaica and Dominican Republic in the Caribbean; Maldives and Sri Lanka in the Indian Ocean; Armenia and Turkmenistan in Central Asia; Nepal and Myanmar in Asia; and Fiji and Guinea in the Pacific Ocean.[33]

2   Legal "Personhood" and Nature's "Personality"

Another legal strategy to protect the nature and ecosystems of the nation was to give the entitlement of legal status as a "natural person" to varied forms of "non-human" ecological entities. In 2014, the Maori Nation of New Zealand led the collaboration with the state by passing a bill to grant legal "personhood" to the forest *Te Urewera* for the first time in New Zealand's history. In 2017, the government and the Maori Nation used the 1840 Treaty of Waitangi to grant legal "personhood" to the Whanganui River, the third largest river in New Zealand.[34] Similar to what the Lakota Nation had done to assert their rights to the ownership of the ancestral homeland under the 1868 Treaty of Fort Laramie in the U.S., the Maori relied on the Treaty of Waitangi to establish the continued ownership of the Maori over their homeland and to give Maori people full rights and protections as British subjects.[35] The legal movement to build Earth Jurisprudence in New Zealand was also based on the Maori Nation's ancestral and spiritual connection to the river, for "the health and well-being of the Whanganui River is intrinsically interconnected with the health and well-being of the people."[36] The state government's pronouncement thereby recognized the river as "a legal entity with standing in its own right."[37]

---

[33] May and Daly (2019, p. 104).

[34] Tutohu Whakatupua Agreement Between Whanganui Iwi and the Crown (hereinafter Tutohu) (2012). ("The purpose of the Whole of River Strategy will be to bring together all those persons and organizations with interests in the Whanganui River (including iwi, local and central government, commercial and recreational users and other community groups) to collaboratively develop a strategy focused on the future environmental, social, cultural and economic health and wellbeing of the Whanganui River.")

[35] O'Malley et al. (2013).

[36] Tutohu (2012).

[37] Ibid.

Also in 2017, soon after New Zealand had granted the river the status of legal personhood, the Constitutional Court of Colombia decided that the Atrato River would be recognized as a legal subject with its own rights of protection, conservation, maintenance, and restoration. The serious pollution of the Atrato River and surrounding regions has been caused by illegal mining, and the Colombian court has responded to the complaints of indigenous and Afro-Colombian communities that depended on the river as ecological guardians of their livelihoods and spiritual well-being.[38] Chapter 4 explored the ways that the Cofán Nation and other original and Afro-Colombian communities have been persecuted by state troopers, left-wing rebels, illegal mining groups, narco-cartel organizations, extractive corporations, and their privately funded security forces. The coordinated political activism of the people began to influence court decisions and legislative actions in Colombia. The Colombian government came to recognize the anthropogenic catastrophes caused by the many ecologically unsustainable human activities in Amazonian communities. For example, a string of court cases led to recognizing wild animals as possessing the "legal personality" and granting them the writ of habeas corpus to free them from unlawful detention from human captivities, including those in zoos.[39]

In Canada, the Inuit Nation has signed an agreement with the state to reclaim their land known as *Nunavut*. After years of indigenous social activism, education, and political negotiations with the state, the *Nunavut* Land Claims Agreement was finally adopted by the Canadian Parliament in 1993. As the law came into effect in 1999, Inuit Tapiriit Kanatami, the organization that represented the Inuit Nation in Canada, reclaimed more than three-quarter million acres of *Nunavut* into their national territory. They also attained local autonomy and political control to ensure the preservation of the environment, Inuit history, tradition, and the self-sustaining culture. In 2013, the Supreme Court of Canada also granted the Tsilhgot'In Nation a declaration of Aboriginal title to nearly 2,000 square kilometers of land in British Columbia.[40] Judicial activism led by the First Nations, environmental activists, and grassroots organizations had effectively protected the nation and their environment from

---

[38] Macpherson and Ventura (2019).

[39] Ibid.

[40] Pfister (2018).

the adverse impact of local mining operations. Because original nations in Canada were able to attain such a high level of political control, government recognition, and public approval, their activism signaled that many original nations around the world could follow suit and accomplish the robust establishment of Earth Jurisprudence in their respective states.[41]

In the U.S., the catalyst for Earth Jurisprudence began in Tamaqua Borough, a small Pennsylvania community, when the borough first drafted legislation to protect the community from the dumping of toxic sewage sludge, seeing it as a violation of the rights of nature. In this community, whose name means "The Land of Running Water" in a local Native American language, the grassroots environmental organization contacted the Community Environmental Legal Defense Fund (CELDF) which helped pass the bill in 2006 making Tamaqua the first municipality in the world to recognize the rights of nature,[42] soon serving as an inspiration for legislative and constitutional activities elsewhere, including Ecuador. As examined earlier, since 2006, many communities and original nations have begun to recognize the ecological benefits of the "Rights of Nature" movement and have enacted Rights of Nature laws in the U.S., Ecuador, Bolivia, and other states across the world.[43] In 2016, the Ho-Chunk Nation of Wisconsin voted overwhelmingly to amend its own national constitution to enshrine the rights of nature, thus becoming the first original nation in the U.S. to do so, claiming that "[e]cosystems and natural communities within the Ho-Chunk territory possess an inherent, fundamental, and inalienable right to exist and thrive."[44] The Ho-Chunk Nation's Constitutional Amendment further prohibited frac sand mining, fossil fuel extraction, and genetic engineering in their territory as violations of the rights of nature.[45] In 2017, the Ponca Nation in Oklahoma became the second to enact the Rights of Nature, acting to ban fracking

---

[41] Inuit still face the threat by multinational corporations that are interested in the exploration of the community for oil and gas extractions in their territories. *See* Rogers (2014).

[42] "Advancing Legal Rights Nature: Timeline" (2018).

[43] Ibid.

[44] Ho-Chunk Nation (2015).

[45] Ibid.

in the ancestral homeland, as it had become the epicenter of earthquakes caused by fracking and injection wells in Oklahoma.[46]

At the global level, Ecuador has been a catalyst in forming the International Rights of Nature Tribunal and granting legal standing to nature for protection and preservation. In 2010, the Global Alliance for the Rights of Nature (GARN) was formed in Patate, Ecuador, with founding members from Ecuador, the U.S., Australia, and many states from Africa, Asia, and Europe, asserting the universal adoption and implementation of legal systems that recognize, respect, and enforce the rights of nature.[47] The GARN then sponsored the first International Rights of Nature Tribunal in Quito, Ecuador.[48] In 2015, the third International Rights of Nature Tribunal was held concurrently with the U.N. Framework Convention on Climate Change (COP21) in Paris, France.[49] To host the tribunal, the GARN partnered with the alliance of nations across the globe, as well as environmental groups such as End Ecocide on Earth, NatureRights, Attac France, and a panel of judges consisting of internationally renowned lawyers and activists.[50] The tribunal ruled that the confluence of global interests, such as multinational corporations, the states, and multilateral institutions, were guilty of crimes against Mother Nature, including greenhouse gas emissions and destructions of ecosystems, life forms, and indigenous cultures.[51] Chief Raoni Metuktire of the Kayapo Nation in Brazil offered a powerful testimony for the urgent need to unite indigenous knowledge about the rights of nature to protect Mother Earth. He declared that "we feel the effects of non-action [on climate change] every day... we feel the effect on our rivers, on our forests, on the animals.... We indigenous continue to speak loudly, but we need your help. We will only stop this madness by working together."[52]

[46] "Ponca Nation of Oklahoma to Recognize the Rights of Nature to Ban Fracking" (2018).

[47] See generally Boyd (2017).

[48] Ibid.

[49] Ibid.

[50] Global Alliance for the Rights of Nature (GARN) (2015).

[51] Lavoto (2015).

[52] Ibid.

Another emergent movement to build the robust system of Earth Jurisprudence has been taking place in Nepal. In its effort to incorporate the Rights of Nature in its constitution, the concept of nature has been extended to include healthy weather and climate. Nepal has suffered serious environmental and ecological catastrophes from the 2015 earthquake that destroyed many buildings and infrastructures. Nepal has also experienced numerous flood disasters due to the rapidly melting glacier at the Himalayan Plateau caused by global warming and climate change. CELDF has worked closely with the Nepalese government and environmental organizations to draft a constitutional amendment to incorporate the rights of nature, including the rights to healthy climate, in order to ensure that the climate has the right to be unaffected by man-made pollution, contamination, and global warming.[53] In 2016, the Nepalese Supreme Court declared that ecologically destructive extractive activities of precious marbles by Godavari Marble Industries Ltd had to be stopped because of water pollution, groundwater contamination, and other environmental concerns. For the first time, Nepal's highest court issued its verdict based on the concept of the rights of nature, ruling that the Godavari marble quarry had to be closed immediately and further prohibiting future mineral extractive operation in the Godavari area.[54] The Supreme Court thus brought the concept of the rights of nature and ecological governance to the forefront of legal discourse and decision-making proceedings.

3   COMMUNITY ENVIRONMENTAL LEGAL DEFENSE FUND (CELDF)

CELDF has been one of the world's leading grassroots organizations to innovate "on-the-ground" strategies to promote the rights of nature in the U.S. and around the world. Since 1995, CELDF has worked on numerous environmental cases to protect the community in Pennsylvania and other states from environmentally harmful corporate projects, such as the construction of hydro-fracking wells, waste sewage facilities, chicken and hog industrial farms, genetically engineered food crop productions;

---

[53] "Community Environmental Legal Defense Fund: Bringing Real Democracy and Protection to Communities and Their Environments" (2016).

[54] La Follette and Maser (2017).

oil, gas, uranium, and coal mining; and other such projects. CELDF has successfully delayed many of these environmentally harmful projects from launching in the community by relying on their masterful interpretation of environmental law and regulations and finding loopholes in government permits and regulatory policies. While many of their efforts have resulted in successful delays, nearly all of the original corporate projects have eventually been implemented, after the corporations developed better permit applications, even helping in some cases to rewrite the law to implement their projects.

CELDF Executive Director Thomas Linzey came to declare that environmental law was not created to protect the environment, but to regulate its use up until its ultimate destruction.[55] Since the early 2000s, CELDF has dramatically changed their approach and their use of legal strategies to protect the community from harmful corporate projects by: (1) empowering the community to create their own structure of law to enshrine the right of local people, community, the nature, and ecosystems from the outreach of the state and corporate sectors, and (2) creating and tailoring legal instruments with specific provisions that nullify the impact of specific mechanisms of the state and corporation that deprive the community of sovereignty and the power to protect their land and ecosystems. CELDF has identified four legal mechanisms on which the state and corporation have relied in stripping away the sovereignty of local communities: (1) Commerce Clause embedded in the U.S. and state constitutions, (2) federal and state preemption law; (3) the Dillion's rule; and lastly (4) the concept of "corporate personhood," which allows the for-profit private firm to be treated as a "natural person" under the rule of law.

The most powerful constitutional instrument that has allowed the corporation to unequivocally engage in the wanton exploitation and destruction of nature, the environment, and ecosystems is called the "commerce clause." This is defined in the U.S. Constitution, stipulating that the U.S. Congress has power to "regulate Commerce with foreign Nations, and among the several States, and with the Indian Tribes."[56] While the commerce clause was intended to federally prohibit states from taxing goods coming from other states, a series of court decisions

---

[55] Linzey (2009).

[56] U.S. Constitution, art. 1 section 8, clause 3.

have developed a doctrine of the "dormant commerce clause," in which Congress was given exclusive power to regulate commerce and to prevent the state from opposing commerce and businesses coming from other states.[57] Thus, local municipalities or counties were incapacitated from prohibiting the importation of "sewage" from larger cities of other states because sewage was considered as part of "commerce." Powerful corporations have used the commerce clause, without local people's consent, to establish factory farms, including industrial hog and chicken farms, and dumping sites of industrial wastes and toxic substances from large-scale agri-business practices.[58]

Another predatory legal mechanism is the federal and state preemption law, in which the higher-level government sets a cap or ceiling on how much they can protect people's civil rights, health, and safety. Once the ceiling is set, the federal and state governments can prohibit local municipalities from enacting more stringent and protective environmental regulations that exceed the government-set standards.[59] This ceiling preemption thereby prohibited local municipalities and counties from protecting their residents, whose lives were more adversely affected than those in other regions, due to dangerous toxic wastes from nearby industrial farms or sewage dumping sites. The 1868 judge-created rule called the "Dillion's rule" is another legal mechanism that has prevented local governments from protecting their own people. The Dillion's rule treats the municipality as the "custodian" of the state, thereby denying the municipal government much-needed power and jurisdiction to take their own actions to protect the community and people.[60]

The concept of corporate personhood is another powerful mechanism that has effectively prioritized the rights and interests of corporate entities over and above the rights of the people, nature, and ecosystems. Since the nineteenth century, an army of corporate lawyers has engaged in judicial activism to argue that the imaginary, collectivist corporate entity should be treated as a "natural person." They have used the rationale that the Fourteenth Amendment's "equal protection clause" and "due

---

[57] Community Environmental Legal Defense Fund (CELDF) (2020, p. 13).
[58] Ibid.
[59] Ibid., p. 11.
[60] Ibid., p. 12.

process clause" should apply to the corporation, although the amendment was originally designed to protect newly freed African slaves, not to create civil rights for the corporation.[61] The term "corporation" does not appear anywhere in the U.S. Constitution, but corporate lawyers' judicial activism and their litigative efforts led to a series of court decisions that established that corporations have equal protection under the law as natural persons.[62]

In order to counter the system of law that prioritized state and corporate interests over the rights of people and the nature, CELDF and other "on-the-ground" environmental organizations and advocacy groups began to initiate Community Bill of Rights Ordinances and to design local self-governing systems of municipal laws to strip the constitutional rights of corporations and prevent egregious and invasive state intrusion into local communities.[63] CELDF also initiated the Community Rights Network at both state and federal levels to propose the draft of state and federal constitutional amendments to establish the Rights of Nature and protect the sovereignty of local communities and peoples.[64] CELDF has helped launch the statewide Community Rights Network in Oregon, Colorado, New Hampshire, Pennsylvania, and Ohio.[65] Such rights-based movements, as noted earlier, have made the natural world into a "rights-bearing" entity, and these grassroots-based alliance building activities have also led to the passage of laws to protect fragile ecosystems from the state and corporate exploitation.

With CELDF's support and collaboration, the town of Lafayette, Colorado in 2017 became the first jurisdiction in the U.S. to enable a "Climate Bill of Rights" ordinance. In recognizing the "Right to a Healthy Climate," it stipulates that "[A]ll residents and ecosystems of the City of Lafayette possess a right to a healthy climate and life sustaining resources, which shall include the right to be free from all activities in the City of Lafayette that interfere with that right, including the extraction of coal, oil, or gas, disposal of drilling waste, contaminated drinking water, lethal carcinogens, toxic gases and other byproducts of industrial activity

---

[61] Ibid., p. 13.
[62] Ibid., p. 14.
[63] Ibid., p. 28.
[64] Ibid., p. 9.
[65] Ibid., p. 18.

which threaten human physical and neurological systems."[66] The town of Exeter in Rockingham County, New Hampshire in 2019 became the second jurisdiction in the U.S. to pass the Right to a Healthy Climate Ordinance. Similar to Lafayette's ordinance, it asserts the community's rights to clean air, pure water, and local community self-government, thereby banning corporate activities that release toxic contaminants into air, water, and grounds as a violation of these rights.[67] CELDF has helped more than three dozen American communities adopt the Rights of Nature into law,[68] including Pittsburgh, Pennsylvania, whose Rights of Nature ordinance was used to prevent fracking inside city limits, on the basis that such industrial extractive activities violated the fundamental rights of natural communities to live, "exist, thrive, and evolve."[69] The city of Santa Monica, California has passed a similar ordinance that acts to "recognize the rights of people, natural communities and ecosystems to exist, regenerate and flourish."[70] In 2019, the city of Toledo, Ohio passed the Lake Erie Bill of Rights, giving one of the Great Lakes the right to "exist, flourish, and naturally evolve," and awarding community residents the right to a "clean and healthy environment."[71]

Since its inception in the 1990s, CELDF has sustained close collaboration with the original nation in North America, and the Board of Advisors includes prominent American Indian activist Winona LaDuke, who is a member of the Anishinaabekwe (Ojibwe) Nation, lives on the White Earth Indian Reservation in Minnesota, and serves as the Executive Director of Honor the Earth, raising public support and funding for frontline native environmental groups. In 2019, the White Earth Band of Ojibwe adopted a Rights of Manoomin (wild rice) law to protect the rights of manoomin and secure the supply of clean and fresh water resources and healthy habitats on which its natural flourishing depended.[72]

[66] Colorado Community Rights Network (2019).

[67] Drugmand (2019).

[68] Bioneers (2020).

[69] Ibid.

[70] Williams (2019).

[71] Zartner (2019).

[72] LaDuke (2019). See also "White Earth Band Enacts First-of-Its Kind Rights of Nature Law" (2019).

4 LIMITATIONS OF THE RIGHTS OF NATURE JURIDICAL MOVEMENT

For the last few decades, the significant pioneering work and tireless effort by legal practitioners and community activists have led to many significant achievements, including the juridical recognition of the rights of nature in multiple states and their municipal and provincial jurisdictions. CELDF, in particular, has played a central role in advancing such recognition by transforming the legal discourse from the property-based system of law to a rights-based system of environmental law. Their work first originated in small towns and municipalities in the state of Pennsylvania, where they worked to prevent the runoff of PCB-contaminated toxic water into the township's river system. Their community organizing efforts around the world eventually led to the creation of the Global Alliance for the Rights of Nature (GARN) in 2007. Collaborative work with the Pachamama Alliance in San Francisco led to the first successful discussion of these themes with lawmakers, along with indigenous nations, their alliances, and grassroots organizations. Working globally, CELDF helped draft and pass a constitutional amendment to establish the juridical recognition of the "Rights of Nature" in Ecuador, which became the first state in the world to recognize nature's rights in its constitutional system.[73]

The efforts to protect nature, indigenous nations, and their people had been propelled by the decades of environmental destruction and pollution of Amazonian forests by ecologically unsustainable corporate development and mining activities. The Ecuadorian Government first allowed the Gulf Oil corporation and Texaco Inc. to conduct oil and gas exploration in eastern regions of Ecuador in 1964, which led to the discovery of oil in 1967. Since then, millions of gallons of toxic materials have been spilled into multiple rivers near oil well operations, causing many deaths as well as extensive health problems among indigenous populations. The first attempt to seek justice by the indigenous nation began in 1993 in the U.S. District Court for the Southern District of New York. The case became to be known as the Aguinda litigation, with 74 plaintiffs who represented more than 30,000 residents affected by oil spills.[74] Chevron, which had purchased Texaco, successfully argued for a change

---

[73] See generally Burdon (2011). See also Boyd (2017).

[74] Dhooge (2010).

of venue and moved the trial from New York to Lago Agrio, Ecuador, in an attempt to avoid an unpredictable jury verdict, noting that Ecuador did not have a civil jury trial and thus ordinary citizens had no direct involvement in legal decision-making on this sensitive environmental issue.[75] Nonetheless, Ecuadorian Judge Nicolas Zambrano found in 2011 that Chevron was to be held liable for causing pollution, ordering Chevron to pay $9 billion and to offer a public apology or to pay double the amount of the compensation award.[76] Chevron subsequently refused to offer a public apology and the compensation was thus increased to nearly $19 billion.[77]

While civil litigation was underway at the Ecuadorian state court, Chevron argued that the Ecuadorian court violated the Ecuador–U.S. Bilateral Investment Treaty (BIT) because the domestic court had failed to resolve commercial cases involving Texaco in the 1990s. A court of international arbitration, the Permanent Court of Arbitration in The Hague, declared its jurisdiction to extend retroactively in 2008, and thus determined that Ecuador had breached the BIT, ruling in favor of awarding Chevron $96 million in 2011.[78] Chevron filed another arbitration case at the Permanent Court of Arbitration, with allegations related to the denial of justice, inequitable treatment, fair case proceeding, corruption, and discrimination in connection with litigation filed by largely indigenous plaintiffs in 2003. The international arbitration court declared once again that it had the jurisdiction over the case in 2012. The Permanent Court of Arbitration issued an award in favor of Chevron and its indirect subsidiary Texaco in 2018, finding that Ecuador had violated its obligation under BIT and other international laws and that the Ecuadorian court decision ordering a $9 billion compensation against Chevron was procured on the basis of fraud, bribery, and corruption, thereby annulling said decision.[79]

Although Ecuador had become the first state in the world to enshrine the Rights of Nature in its constitution in 2008, under the current system of the BIT agreement and the international arbitration system, the

---

[75] Lerner (2020).

[76] Romero and Krauss (2011).

[77] "Texaco/Chevron Lawsuits (re: Ecuador)" (2020).

[78] Ibid.

[79] Ibid.

supra-state arbitration decisions superseded the jurisdiction of the state court, state sovereignty, the constitutional recognition of the rights of nature, and even the human rights of the indigenous nation and people. The establishment of supra-state international arbitration institutions, such as the Permanent Court of Arbitration in The Hague, the Netherlands, and the International Center for the Settlement of Investment Disputes (ICSID) in Washington, DC, continued to serve the interest of powerful transnational fossil fuel industries, international banks, investment firms, and private corporate wealth over and above the rights of the state, its judicial bodies, government, general populations, and indigenous communities.

The limitation of the Rights of Nature movement may be that the legal strategies and law-making activities involved had to depend on the existent system of law that had long protected private wealth and corporate interests. CELDF's activism in rights-based movements led to the awareness that local communities were legally denied fundamental rights to exercise their own local sovereignty. The architecture of law, at least in the U.S., has been constructed to ensure that the superior and plenary rights of the state and corporate entities are deeply embedded in the legal culture, juridical custom, and legal systems. Given these fundamentally inequitable systems of law, other revolutionary strategies were desperately needed in order to engineer much larger, more powerful movements and organizing efforts. The CELDF's struggles and its reliance on the structure of existing legal mechanisms have served as a powerful reminder for the original nation, political activists, and grassroots environmental protectors that the state legal system, political apparatus, and court administrations have emerged from the tenuous process of "state-building" and "nation-destroying" projects, through which the system of law was developed to serve as a perfect instrument of a state empire to maintain its dominion over the original nation, people, the nature, and ecosystems.

The inevitable irony today is that nonindigenous communities and descendants of European settlers and other migrants have been exposed to the same predatory governmental programs and legal maneuvers imposed on nations and peoples in North America. In responding to this idea, prominent American lawyer and legal scholar Felix S. Cohen prophetically declared in 1953 that indigenous people in North American had served as the proverbial "Miner's Canary" of U.S. colonial experiments.[80] Cohen predicted that the assault of predatory state programs on the indigenous nation and people would inevitably serve as an idealized prototype for events and projects by the state and corporate elites intended for application to the U.S. as a whole and even beyond. The impacts of the "nation-destroying" policy and its legal implementation upon the indigenous nation and people, according to Cohen, should be viewed as "early warning signs" of the cost and consequences of state policies and legal applications for the broader society.[81] He warned that close examination of this trajectory should equip the larger society to formulate means of self-defense in building a greater alliance to oppose future state and corporate encroachment. Indeed, the deeper understanding of the projection of the "nation-destroying" or modern-day "municipality-destroying" agendas has begun to ignite widespread support for grassroots movements advocating for greater social changes. U.S. municipalities and rural communities have begun to enact laws and policy measures to defend their sovereignty and to protect the rights of residents, the nature, and ecosystems, with the support of CELDF and other "on-the-ground" environmental activists. Multiple grassroots organizations, political activists, and environmental organizations across the U.S. and the globe have come to resonate with the prophetic wisdom embodied in Cohen's foresight, beginning to initiate a global movement to mount robust opposition to the state and to corporate exploitation and depredation.

5   The Nation's International Rights of Nature Tribunals to Address State and Corporate Crimes

An effective strategic maneuver to ensure compliance with the international agreements on the protection of the rights of indigenous peoples and nature may be achieved through the establishment of international tribunals organized by the original nation, people, and their allies. The chief objective of the inter-national tribunal has been to ensure that state and corporate actions work to preserve nature, the environment, and ecosystems and to deter such anthropogenic catastrophes as climate

---

[80] Cohen (1953, p. 390).

[81] See also Churchill (1997, p. 361) and Ward Churchill (1999, 128).

change, global warming, sea-level rising, and other ecological disasters that not only harm the original nation, but also devastate the state.

However, the state has largely failed to recognize the importance of the international tribunals that have been organized by the nations, political activists, and environmental organizations. The first of these international tribunals to enshrine the Rights of Nature emerged in Ecuador in 2014. Renowned physicist and environmental activist Vandana Shiva presided over the historic tribunal along with nine other distinguished judges from seven states and five continents.[82] This international tribunal presided over nine cases that allegedly violated the Universal Declaration of the Rights of Mother Earth (UDRME), which had been adopted in Cochabamba, Bolivia in April 2010.[83] These nine specific violations included: (1) the Chevron–Texaco pollution case in Ecuador; (2) the British Petroleum (BP) Deep Horizon oil spill in the U.S.; (3) the Yasuni-ITT oil project in Ecuador; (4) hydraulic fracturing ("fracking") in the U.S.; (5) the prosecution of Defenders of Nature in Ecuador; (6) the threats of genetically modified organisms (GMOs); (7) the Great Barrier Reef and its survivability in Australia; (8) the gigantic open-pit mining called *Minería* Condor Mirador in Ecuador; and (9) climate change affecting the well-being of the global community.[84]

The second international tribunal was convened in Lima, Peru in December 2014, parallel to the U.N. Framework Convention on Climate Change in Peru (COP20).[85] A collegial panel of thirteen judges, after hearing evidence and testimony, ordered BP to abstain from any future underwater oil exploration. Chevron was found guilty of ecocide and ordered to pay the $9 billion in damages previously ordered by an Ecuadorian court in relation to the massive oil spills in the Amazon River basin. The Ecuadorian government was ordered to suspend the operation of the Mirador open-pit mine and compensate the victims of ecological devastations. The tribunal concluded by stating that future cases would place Exxon and Monsanto on trial for the violation of the rights of nature and the crime of committing ecocide.[86]

---

[82] *See* Borras (2016).

[83] Recinos (2014).

[84] Milam (2014).

[85] Ibid.

[86] "2nd International Rights of Nature Tribunal: Lima" (2014).

The third international rights of nature tribunal was held in Paris in December 2015, which coincided with the U.N. Framework Convention on Climate Change (COP21).[87] As in the previous international tribunals, the judges examined what they called "climate crimes" against nature, including the criminal offenses committed against Mother Earth by GMO and agro-food industry, tar sands in Canada, mega-dams in the Brazilian Amazon, oil drilling and catastrophic spills and ecological damages in Ecuador, and international ocean management.[88]

The fourth international tribunal, held in Bonn, Germany in 2017, adjudicated seven cases in the violation of the Rights of Nature: (1) climate change and false energy solutions, i.e., fracking, coal, nuclear, and the consolidation of fossil fuel industries in North America; (2) the financialization of nature and the REDD (Reducing Emissions from Deforestation and Forest Degradation); (3) the lignite mining at Hambach Forest in Germany; (4) violations of Mother Earth defenders at Standing Rock, as well as elsewhere in the U.S., Russia, and Scandinavia; (5) water deprivation in Almeria, Spain; (6) threats to the Amazon in Ecuador, Brazil, Bolivia, and French Guyana; and (7) international free trade agreements (FTAs) and their egregious impact on nature. The representatives of multiple indigenous nations around the globe gave powerful testimonies as expert witnesses throughout the tribunal. The tribunal became a permanent platform for hearing and judging cases from "on-the-ground" activists and protectors around the world.

The fifth, and most recent, international rights of nature tribunal was held at the University of Chile in Santiago, Chile in December 2019. The COP25 meeting scheduled to be held in Santiago had been transferred to Madrid, Spain. Three litigations were adjudicated: (1) Lithium mining in the Atacama Desert in Chile; (2) threats to Patagonia in terms of water and life reserve in Chile; and (3) water privatization in Chile. The tribunal also deliberated on cases for admission to future adjudication, including: (1) the Vaca Muerta Region in Neuquén, Argentina, which was estimated by the Energy Information Administration of the U.S. government to hold the largest reserve of gas shales outside North America; and (2) ecocide in the Amazon, including Chiquitania in eastern

[87] Ramsden (2015).
[88] Schuele (2015).

Bolivia and Pantanal which is the world's largest tropical wetland in the Brazilian state of Mato Grosso do Sul, and other surrounding areas.[89]

The oil and natural gas production in the region known as Vaca Muerta, in the Neuquén Basin located in northern Patagonia in Argentina is, according to the Energy Information Administration, "one of the greatest potential worldwide, outside of North America."[90] The Neuquén Basin corresponds to the jurisdiction of three Argentinian provinces: Neuquén, Rio Negro, and Mendoza. The Provinces of Neuquén and Mendoza have recently adopted the criminal jury system called *El Jurado Indígena* (the Indigenous Jury) that guarantees equal representation of indigenous and nonindigenous jurors in criminal cases when the defendant is a member of the indigenous nation,[91] and also guarantees that half of the jurors should be women. Many indigenous activists, including those from the Mapuche Nation, have been arrested, convicted, and sentenced to prison for their anti-corporate mining projects in their homeland. Furthermore, in May 2020, the Province of Mendoza adopted the civil jury system to ensure the protection of the economic interests of residents of local communities, including the indigenous nation. The significant socio-political ramifications of direct citizen participation in Argentina's newly adopted criminal and civil trials are explored in the following chapter.

Despite the multiple international rights of nature tribunals and their repeated condemnations of egregious state and corporate activities, the states' refusal to recognize the legitimacy of these tribunals and their verdicts has resulted in the lack of proper jurisdiction and powers needed to enforce compliance with their judgments by the respective states. The international tribunals are autonomous peoples' institutions unconstrained by states' legal systems, and have thus created the opportunity for many important cases to be heard that would be difficult to adjudicate in most state or international courts, including the International Criminal Court (ICC) or the International Court of Justice (ICJ).

---

[89] "International Rights of Nature Tribunal, Final Verdict: Fifth International Rights of Nature Tribunal" (2019).

[90] Ibid., p. 52.

[91] Harfuch et al. (2016).

Powerful western states have also routinely ignored the judgments and rulings of international courts that are properly recognized under international law, including the International Court of Justice (ICJ) and the International Criminal Court (ICC). The ICJ was established in 1945 and headquartered in The Hague, the Netherlands, becoming the principal judicial organ and branch of the U.N. with the objective to settle legal disputes between member states and to provide advisory opinions and judgments to other U.N. organizations and agencies. The ICC was created in 2002 and is also headquartered in The Hague, having the jurisdiction to prosecute individuals, including heads of state, for international crimes of genocide, crimes against humanity, war crimes, and crimes of aggression. The U.S. played an important role in establishing the 1998 Roma Statute that created the ICC, but today the U.S. is no longer a signatory state party to the ICC statute.

While remaining a signatory party to the ICJ statute, the U.S. has decided to either ignore or withdraw from its protocol or rulings on numerous occasions. For example, the U.S. government withdrew from the ICJ's protocol when the court determined that the U.S. should hold new hearings for fifty-one Mexican nationals who had been placed on death rows in the U.S.[92] The U.S. government considered the ICJ decision on inmates' review to be an international interference in its domestic affairs, as the decision required that American courts must grant "review and reconsideration" to claims that the Mexican citizens' rights had been violated by the failure of American authorities to allow them to contact Mexican consular officials.[93]

The U.S. government has also rejected ICJ decisions on international affairs, including the matter of *The Republic of Nicaragua v. The United States of America* (1986), which ruled that the U.S.'s covert war in the 1980s against the *Sandinista* government in Nicaragua was in violation of international law. The ICJ also ordered the U.S. to terminate the "unlawful use of force" and illegal interruption of "peaceful maritime commerce" against the *Sandinista* government of Nicaragua and to pay substantial reparations to the country.[94] The U.S. immediately withdrew from ICJ's compulsory jurisdiction in 1986, declaring that it would

---

[92] *See* Liptak (2005).

[93] Ibid.

[94] International Court of Justice (1986, pp. 118, 137).

accept the court's jurisdiction only on a case-by-case basis in the future. Although Chapter XIV of the U.N. Charter authorizes the U.N. Security Council to enforce court rulings, the U.S. moved to veto two U.N. Security Council resolutions affirming the ICJ judgment that called on all states, including the U.S., to observe and respect international law.[95] The U.S.'s clandestine operations continued in Nicaragua until the *Sandinista* government was finally toppled in 1990.

The U.S. has not been the only state to sidestep the ICJ decisions. In a 2004 ruling, the ICJ determined that Israel's building of walls in the occupied Palestine territory was illegal under international law, that the construction had to stop immediately, and that Israel should make reparations for any damages caused.[96] The ICJ's decision also called for the demolition of the wall within the occupied Palestinian territory, and the return of land, orchards, olive groves, and other property to the original Palestinian owners. If this were not possible, compensation would be required. Israel, however, ignored the ICJ rulings and continued constructing its own walls in the occupied territory.[97]

The i\International Rights of Nature Tribunal has been organized by a multiplicity of the nations, indigenous activists, feminist advocacy groups, civic political organizations, and grassroots environmental groups, along with those who have represented victims of predatory state policies around the globe. Many important cases have been presented by a group of activists called "Earth Defenders," including experts, witnesses, and victims who have observed the consequences of the violation of human rights and rights of nature that were guaranteed under the Universal Declaration of the Rights of Mother Earth (UDRME). In their testimonies and presentations, these experts proposed innovative strategies for restorative justice measures. The internationally organized, "bottom-up" tribunals also began to challenge existing conceptions of "inter-state" law, along with the matrix of legal institutional mechanisms designed to set aside the common interest of the nation, people, earth defenders, eco-feminists, environmental activists, and other reform-oriented progressive groups who have been striving to ensure the preservation of nature and

---

[95] *See* Marshall (1986).

[96] International Court of Justice (2004).

[97] United Nations (2008). ("Israel continues to carry out its illegal colonial campaign in grave violation of international law ... in defiance of the 9 July 2004 advisory opinion of the International Court of Justice.")

ecosystems, in opposition to the short-term interests and profit-oriented goals of the powerful constituency of corporate power and private wealth.

Furthermore, international tribunals created to develop strong and robust Earth Jurisprudence have been considered to provide a permanent legal platform to hear cases from the nation, environmental activists, and earth defenders across the globe in response to concerns that state and international legal mechanisms do not protect or respect the rights of the original nation, the nature, and ecosystems. In order to assure that international tribunals' rulings, orders, and pronouncements are legally binding, the horizontally aligned, global "alliance-making" activities of the original nation and allies may be necessary to counter the hegemonic influences of the state and international institutions.

6   CONCLUSIONS

This chapter explored areas of possible nation-state collaboration, particularly in the realm of the state's judiciary and legislature, that could serve to transform nature and Mother Earth into rights-bearing entities. The original nation's collaboration with state sectors has been sought to facilitate the juridical establishment and recognition of the "Rights of Nature" through constitutional and legislative processes, and to build a robust system of Earth Jurisprudence to protect the original nation, people, the nature, and ecosystems. Ecuador, Bolivia, Colombia, New Zealand, India, Nepal, and other states primarily located in the Global South, as well as indigenous nations in North America, have adopted the rights of nature in their constitutions, ordinances, and local policies. These states and nations have worked closely with the U.S. grassroots environmental organization known as the Community Environmental Legal Defense Fund (CELDF), which has become a pioneer in transforming nature, the environment, and ecosystems into rights-bearing entities so that the existing legal system can be mobilized to protect their rights to exist, flourish, and run through their natural life cycles.

The limitation of the rights-based jurisprudence was also examined. While the state and the nation have worked collaboratively to insert the rights of nature into their respective systems of law and government policies, the powerful states have also created international arbitration courts which have often rendered decisions that supersede and nullify those environmental laws and ecological policies that had been painstakingly developed through the close collaboration among the state, indigenous nations, and environmental groups. Another limitation was seen to be the realization that rights-based legal strategies and judicial activism still had to rely upon the existing systems of legal doctrine, legal culture, court procedures, and judicial personnel who often fail to incorporate the worldview of the original nation and people into legal decision-making. The last section of the chapter examined the evolution and efficacy of the international rights of nature tribunals. Indigenous activists, nature protectors, and environmental groups have testified before renowned judges and specialists who have then condemned powerful states and transnational corporations for their egregious activities and exploitive projects in the homelands of nations across the globe.

The following chapter focuses on the recent social, political, and economic transformation of indigenous nations which have successfully established local sovereignty over the land, culture, and natural wealth without the assistance of the rights-based system of legal changes initiated by CELDF or other progressive environmental groups. Specific attention is directed to two indigenous communities in southern Mexico, the Zapatista Army of National Liberation (aka the Zapatista) in Chiapas, and the indigenous P'urhépecha town of Cherán in Michoacán, in an exploration of the new initiatives of independent, indigenous nations that have embraced and incorporated a self-sustaining culture and the principle of self-governance into their polity.

BIBLIOGRAPHY

"2nd International Rights of Nature Tribunal: Lima" (2014) GARN, December. available at https://therightsofnature.org/lima-2014-tribunal/.

Adam, Adam Hussein (2012) "Report: Recognising Sacred Natural Sites and Territories in Kenya: An Analysis of How the Kenyan Constitution, National and International Laws Can Support the Recognition of Sacred Natural Sites and Their Community Governance Systems," available at https://cmsdata.iucn.org/downloads/gaiasns_1.pdf.

"Advancing Legal Rights Nature: Timeline" (2018) Community Environmental Legal Defense Fund (accessed 21 November 2018), available at https://celdf.org/rights/rights-of-nature/rights-nature-timeline/

"American Indian in 1890 " (2020) Native American Netroots (accessed 15 May 2020), available at https://nativeamericannetroots.net/diary/1716.

Andersen, Pamela Jacquelin (2017) "Indigenous Peoples Are Dying for a Global War for Their Lands, Climate Home News, 13 September.

Barros, Maria Valeria (2015) "The Constitution of the Republic of Ecuador: Pachamama Has Rights," Environment & Society 11 (2015), available at https://www.environmentandsociety.org/arcadia/constitution-republic-ecuador-pachamama-has-rights.

Berry, Thomas (1999) The Great Work: Our Way into the Future. NY: Broadway Books.

Bioneers (2020) "Bioneers Partners with Community Environmental Legal Defense Fund on Rights of Nature in Indigenous Communities" (accessed 15 May 2020).

Bolivia: Pacto de Unidad Exige al Gobierno la Aprobación de la Ley de la Madre Tierra [Bolivia: The Pact of Unity Requires the Government to Approve the Law of Mother Earth]" (2011) Enlace Indigena, 18 July, available at https://movimientos.org/node/19600?key=19600.

Borie, Maud & Mike Hulme (2015) "Framing Global Biodiversity: IPBES Between Mother Earth and Ecosystem Services," Environmental Science and Policy 54: 487-498.

Borras, Susana (2016) "New Transitions from Human Rights to the Environment to the Rights of Nature," 5 Transnational Environmental Law 5(1):113–43.

Boyd, David R. (2017) The Rights of Nature: A Legal Revolution That Could Save the World. Toronto, Canada: ECW Press.

"Brazil 'Invites Deforestation' With Overhaul of Environmental Law" (2018) Guardian, 1 March.

Burdon, Peter (2011) Exploring Wild Law: The Philosophy of Earth Jurisprudence. Cambridge, MA: Wakefield Press.

Calmon, Miguel Mariana Oliveira & Rachel Biderman (2019) "The Other Brazilian Rainforest: Why Restoration of the Atlantic Forest Can Help Tackle Climate Change," World Resources Institute, 14 August.

"Canada Votes 'No' as UN Native Rights Declaration Passes" (2007) CBC, 13 September.

Charny, Israel W. (1999) Encyclopedia of Genocide. Santa Barbara, CA: ABC-CLIO.

Churchill, Ward (1997) A Little Matter of Genocide: Holocaust and Denial in the Americas 1492 to the Present. San Francisco, CA: City Lights Publishers.

Churchill, Ward (1999) Acts of Rebellion: The Word Churchill Reader. London, UK: Routledge.

Churchill, Ward (2004) Kill the Indian, Save the Man: The Genocidal Impact of American Indian residential Schools. SF, CA: City Lights Publishers.

Cohen, Felix S. (1953) "The Erosion of Indian Rights," Yale Law Journal 62: 348-390.

Colorado Community Rights Network (2019) Lafayette Climate Bill of Rights (accessed 14 November 2019), available at https://cocrn.org/lafayette-cli mate-bill-rights/.

"Community Environmental Legal Defense Fund: Bringing Real Democracy and Protection to communities and Their Environments" (2016) Radical Ecological Democracy, 6 April.

Community Environmental Legal Defense Fund (2020) Community Rights Do-It-Yourself Guide to Lawmaking (accessed 15 May 2020), available at https://celdf.org/diyguide.pdf.

Cullinan, Cormac (2001) Wild Law: A Manifesto for Earth justice. Jackson, VT: Chelsea Green Publishing.

Dhooge, Lucien J. (2010) "Aguinda v. Chevron-Texaco: Discretionary Grounds for the Non-recognition of Foreign Judgments for Environmental Injury in the United States," Virginia Environmental Law Journal 28(2): 241-298.

Drugmand, Dana "N.H. Town Passes Law Recognizing Right to a Healthy Climate," Climate Liability News, 14 March.

Freeman, Andrew (2019) "Amazon Fires Could Accelerate Global Warming and Cause Lasting Harm to a Cradle of Biodiversity," Washington Post, 21 August.

Global Alliance for the Rights of Nature (2015) "Video: International Rights of Nature Tribunal Introduction, Global Alliance for the Rights of Nature," available at https://therightsofnature.org/rights-of-nature-tribunal-paris/.

Hall, Anthony J. (2003) The American Empire and the Fourth World: The Bowl with One Spoon. Montreal, Canada: McGill-Queen's University Press.

Harfuch, Andres, Mariana Bilinski & Andrea Ortiz (2016) "El Jurado Indí-genas en Argentina [Argentina's Indigenous Jury]," Juicio por Jurados y Procedimiento Penal, 25(2016), available at https://inecip.org/wp-content/uploads/JxJ-JusBaires-JuradoIndigena.pdf. The English version is available at https://inecip.org/wp-content/uploads/Argentina%C2%B4s-Indigenous-jury-by-Harfuch-Bilinski-and-Ortiz-6.pdf

"History of Earth Jurisprudence" (2020) The Ecozoic Times (accessed 15 May 2020), available at https://ecozoictimes.com/ecozoic-movements/earth-jur isprudence/history-of-earth-jurisprudence/

Ho-Chunk Nation Legislature (2015) "Acknowledgement of General Council Resolution 9/19/2015–09 and Legislative Action Regarding the Resolu-tion to Amend the Constitution and Provide for the Rights of Nature," 20 October.

International Court of Justice (ICJ) (1986) "Reports of Judgements, Advisory Opinions and Orders: Case Concerning Military and Paramilitary Activities in and Against Nicaragua," available at https://www.icj-cij.org/files/case-rel ated/70/070-19860627-JUD-01-00-EN.pdf

International Court of Justice (2004) "Legal Consequences of the Construction of a Wall in the Occupied Palestinian Territory, Advisory Opinion of 9 July, 2004," available at https://www.icj-cij.org/files/case-related/131/131-200 40709-PRE-01-00-EN.pdf.

"International Rights of Nature Tribunal, Final Verdict: Fifth International Rights of Nature Tribunal, Gathered in the City of Santiago De Chile, December 05, 2019: Resolution No.5/2019." (2019) 5 December, available at https://therightsofnature.org/wp-content/uploads/2020/03/VER DICT-TRIBUNAL-Chile-English-.pdf.

La Follette, Cameron and Chris Maser (2017) Sustainability and the Rights of Nature: An Introduction. Boca Raton, FL: CRC Press.

LaDuke, Winona (2019) "The Rights of Wild Rice," In These Times, 21 February.

Langevin, Michael (2016) *The Secrets of Amazon Shamans: Healing Traditions from South America*. Hertford, NC: Crossroad Press.

Lavoto, Robert (2015) "COP21: International Rights of Nature Tribunal Finds Corporations, Governments Guilty of Crimes Against Nature," Alernet, 10 December, available at https://www.alternet.org/environment/cop21-intern ational-rights-nature-tribunal-finds-corporations-governments-guilty-crimes.

Layton Robert & Peter Ucko (2000) The Archeology and Anthropology of Landscape: Shaping Your Landscape. London, UK: Routledge.

Lemkin, Raphael (2011) Lemkin on Genocide. Lanham, MD: Lexington Books.

Lerner, Sharon (2020) "How the Environmental Lawyer Won a Massive Judgment Against Chevron Lost Everything," The Intercept, 29 January.

Liptak, Adam (2005) "U.S. Says It Has Withdrawn from World Judicial Body," N.Y. Times, 10 March.

Linzey, Thomas (2009) Be the Change: How to Get What You Want in Your Community. Layton, UT: Gibbs Smith Publisher.

Macpherson, Elizabeth & Julia Torres Ventura (2019) "The Tour to Save the World: Colombia Wins the Yellow Jersey for the Rights of Nature," IUCN, International Union for Conservation of Nature, 3 September.

Marshall, Tyler (1986) "World Court Rules U.S. Aid to Contras is Illegal," LA Times, 28 June.

May, James R. & Erin Daly (2019) Global Judicial Handbook on Environmental Constitutionalism. Cambridge, UK: Cambridge University Press.

McNeish, John-Andrew (2013) Extraction, Protest and Indigeneity in Bolivia: The TEIPNIS Effect, Latin American and Caribbean Ethnic Studies 8(2): 221-242.

Milam, Robin R. (2014) "First Global Tribunal on Rights of Nature Hears 9 Cases," GARN, 17 January.

O'Malley, Vincent, Bruce Stirling & Wally Penetito (2013) The Treaty of Waitangi Companion: Maori and Pakeha from Tasman to Today. Auckland, New Zealand: Auckland University Press.

Pagliarini, Andre (2019) "What Indigenous Rights Have to Do with Fighting Climate Change," The New Republic, 7 August.

Pfister, Tom (2018) "Gaining Ground From Reclaimed Abandoned Mine Lands," Forbes, 3 September.

Pietari, Kyle (2016) "Ecuador's Constitutional Rights of Nature: Implementation, Impacts, and Lessons Learned," Willamette Environmental Law Journal (Fall 2016): 37–94.

"Ponca Nation of Oklahoma to Recognize the Rights of Nature to Ban Fracking" (2018) GARN, 29 January.

"Press Release: Colombia Supreme Court Rules That Amazon Region is 'Subject of Rights'" (2018) CELDF, 4 April.

Ramsden, Che (2015) "International Rights of Nature Tribunal: Pachamama vs. ' Macho Papas,'" Open Democracy, 9 December.

Recinos, Ada (2014) "First International Tribunal on Rights of Nature: Inaugural Session in Ecuador Admits Nine Cases," Amazon Watch, 21 January.

Recinos, Ada (2019) "New Report: European and North American Companies Support Soy, Cattle, and Timber Companies Responsible for Recent Surge in Amazon Deforestation," Amazon Watch, 25 April.

"Revised Brazilian Forest Code May Lead to Increased Legal Deforestation in Amazon" (2019) Phys.org, 7 January.

Rogers, Sarah (2014) "Frustrated Nunavut Protesters Look to Federal MP for Support," NUNATSIAQ Online, 23 July, available at https://www.nunatsiaqonline.ca/stories/article/65674frustrated_nunavut_protesters_look_to_federal_government_for_support/.

Romero, Simon & Clifford Krauss (2011) "Ecuador Judge Orders Chevron to Pay $9 Billion," NY Times, 14 February.

Scanlan, Melissa K. (2016) Law and Policy for a New Economy: Sustainable, Just, and Democratic. Northampton, MA: Edward Elgar Pub.

Schipani, Andres (2010) "Grassroots Summit Calls for International Climate Court," Guardian, 23 April.

Schuele, Waleria (2015) "Giving Nature Legal Rights, Tribunal Puts Environmental Damage on Trial," ProJourno, 4 December.

Smith, Gar (2009) "In Ecuador, Tree Now Have Rights," Earth Island Journal 23(winter 2009), available at https://www.earthisland.org/journal/index.php/magazine/entry/in_ecuador_trees_now_have_rights/

"Texaco/Chevron Lawsuits (re Ecuador)" (2020) Business & Human Rights Resource Center (accessed 15 May 2020), available at https://www.business-humanrights.org/en/texacochevron-lawsuits-re-ecuador

Tucker, Mary Evelyn John Grim, and Andrew Angyal (2019) Thomas Berry: A Biography, NY: Columbia University Press.

Tutohu Whakatupua (2012) "Agreement Between Whanganui Iwi and the Crown." 30 August, available at https://www.govt.nz/dmsdocument/3706.pdf

United Nations (2008) "Israel's 'Enormous Web of Unlawful Practices' Devastating Palestinian Society, Palestine's Observer Says, as Fourth Committee Debates Situation in Territory," 4 November.

U.S. Constitution (1787), available at https://constitutionus.com/

Velasco, Luis Francisco Valle (2013) The Rights of Mother Earth in Bolivia. Scotts Valley, CA: CreateSpace Independent Publishing.

Vidal, John (2011) "Bolivia Enshrines Natural World's Rights with Equal Status for Mother Earth, Guardian, 10 April.

Watson, Irene (2018) Indigenous Peoples as Subjects of International Law: We Were Here First. NY: Routledge.

"White Earth Band Enacts First-of-Its Kind Rights of Nature Law" (2019) IC Magazine, 7 February.

Williams, Timothy (2019) "Legal Rights for Lake Erie? Voters Ohio City Will Decide," NY Times, 17 February.

World People's Conference on Climate Change and the Rights of Mother Earth (2010), available at https://therightsofnature.org/universal-declaration/.

Zartner, Dana (2019) "How Giving Legal Rights to Nature Could Help Reduce Toxic Algae Blooms in Lake Erie," The Conversation, 10 September.

CHAPTER 7

The Original Nation's Path to Recognition Under International Law: The Sovereignty-Making of Zapatista, Cherán, and Neuquén

ONAIL holds that the legal recognition of the nation under international law is important in establishing the nation's right to self-determination. Nonetheless, achieving such recognition has been a tortuous process. Chief Deskaheh of the Haudenosaunee Six-Nation Confederacy in North America and Te Haahi Ratana of New Zealand's Maori Nation first attempted to gain legal recognition of their nations and peoples under international law in the aftermath of World War I in the 1920s. They sought access to the League of Nations in order to contest the state's failure to respect and honor their treaty rights before the international legal community. The League of Nations determined that treaties between the states and the nations were *domestic* matters and denied the nations' legal standing before the international community and access to remedies under international law.[1] This characterization of the nation's affairs as "domestic" issues to be solved within the state domain established legal precedent for the subsequent negotiation of rights of the nation under international law.[2]

---

[1] *See* Smith (2018). See also Woo (2003); *see also* Bhatia (2012, pp. 159–171).

[2] *See* Burns (2013, pp. 154–155).

© The Author(s), under exclusive license to Springer Nature Switzerland AG 2021
H. Fukurai and R. Krooth, *Original Nation Approaches to Inter-National Law*,
https://doi.org/10.1007/978-3-030-59273-8_7

Major trends of indigenous nationalism, or political and economic independence of the nation and people, only began to emerge under international law in the post-WWII era. The 1948 Universal Declaration of Human Rights (UDHR) became the first postwar international document to recognize the necessity to protect the rights of the nation and people. In 2007, to proclaim the place of the nation in the global community, the U.N. General Assembly adopted the U.N. Declaration on the Rights of Indigenous Peoples (UNDRIP), which established the need for free prior informed consent (FPIC) and demanded respect for the nations' collective rights to their ancestral homeland, culture, identity, management systems, self-determination, and the application of international legal standards in negotiations and agreements.[3]

The intent of UNDRIP was noble and significant, but it was not legally binding and lacked an effective enforcement mechanism in its signatory states. Thus, unsustainable corporate development projects continued to destroy the biological and cultural diversity, ecosystems, and traditional knowledge that had historically sustained the original nation and people. Furthermore, many states adopted UNDRIP and supported the nation's right to self-determination only as long as those rights did not directly interfere with the territorial integrity of their own state system and policies. As stated earlier, four leading states—the U.S., Canada, Australia, and New Zealand—voted against the adoption of UNDRIP. These are states that have historically pursued settler-state colonial policies to subordinate, if not to exterminate altogether, original nations and peoples.[4]

The first section of this chapter explores an independent movement by the original nation, indigenous activists, and political supporters that has thus far achieved some degree of success in attaining independence: the Zapatista Army of National Liberation (aka the Zapatista) in Chiapas, Mexico. Since its declaration of popular uprising in 1994, the Zapatista has created the Rebel Zapatista Autonomous Municipalities in a substantial range of territory in Chiapas, the southernmost state of Mexico.

---

[3] *See* United Nations (2008). For the significance of international law and the rights of indigenous peoples, see Thompson (1987), Brolmann (1993), Chakma and Jensen (2001), Anaya (2000), Castellino and Walsh (2005), Gilbert (2016), Iankova et al. (2016), Tobin (2016), Watson (2016), Barelli (2018), Nielsen and Jarrat-Snider (2020).

[4] The four countries later reversed their position. See Morin (2017).

Many indigenous organizations, including its military troops, were organized through the active participation of Zapatista women. They aligned their political ideologies with those of the wider alter-globalization and anti-neoliberal social organizations, seeking indigenous sovereignty and indigenous control over local resources, land, the nature, and ecosystems.

The second section explores the Municipio of Cherán in the state of Michoacán, Mexico, examining the strategies and philosophies that propelled them to establish their regional autonomy and build a self-governed community. The indigenous P'urhépecha town of Cherán has practiced self-governance since 2011 as a result of the "Cherán Revolution." In April 2011, after many decades of illegal logging, kidnapping, extortion, murders, and sexual violence unleashed by illegal loggers and drug trafficking cartels, the popular uprising led by local women finally succeeding in throwing out the mayor, the entire police apparatus, politicians, illegal loggers, and drug gangs, and then moving on to create a self-sustaining and self-governing community. Cherán's autonomy as an indigenous P'urhépecha community has now been recognized by the Mexican government.

The third section examines yet another state-supported legal strategy to protect the original nation, people, the nature, and ecosystems. In 2011, the Province of Neuquén in Argentina adopted the jury trial, known as *El Jurado Indigena* (the indigenous jury), for the first time in its state history. This affirmative jury trial has mandated the equal representation of indigenous people and nonindigenous peoples, in cases when the one accused of alleged crimes was a member of the indigenous nation. This jury structure also required the equal representation of women and men among its 12-member jury. This section examines the historical background of such innovative adjudicative structures, dating back to the Roman civil trial, known as the *Recuperatores* (the international jury with mixed nationalities), in the Mediterranean city-state under Roman control in 200 BCE, as well as the Jury *de Medietate Linguae* (the split jury) which was first instituted in England in the early thieteenth century, in which half of the jury was composed of Jews and the other half were non-Jewish groups, so as to ensure trial fairness and verdict legitimacy.

The Nation of Mapuche and their activists in Neuquén have been protecting their ancestral land from the state and corporate outreach and have been targeted for prosecution as environmental terrorists and insurgents. Similar to the Jury *de Medietate Linguae*, the indigenous jury in Neuquén has provided indigenous activists with much-needed protection from overzealous state prosecution, as evidenced in a 2017 trial in which the Mapuche woman leader was acquitted by the hybrid jury of an attempted murder charge.

1   THE ZAPATISTA UPRISING IN CHIAPAS, MEXICO

On January 1, 1994, the Zapatista Army of National Liberation, known as *Ejercito Zapatista de Liberacion Nacional* (EZLN) or Zapatista, rose up in the southern Mexican town of San Cristobal de las Casas, Chiapas under slogans for humanity and against globalization and neoliberalism. Soon after the Zapatista uprising in Chiapas, the EZLN, made up of many rural poor peasants, including indigenous peoples, announced the adoption of the Women's Revolutionary Law, a set of ten gender-equality laws that granted rights to women in the areas of marriage, children, work, health, education, political and military participation, and protection from violence. The EZLN membership also included supporters in urban sectors, both domestic and international. Subcomandante Marcos, the most prominent and frequently identified member of the EZLN leadership, for example, was not himself indigenous. He described the Zapatista cause in the following declaration: "We are a product of 500 years of struggle: first against slavery, then during the War of Independence against Spain led by insurgents, then to avoid being absorbed by North American imperialism ... We, the men and women, are conscious that the war that we have declared is our last resort, but also a just one. The dictators are applying an undeclared genocidal war against our people for many years. ... We declare that we will not stop fighting until the basic demands of our people have been met by forming a government of our country that is free and democratic."[5]

Mexico has the largest indigenous population in the Americas, with 17 million people and 78 indigenous nations, which make up 21.5% of the entire population.[6] One study showed that 28% of Mexicans identified themselves as either predominantly or totally Indian, and more than 7% of the population remained either complete or partial indigenous

---

[5] "General Command of the EZLN, First Declaration of the Lacondona Jungle: EZLN's Declaration of War, Today We Say 'Enough is Enough! (Ya Basta!)" (1993).

[6] INEGI (2015, p. 3).

language speakers.[7] Indigenous Maya people of the Tzeltal Nation and the Tzotzil Nation, for example, have lived in the highlands of Chiapas for centuries. Together with other highland Maya people, Tzeltal and Tzotzil people joined in the 1994 Zapatista uprising, and indigenous women actively participated in the Zapatista army, holding prominent leadership positions, including Comandante Esther, a Tzeltal woman who became a spokesperson for the Zapatistas.[8] Comandante Ramona, a Tzotzil woman, became the first Zapatista member to speak in the Mexican Congress, where she expressed the plight of the indigenous nations, peoples, women, and other underrepresented and marginalized communities in rural Mexico.[9]

Despite the diversity of indigenous nations, the Mexican government has a history of disregarding its diverse populations. It was not until the 1992 revision of the Mexican Constitution that the government officially recognized that "the Mexican nation has a multicultural composition, stemming originally from its indigenous communities."[10]

The 1992 Constitutional amendment also included the modification of Article 27 to allow privatization of collective peasant holdings, the rights to which were previously guaranteed in the 1917 Constitution and had also been the cornerstone of Emiliano Zapata's armed uprising of 1910–1919 during the Mexican Revolution. Under the historic Article 27 in the 1917 Mexican Constitution, Indian communal landholdings were protected from sale or privatization. Newly amended Article 27 in 1992 effectively took that protection away from indigenous communities, stating that "Ownership of the lands and waters within the boundaries of the national territory is vested originally in the Nation, which has had, and has the right to transfer title thereof to private persons, thereby constituting private property."[11]

The Zapatista's uprising on New Year's Day of 1994 paralleled the date on which the North America Free Trade Agreement (NAFTA) was put into effect. NAFTA had been signed between Mexico, the U.S., and Canada and was believed to be destructive of the livelihood of many

---

[7] Central Intelligence Agency (2019).

[8] Danver (2012, p. 166).

[9] Ibid., p. 167.

[10] Ibid., p. 641. See also Herrera (2015).

[11] Kelly (1994, p. 542).

independent *campesinos* in Mexico. Indigenous farmers feared the loss of their lands and the negative impacts of the U.S. dumping of the highly government-subsidized, cheap substitute crops, including Mexico's main staple of corn, into the Mexican food market. Many feared that they would be driven out of agriculture, with many more losing farms to become contract workers or being forced to migrate to the U.S. to seek jobs. In 1994, U.S. Attorney General Janet Reno announced the execution of Operation Gatekeeper, to close and militarize the U.S.–Mexico border in order to prevent the projected influx of Mexican farmers, preventing them from migrating to the U.S. in order to find jobs in a less-stable, secondary labor market.[12]

The Zapatista additionally relied on Mexico's mainstream NGOs in all of Mexico, using civil society that also opposed globalization as a political leverage to force Mexican politicians and government officials into a prolonged negotiation process, rather than allowing the government to settle the rebellion and armed uprising in Chiapas with a quick military solution.[13] The Zapatista's initial political objective was to transform the polity of Mexico and energize civil society in Mexico and neighboring regions.

The Zapatista signed the San Andres Accords with the Mexican government in 1996, which granted them autonomy, recognition, and rights to participate in the political process, as well as the preservation of natural resources within the lands occupied by them. Also in 1996, the Zapatista also helped organize the National Indigenous Congress (*Congreso Nacional Indígena* or CNI), the first nationwide indigenous congress ever held in Mexico, after the call from the EZLN to all indigenous nations and peoples to participate in the Special National Forum on Indigenous Rights and Culture, as a follow-up to the San Andres Accords that the Zapatista signed with the Mexican government earlier in the same year. The CNI received support from a wide political spectrum, from labor unions to student organizations and feminist groups. Between 1996 and 1998, many original nations and indigenous communities also established political alliances with the CNI and the Zapatista and demanded

---

[12] Sander (1995).

[13] Day (2005, pp. 190–192).

the constitutional recognition of rights of indigenous nations and peoples in Mexico.[14]

The Zapatista recognized that Mexico has already lost its national sovereignty in the international community and had been captured by the powerful matrix of international finances, political forces, and neoliberal policies. The Zapatista thus began to "internationalize" their efforts, making effective use of the media and internet cyber-space to build strong solidarity with other indigenous nations and peoples, as well as feminist organizations, labor and trade activists, farmworkers, student groups, progressive political organizations, and other grassroots environmental groups across the globe.[15] In July 1996, the Zapatista organized the First Intercontinental Gathering for Humanity and Against Neoliberal Practices, which attracted large numbers of delegates from 42 countries. In 1997, the EZLN initiated the formation of the Peoples' Global Action Against "Free" Trade and the WTO (aka PGA) and developed a network of organizations that included large workers' movements in Brazil (*Movimento Sem Terra*), European anti-authoritarian groups such as Reclaim the Street (RTS), Play Fair Europe!, and Ya Basta! in Italy, indigenous communities such as Movement for the Survival of the Ogoni People (MOSOP) in Nigeria, Karnataka State Farmers' Association in India, and other progressive environmental organizations that opposed globalization and neoliberalism on varied grounds.[16] Many of the same groups were involved in the uprising for the Battle of Seattle in 1999, including PGA, Direct Action Network (DAN), and the first Independent Media Center (IMC), and they had developed close links with the Zapatista.[17]

The Zapatista's activities inspired and promoted a philosophical "cocktail" of multiple progressive ideologies through their outreach efforts to build strong solidarity. Among these were ideologies related to indigenous knowledge on self-sustenance and self-governance; anarchism that stressed direct "on-the-ground" actions of physical resistance, opposition, and confrontation with state power; feminist principles for achieving gender equality; and progressive Euro-American democratic traditions

---

[14] Solano (2007).

[15] See generally Subcomandante Marcos and De Leon (2011).

[16] Austin (1997).

[17] Callahan (2005).

for political and economic equality. The Zapatista advocated the possibility of reimagining an alternative world—through direct, horizontal, and "full-community" participatory democracy, fighting for rights to self-determination, and the construction of social and political relationships among indigenous nations, peoples, women, students, labor organizers, and grassroots environmental activists in Mexico and across the globe.

2   The Municipio of Cherán in Michoacán, Mexico

On April 15, 2011, the Municipio government of Cherán in Michoacán was forcefully taken over by a group of women and men who used rocks and fireworks to expel the police force and politicians. When the residents realized that the organized criminal gangs had attempted to seize the forests near the community water source, they set up barricades at all entry points into the town. They also blocked roads leading to the forests on a nearby mountain that had been subject to illegal loggings by those who were closely affiliated with the Mexican drug cartel *La Familia Michoacana* and the *Caballeros Templarios* (Knights Templar).[18] Townspeople soon expelled the gangs, along with local authorities and politicians who had been bribed by organized criminal organizations. Cherán residents also demanded that the federal and state governments guarantee the community's security under Article 2 of the Mexican Constitution, which granted self-governance and self-defense rights to the indigenous nations, stipulating that the Mexican Constitution "recognizes and the protects the indigenous peoples' right to self-determination and, consequently, the right to autonomy."[19] Article 2 also defines the indigenous community as a collective that "constitute[s] a cultural, economic and social unit settled in a territory and that recognized its own authorities, according to their customs."[20]

The autonomous municipal government of Cherán was then established, composed of twelve council members who were elected directly and democratically by all adult residents in the town. The townspeople also decided to revitalize the P'urhépecha custom that stressed reciprocity

---

[18] Ojeda (2014).

[19] Mexican Constitution, art. 2.

[20] Ibid.

and mutual aid, and Cherán residents chose to make contributions to the community work aimed at maintaining the self-governing society. For example, each member of the community, including those who have migrated to the U.S. (i.e., approximately 40% of the population), contributes funds, labor, or time to support community work. After three months of round-the-clock vigils, the community organized their own forest patrols to prevent illegal logging, drug corruption, and gang activities.[21] They also formed *Guardias Comunitarias* (community guards) and *Rondas Comunitarias* (community police), who were made up of women and men working to protect their new community in the heart of the P'urhépecha Nation.

As the second largest empire in Mexico, and contemporary of the Aztecs at the time of the Spanish conquest, the P'urhépecha Nation has maintained a distinct culture throughout their history.[22] Of the more than 100,000 P'urhépecha people who live in the state of Michoacan, 91,000 still speak the native language along with Spanish, while 15,000 speak no Spanish.[23] P'urhépecha people have been known for their craftsmanship in bronze, copper, stone, wood, and lacquerware since pre-Columbian times. Because of their invention of bronze tools and weaponries, the P'urhépecha Nation was not conquered by the Aztecs and was able to establish an extensive network of trade routes and cultural relationships with indigenous communities in the American Southwest and South America.[24] Yet as a consequence of the Spanish conquest and then the Mexican Revolution, the P'urhépecha Nation and people began to suffer from poverty, discrimination, alcohol and drug addiction, lack of education, and loss of language and culture. After the signing of NAFTA in 1994, the failure of small farms became endemic, and the migration of P'urhépecha people to California accelerated.[25]

The Municipality of Cherán, with more than 12,000 residents, lies in the homeland of the P'urhépecha Nation in the northwestern region of the State of Michoacán. Cherán in the P'urhépecha language means "a

[21] Soloff (2018).

[22] Danver (2012, p. 153).

[23] Ibid.

[24] Ibid.

[25] Ibid.

place of fear," reflecting the dangers inherent in a landscape of irregular peaks and chasms. However, the fearless P'urhépecha resistance to political corruption, drug trafficking, and illegal logging has led to the strengthening of community ties and to new demands on the federal and state governments for the recognition of its sovereignty and rights to self-determination. Since the autonomous government was established, Cherán in the state of Michoacán has not had a slaying or any other serious crimes. This is despite the fact that in 2019, Michoacán had the fifth highest number of homicides in Mexico ($n = 2,625$), and the U.S. State Department issued a warning to U.S. citizens not to travel to Michoacán for reasons of danger and security.[26]

2.1   P'urhépecha Women and Their Revolutionary Role

As with the Zapatista movement, the democratization of the Municipio of Cherán was led by indigenous women who initially organized secret meetings to develop their plan to transform the city. They had witnessed years of killings and kidnaps that became routine in Cherán. Although Mexico's drug cartels had once profited mainly on the drug trades, they had begun to diversify, seeking to dominate in the business of lucrative timber industries, which has been the foundation of Cherán's economy.[27] P'urhépecha women had been going to the forest and trying to reason with and persuade the armed men for years, but to no avail.

On the day of the mass revolt, April 15, 2011, soon after the Church bell rang alerting the arrival of illegal loggers, a group of P'urhépecha women who had covered their faces began to build a human wall to blockade the loggers' pick-up trucks. They also took some of the illegal loggers as hostages, and set off homemade fireworks, alerting the community to the arrival of the gangs, and calling for support and solidarity. The townspeople gathered, coming together with firearms, shovels, and rocks in their hands, demanding that the drug cartels, local police, and politicians all leave.[28] After a tense confrontation, local police and politicians

---

[26] "States with the Highest Number of Homicides in Mexico in 2019" (2020).

[27] Pressly (2016).

[28] Miroff (2013). ("Michoacán … has been a smoldering battleground for years … [and] drug gangs also squeeze local businesses and villagers with schemes to extort payments.")

were driven out of Cherán. Shortly after that, all political parties were abolished.

P'urhépecha women then spearheaded efforts to rehabilitate the deforested ancestral homeland. Cherán was made up of 27,000 hectares of forest, which had been substantially destroyed, leaving a mere 7,000 hectares, thereby affecting the lives and self-sustaining culture of the P'urhépecha. Since the autonomous government was established, seedlings for reforestation have been nurtured in the town's own tree nursery managed by women, and more than one million trees have been replanted.[29] While Cherán receives state and federal funding, its autonomy as an indigenous P'urhépecha community has been recognized and underwritten by the Mexican government. The city ban on political parties has also been upheld by the courts, confirming its right not to participate in local, state, or federal elections.[30]

In a similar way to the Zapatista movement, Cherán has maintained its autonomy and sovereignty through its international media campaigns and open collaborations with other autonomous communities, as well as through its effective use of alternative media. The documentation needed to protect the indigenous traditions has been disseminated through such social media as a blog, Facebook page, and YouTube channel. Additionally, in 2014, TV Cherán was launched to help the voice of the people of Cherán to be heard by other indigenous nations and peoples who are struggling to obtain their own independence and sovereignty across the world.[31]

In January 2018, the murder of a P'urhépecha activist, 32-year-old Guadalupe Campanur Tapia, resurrected the horrific memory of violence, rape, and murders in pre-2011 Cherán. Campanur's strangled body with signs of rape and torture was found on the side of a highway in the nearby municipality of Chilchota, nearly 30 km north of Cherán. Campanur had been involved in the fight against gang activities and violence in Cherán, helping to overthrow the corrupt local government in April 2011, and participating in local security patrols, including those in municipal forests.[32] Her murder was the first homicide in the municipality since

---

[29] Lopez (2020). See also Agren (2018).

[30] Pressly (2016).

[31] Salazar (2015).

[32] "Community Shaken by Woman's Murder" (2018).

2012. The perpetrator of her death has yet to be found, and a score of indigenous woman activists have also been murdered in neighboring Mexican states and regions. In June 2017, indigenous radio host Marcela de Jesus Natalia was murdered in the Mexican state of Guerrero, and was the sixth journalist killed that year. In June 2018, Juana Raymundo, a 25-year-old indigenous Mayan Ixil and Guatemala nurse who also fought for indigenous rights, was tortured and then murdered. She had been a coordinator of Peasant Development Committee (*Comite de Desarrollo Campesino*, or CODECA) and a prominent member of the Movement for the Liberation of Peoples (*Movimiento para la Liberacion* de los Pueblos, or MLP), which served as a political arm of CODECA. She was the eighth member of the CODECA to be murdered.

Violence against indigenous women originates not only from organized crime and their so-called "hit units," but also from government authorities, including politicians and law enforcement agencies at the local, state, and federal levels.[33] A recent study by the Mexico's Center for Environmental Rights (CEMDA) found that "43 percent of attacks carried out against the environmentalists came from the [government] authorities themselves."[34] Parallel to the increased assassination of indigenous women activists, a strong sense of impunity has developed among organized criminal groups and government authorities, due largely to the inequities of Mexico's criminal justice system, as well as the inability of the government to prosecute those who have targeted indigenous women, environmental activists, and earth protectors. The following section explores the innovative methods devised in Argentina to develop close collaboration with state sectors in order to protect the rights of indigenous activists and land protectors from overzealous state prosecution and ideological condemnation by private corporate sectors.

3   THE MODERN-DAY "*JURY DE MEDIETATE LINGUAE*": "*EL JURADO INDÍGENA*" (THE INDIGENOUS JURY)

After many years of political struggles and social movements by grassroots lawyers, political activists, and indigenous organizers to democratize the

---

[33] Morris (1991), Botello and Rivera (2000), Morris (2009), Nagle (2010), and Jaramillo (2019).

[34] "Cultural Survival, Observations on the State of Indigenous Women's Rights in Mexico: Alternative Report Submission" (2018, p. 14).

legal system of Argentina, the system known as *"El Jurado Indígena* (the Indigenous Jury)" was finally introduced in 2011. Argentina thus became the first country in the world to require the inclusion of indigenous jurors in the adjudication of criminal disputes. The law mandated that the jury must have equal representation of indigenous and nonindigenous jurors randomly selected from the community in the impanelment of the 12-member criminal jury.

The establishment of the hybrid jury in Argentina, a country that had suffered under political repression by the military dictatorship from 1974 to 1983, is truly a remarkable achievement. In examining the original creation of the multiracial or ethnic jury, we must go back to the Roman Republic more than two thousand years ago, when Rome had successfully colonized the multiplicity of indigenous societies, autonomous nations, and other nucleated city-states in and around the Mediterranean region, including southern Europe, the Middle East, northern Africa, and beyond. In the colonized city-states, towns, and municipalities, the Roman government adopted the hybrid judicial system called *Recuperatores*, which selectively incorporated the local culture, legal tradition, and local people in resolving the disputes that involved litigants who resided in colonized regions. The tribunal of *Recuperatores* was adopted to solve private and civil disputes according to the following procedural precepts: (1) applicable law should be the legal customs of the tribe or city-state of which the litigant is a member; (2) access to courts is restricted to members of the court-keeping tribe or city-state; (3) the solution arrived at by this special tribunal is for cases of mixed citizenship; (4) the number of laypersons included as court's members range from three to five; and (5) the application of *voir dire* is used for lay-judges selection, i.e., a principle in which candidates are potentially eliminated through questions and answers until the final adjudicators are chosen.[35]

Private and civil disputes were thus resolved with the participation of two mixed groups of citizens. The tribunal of *Recuperatores* was characterized by its speed and informality, as legal disputes were decided within ten days from the start of private suit.[36] The resolution of disputes by *Recuperatores* served to provide a considerable sense of trial fairness and verdict legitimacy to people in the city and municipality in the colonized

---

[35] Dawson (1960, pp. 20–21).

[36] Ibid.

regions. The use of the mixed-citizenship panel in deliberating the civil disputes also created a strong sense of semi-sovereignty shared among local residents in many Mediterranean city-states that were subjected into Roman jurisdiction. While the true intent of *Recuperatores* may have been to "pacify" the colonized subjects and to maintain the stable relationship between the Roman occupiers and those of Mediterranean city-states, the fact that the use of this mixed-citizenship tribunal lasted even up until 100 CE, during the era of Roman Empire, suggests that the sense of trial fairness and verdict legitimacy had been widely accepted among the colonized population.[37]

Nearly one thousand years after the Roman conquest of the British Isles, a similar mixed tribunal emerged in late twelfth-century Medieval England. King Richard I of England enacted a charter to give Jews the right to the jury *de medietate linguae*, a half-Jewish jury in both civil and criminal disputes.[38] This practice of mixed juries, with half English natives and half Jews, was essential in England because of the danger that inhered in allowing members of minority communities to be tried entirely by English jurors. The Latin term, *de medietate linguae*, literally meant the jury of a "half tongue or culture/language/tradition," for this affirmative jury method applied to people who spoke a foreign language or exercised a different alien culture. Due to mass riots and frequent violence in England against wealthy and influential Jews, who were then considered the King's property, a trial loss effectively diminished the King's wealth and power. While England subsequently banished all Jews in 1290, they were replaced as the King's financial agents by foreign merchants from Italy and other European countries who were also given the privilege of a trial *de medietate linguae*, i.e., a trial heard by a jury composed of two equal numbers of members: their own country persons and English persons qualified to serve as jurors. The King's economic motive was the underlying factor in the establishment of the first hybrid jury in England, which effectively served to prevent diminution of the King's resources and wealth. However, this affirmative, culturally mixed jury provided substantial fairness and protection against unfair verdicts derived from prejudice against ethnically and culturally marginalized groups in England, enduring for almost seven hundred years until 1870.

[37] Ibid.

[38] See generally Fukurai and Krooth (2003).

English colonies in North America inherited the English legal tradition, adopting the hybrid jury, which remained in practice from the sixteenth to the beginning of the twentieth century. In Northeastern regions, the Jury *de Medietate Linguae* had been applied in early trials involving American Indians, and by the eighteenth century, it had become routine whenever Indians were involved in major crimes. These states included Kentucky, Maryland, Massachusetts, Pennsylvania, New York, Virginia, and South Carolina.[39] Although the racially and nationally diverse jury had been in use at multiple state courts, the U.S. Supreme Court in *the U.S. v. Wood* (1936) abandoned the use of the hybrid jury at federal courts, stating that "the ancient rule under which an alien might have a trial by jury *de medietate linguae* ... no longer obtains."[40]

Because of the substantive appearance of trial fairness and protection against biased verdicts, the mixed jury was also adopted in other British commonwealth countries, including Aden, Barbados, Brunei, the Federated Malay States, Gold Coast, Johore, Kelantan, Kenya, Nigeria, North Borneo, Nyasaland, and New Zealand.[41] In criminal trials that raised potential issues involving clear cultural, ethnic, and racial differences and unmistakable elements of prejudice against the marginalized community, there has been a widespread consensus that the affirmative hybrid tribunal offers many benefits. Such an affirmative mixed jury may also provide an important mechanism of checks-and-balances necessary to insure that superior government officers, including the police, prosecutors, judges, and other legal specialists, do not discriminate against the marginalized segments of the indigenous nation and other nucleated communities.

3.1 El Jurado Indígena *(an Indigenous Jury) in Argentina*

While the mixed tribunals of *Recuperatores* and Jury *de Medietate Linguae* in varied forms had been historically used in multiple regions across the globe, none of these hybrid jury models had incorporated the inclusion of women to guarantee their representation in the trial proceeding. An unprecedented and innovative introduction of such an equitable jury

---

[39] Ramirez (1994, pp. 777–818).

[40] *U.S. v. Wood*, 299 U.S. at 132-33 (citing Crawford v. United States, 212 U.S. 183, 1908).

[41] Ramirez (1994).

model has taken place in recent times. For the first time in the history of lay-adjudication system, the gender-parity jury model was adopted, in which the twelve-member, all-layperson jury must be composed of an equal number of women and men.[42] Argentina became the first country to adopt such a model, through legislation adopted in the province of Neuquén in 2011, in Buenos Aires in 2013, and in Chaco in 2015.[43]

The provincial governments of Neuquén and, later, Chaco, went one step further than the gender-parity provision, by declaring that the twelve-member jury panel must also be equally composed of indigenous and nonindigenous members in cases when the defendant comes from the indigenous community. This hybrid jury model, known as *Jurado Indígena* (an indigenous jury), is somewhat similar to the hybrid tribunal that had solicited the participation of colonized subjects in the Mediterranean city-states under the Roman jurisdiction, Jews and other foreigners who resided in England, indigenous people in the U.S., and aboriginal populations in former British colonies throughout the world. The affirmative hybrid jury was applied to ensure the representation of indigenous voices in the adjudication of crimes allegedly committed by indigenous people, which is of critical importance, given that there are thirty-eight major indigenous groups in Argentina, with most of them living in the Argentine Provinces of Chaco and Neuquén. The Mapuche—whose name is derived from the words for "earth" and "people" in the Mapudungun language—is one of the most populous indigenous people in Argentina and Chile.[44] The split jury adopted in Chaco stipulates, "when the accused belongs to the Native People, Qom, Wichi or Mocovi, half the jury of twelve members shall consist compulsory for [must consist of] men and women of the same original community."[45] Similarly, Neuquén's jury "must be integrated, including alternates, by men and women equally. It will be required that at least half the jury belongs to the same social and cultural environment of the accused. It will also try, whenever possible, to have seniors, adults and youth in the panel of juries."[46]

---

[42] See generally Scherr (2016).

[43] Ibid.

[44] Danver, supra, note 137.

[45] Harfuch et al. (2016).

[46] Ibid.

The Vaca Muerta Formation in the Neuquen Basin has been known as the host rock for major deposits of shale oil and shale gas. Multinational fossil fuel industries have been involved in the development of Vaca Muerta that has been divided into industrial blocks. The industrial consortium for development included Petroleo Brasileiro S.A. (or Petrobras) of Brazil; Royal Dutch Shell of the Netherlands; Chevron and ExxonMobil of the U.S.; Americas Petrogas of Canada; Repsol S.A. of Spain; Wintershall of Germany; and Pan American Energy of Argentina, among many others. The indigenous nations in Argentina have opposed the extractive activities in their ancestral homeland and have been arrested and prosecuted by the state government. Argentina, since its independence from Spain in 1810, has expropriated the indigenous lands and subjugated indigenous people as a labor force. It was not until 1983 that indigenous nations were able to begin to effectively protest state policies of cultural repression, land appropriation, and forced assimilation. Today, Argentina has more than 30 indigenous nations, including Mapuche, Toba, Guarani, Diaguita, Kolla, Quechua, Wichí, Comechingon, and many others.[47]

The adoption of the indigenous jury has had a significant impact upon the protection of ancestral lands, ecosystems, and the integrity of indigenous nations and people. The first use of the indigenous jury took place in 2015 in the mining town of Zapala, Neuquén, where indigenous activists and environmental protectors have long participated in demonstrations against ecologically unsustainable, state-supported corporate projects. Zapala is situated at the confluence of national and provincial roads to the Andes and Chile, and the specific corporations involved in the mining project there have included the Apache Corporation, a U.S. petroleum and natural gas exploration and production company headquartered in Houston, Texas; Repsol S.A., Spain's energy company based in Madrid; and Argentina's own state-run energy corporation, YPF (*Yacimientos Petrolieros Fisales*).

In December 2012, a criminal case began when a court officer, together with representatives of the Apache Oil Company, corporate security guards, and a contingent of police, arrived with an eviction notice for indigenous residents who had long resisted extractive activities in their ancestral homeland. Indigenous people defended themselves against their forceful removal from their land by throwing stones at the entourage of

---

[47] "Censo Nacional de Poblacion, Hogares y Viviendas 2010: Pueblos Originarios: Region Noroeste Argentino: Serie D N 1" (2020).

visitors, thus hitting and injuring a court officer and damaging a vehicle. The public prosecutor charged Mapuche leader Relme Ñamku with attempted homicide and charged two other land protectors with serious damages to properties. Prior to the trial, in the province of Neuquén, 241 indigenous leaders and activists who had tried to defend their ancestral homeland had been charged with criminal offenses, and 60% of prosecuted cases were directly related to indigenous land struggles.[48] Additionally, more than 350 Mapuche residents had been prosecuted, and many of them were accused as usurpers of the very territories where they had lived for many generations.[49]

The trial began on October 28, 2015, with an indigenous jury composed of six men and six women, and six of the twelve were Mapuche members.[50] Over the next eight days of trial, many instances of human rights violation by international oil conglomerates were exposed, including the use of child labor, numerous oil spills, pollutions of community water sources, and multiple instances of violence against indigenous residents by paramilitary security guards hired by oil industries.[51] The testimony also revealed that, while these instances of violence and environmental damages had been reported to the Office of the Public Prosecutors, no action had been taken by the government.[52]

On November 4, 2015, after only two hours of deliberation, the jury handed down a not guilty verdict for the Mapuche leader and the two indigenous activists who had defended their land against the advances of oil exploitation in their ancestral land.[53] The gender and indigenous split jury system adopted in Neuquén had begun to exert a significant impact on the preservation of legal and socio-political rights of the indigenous nation and peoples in Argentina. Women's and all indigenous people's direct access to criminal trials as jurors further solidified their efforts to protect their ecosystems and the integrity of ancestral lands in Neuquén and neighboring regions. After the historic trial and acquittal verdict, Ñamku declared that "this decision marks a historic precedent. Now we

---

[48] Ibid.

[49] Amnistía Internacional (2017).

[50] Ibid.

[51] Cregan (2015).

[52] Ibid.

[53] Ibid. The indigenous leader was found guilty of simple damage to a vehicle.

have the enormous responsibility of bringing our message of resistance to all the indigenous peoples who are prosecuted and criminalized (across the globe)."[54]

4 Conclusions

ONAIL supports the international movements and organizing efforts for building strong solidarity and alliance across nations, peoples, and their supporters around the globe. In an era when no widespread internet was available for the original nation and people in the early 1990s, the Zapatista in the rugged mountains of Chiapas in southern Mexico succeeded in developing a direct and participatory democratic society. Escaping from the Mexican government's surveillance and intelligence monitoring, the rural poor of many farmers, indigenous women, and their supporters relied on the means of person-to-person communication, developing a deep social fabric of mutual support and strong solidarity in organizing a successful armed uprising whose mission was to explore the creation of a better, alternative world.

The Zapatista's uprising and declaration of autonomy in Mexico followed a similar history of large-scale movements in Haiti, the poorest country in the Western Hemisphere, where in 1990 the urban and rural poor in the slums and hills organized a grassroots movement to support the birth of another, alternative society. As the first African republic built on the successful slave revolution that lasted from 1791 to 1804 in the island of Hispaniola, Haiti had been subjected to brutal colonial and imperial projects largely unleashed by the U.S. and France, due to the "crime" of freeing themselves from the grips of colonial masters for the previous two hundred years. In 1990, in the first democratic election to take place in Haiti, the democratic movement successfully organized and elected a 37-year-old populist and liberation theology priest, Jean-Bertrand Aristide, as Haiti's first democratically elected president. Defeated was Marc Louis Bazin, a former World Bank official and Minister of Finance and Economy under the dictatorship of Jean-Claude Duvalier, who had been driven out of the country by a popular uprising in 1986. The election was backed by a vigorous grassroots movement,

[54] Ibid.

largely emerging from the urban and rural poor in the slums and impover-ished hills of Port-au-Prince. The election of Aristide began to transform the Haitian society, which was still the poorest country in the Western Hemisphere. However, the U.S. soon acted to undermine the demo-cratically elected government, with a U.S.-supported military coup taking place in September 1991. Marc Louis Bazin was soon appointed as prime minister by the military government that seized power after the coup.[55]

In contrast, the Zapatista and the Municipio of Cherán have thus far escaped the military wrath of the state. The Mexican government sent a large-scale military force to Chiapas to subdue the Zapatista autonomy in 1995. Then-President Ernesto Zedillo also decided to launch a military offense to capture Subcomandante Marcos and other Zapatista leaders after arrest warrants were issued against them. Although the Mexican army took action to restore the rule of law in the Zapatista-occupied territories, they failed to arrest Subcomandante Marcos and other EZLN leaders. Later, in 1997, the state paramilitary troops killed 45 indige-nous people, including 15 children and many women, using machetes and AK-47 assault rifles in the village of Acteal, Chiapas. The paramilitary group also attacked bishops of the Diocese of San *Cristóbal* de las Casas, Chiapas. Even though violent incidents continued, the Zapatista success-fully defended the further state military excursion and maintained their independence in the autonomous regions of Chiapas. The Zapatista and their uprising against the state seemed to have struck a powerful chord with a large segment of the Mexican population, indigenous nations, and grassroots environmental organizations across the globe.

The original nations of Argentina have relied on a distinct justice system to protect the nation, people, and the integrity of their ances-tral homeland. After decades of grassroots activism by political lawyers, legal scholars, environmental activists, and indigenous organizers, the Province of Neuquén introduced in 2011, for the first time in the world, a criminal jury trial system that guaranteed the equal representation of women and indigenous people. When the Mapuche woman leader who led the indigenous protest against state-assisted corporate mining projects in the homeland was arrested and prosecuted for the charge of attempted murder, she was subsequently acquitted by the hybrid jury that included six women and six indigenous jurors chosen from the local community.

---

[55] Horne (2015).

The strategies and methods used to protect the rights of indigenous people, nature and ecosystems have varied among the original nations. The Zapatistas have relied on armed uprisings and the powerful and active participation of indigenous women in prominent leadership positions, and have created a democratic and horizontally rooted community based on a culture of self-sustenance and self-governance. The Municipio of Cherán has also relied on full-scale uprisings against organized gang cartels, illegal loggers, corrupted politicians, party officials, and law enforcement personnel, all of whom have been physically driven out of the city. Women have also been active participants in Cherán's newly constituted government and community policing. The autonomy of the city has subsequently been established and recognized by the state. Argentina's innovative and affirmative jury model, as a realistic alternative to traditional criminal process, also represents a symbol of viable hope. In 2020, the Province of Mendoza has also decided to adopted the same hybrid jury in the resolution of civil disputes.[56] The original nation in Argentina can now rely on the civil jury trial to ensure that civil litigation involving the destruction and damage caused by corporate projects will be adjudicated by the indigenous- and gender-parity jury. ONAIL supports the further adoption of democratic and affirmative jury models in order to protect the rights of indigenous people, nature, and ecosystems in other states across the globe.

Bibliography

Agren, David (2018) "Mexican Indigenous Community That Ran Politicians Out of Town," Guardian, 3 April.

Amnesty International (2017) "Amnesty International Report 2016/17: The State of the World's Human Rights," available at https://www.amnesty.org/download/Documents/POL1048002017ENGLISH.PDF.

Anaya, S. James (2000) Indigenous People in International Law. Oxford, UK: Oxford University Press.

Austin, Accion Zapatista de (1997) "Peoples' Global Action Against 'Free' Trade and the World Trade Organizaton," 29 November, available at https://www.hartford-hwp.com/archives/25a/024.html.

---

[56] "Mendoza, Argentina: Governor Suarez Announced the Expansion of the Jury to More Crimes and the Implementation of the Civil Jury" (2020).

Barelli, Mauro (2018) *Seeking Justice in International Law: The Significance and Implications of the UN Declaration on the Rights of Indigenous Peoples*, NY: Routledge.

Bhatia, Amar (2012) "The South of the North: Building on Critical Approaches to International Law with Lessons from the Fourth World," 14 *Oregon Review of International Law* 131–176.

Botello, Nelson Arteaga & Adrian Lopez Rivera (2000) "Everything in This Job is Money: Inside the Mexican Police," 17 World Policy Journal 17(3): 61–70.

Brolmann, Catherine, Rene Lefeber & Majoline Zieck (1993) *Peoples and Minorities in International Law*. Dordrecht, Netherlands: Martinus Nijhoff.

Burns, Marcelle J. (2013) "Shifting Global Power and Shifting State Power." In Maguire et al., eds., Shifting Global Powers and International Law: Challenges and Opportunities. London, UK: Routledge.

Callahan, Manuel (2005) "Why Not Share a Dream? Zapatista as Political and Cultural Practice," Humboldt Journal of Social Relations 29(1): 6-37.

Castellino, Joshua and Niamh Walsh (2005) *International Law and Indigenous People*. Leiden: M. Nijhoff Publishers.

"Censo Nacional de Poblacion, Hogares y Viviendas 2010: Pueblos Originarios: Region Noroeste Argentino: Serie D N 1," (2020) INDEC (accessed 15 May 2020) at https://web.archive.org/web/20080611004448/http://www.indec.gov.ar/webcenso/ECPI/index_ecpi.asp.

Central Intelligence Agency (2019) The World Factbook (accessed 14 March 2019), available at https://www.cia.gov/library/publications/the-world-factbook/geos/mx.html

Chakma, Suhas & Marianne Jensen (2001) *Racism against Indigenous Peoples*. Copenhagen, Denmark: IWGIA.

"Community Shaken by Woman's Murder" (2018) Mexico News Daily, 24 January.

Cregan, Fionuala (2015) "Mapuche Leader Found 'Not Guilty' in Unprecedented Trial in Argentina," Intercontinental Cry, 6 November, available at https://intercontinentalcry.org/mapuche-leader-found-not-guilty-in-unprecedented-trial-in-argentina/.

"Cultural Survival, Observations on the State of Indigenous Women's Rights in Mexico: Alternative Report Submission" (2018), available at https://www.culturalsurvival.org/sites/default/files/CEDAW_Report_Mexico_2018.pdf.

Danver, Steven (2012) The Native Peoples of the World: An Encyclopedia of Groups, Cultures, and Contemporary Issues. Armonk, NY: Sharpe Reference.

Dawson, John Philip (1960) A History of Lay Judges. Cambridge, MA: Harvard University Press.

Day, Richard J.F. (2005) Gramsci is Dead: Anarchist Currents in the Newest Social Movements. London, UK: Pluto Press.

Fukurai, Hiroshi & Richard Krooth (2003) Race in the Jury Box: Affirmative Action in Jury Selection. Albany, NY: SUNY Press.

"General Command of the EZLN, First Declaration of the Lacondona Jungle: EZLN's Declaration of War, Today We Say 'Enough is Enough! (Ya Basta!)'" (1993), available at https://woocommerce-180730-527864.cloudwaysapps. com/wp-content/uploads/2014/03/1st-Declaration-of-the-Lacandona-Jun gle.pdf

Gilbert, Jeremie (2016) *Indigenous Peoples' Land Rights Under International Law*. Boston, MA: Brill Nijhoff.

Harfuch, Andres, Mariana Bilinski & Andrea Ortiz (2016) "El Jurado Indígenas en Argentina [Argentina's Indigenous Jury]," Juicio por Jurados y Procedimiento Penal, 25(2016), available at https://inecip.org/wp-content/ uploads/JxJ-JusBaires-JuradoIndigena.pdf. The English version is available at https://inecip.org/wp-content/uploads/Argentina%C2%B4s-Indigenous-jury-by-Harfuch-Bilinski-and-Ortiz-6.pdf

Herrera, Jose Israel (2015) "The Challenge of the Cultural Diversity in Mexico Through the Official Recognition of Legal Pluralism," The Age of Human Rights Journal 4 (June): 60-80.

Horne, Gerald (2015) Confronting Black Jacobins: The U.S., the Haitian Revolution, and the Origins of the Dominican Republic. NY: NYU Press.

Iankova, Katia, Azizul Hassan & Rachel L'Abbe (2016) *Indigenous People and Economic Development*. NY: Routledge.

INEGI (2015) "Resultados Definitivos de la Encuesta Intercensal 2015." Aguascalientes, AGS: INEGI. 8 December. available at https://www.inegi.org.mx/ saladeprensa/boletines/2015/especiales/especiales2015_12_3.pdf

Jaramillo, Juan Camilo (2019) "Entire Police Forces Continue to be Arrested in Mexico," InSight Crime, 21 August.

Kelly, James J. (1994) "Article 27 and Mexican Land Reform: The Legacy of Zapatista's Dream," Columbia Human Rights Law Review 25: 541-570.

Lopez, Oscar (2020) "A Town Torn Apart: Mexico's Indigenous Communities Fight for Autonomy," Place, 2 January.

"Mendoza, Argentina: Governor Suarez Announced the Expansion of the Jury to More Crimes and the Implementation of the Civil Jury" (2020) AAJJ, 9 May.

Mexican Constitution (1917), available at https://www.constituteproject.org/ constitution/Mexico_2015.pdf?lang=en.

Miroff, Nick (2013) "On Mexico's Western Front, Cartel Violence Escalates," Washington Post, 25, July.

Morin, Brandi (2017) "Where Does Canada Sit 10 Years After the UN Declaration on the Rights of Indigenous Peoples?" CBC, 13 Sept.

Morris, Stephen D. (1991) Corruption & Politics in Contemporary Mexico. Tuscaloosa, AL:

Morris, Stephen D. (2009) Political Corruption in Mexico: The Impact of Democratization Boulder, CO: Lynne Rienner Pub.

Nagle, Luz E. (2010) "Corruption of Politicians, Law Enforcement, and the Judiciary in Mexico and Complicity Across the Border," Small Wars & Insurgencies, 21: 95-122.

Nielsen, Marianne O. & Karen Jarratt-Snider (2020) *Traditional, National, and International Law and Indigenous Communities.* Tucson, AZ: University of Arizona Press.

Ojeda, Lorena "Mexico: Communities Up in Arms," Berkeley Review of Latin American Studies, (Spring, 2014):, available at https://clas.berkeley.edu/res earch/mexico-communities-arms.

Pressly, Linda (2016) "Cherán: The Town That Threw Out Police, Politicians, and Gangsters," BBC News, 13 October.

Ramirez, Deborah A. (1994) "The Mixed Jury and the Ancient Custom of Trial by Jury De Medietate Linguae: A History and Proposal for Change," Boston University Law Review, 74: 777-818.

Salazar, Giovanna (2015) "The Cherán Indigenous Community's Remarkable Road to Self-Rule in Mexico," Our World, 24 April.

Sander, Ernest (1995) "From Operation Gatekeeper to Operation Hardline: What's in a Name?" Associated Press, 9 May.

Scherr, Caitlyn (2016) "Chasing Democracy: The Development and Acceptance of Jury Trials in Argentina," University of Miami Inter-American Law Review 47: 316-353.

Smith, Donald B. (2018) Deskaheh (Levi General), Dictionary Canadian Biography (accessed 21 November 2018), available at https://www.biographi.ca/ en/bio/deskaheh_15E.html.

Solano, Xochitl Leyva (2007) "Indigenismo, Indianismo and 'Ethnic Citizenship' in Chiapas," Journal of Peasant Studies 32(3-4): 555-83.

Soloff, Andalusia Knoll (2018) "After Long Fight for Self-Government, Indigenous Town of Cherán, Mexico Ushers in New Council," NBC News, 4 September.

"States with the Highest Number of Homicides in Mexico in 2019" (2020) Statista (accessed 15 May 15).

Subcomandante Marcos & John Ponce De Leon (2011) Our Word is Our Weapon: Selected Writings. NY: Seven Stories Press.

Thompson, Ruth (1987) *The Rights of Indigenous Peoples in International Law: Selected Essays on Self-Determination.* Saskatoon, Canada: University of Saskatchewan, Native Law Center.

Tobin, Brendan (2016) *Indigenous Peoples, customary Law and human Rights: Why Living Law Matters.* London, UK: Routledge.

United Nations (2008a) Achieving Sustainable Development and Promoting Development Cooperation: Dialogues at the Economic Social Council, available at https://www.un.org/en/ecosoc/docs/pdfs/fina_08-45773.pdf.

U.S. v. Wood, 299 U.S. 123 (1936).

Watson, Irene (2016) *Aboriginal Peoples, Colonialism and International Law.* NY: Routledge.

Woo, Grace Li Xiu (2003) "Project, Canada's Forgotten Founders: The Modern Significance of the Haudenosaunee (Iroquois) Application for Membership in the League of Nations," *LGD 2003*, (1) at n. 19, available at https://war wick.ac.uk/fac/soc/law/elj/lgd/2003_1/woo/.

Conclusion: The Future of the Original Nation and the Global Nation in the Age of Anthropocene

The struggle of the original nation continues in various regions of the world today. The Original Nation Approaches to Inter-National Law (ONAIL) was proposed to offer fundamentally differing interpretations and narratives of history, geography, politics, and the role of international law, ones in which the perspective of the nation is placed at the center of geopolitical analyses. ONAIL was devised to serve as a critical theoretical tool to explain and understand persistent global patterns of ethnocide and ecocide resulting from predatory policies of the state that continue to capture, occupy, oppress, and exploit original nations. ONAIL was proposed to promote cooperation and collaboration among diverse groups of individuals and organizations, including progressive political activists, human rights lawyers, feminist groups, academics, and most importantly, peoples of resisting original nations and autonomous communities. ONAIL exposed the history of the "state-making" and "nation-destroying" project and examined the original nation's powerful resistance in multiple regions in the world, including the Lakota Nation in North America; Okinawa, the southernmost island of Japan; the Kurdistan in the Middle East and its forced partition into Turkey, Syria, Iraq, and Iran; the P'urhépecha Nation in the deep forest of Chiapas in southern Mexico; and the Cofán Nation in the Amazonian border of Ecuador and Colombia, among many others. This last

© The Author(s), under exclusive license to Springer Nature Switzerland AG 2021
H. Fukurai and R. Krooth, *Original Nation Approaches to Inter-National Law*,
https://doi.org/10.1007/978-3-030-59273-8_8

chapter explores two distinct sets of revolutionary cognitive approaches to address the anthropogenic disasters that continue to pose serious threats to the nation, to the people, and to ecosystems. They include: (1) the paradigmatic cognitive shift involved in deconstructing the "legal fiction" concept as applied to both the state and the corporation, and (2) the potential cognitive adoption of the Inter-National Grand Jury (IGJ) and the robust transformation of the International Rights of Nature Tribunal (IRNT) into a set of more inclusive and expansive global adjudicative panels. ONAIL asserts that such cognitive transformation is of great importance, as the oppressive entities of the state and the corporation, with their masterful deployment of predatory international law, have "outlived" their useful life trajectory, as they no longer serve the interests of populous constituents all across the globe. ONAIL, coupled with affirmative cognitive transformations, provides stronger hope for the future, one in which the state, the corporation, and other oppressive legal fictions may eventually be consigned to the dustbin of history. Lastly, given the transitory and ephemeral life cycle of the state and modern corporations, it is imperative to realize that the original nation and people must persist in their contribution to the preservation of life on Mother Earth, as has been done for thousands of years. The original nation has outlasted historical residues of powerful empires, monarchies, kingdoms, dynasties, and other imperial entities of the past. As these entities may come and go, the original nation, imbued with its emancipatory spirit and impetus, must persist and flourish into the foreseeable future.

1   ONAIL AND "BOTTOM-UP" PERSPECTIVES

Unlike traditional geopolitical perspectives that have envisioned the globe as consisting of fixed legal entities joined in a network of 193 sovereign states, ONAIL offers a geographic vision of a world whose ecosystems and natural features have been carefully maintained by self-sustaining cultures and self-governing communities of thousands of original nations for many centuries. ONAIL introduces a "bottom-up" and "on-the-ground" history in contrast to traditional and canonical state-centric approaches, adding modern-day portraits of the resilience and potency of the original nation and peoples to substantive analysis of international political affairs, regional conflicts, human struggles, and ecological survival. Critical lenses and discourses catalyzed by the Original Nation scholarship provide a powerful critique of state-sponsored predatory geopolitical processes, thus exposing the state's role as an intermediary agency of international law which is weaponized to serve the objectives of profit-driven transnational corporations and multilateral institutions. ONAIL offers an active voice to the nation and people, helping to build strong global solidarity for an international network opposing the hegemonic legal framework of the state, government agencies, private power, corporate interests, and predatory international organizations. ONAIL explores the prospect of active judicial collaboration with the state, for the time being, in order to develop robust Earth Jurisprudence that can protect the rights of nature and ecosystems preserved in the original nation across the globe. ONAIL supports the use of the state's power to mobilize the International Criminal Court (ICC) to investigate human rights violations of indigenous peoples. For example, ONAIL contends that human experiments at global clinical trials and the corporate theft of indigenous bodies and knowledge in the form of intellectual property rights for profit maximization should be seen as constituting crimes against humanity under international law.

ONAIL also interrogates the predatory effect of the international legal mechanism known as the Investor State Dispute Settlement (ISDS), which has prioritized economic growth, corporate profits, and private wealth over the rights of the nation and people. ISDS, as inscribed in the 1994 NAFTA signed by the U.S., Mexico, and Canada, has had an egregious and disparate impact on the economic, social, and ecological well-being of the indigenous nation and peoples, including the P'urhépecha Nation, the Tzeltal Nation, the Tzotzil Nation and other indigenous communities in southern Mexico, as well as the Lakota Nation and other first nations in North America. ONAIL proposes the greater expansion of international tribunals such as the International Rights of Nature Tribunals (IRNT), organized by the greater alliance of the original nation, ecological activists, and environmental organizations. Since the IRNT verdicts are not legally binding, ONAIL suggests the creation of a robust socio-legal framework to protect ecosystems and cultural and biological diversity through education, activism, collaboration, and negotiations with the state sectors. Finally, ONAIL offers a prescient approach to the preservation of indigenous knowledge and the natural environment necessary for the survival of humans and nonhuman species in coming generations.

The future power position of the original nation and peoples living in tenuous territories throughout the world is still uncertain, due to their continuing struggles against such devastating activities of central-ized states as engaging in wars, killing indigenous resisters, extending corporate empires, and colonizing territories without restraints. An exam-ination of the history of the relatively recent evolution of the predatory state as compared to the long resilience and durability of the original nations reveals that the original nations have outlived great numbers of powerful kingdoms, dynasties, and empires. Many of these have collapsed from internal economic meltdowns, over-extended military outreach, internal revolts, and bureaucratic complexities beyond the possibility of fixture,[1] while others have faced external enemies, internal convulsion, economic competition or have simply broken apart.[2] The original nation, in contrast, has existed for many centuries, and it seems safe to assume that the original nation will, in time, outlast the predatory state and state-centric institutions. Indeed, the alliance and cooperation of the original nation and peoples attempting to securing their land and biodiversity is a tenacious force globally. Their collective aspirations contribute to a portrait of the possibility of successful defiance against centralized states and corporate allies whose drives to accumulate wealth involve destroying nations, waging wars, expanding colonies, and creating neoliberal spheres of hegemonic influence.

1.1   The Original Nation in the Age of Anthropocene

ONAIL examines predatory state and corporate activities and explores the creation of socio-legal mechanisms to protect the original nation, people, and homeland from state encroachment and exploitation. Today there arises yet another significant cause of concern over the future of the original nation, people, the nature and ecosystems. The anthropogenic catastrophes have come to threaten the survival not only of humans, but also of all living creatures on earth. The rapid globalization and neoliberal policies of state and corporate sectors have accelerated the mass extinc-tion of many species through the destruction of their natural habitats.[3]

---

[1] Tainter (1988).

[2] For detailed examinations of the collapse of Rome, Britain, and the U.S. hegemony, see Johnson (2008, pp. 54–89).

[3] Piper (2009). See also McMullan (2018).

Campaigns of the state and corporations have already led to multiple instances of ecological disaster, environmental collapse, and pandemics.[4]

The Anthropocene refers to the current geological age, a period in which human activity has exerted the dominant force on the climate, environment, and human and nonhuman society. The ONAIL scholarship attributes the arrival of the Anthropocene to the last two centuries' overarching emphasis on industrial development and technological innovation as well as the unceasing thirst for corporate profits, resulting in endless industrial extraction and pollution of the earth; privatization, commodification and legalized enslavement of nature and people for profit-extraction; and institution of economic systems of supply–demand expansion, without taking account of their "externalities" on the planet and ecosystems.[5] The original nation has witnessed the escalation of militarism and endless war as a means of achieving governance over the nation, peoples, and lands, in order to expand profit exploitation, along with the expansion of legal systems that ennoble private property at the expense of the nation, people, ecology, and equity. Such systems of exploitation have relied on a worldview that places humans above nature, leading to the ongoing destruction of self-governing communities and self-sustainable cultures which had long been preserved by the indigenous nation and people across the world, who now struggle to try to protect what they have left of their ancestral homelands.

ONAIL has warned that we are already facing numerous deadly effects of such anthropogenic activities, in the form of global warming, climate change, rising sea levels, cultural and biological diversity depletion, ecological destruction, and even threats of nuclear war.[6] Critical scientists have also warned that anthropogenic catastrophes could imply the impending sixth extinction of all species on the planet.[7] The World Wildlife Fund (WWF) reported that human activities since 1970 have wiped out 60% of mammals, birds, fish, and reptiles, as well as nearly

---

[4] The Asian Law and Society Association (ALSA) Annual Conference in Osaka, Japan held the presidential session, "Anthropocene and the Law in Asia" in December 2019. The first author, then-President of ALSA, organized the session, and many of the session papers will appear in a future issue of the *Asian Journal of Law and Society* (Cambridge University Press).

[5] See generally Chomsky (2020).

[6] Ibid.

[7] Elmore (2020).

80% of freshwater species.[8] The fifth extinction of species took place 65 million years ago when a meteor hit the earth.[9] Today, humankind can metaphorically be seen as another powerful asteroid, threatening the future of human and nonhuman species on the entire planet.

Scientists have also warned about the possibility of increased future frequencies of animal-borne virus pandemics, due to the effects of anthropogenic disasters.[10] For the last several decades, nearly all pandemics have been caused by "cross-species" zoonotic viruses, such as HIV, SARS, MERS, Ebola, and COVID-19. The causes for the pandemics were well-known, as the natural habitats of animals of many species have been systematically eradicated by globalization and neoliberal policies that have accelerated the process of the deforestation, environmental pollution, and ecological destruction, thereby eliminating the "borders" that once existed between the animal and human worlds.[11]

1.2   Asia as the Epicenter of the Anthropogenic Disaster: The Original Nations at Risk

In line with the prophetic vision offered by the U.S. government and its intelligence community in the 1950s that the epicenter of the state-nation conflicts would be in Asia, recent research on the anthropogenic disaster has also warned that Asia would become the epicenter of climate catastrophes and environmental disasters in coming decades.[12] *Nature Communications*, a popular multidisciplinary journal of natural science, warned in 2019 that the regions mostly affected by anthropogenic disasters would be "developing countries across Asia, … including Bangladesh, Vietnam, and many Small Island Developing States (SIDS)."[13] A series of significant climate changes have already been observed in multiple Asian countries and neighboring regions. For example, in summer 2019, Mumbai in India experienced their average monthly rainfall in just one

---

[8] Carrington (2018).
[9] Carrington (2017).
[10] Elegant (2020).
[11] Brown (2020).
[12] Wood (2018).
[13] Kulp and Strauss (2019).

48-hour period.[14] The flooding from a 2019 summer monsoon killed more than six hundred people in India, Nepal, Bangladesh, and Pakistan, and displaced millions of people in South Asia, including 800,000 Rohingya Muslim refugees in Cox's Bazar, the largest refugee camp in the world.[15] Further, more than 300 million people in Asia face the risk of being displaced due to rising sea levels, three times more than previous estimates, and the vast majority of the most vulnerable populations in the world are concentrated in east and southeast Asia, including China, Bangladesh, India, Vietnam, Indonesia, and Thailand.[16] All of these Asian countries will soon face the gravest threat, with coastal elevations of more than six feet or two meters.[17] Much of southern Vietnam, including Ho Chi Minh City, the country's economic center, for instance, could all but completely disappear by 2050.[18] And in northern Asia in Siberia, wild fires have burned more than 200,000 hectares, an area larger than the whole island of Maui, Hawaii.[19]

Asia's island states have been no exception in facing the consequences of anthropogenic disaster. On Christmas Day 2019, Typhoon Phanfone with winds of up to 118 miles (190 km) per hour slammed into the Philippines, killing 28 residents and forcing evacuation of more than 50,000.[20] On New Year's Eve 2019, the torrential rainfall in the capital city of Jakarta in Indonesia also led to massive flooding and landslides that instantly took the lives of 66 people and forced more than 60,000 to evacuate their homes.[21] The Indonesian government has already decided to move Jakarta, the metropolitan city of 30 million on the island of Java, to East Kalimantan on the world's third largest island, Borneo, because a quarter or more of the capital city has been projected to be under water within the next ten years. Australia, Indonesia's southern neighbor, has also been affected by climate change. In January 2020, Australia launched the largest peacetime maritime rescue mission in its national history to

---

[14] Vaktania (2019.

[15] Milko and Hammond (2019) and Ferguson (2019).

[16] Kulp and Strauss (2019).

[17] Ibid.

[18] Lu and Flavelle (2019).

[19] Bowler (2020).

[20] Rosane (2019).

[21] Berlinger (2019) and John (2019).

save thousands of residents and tourists who had been stranded on the beach after being forced to flee uncontrollable wildfires.[22] The unprecedented climate-fueled wildfire killed at least 33 people, scorched more than 26 million acres of land, an area larger than the state of Indiana, while killing more than a billion animals, and blanketing the country in smoke.[23] The states of Victoria and New South Wales, in which Sydney is located, declared a state of emergency, forcing more than 4,000 to flee to the beach to escape the approaching blazes, while Australia's Bureau of Meteorology confirmed that 2019 was the continent's hottest year on record.[24] Climate activists and scientists have pointed to Australia as an example of what is to come in the decades ahead, if radical steps are not taken to curb global carbon emission.[25] The thick smoke from Australia traveled almost 7,000 miles across the Pacific Ocean, reaching Chile and Argentina.[26] All Asian states and neighboring regions will be affected by anthropogenic disasters, but anthropogenic catastrophes will have even greater consequences for Asia's "developing" states, as well as original nations, impoverished regions, and rural communities.

The original nation in Asia and across the globe has suffered greatly from globalization and the neoliberal assault against their people, land, and ecosystems. The original nation has also experienced the escalating calamitous impact of climate changes, environmental destruction, and ecological disasters, all of which can be viewed as the externalities of desperate state policies and profit-driven corporate projects across the globe. Anthropogenic crises do not recognize state borders, national boundaries, or even military blockades set up by the state, international institutions, or supra-state continental federations. The state can never be ecologically sovereign, and no state can shield itself completely from anthropogenic disasters simply by building a border wall or sealing its state. This is true for all states, even such powerful ones as the U.S., Russia, China or even the European Union, for none enjoy ecological sovereignty.[27]

[22] Albeck-Ripka et al. (2020).

[23] Flanagan (2020) and Kahn (2020). See also Cohen (2020).

[24] Klein (2020).

[25] Gander (2020).

[26] Ibid.

[27] United Nations (2008). See also Harari (2020).

The anthropogenic threat also does not discriminate on the basis of national origin, political affiliation, religion, race, ethnicity, sexual orientation, or any other "imaginary" boundaries or socially constructed identities. Effective approaches to dealing with the anthropogenic threat can come only through the strength of global cooperation and mutual collaboration. This international cooperation and movement of solidarity may be only achieved by recognizing that "we are all part of Mother Earth, an indivisible, living community of interrelated and interdependent beings with a common destiny."[28] Such a sense of global nationalism must also be predicated on the protection of interconnected and interdependent ecosystems through "teaching, education, and consciousness raising."[29]

2   ZOONOTIC VIRUS PANDEMICS AND GLOBAL SOLIDARITY

The 2014 Ebola pandemic demonstrated the importance of protecting the health and welfare of every single individual on earth in order to prevent future zoonotic pandemics and possible deaths of millions. That pandemic originated in a single transmuted gene of the Ebola virus in a single person in West Africa, and the higher infectious doses of the mutated Ebola virus soon began to spread around West Africa.[30] Similarly, the COVID-19 originated in a tiny Wuhan market in China, in a mutated gene of the bat-borne, zoonotic coronavirus that led to the infection of hundreds of millions of people, the deaths of millions, and healthcare disasters around the world.[31] There is also the likelihood of the gene mutation of the COVID-19 virus in a single infected person somewhere in Yemen, Somalia, Iraq, or other conflict zones where there are no adequate healthcare facilities to treat infected patients. The mutated gene of coronavirus or any of the other zoonotic viruses could possibly infect millions in the future, creating another disastrous pandemic.

In the past, the U.S. has assumed global leadership in dealing with such pandemics. Under Operation United Assistance, for example, the

---

[28] Universal Declaration of the Rights of Mother Earth, Preamble (2010).

[29] Ibid.

[30] Maron (2016) and Dietzel et al. (2017).

[31] Ortiz and Miller (2020) and Mendal et al. (2020).

U.S. Africa Command, which is one of the eleven combatant commands of the U.S. Armed Forces headquartered in Stuttgart, Germany, led a global effort to successfully deal with the last Ebola pandemic, which first appeared in Liberia and began to spread to other regions in West Africa in 2014.[32] In 2018, however, the U.S. abruptly abdicated its global leadership role, with the U.S. administration decision to dismantle the team in charge of global pandemic response.[33] A further abdication of global leadership occurred in April 2020, when the U.S. announced it would halt its funding to the World Health Organization (WHO) in the midst of the global COVID-19 pandemic.[34] As a consequence, regulatory responses to the coronavirus pandemic have fallen to individual states around the world, without benefit of U.S. assistance or coordinated global strategies.

The dual crises of the coronavirus pandemic and anthropogenic natural disasters have had a devastating impact upon indigenous nations and peoples across the globe.[35] The Navajo Nation of approximately 17,000 people, and others in the reserved territories in North America, for example, have been hit hard by the COVID-19 pandemic, exhibiting higher infection and death rates than other groups.[36] The indigenous people in North America have already suffered from higher rates of asthma, diabetes, obesity, and heart disease, making them more susceptible to the deadly pandemic. Since effective federal aid programs were almost nonexistent in the Indian reservation, the Navajo Nation and the Choctaw Nation have been forced to resort to a donation campaign from private citizens and charities across the world for monetary assistance.[37] In May 2020, people in Ireland raised and donated more than $2.6 million to help supply clean water, food, and health supplies to the Navajo and Hopi Nations. This generous donation was in direct response to the 173-year-old act of generosity by the Choctaw Nation, whose people had pooled together $170 in 1847 to donate to Irish families struggling to

---

[32] U.S. Department of Defense (2020).

[33] Shesgreen (2020).

[34] Yeung (2020).

[35] Norton (2020), "The Double Crisis: How Climate Change Impacts Aggravate Dealing with Coronavirus in Countries of the Global South" (2020), and "Pandemics, Climate Change and UN Reform" (2020).

[36] Da Costa (2020).

[37] Roper (2020).

survive the infamous Potato Famine. The Choctaw Nation had endured the Trail of Tears sixteen years earlier, with many of them also suffering from hunger, starvation, and deaths among their people. Their donation displayed their empathy and depth of humanity on behalf of the Irish people who had faced similar colonial repression by Britain for many centuries.[38]

Many indigenous people in Brazil, including those in the Amazon, have died from the coronavirus pandemic.[39] The Brazilian government has provided indigenous nations minimal if any assistance to deal with the pandemic.[40] Prior to the arrival of the Portuguese in 1500, there were more than 2,000 indigenous nations in the region, with a total population of two to five million.[41] The 2006 Brazilian census reported that there were only 519,000 native people speaking 180 distinct indigenous languages.[42] Indigenous nations and peoples in the Amazon have long been targeted for extermination, and their lands and natural resources have been usurped and exploited by agri-business, logging, and mining corporate interests.[43] Kevin Mayoruna, a leader of the Matsés Nation in the Amazon, declared that "the government's dream is to exterminate the indigenous people so they can take our land."[44] The deforestation, mining explorations, ecological contaminations, and the accelerated impacts of anthropogenic catastrophes continue to hamper the welfare of indigenous nations in the entire Amazonian region. The indigenous nations and people are in desperate need of global support and mutual aid for their very survival.

The remaining section of this final chapter explores two sets of suggestions for approaches to the anthropogenic disasters that pose serious threats to the survival of original nations, nature and ecosystems around the world. The first suggestion is to promote the cognitive deconstruction of the "legal fiction" concept as applied to both the state and the corporation.

---

[38] Hedgpeth (2020) and Kirby (2020).

[39] Darlington et al. (2020).

[40] Ibid.

[41] Danver (2012, p. 579).

[42] Ibid.

[43] Wallace (2019). See also McElvaney (2019).

[44] Phillips (2019).

ONAIL recognizes that the state as a dominant and oppressive geopolitical entity has outlived its useful life cycle, as it no longer serves the interest of its most populous constituents. In the Age of Anthropocene, ONAIL suggests the active cognitive engagement in the reimagining of the global community as an interrelated and interdependent assemblage of original nations and their allies, rather than of the state or state-centric international organizations.[45] The second suggestion is to propose the creation of collaborative legal agreements by original nations and allies to ensure the protection of the rights of nature and Mother Earth. Specific approaches include the establishment of the Inter-National Grand Jury System (IGJ) and the transformation of the International Rights of Nature Tribunal (IRNT) into a world jury panel composed of vital constituents of the global community. These institutional mechanisms are proposed for the purpose of identifying and deterring human activities that lead to the violation of the rights of the original nation, nature, and ecosystems that need to be preserved for coming generations.

3   THE COGNITIVE DECONSTRUCTION
OF THE STATE AND CORPORATION

A new paradigmatic shift in confronting the anthropogenic endgame is in order. This section explores the possibility of a new cognitive shift which would promote global cooperation and collaboration in the Age of Anthropocene in order to protect the indigenous nation and to preserve self-sustaining cultures, self-governing communities, and diverse ecosystems in their homelands. The ONAIL scholarship offers the following bifurcated steps of this cognitive shift: (1) to make a clear conceptual demarcation between what is true and what is fiction in the dual realities of our cognitive world—that is, to draw an intelligible boundary between objective and imaginative realities; and (2) to develop a cognitive commitment to the construction of the imaginary collective of the "global nation" through the ideology of "global nationalism."

The first step begins with the cognitive realization that the state is a geopolitical fiction rather than an embodied entity that possesses physical bearing. It came into existence following the 1648 Westphalian Peace Treaty in Europe. Delegations of kings, nobles, and other stakeholders of

---

[45] Universal Declaration of the Rights of Mother Earth (2010), preamble.

multiple power centers in Europe congregated in Westphalia, Germany and agreed to create the imaginary geographical entity called a "sovereign state" which was fortified by its delimited geopolitical boundary. The corpus of the resulting inter- "state" treaty ensured the nonintervention by other external states into a state's internal affairs, thereby minimizing potential conflicts among states in Europe. European states proceeded to export this concept of state sovereignty abroad, conquering original nations overseas and creating colonies across the globe, many of which later became independent states by adopting the legal fiction of European-imposed "statehood," actions which were to occur due to either U.N.-led decolonization efforts or to their own anti-colonial struggles against imperial masters.[46]

This newly emerged, collectivist "story" of the state also invented a new script of history, geography, ideology, religion, memory, as well as a system of law to self-justify its existence. In the 1970s, the state's globalization and neoliberal policies began to accelerate the polarization of economic wealth in the state and the world, so that by 2017, the eight richest individuals, all men, and mostly American entrepreneurs and European descendants, owned an amount of wealth equal to that of the 3.6 billion people who make up the poorest half of all humanity on earth.[47]

The state also invented another new story of the corporation as it introduced the concept of "corporate personhood" and "corporate personalities" into the legal system. The corporation was authorized by the state to act as a single entity and was defined as a"legal fiction" that accompanies no embodied objective entity. Today, a "corporate person" has acquired many legal rights and freedom enjoyed by natural persons. In particular, the state granted the corporation the following five

---

[46] Onuma (1997, 2000, 2003, 2017), Glenn (2007), and Darian-Smith (2010). Onuma, for example, identified the necessity to engage in a significant cognitive shift for the understanding of international law from multipolar, trans-civilizational perspectives, thereby going beyond what he called "West-centric" views of international law that had long been dominated by powerful North Atlantic countries in Europe and North America with their "state-centric" canonical narratives and generative discourses. See also Neuwirth (2018, 2020) and Neuwirth et al. (2017). Neuwirth suggested that a radical cognitive transformation was needed for the survival of civilization in a highly complex, technological society where oxymoronic concepts began to dominate legal concepts and activities. These cognitive shifts, according to Neuwirth, were also needed to ensure the survival of humanity in the Age of Anthropocene, especially BRICS states and other "developing" states around the world.

[47] "Just 8 Men Own Same Wealth as Half the World" (2017).

legal personalities, enabling it to: (1) own property; (2) make and sign contracts; (3) enforce contracts; (4) employ workers and agents; and (5) make by-laws and exercise self-governance.[48] These new legal personalities have helped justify destructive corporate projects, maximize corporate profits without restriction, increase market shares, and expand neoliberal projects all across the globe.

ONAIL opposes the hegemonic existence of the "fictitious entities" of the oppressive state and exploitive corporations. According to James Madison, known as one of America's Founding Fathers and principal architects of state policies, the state's primary objective has been "to protect the minority of the opulent against the majority"[49] and to enslave and incorporate the majority into the expanding hierarchical and tyrannical power structure of the state. In responding to this cruelly ironical situation in which the majority can be governed so easily by the opulent minority, English historian and legal scholar David Hume curiously noted that "Force is always on the side of the governed, [while] the governors have nothing to support them but opinion. It is therefore, on opinion only that government is founded; and this maxim extends to the most despotic and most military government, as well as to the most free and most popular."[50] ONAIL supports the "cognitive deconstruction" of the hegemony of "opinion" concerning the story of the state and corporations, proposing that this story represents cognitive manifestations of fictitious entities created and supported by political elites to subordinate the majority and to instill in them "sufficient humility" so that they will submit to decisions of the elite, without pressing for their own demands in the political arena.[51]

As a second step, ONAIL urges the construction of a democratic and equitable global geopolitical community, the "global nation." Unlike the United Nations which is the global management institution composed of 193 independent "member states," the global nation may be perceived as a large assemblage of interconnected and interdependent networks of original nations and their allies. This vision of the interrelated network of the world has had both cognitive and historical precedence. Prior to the

---

[48] Saha (2010, pp. 77–100).

[49] Bailey (2015, p. 160).

[50] Hume (2020).

[51] See generally Herman and Chomsky (1988).

advent of the state, many interconnected networks among original nations and peoples had long existed in various regions across the globe.[52]

Prior to the 1648 Westphalian Treaty, for example, many original nations and peoples around the world had already established intricate networks of communication, commerce, and trade. In North America, for example, indigenous nations had built a complex system of trails and roadways that tied multiple nations and communities together across the landmass of much of the Americas in the Western Hemisphere. In pre-Columbian America, this infrastructure, with its network of commercial paths and trade routes, was so expansive that "they constituted an extensive system of roadways that spanned the Americas, making possible short, medium, and long distance travel. ...[and] a complex system of roads and paths which became the roadways adopted by the early [European] settlers ... were ultimately transformed into major highways."[53] The same system of roadways, seaways, and coastal routes for trade, commerce, and travel had been established throughout multiple parts of the world prior to the forceful reconfigurations of global networks by the Europeans. Such ancient roadways included the Silk Road and its regional roadways that spanned East Asia to the Middle East and Europe; advanced networks of "Ancient Roman Highways" in North Africa, Middle East, and Europe; and the "Great Trunk Road" in South Asia, among many others.[54]

ONAIL recognizes that prior to the advent of the state, the world had been constituted of expansive networks of trade, commerce, travel, and communication among original nations and peoples. ONAIL also recognizes the need to engage in a cognitive reimagination of the role of original nations and their allies to serve as the foundations of cohesive geopolitical communities of the global nation in the Age of Anthropocene. The question, then, is this: Is the human community as a

---

[52] Another cognitive field exploring the survivability of human society is the new conceptual recapitulation of human organizations as a multi-sectored, multi-level global governance system, as suggested by the "Theory of Gestalt." Gestalt science understands humanity as a "grouping" organization with a web woven by each person, nation peoples included, with all constituent individuals together supporting humanity as a new holistic entity. See, for example, Banerjee (1994, pp. 107–109), Palmer (2003), Wolfe et al. (2008), and Goldstein (2009).

[53] Dunbar-Ortiz (2014, pp. 28–29) (citing David Wade Chambers, "Native American Road Systems and Trails," *Udemy* (accessed on Sep. 24, 2013).

[54] Elisseeff (1999).

whole capable of reimagining a world of nearly eight billion strangers on the planet and recognizing them, and thus "recognizing" them as members of a single community of global nation. Cognitive science scholars have substantiated that such cognitive reconfiguration is possible because our cognitive abilities have already been embedded in the human DNA.[55] Evolutionary scholars and cognitive scientists have suggested that humankind, i.e., Homo *sapiens*, acquired the cognitive ability to invent "unlimited" imaginative stories and myths that transcended the objective confines of physical and biological reality nearly 70,000 years ago.[56] The cognitive ability to engage in free, independent, and creative activities also served to separate Homo *sapiens*, today's only surviving human species, from such other human species as Homo *erectus*, Homo *neanderthalensis* (i.e., Neanderthals), Homo *floresiensis*, Homo *naledi*, and Homo *habilis*, among many others.

Prior to the inventive mythologies of the state and corporation, folklore and imagined stories about gods and spirituality, for instance, had allowed Homo *sapiens* to congregate *en masse* and engage in group-based, cooperative activities.[57] Scientists have argued that the cognitive activity of free and creative imagination was developed without being hindered by surrounding physical environments or external circumstances.[58] This cognitive ability has led to rapid developments and spectacular advancements in science, math, medicine, technology, and industry. Such aspects of human cognition also made it possible to invent fictitious entities such as the state and the corporation, to obtain group collaboration and cooperation. As with past kingdoms, monarchies, oligarchies, and empires, many of which no longer exist, the hegemony of the oppressive state and exploitive corporations must now be subjected to a critical reconfiguration, if not total deconstruction and dissolution. ONAIL urges the reimagining of an alternative collectivist entity of the global nation, which is more responsive to the interests and welfare of original nations, peoples, nature, and ecosystems.

---

[55] Harari (2015).

[56] Ibid. See also Diamond (1991).

[57] Diamond (1997) and Gibbons (2012).

[58] Harari (2015).

4 The "Inter-National" Grand Jury (IGJ) and International Rights of Nature Tribunal (IRNT)

In order to complete this transformative cognitive shift, ONAIL contends that the shift in cognitive focus must be accompanied by a new set of democratic institutions and a robust rubric and rule of law. Until the oppressive state and exploitive corporations are deconstructed and dissolved, it is imperative to create "inter-national" legal mechanisms that will discourage and eliminate egregious activities of such entities and promote global collective action to avert impending anthropogenic disasters.

First, ONAIL suggests that the global system of law requires the genuine form of "international law," i.e., the structure and rubric of legal agreement that defines the obligation, responsibility, and relationship among original nations, their allies, and living communities across the globe in order to establish precautionary and restrictive measures to identify, discourage, and prevent all state, corporate, and other predatory activities that can lead to the destruction of the nation and ecosystems, species extinction, and the disruption of ecological cycles. This structure of "inter-national" law must also establish a nation-based network of legal aids, services, and support mechanisms designed to reflect and respond to the needs, interests, and rights of the original nation and nature, as defined by the UNDRIP and the UDRME.

Second, the global system of law must organize and mobilize a global investigative body, the Inter-national Grand Jury (IGJ), to monitor egregious activities that violate the rights of the original nation and nature. IGJ is conceived as the investigative body of the global nation which serves to examine allegations of the violation of the inherent rights of the original nation and nature. It would be similar to the criminal grand jury in Okinawa, in which a group of native inhabitants of the island was empowered to investigate alleged wrongdoings of foreign soldiers, nullify the "exterritorial" immunity of the powerful state, and restore the rights to exercise the primary jurisdiction over alleged crimes that occurred in their own communities.

Specifically, the IGJ proposed differs from the traditional form and adjudicative function of grand jury that has been adopted and practiced in the Euro-American states, in which the panels of jurors were limited to reviewing and deliberating their verdict based on the evidence presented by the state's prosecutors and their investigators. The IGJ's juridical function, on the other hand, parallels that of Okinawa's Prosecution Review Commission (PRC), in which a select group of jurors are empowered to evaluate the authenticity and appropriateness of "non-indictment" decisions rendered by state prosecutors. Given the fact that state prosecutors have been reluctant to prosecute privileged elites and powerful organizations, including prominent politicians, high-ranking government officials, criminal justice officers, military personnel, and civilian contractors, including those from abroad, and transnational corporations, the IGJ's primary function is to critically investigate and assess the cases that resulted in prosecutors' failure to indict and prosecute. This IGJ's review process, however, will still be predicated upon the active "on-the-ground" political activism and robust litigative processes that promote the critical investigation of the state's prosecutorial actions and criminal procedures. For instance, Okinawa's PRC has reviewed the Japanese prosecutors' non-indictment decision against the alleged killing of a local youth by military personnel who had been shielded from prosecution in local courts due to the U.S.-Japan Status of Forces Agreement (SOFA). The PRC's indictment decision ultimately invalidated the SOFA's immunity clause and led to the prosecution, conviction, and incarceration of military personnel. It would be ideal if many jurisdictions were urged to adopt the PRC-style grand jury system in their respective justice systems. A select group of IGJ jurors, including original nation people, could be empowered to evaluate and interrogate state prosecutors' non-indictment cases on the alleged exploitation, degradation, and annihilation of the rights of nation peoples and nature.

Third, ONAIL suggests that the International Rights of Nature Tribunal (IRNT) be elevated to serve as the principal international court to adjudicate the indicted cases submitted by the IGJ. The UDRME suggests the importance of criminal justice investigation and adjudication, stating that "the damages caused by human violations of the inherent rights [Mother Earth] ... are rectified and... those responsible are held accountable for restoring the integrity and health of Mother Earth."[59] ONAIL supports the prospect of the global panel of the IRNT serving to adjudicate IGJ-indicted cases, with the power to render the court's final decision and to determine the severity of sentences in case of conviction.

---

[59] Universal Declaration of the Rights of Mother Earth (2010), art. 3 (g).

Fourth, ONAIL proposes to create an expansive and representative panel of international investigators and judges in both IGJ and IRNT. The IRNT statute mandates that "the tribunal should be composed of at least three and not more than twenty members [of judges]."[60] Because of the magnitude of the impact of the anthropogenic threat on earth, a greater number of participants needs to be solicited for the investigation and adjudication processes. In the first IRNT meeting, a total of 10 tribunal judges have participated, while 13 judges have presided over the second and third IRNTs. ONAIL proposes that the size of both IGJ and IRNT should be increased and also made more inclusive.

ONAIL recognizes that a tribunal with a large panel of jurors has had prominent historical precedence. The first all-citizen democratic jury was created nearly 2,500 years ago in the City-Polis of Athens in Ancient Greece. The typical size of the Athenian jury, the *Dikasteria*, was 501, although it could range from 51 to 1,501, depending upon the seriousness of criminal charges and extent of monetary damages involved in litigations. All jurors were randomly chosen from eligible members of the entire Athenian society.[61] After all evidence and testimonies were presented in the tribunal, hundreds of jurors cast their votes to determine the outcome of the trial. A decision by a larger panel of both IGJ and IRNT, with hundreds of participants chosen randomly from all over the world, would provide a greater perception of trial fairness and verdict legitimacy in the eyes of the global nation. Technological advancement should also make it possible and relatively easy to create a virtual panel of a large number of jurors across the globe for the adjudication of given cases.

ONAIL recommends that the collegial panel of both IGJ and IRNT also incorporate the affirmative participation of jurors on the basis of national affiliation and gender. If any other considerations, such as political identity, sexuality, religion and other ideological affiliations, are necessary, the affirmative inclusion of special groups should be considered in the formation of diverse jury panels. For instance, the Argentinean jury known as *El Jurado Indigena* (an Indigenous Jury) that was adopted in Neuquén and Chaco has relied on the affirmative action model in

---

[60] Statute of the international Tribunal of Mother Earth, art. 5 (1).

[61] Hansen (1991).

guaranteeing equal representation of jurors based on indigenous nationality as well as gender. The active participation of indigenous people and of women in both IGJ and IRNT panels is important to ensure that varied perspectives, life experiences, human ingenuity, and indigenous knowledge are incorporated into the adjudication process. The active participation of women in politics, cultural affairs, ecosystem preservation, and the armed defense have already been observed in many original nations around the world, including the Zapatista in Chiapas, Mexico; Jeju people in South Korea; the Municipio of Cherán in Michoacán, Mexico; and nearly all matriarchal tribal societies of indigenous nations in North American.

Lastly, ONAIL supports the development of the system of "international" law that promotes global nationalism, not "global statism." Global nationalism is a political ideology and movement to promote the interests of the global nation, based on the cognitive realization that "we are all part of Mother Earth, an indivisible, living community of interrelated and interdependent beings with a common destiny."[62] The ideology of "global statism" along with its predatory policies has persisted for the last several hundred years. In order to prevent the possibility of a sixth mass extinction on the planet, ONAIL recognizes the need for a paradigmatic cognitive shift to ensure the urgent transformation of the oppressive state, inter-state institutions, and corporate systems that have given rise to climate change and other anthropogenic disasters.

5   CONCLUSIONS

In observing the destruction, plunder, and pillage of the original nation of Latin America by powerful North Atlantic states in Europe and North America, Uruguay's renowned political critic and poet Eduardo Galeano once asserted that "the development [by Western powers] is a voyage with more shipwrecks than navigator,"[63] and that the majority of indigenous populations in "America, Australia, and Oceania died from the contamination of first contact with Europeans."[64] The indigenous navigators who

---

[62] Universal Declaration of the Rights of Mother Earth (2010), preamble.

[63] Galeano cited Brazilian anthropologist Darcy Ribeiro's work. See Galeano (1997, p. 171).

[64] Ibid., p. 18.

once stewarded the large swaths of ancestral homelands in Latin America have been subjected to five centuries' genocidal war against their culture, indigenous knowledge, memory, and ecology. The plunder and pillage of the original nation and peoples by powerful states has also been extended to the rest of humanity all across the globe.

Against the West-centric normative framework of the predatory international system, ONAIL provides critical scholarship and alternative voices in relation to the state-centric canonical narrative of current geopolitical analyses. In examining the historical background of the state, ONAIL recognizes that, despite the continual state assault against nation peoples, the original nation has clearly outlived many of its predatory predecessors, such as the powerful kingdom, monarchy, aristocracy, dynasty, and empire. The original nation has persisted for many centuries, and it is safe to assume that the original nation's ability to resist the state should outlast the state's efforts to oppress and destroy it. ONAIL also examines the resilience of the original nation in the face of predatory state policies, state-empowered institutions, and inter-state laws which have been weaponized to serve as ultimate instruments of the "state-building" and "nation-destroying" projects that still continue to manifest in today's world.

ONAIL has focused on the anthropogenic threat to the original nation and people, including natural and climate disasters. Globalization and neoliberal policies have accelerated the devastating human activities that have adversely affected the environment, climate, and both human and nonhuman society. As predicted by many scientists, Asia was positioned to become the epicenter of future anthropogenic disasters, a region where some coastal areas in the southeast and south have already disappeared into the ocean due to rising sea levels. More than 60% of the world population lives in Asia, and many original nations, particularly in South, Southeast, and Western Asia and neighboring regions, are already facing serious ecological threats to survival.[65]

ONAIL has proposed key suggestions for approaches to averting the threat of anthropogenic disasters. The first of these requires a cognitive shift in deconstructing the assumption that the state is an embodied entity rather than a "legal fiction," a story only supported by West-centric hegemonic belief and presupposition. The second suggestion involves creation

[65] See "Asian Region is Vulnerable to Natural and Man-Made Disasters: Rajnath" (2016).

of the new cognitive manifestation of a "global nation," comprised of geopolitical communities—a necessary reconceptualization, given that the threat of anthropogenic disaster requires concerted action beyond the level of the state or the corporation, neither of which are ecologically sovereign.

ONAIL—The Original Nation Approaches to Inter-National Law, provides strong hope for the future, a future in which the state ceases to perpetrate its egregious policies resulting in harm to nature and ecosystems, and one in which the original nation can persist in its contributions to the preservation of life on earth, as it has done for thousands of years.

Bibliography

Albeck-Ripka, Livia, Isabella Kwai, Thomas Fuller, & Famie Tarabay (2020) "It's an Atomic Bomb: Australia Deploys Military as Fires Spread," NY Times, 4. January.

"Asian Region is Vulnerable to Natural and Man-Made Disasters: Rajnath" (2016) Business Standard, 3 November.

Bailey, Jeremy D. (2015) James Madison and Constitutional Imperfection. NY: Cambridge University Press.

Banerjee, J. C. (1994) *Encyclopaedic Dictionary of Psychological Terms*. New DelhiL M.D. Publications Pvt Ltd.

Berlinger, Joshua (2019) "66 People Now Killed by Flooding in Jakarta, and More Rain Appears to be on the Way," CNN, 6. January.

Bowler, Jacinta (2020) "We Don't Want to Alarm Anyone, But a Large Amount of Siberia Is on Fire Right Now," Science Alert, 4 May.

Brown, Kate (2020) "The Pandemic Is Not a Natural Disaster," New Yorker, 13 April.

Carrington, Damian (2017) "Earth's Sixth Mass Extinction Event Underway, Scientists Warn," Guardian, 10, July.

Carrington, Damian (2018) "Humanity Has Wiped out 60% of Animal Populations Since 1970, Report Finds," Guardian, 19 October.

Chambers, David Wade (2020) "Native American Road Systems and Trails," Udemy (accessed September. 24, 2013).

Chomsky, Noam (2020) Internationalism or Extinction. England, UK: Routledge.

Cohen, Li (2020) "Australian Bushfire Smoke Killed More People Than the Fires Did, Study Says," CBS News, 20 March.

Da Costa, Pedro Nicolaci (2020) "Native Americans Are Being Hit Hard by Coronavirus, An Echo of Colonial Pandemics That Nearly Wiped Them Out," 13 March.

Danver, Steven (2012) The Native Peoples of the World: An Encyclopedia of Groups, Cultures, and Contemporary Issues. Armonk, NY: Sharpe Reference.

Darian-Smith, Eve (2010) *Religion, Race, Rights: Landmarks in the History of Modern Anglo-American Law.* Oxford, U.K.: Hart Publishing Ltd.

Darlington, Shasta, Jose Brito, and Flora Charner (2020) "Report: Brazil's Indigenous People Are Dying at an Alarming Rate from Covid-19," CNN, 24 May.

Diamond, Jared (1991) The Third Chimpanzee: The Evolution and Future of the Human Animal. NY: HarperCollins.

Diamond, Jared (1997) Guns, Germs, and Steel: The Fates of Human Societies. NY: W.W. Norton & Co.

Dietzel, Erik, Gordian Schudt, Verena Krahling, Mikhail Matrosovich, and Stephan Becker (2017) "Functional Characterization of Adaptive Mutations During Ebola Virus Outbreak," Journal of Virology, 91(2): 1-13.

Dunbar-Ortiz, Roxanne (2014) An Indigenous Peoples' History of the United States. Boston, MA: Beacon Press.

Elegant, Naomi Xu (2020) "Before the New Coronavirus, There was SARS, and MERS: Do Epidemics Ever Really End?" Fortune, 29 February.

Elisseeff, Vadime (1999) The Silk Roads: Highways of Culture and Commerce. Paris, France: UNESCO.

Elmore, Jonathan (2020) Fiction and the Sixth Mass Extinction: Narrative in an Era of Loss. Lanham, MD: Lexington Books.

Ferguson, Sarah (2019) "Heavy Monsoon Rains Drench Rohingya Refugee Camps in Bangladesh," UNICEF, 9 July.

Flanagan, Richard (2020) "Australia is Committing Climate Suicide," NY Times 3, January.

Galeano, Eduardo (1997) *Open Veins of Latin America: Five Centuries of the Pillage of a Continent.* NY: NYU Press.

Gander, Kashmira (2020) "Smoke From Australia's Fires Has Traveled 6,800 Miles Across the Ocean to Chile," Newsweek, 7, January.

Gibbons, Ann (2012) "Bonobos Join Chimps as Closest Human Relatives," Science, 13 June.

Glenn, H. Patrick (2007) *Legal Traditions of the World: Sustainable Diversity in Law.* Oxford, U.K.: Oxford University Press.

Goldstein, E Bruce (2009) *Sensation and Perception.* Boston, MA: Cengage Learning.

Hansen, Mogens Herman (1991) The Athenian Democracy in the Age of Demosthenes: Structure, Principles, and Ideology. Oxford, UK: Bristol Classical Press.

Harari, Yuval Noah (2015) Sapiens: A Brief History of Humankind. NY: HarperCollins.

Harari, Yuval Noah (2020) "Yuval Noah Harari: The World After Coronavirus," Financial Times, 19 March.

Hedgpeth, Dana (2020) "The Irish are Repaying a Favor From 173 Years Ago in Native Americans' Fight Against Coronavirus," Washington Post, 13 May.

Herman, Edward S. & Noam Chomsky (1988) Manufacturing Consent: The Political Economy of the Mass Media. NY: Pantheon Books.

Hume, David (2020) "Of the First Principles of Government," (accessed 15 May 2020), available at https://www.constitution.org/dh/pringovt.htm.

John, Tara (2019) "Jakarta Floods Leave Dozens Dead and 60,000 Displaced," CNN, 2, January.

Johnson, Chalmers (2008) Nemesis: The Last Days of the American Republic. NY: Metropolitan Books.

"Just 8 Men Own Same Wealth as Half the World" (2017) OXFAM International, 16 January.

Kahn, Brian (2020) "An Estimated 1.25 Billion Animals Have Perished in Australia's Bushfires," Gizmodo, 8, January.

Kirby, Ben (2020) "US Native Tribes and Ireland's 170-Year-Old Connection is Renewed in the Pandemic," Vox, 13 May.

Klein, Alice (2020) "2019 Was Australia's Hottest and Driest Year on Record, New Scientist, 8 January. 8.

Kulp, Scott A. & Benjamin H. Strauss (2019) "New Elevation Data Triple Estimates of Global Vulnerability to Sea-Level Rise and Coastal Flooding," Nature Communications, 29 October.

Lu, Denise & Christopher Flavelle (2019) "Rising Seas Will erase More Cities by 2050, New Research Shows," NY Times, 29, October.

Maron, Dina Fine (2016) "Ebola's West African Rampage Was Likely Bolstered by a Mutation," Scientific American, 3 November.

McElvaney, Kevin (2019) "The Murders of Indigenous Activists in the Amazon Continue to Rise," Yale Environment 360, 17 December.

McMullan, Thomas (2018) "Only Dramatic Action Can Save Us from the Sixth Mass Extinction," Wired, 1 November.

Mendal, Sudip Kumar, Sourav Bhattacharya and Dhrubo Jyoti Sen, "Coronavirus: COVID-19 is Now a Pandemic," ACTA Scientific Pharmacology 1(6): 2–7.

Milko, Victoria & Clare Hammond (2019) "The World's Largest Refugee Camp is Becoming a Real City," Citylab, 27, September.

Neuwirth, Rostam J. (2018) Law in the Time of Oxymoron: A Synaesthesia of Language, Logic and Law. NY: Routledge.

Neuwirth, Rostam J. (2020) "GAIA 2048: A 'Glocal Agency in Anthropocene': Cognitive and Institutional Change as 'Legal Science Fiction,'" in, Kolsky, Meredith, et al., A Post-WTO-International Legal Order: Utopian, Dystopian and Other Scenarios. Cham, Switzerland: Springer, pp.71–93.

Neuwirth, Rostam J., Alexandr Svetlicinil, & Denis De Castro Halis (2017) *The BRICS-Lawyers' Guide to Global Cooperation*. NY: Cambridge University Press.

Norton, Andrew (2020) "Coronavirus and Climate Change Are Two Crises That Need Humanity to Unite," Climate Home News, 12 March.

Onuma, Yasuaki (1997) "Towards an Intercivilizational Approach to Human Rights: For Universalization of Human Rights Through Overcoming of a Westcentric Notion of Human Rights," 7 *Asian Yearbook of International Law* 21-81.

Onuma, Yasuaki (2000) "When was the Law of International Society Born? An Inquiry of the History of International Law from an Intercivilizational Perspective," 2 *Journal of the History of International Law* 1-66.

Onuma, Yasuaki (2003) "International Law in and with International Politics: The Functions of International Law in International Society," 14 *European Journal of International Law* 105-139.

Onuma, Yasuaki (2017) A *Transcivilizational Perspective on International Law: Questioning Prevalent Cognitive Frameworks in the Emerging Multi-Polar and Multi-Civilizational World of the Twenty-First Century*. Leiden, Belgium: Martinus Nijhoff Publishers.

Ortiz, Jorge L. and Ryan W. Miller (2020) "Coronavirus live Update: Global Cases Top 5M: Donald Trump Says He Has Almost Completed Hydroxy-chloroquine Regimen: 93K US Deaths," Post Crescent, 20 May.

Palmer, Stephen E. (2003) "Visual Perception of Objects," in Healy, Alice F. and Robert W. Proctor, *Handbook of Psychology: Experimental Psychology*. Hoboken, NJ: John Wiley and Sons.

"Pandemics, Climate Change and UN Reform" (2020) Global Geneva, 19 May.

Phillips, Tom (2019) "'He Wants to Destroy Us': Bolsonaro Poses Gravest Threat in Decades, Amazon Tribes Say," Guardian, 26 July.

Piper, Ross (2009) Extinct Animals: An Encyclopedia of Species That Have Disappeared During Human History. Westport, CT: Greenwood Press.

Roper, Willem (2020) "Navajo Nation Hit Hard by COVID-19," Statista, 26 May.

Rosane, Olivia (2019). "Typhoon Kills 28, Displaces More Thank 50,000 in the Philippines," EcoWatch, 27 December.

Saha, Tushkar Kanti, (2010) Textbook on Legal Methods, Legal Systems and Research. India: Universal Law Publishers.

Shesgreen, Deirdre (2020) "'Gross Misjudgment': Experts say Trump's Decision to Disband Pandemic Team Hindered Coronavirus Response," USA Today, 18 March.

Statute of the international Tribunal of Mother Earth (2015), available at https://therightsofnature.org/wp-content/uploads/Statute-of-the-International-Tribunal-of-Mother-Earth-Rights4Dec2015.pdf.

Tainter, Joseph A. (1988) The Collapse of Complex Societies. NY: Cambridge University Press.

"The Double Crisis: How Climate Change Impacts Aggravate Dealing with Coronavirus in Countries of the Global South" (2020) PreventionWeb, 14 April.

United Nations (2008) Achieving Sustainable Development and Promoting Development Cooperation: Dialogues at the Economic Social Council, available at https://www.un.org/en/ecosoc/docs/pdfs/fina_08-45773.pdf.

Universal Declaration of the Rights of Mother Earth (2010), available at https://therightsofnature.org/universal-declaration/.

U.S. Department of Defense (2020) "DOD Helps Fight Ebola in Liberia and West Africa" (accessed May 15 2020), available at https://archive.defense.gov/home/features/2014/1014_ebola/.

Vaktania, Saurabh (2019) "Mumbai Receives Record Monsoon Rains in 2019," India Today, 16, September.

Wallace Scott (2019) "Murder in the Amazon Heightens Fears for Isolated Tribes," National Geographic, 27 September.

Wolfe, Jeremy, Keith R. Kluender, Dennis M. Levi, Linda M. Bartoshuk, Rachel S. Herz, Roberta L. Klatzky, Susan J. Lederman & Daniel M. Merfeld (2008) Sensation and Perception. Sunderland MA: Sinauer Associates.

Wood, Johnny (2018) "Why Asia-Pacific is Especially Prone to Natural Disasters," World Economic Forum, 6 December.

Yeung, Jessie (2020) "The US Is Halting Funding to the WHO: What Does This Actually Mean?" CNN, 16 April.

Bibliography

"09-Biodiversity Management" (2015) Scottish Canals, Theme 9: Biodiversity Management, available at https://www.scottishcanals.co.uk/wp-content/uploads/sites/2/2015/12/9-Biodiversity-Management.pdf (accessed 22 October 2020).

"2nd International Rights of Nature Tribunal: Lima" (2014) *GARN*, December, available at https://therightsofnature.org/lima-2014-tribunal/ (accessed 22 October 2020).

1852 Treaty of Fort Laramie, September. 17 (1851) article 1, https://www.republicoflakotah.com/2009/1851-treaty/ (accessed 15 March 2019).

1868 Treaty of Fort Laramie, April 29 (1868) article 1, https://www.republicoflakotah.com/2009/1868-treaty/ (accessed 15 March 2019).

"89% of Veneto Residents Vote for Independence from Rome" (2014) *Reuters*, 23, March.

"A Returned US Base in Jeju, Proved to Be 'Most Oil-Contaminated,' Will be Used Again to Militarize Jeju?"(2013) *Save Jeju Now*, 28 June, available at http://savejejunow.org/p7989/.

Aba, Jerome Succor (2018) "First Person Account: I Am Jerome Succor Aba. I Am a Muslim Human Rights Worker from Mindanao, NOT a Terrorist," *MindaNews*, 25 April, available at http://www.mindanews.com/mindaviews/2018/04/first-person-account-i-am-jerome-succor-aba-i-am-a-muslim-human-rights-worker-from-mindanao-not-a-terrorist/.

Abate, Randall Abate & Elizabeth Ann Kronk (2013) *Climate Change and Indigenous People: The Search for Legal Remedies*. Northampton, MA: Edward Elgar Publishing.

"Abolition of Main Crop Seeds Law Puts Nation at Risk" (2018), *Japan Times*, 20 March.

"About the Summit" (2020) *Advantage Assam* (accessed 15 May 2020), available at https://advantageassam.com/about-the-summit.

Achiume, E. Tendayi (2016) "Syria, Cost-Sharing, and Responsibility to Protect Refugees," 100 *Minnesota Law Review* 687–761.

Achiume, E. Tendayi (2019) "Migration as Decolonization," 71 *Stanford Law Review* 1509–1574.

"Advancing Legal Rights Nature: Timeline" (2018) Community Environmental Legal Defense Fund (accessed 21 November 2018), available at https://celdf.org/rights/rights-of-nature/rights-nature-timeline/.

Adam, Adam Hussein (2012) "Report: Recognising Sacred Natural Sites and Territories in Kenya: An Analysis of How the Kenyan Constitution, National and International Laws Can Support the Recognition of Sacred Natural Sites and Their Community Governance Systems," available at https://cmsdata.iucn.org/downloads/gaiasns_1.pdf.

Adams, Brad (2020) "Philippines Soldiers Accused of Beating Indigenous People," *Human Rights Watch*, 4 September.

Agarwal, Bina (2010) *Gender and Green Governance: The Political Economy of Women's Presence Within and Beyond Community Forestry*. Oxford, U.K.: Oxford University Press.

Aginam, Obijiofor (2003) "The Nineteenth Century Colonial Fingerprints on Public Health Diplomacy: A Postcolonial View," 2003 *Law, Social Justice and Global Development Journal* 1–15.

Agonito, Joseph (2011) *Lakota Portraits: Lives of the Legendary Plains People 101*. Guilford, CT: Atwodat Book.

Agren, David (2018) "Mexican Indigenous Community That Ran Politicians Out of Town," *Guardian*, 3 April.

Aguilera-Barchet, Bruno (2013) *A History of Western Public Law: Between Nation and State*. NY: Springer.

Ahae, Jo (2018) "Symposium on the US Base in East Asia," *Gangjeong Village Story*, August/September.

Al Attar, Mohsen (2012) "Third World Approaches to International Law and the Rethinking of International Legal Education in the 21st Century." York University, Ph.D. Dissertation.

Al Attar, Mohsen (2013) "Reframing the 'Universality' of International Law in Globalising World," 59 *McGill Law Journal* 95–139.

Al Attar, Mohsen & Vernon Tava (2010) "TWAIL Pedagogy: Legal Education for Emancipation," 15 *Palestine Yearbook of international Law* 7–39.

Al Attar, Mohsen & Rebekah Thompson (2011) " A Multi-Level Democratisation of International Law-Making: Popular Aspirations Towards Self-Determination," 3 *Trade, Law and Development* 65–102.

Alawi, Hayla (2020) :Jeju Island, the Three Clans Myth, and Women Divers: Female Importance in Jeju's Cultural History," Pamela J. Mackintosh Undergraduate Research Award, https://deepblue.lib.umich.edu/bitstream/handle/2027.42/156011/haylaalawiresearchpaper.pdf?sequence=1&isAllowed=y (accessed 22 October 2020).

Albeck-Ripka, Livia, Isabella Kwai, Thomas Fuller, & Famie Tarabay (2020) "It's an Atomic Bomb: Australia Deploys Military as Fires Spread," *NY Times*, 4. January.

Ali, Saleem H. (2001) *Mining, the Environment, and Indigenous Development Conflicts*. Tucson, AZ: University of Arizona Press.

Ali, Sangar P. (2017) "KK Leader: Referendum a Democratic Right, No One Should Stand Against it," *Kurdistan24*, 13 June, available at http://www.kurdistan24.net/en/news/1ba4d164-3e06-431d-9a14-e83370cb869a.

Allen, Charles W. & Richard E. Jensen (2001) *From Fort Laramie to Wounded Knee: In the West That Was*. Lincoln, NE: University of Nebraska Press.

Allen, Nathan and Inti Landauro (2020) "Coronavirus Traces Found in March 2019 Sewage Sample, Spanish Study Shows," *Reuters*, 26 June.

"Allow Jerome Succor Aba Entry to the US Now!" (2018) NY Committee for Human Rights in the Philippines, 18 April.

Amaline, William T. et al. (2011) *Human Rights in Our Own Backyard: Injustice and Resistance in the United States*. Philadelphia, PA: University of Pennsylvania Press.

Amah Mutsun Land Trust (2020) "Our Mission," (accessed 15 May 2020), available at https://www.amahmutsunlandtrust.org/our-mission.

Aman, Alfred C. Jr. & Carol Greenhouse (2017) *Translational Law: Cases and Problems in an Interconnected World*. Durham, NC: Carolina Academic Press.

"American Indian in 1890 " (2020) Native American Netroots (accessed 15 May 2020), available at http://nativeamericannetroots.net/diary/1716.

Amnesty International (2017a) "Amnesty International Report 2016/17: The State of the World's Human Rights," available at https://www.amnesty.org/download/Documents/POL1048002017ENGLISH.PDF.

Amnesty International (2017b) "All the Civilians Suffer": Conflict, Displacement, and Abuse in Northern Myanmar," available at https://www.amnesty.org/en/documents/asa16/6429/2017/en/.

Amnesty International (2019) "Nepal 2017/2018," available at https://www.amnesty.org/en/countries/asia-and-the-pacific/nepal/report-nepal/.

Amnistía Internacional (2015) "Diario del Juicio a Relmu Namku," 17 November, available at https://amnistia.org.ar/relmu/.

Anaya, S. James (2000) *Indigenous People in International Law*. Oxford, UK: Oxford University Press.

Andersen, Pamela Jacquelin (2017) "Indigenous Peoples Are Dying for a Global War for Their Lands," *Climate Home News*, 13 September.

Anderson, Benedict (1983) *Imagined Communities: Reflections on the Origin and Spread of Nationalism.* London, UK: VERSO.

Andersson, Rani-Henrik (2019) *A Whirlwind Passed Through Our Country: Lakota Voices of the Ghost Dance.* Norman: University of Oklahoma Press.

Anghie, Antony (2002) "Colonialism and the Birth of International Institutions: Sovereignty, Economy, and the Mandate System of the League of Nations," 34 *NY University Journal of International Law and Politics* 513–634.

Anghie, Antony (2004) *Imperialism, Sovereignty and the Making of International Law.* Cambridge, UK: Cambridge University Press.

Anghie, Antony (2006) "Nationalism, Development and the Postcolonial State: The Legacies of the League of Nations," 41 *Texas International Law Journal* 447–463.

Anghie, Antony (2008) "TWAIL: Past and Future," 10 *International Community Law Review* 479–482.

Anghie, Anton & B.S. Chimni (2003) "Third World Approaches to International Law and Individual Responsibility in Internal Conflicts," *Chinese Journal of International Law* 2:77–103.

"Area 1. B.O.S.S. Jeju Island Trip" (2020) *MWR: Camp Casey*, https://casey.armymwr.com/calendar/jeju-island (accessed 22 October 2020).

Appiagyei-Atua, Kwadwo (2015) "Ethical Dimensions of Third-World Approaches to International Law (TWAIL): A Critical Review," 8 *African Journal of Legal Studies* 209–235.

Arsel, Murat & Bram Buscher (2012) "Nature Inc.: Changes and Continuities in Neoliberal Conservation and Environmental Markets," 43 *Development and Change* 53–78.

Asia Foundation (2017) Nepal at a Glance, available at https://asiafoundation.org/wp-content/uploads/2017/10/Nepal-StateofConflictandViolence.pdf.

"Asian Region is Vulnerable to Natural and Man-Made Disasters: Rajnath" (2016) *Business Standard*, 3 November.

Auken, Bill Van (2015) "US Troops Immune from Prosecution, Raped Dozens of Colombian Children," *World Socialist Web Site*, 28 March.

Austin, Accion Zapatista de (1997) "Peoples' Global Action Against 'Free' Trade and the World Trade Organizaton," 29 November, available at http://www.hartford-hwp.com/archives/25a/024.html.

Aveling, Harry and Damien Kingsbury (2003) *Autonomy and Disintegration in Indonesia.* NY: Routledge.

Bachelet, Michelle (2019) "Human Rights and Climate Change," United Nations Human Rights Office of the High Commissioner, 9 September, available at https://www.ohchr.org/EN/Issues/HRAndClimateChange/Pages/HRClimateChangeIndex.aspx.

Bacon, John (2017) "Kurds Vote for Independence Amid U.S. Concerns," *USA Today*, 27 September.

Badaru, O.A. (2008) "Examining the Utility of Third World Approaches to International Law for International Human Rights Law," 10 *International Community Law Review* 379–387.

Bailey, Jeremy D. (2015) *James Madison and Constitutional Imperfection*. NY: Cambridge University Press.

Balisacan, Arsenio M. & Hal Hill (2002) "The Philippine Development Puzzle," 2002 *Southeast Asian Affairs* 237–252.

Banerjee, J.C. (1994) *Encyclopaedic Dictionary of Psychological Terms*. New Delhi: M.D. Publications Pvt Ltd.

Barros, Maria Valeria (2015) "The Constitution of the Republic of Ecuador: Pachamama Has Rights," *Environment & Society* 11 (2015), available at http://www.environmentandsociety.org/arcadia/constitution-republic-ecuador-pachamama-has-rights.

Baslar, Kemal (1998) *The Concept of the Common Heritage of Mankind in International Law*. Leiden, Neatherlands: Martinus Nijhoff Pubs.

Bayani, Makisig (2011) "Wikileaks: US Says Island Mindanao Has $1-Trillion Dollar Untapped Mineral Resources," *Peso Reserve News*, August, available at https://www.pesoreserve.com/2011/08/wikileaks-us-says-island-mindanao-has-1.html.

Bender, Thomas (2006) A Nation Among Nations: America's Place in World History, NY: Hill and Wang.

Barsocchini, Robert (2015) "US Now Has Over 1,400 Foreign Military Bases Spread Over 120 Countries: Assange," *Countercurrents.org*, 10 September, available at https://www.countercurrents.org/barsocchini100915.htm.

Barelli, Mauro (2018) Seeking Justice in International Law: The Significance and Implications of the UN Declaration on the Rights of Indigenous Peoples, NY: Routledge.

Barrow, Amy (2010) "History and Theory of International Law: A Transcivilizational Perspective on International Law," 3 *Asian Journal of International Law* 192–193.

Bassiouni, M. Cherif (2010) "Legal Status of US Forces in Iraq from 2003–2008," *Chicago Journal of International Law* 11:1–38.

Bear, Sarah (2020) "Mining on Indigenous Territories in the Philippines: Geological Features, Environmental, Socioeconomic Impacts on the Indigenous Population of the Philippines," *Storymaps*, 16 August, https://storymaps.arcgis.com/stories/de2c08a0b1cd4d08a4f7e728adc0c22e (accessed 22 October 2020).

"Bearing the Brunt: The Impact of Government Responses to COVID-19 on Indigenous Peoples in India" *International Working Group for Indigenous Affairs (IWGIA)*, 10 September, https://www.iwgia.org/en/news-alerts/news-covid-19/3839-bearing-brunt-covid-19.html.

"Beigunzoku, Kisosoto Chiikyotei ga Hikokusekini ["Indictment is Proper" for Military Employee: SOFA is on Defendant's Seat] (hereinafter Beigunzoku)" (2011) *Okinawa Times*, 29 May.

"Beiheihanzai Fukiso ni Kogi [Protest against Non-Prosecutorial Decision] (2011) *Akahata Shimbun*, 19 April.

Berlinger, Joshua (2019) "66 People Now Killed by Flooding in Jakarta, and More Rain Appears to be on the Way," *CNN*, 6. January.

Berner, Brad K. (2014) *The Spanish-American War: A Documentary History with Commentaries*. Lanham, MD: Fairleigh Dickinson University Press.

Berry, Thomas (1999) *The Great Work: Our Way into the Future*. NY: Broadway Books.

Bevins, Vincent (2018) "Instead of Peace, Indigenous Filipinos Get the Duterte Treatment," *Washington Post*, 22 April.

Bhatia, Amar (2012) "The South of the North: Building on Critical Approaches to International Law with Lessons from the Fourth World," 14 *Oregon Review of International Law* 131–176.

Bhatt, Kinnari (2019) "A Post-Colonial Legal Approaches to the Chagos Case and the (Dis)Application of Land Rights Norm," 15 *International Journal of Law in Context* 1–19.

Biggs, Shannon, Goldtooth, Tom B.K. and Lake, Osprey Orielle (2017) *Rights of Nature and Mother Earth Rights-Based Law for Systemic Change*, https://www.ienearth.org/wp-content/uploads/2017/11/RONME-Rights BasedLaw-final-1.pdf.

"Biodiversity Strategy of the Basque Autonomous Community: 2030 and First Action Plan 2020" (2019) *Regions4*, available at https://www.regions4. org/resources/biodiversity-strategy-for-the-basque-autonomous-community-2030-and-first-action-plan-2020/.

Bioneers (2020) "Bioneers Partners with Community Environmental Legal Defense Fund on Rights of Nature in Indigenous Communities" (accessed 15 May 2020), available at https://bioneers.org/bioneers-partners-commun ity-environmental-legal-defense-fund-rights-nature-indigenous-communities/.

Bird, John Samuel (2018) "Bio-Piracy on the High Sea? Benefit Sharing from Marine Genetic Resources Exploitation in Areas Beyond National Jurisdiction," 9 *Natural Resources* 413–428.

Blum, William (2014) *Killing Hope: U.S. Military and CIA Interventions Since World War II*. London, UK: Zed Books.

Bociago, Robert (2020) "For the Philippines' Mangyans, COVID-19 Extends a Long History of Discrimination," *Mongabay*, 7 August.

Bogota, John Otis (2015) "Colombians Accuse U.S. Soldiers and Officials of Sexual Assault and Rape," *Time*, 15 April.

Bolivia: Pacto de Unidad Exige al Gobierno la Aprobación de la Ley de la Madre Tierra [Bolivia: The Pact of Unity Requires the Government to Approve the

Law of Mother Earth]" (2011) *Enlace Indigena*, 18 July, available at https:// movimientos.org/node/19600?key=19600.

Bonn, Keith E. & Anthony E. Baker (2000) *Guide to Military Operations Other War: Tactics, Techniques & Procedures for Stability & Support Operations: Domestic & International*. Mechanicsburg, PA: Stackpole Books.

Borie, Maud & Mike Hulme (2015) "Framing Global Biodiversity: IPBES Between Mother Earth and Ecosystem Services," 54 *Environmental Science and Policy* 487–498.

Bornemann, Alberto Ulloa, Arthur Schmidt, and Aurora Camacho de Schmidt (2007) *Surviving Mexico's Dirty Wr: A Political Prisoner's Memoir*. Philadelphia, PA: Temple University Press.

Borrows, John (2010) *Canada's Indigenous Constitutio*. Toronto: University of Toronto Press.

Borras, Susana (2016) "New Transitions from Human Rights to the Environment to the Rights of Nature," 5 *Transnational Environmental Law* 113–143.

Bosselmann, Klaus (2015) *Earth Governance: Trusteeship of the Global Commons*. Cheltenham, U.K.: Edward Elgar Publishing.

Botello, Nelson Arteaga & Adrian Lopez Rivera (2000) "Everything in This Job is Money: Inside the Mexican Police," 17 *World Policy Journal* 61–70.

Bowler, Jacinta (2020) "We Don't Want to Alarm Anyone, But a Large Amount of Siberia Is on Fire Right Now," *Science Alert*, 4 May.

Boyd, David R. (2017) *The Rights of Nature: A Legal Revolution That Could Save the World*. Toronto, Canada: ECW Press.

"Brazil: Indigenous Peoples Participate in World Social Forum" (2018) *Cultural Survivor*, (accessed 21 November 2018), available at https://www.culturalsurvival.org/news/brazil-indigenous-peoples-participate-world-social-forum.

"Brazil 'Invites Deforestation' With Overhaul of Environmental Law" (2018) *Guardian*, 1 March.

Breitenbach, Dagmar (2014) "A Free and Independent Free State of Bavaria?" *DW*, 19 September.

Broadman, Harry G. (2019) "Arbitration of International Investor-State Disputes Sorely Needs Reform," *Forbes*, 30 October.

Brockington, Dan and Rosaleen Duffy (2010). "Capitalism and Conservation: The Production and Reproduction of Biodiversity Conservation," 3 *Antipode* 469–482.

Brockington, Dan, Rosaleen Duffy and Jim Igoe (2008) *Nature Unbound: Conservation, Capitalism, and the Future of Protected Areas*. London, UK: Earthscan.

Brodzinsky, Sibylla (2015) "US Army Investigates Reports That Soldiers Raped Dozens in Colombia," *Guardian*, 7 April.

Brolmann, Catherine, Rene Lefeber & Majoline Zieck (1993) *Peoples and Minorities in International Law.* Dordrecht, Netherlands: Martinus Nijhoff.

Brown, Alleen (2017) "Approves Keystone XL Pipeline as Opponents Face Criminalization of Protests," *The Intercept,* 20 November.

Brown, Alleen (2018a) "Five Spills, Six Months in Operation: Dakota Access Track Record Highlights Unavoidable Reality: Pipelines Leak," *The Intercept,* 9 January,

Brown, Alleen (2018b) "The Infiltrator: How an Undercover Oil Industry Mercenary Tricked Pipeline Opponents into Believing He was One of Them," *The Intercept,* 30, December.

Brown, Alleen, Will Parrish & Alice Sper (2017) "Leaked Documents reveal Counterterrorism Tactics Used at Standing Rock to 'Defeat Pipeline Insurgencies'," *The Intercept,* 27 May.

Brown, Kate (2020) "The Pandemic Is Not a Natural Disaster," *New Yorker,* 13 April.

Buchan, Bruce (2001) "Subjecting the Natives: Aborigines, Property and Possession Under Early Colonial Rule, 45 *Social Analysis* 143–162.

Buck, Susan J. (1998) *The Global Commons: An Introduction.* Washington, DC: Island Press.

Burdon, Peter (2011) *Exploring Wild Law: The Philosophy of Earth Jurisprudence.* Cambridge, MA: Wakefield Press.

Burgess, John (1986) "Japanese Proud of Their Homogeneous Society," *Washington Post,* 28 September.

Burnett, Peter H. (1851) "Executive Order, Peter Burnette, 1st Governor, Independent Democrat 1849–1851: State of the State Address," 6 January, available at https://governors.library.ca.gov/addresses/s_01-Burnett2.html.

Burnette, Ryan (2013) *Biosecurity: Understanding, Assessing, and Preventing the Threat.* Hoboken, NJ: Wiley.

Burns, Jim (2010) "'UC Santa Cruz Makes' Most Beautiful College Campuses' List," *UCSC Santa Cruz News Center,* 10, March.

Burns, Marcelle J. (2013) "Shifting Global Power and Shifting State Power." In Maguire et al., eds., *Shifting Global Powers and International Law: Challenges and Opportunities.* London, UK: Routledge.

Buscher, Bram (2012) "Payments for Ecosystem Services as Neoliberal Conservation: (Reinterpreting) Evidence from the Maloti-Drakensberg, South Africa," 10 *Conservation and Society* 29–41.

Buscher, Bram, Sian Sullivan, Katja Neves, Jim Igoe & Dan Brockington (2012) "Towards a Synthesized Critique of Neoliberal Biodiversity Conservation," 23 *Capitalism, Nature, Socialism* 4–30.

Buxton, Julie (2006) *The Political Economy of Narcotics: Production, Consumption and Global Markets.* London, UK: Zed Books.

"California Military Bases" (2020), https://militarybases.com/california/#: ~:text=California%20has%20more%20military%20bases,most%20heavily%20a round%20San%20Diego (accessed 22 October 2020).

Callahan, Manuel (2005) "Why Not Share a Dream? Zapatista as Political and Cultural Practice," 29 *Humboldt Journal of Social Relations* 6–37.

Calloway, Colin G. (1998) *New Worlds for All: Indians, Europeans, and the Remaking of Early America*. Baltimore, MD: The John Hopkins University Press.

Calmon, Miguel Mariana Oliveira & Rachel Biderman (2019) "The Other Brazilian Rainforest: Why Restoration of the Atlantic Forest Can Help Tackle Climate Change," *World Resources Institute*, 14 August.

Campbell, Alexia Fernandez & Carrie Levine (2020) "Native Americans, Hit Hard by Covid-19, Faced Major Barriers to Vote," *The Center for Public Integrity*, 5 November.

Campbell, Duncan (2004) "Energy Giant Agrees Settlement with Burmese Villagers," *Guardian*, 14 December.

"Canada Votes 'No' as UN Native Rights Declaration Passes" (2007) *CBC*, 13 September.

Canny, Nicholas (2012) "A Protestant or Catholic Atlantic World? Confessional Divisions and the Writing of Natural History," 181 *Proceedings of the British Academy* 83–121.

Capdevila, Gustavo (2009) "Indigenous People Troubled by US Military Presence in Colombia," *TNI*, 14 August, available at https://www.tni.org/my/node/4501.

Carey, Peter (1995) "Letter: State Terrorism in East Timor," *Indep.*, 2 October, available at https://www.independent.co.uk/life-style/letter-state-terrorism-in-east-timor-1575579.html.

Carrington, Damian (2017) "Earth's Sixth Mass Extinction Event Underway, Scientists Warn," *Guardian*, 10, July.

Carrington, Damian (2018) "Humanity Has Wiped out 60% of Animal Populations Since 1970, Report Finds," *Guardian*, 19 October.

Carson, Catherine & Kenneth Iain McDonald (2012) "Enclosing the Global Commons: The Convention on Biological Diversity and Green Grabbing," 39 *Journal of Peasant Studies* 263–283.

Castellino, Joshua and Niamh Walsh (2005) *International Law and Indigenous People*. Leiden: M. Nijhoff Publishers.

Castells, Manuel (2010) *End of Millennium, in The Information Age: Economy Society, and Culture*. Oxford, UK: Blackwell.

Castets, Remi (2019) "What's Really Happening to Uighurs in Xinjiang?" *Nation*, 19 March.

Castillo, Elias (2004) "The Dark, Terrible Secret of California's Missions," *SF Chronicle*, 8 November.

"Catalan Referendum: Preliminary Results Show 90% in Favor of Independence" (2017) *Guardian*, 1 October.

"Censo Nacional de Poblacion, Hogares y Viviendas 2010:Pueblos Originarios" Region Noroeste Argentino: Serie D N 1," (2020) *INDEC* (accessed 15 May 2020) at https://web.archive.org/web/20080611004448/http://www.indec.gov.ar/webcenso/ECPI/index_ecpi.asp.

Central Intelligence Agency (1950) "CIA-RDP67, Review of the World Situation as it Relates to the Security of the United States," 16 January, available at https://www.cia.gov/library/readingroom/docs/CIA-RDP67-00059A000500100009-6.pdf.

Central Intelligence Agency (2019) *The World Factbook* (accessed 14 March 2019), available at https://www.cia.gov/library/publications/the-world-factbook/geos/mx.html.

Center for the Study of Ethnicity and Race (2017) "Indigenous People's Rights and Unreported Struggles: Conflict and Peace," available at https://academiccommons.columbia.edu/doi/10.7916/D82R5095.

Cepek, Michael (2012) *A Future for Amazonia: Randy Borman and Cofán Environmental Politics*. Austin, TX: University of Texas Press.

Cerney, Jan & Roberta Sago (2010) *Images of America: Black Hills Gold Rush Towns*. Chicago, IL: Arcadia Publishing.

Chakma, Suhas & Marianne Jensen (2001) *Racism against Indigenous Peoples*. Copenhagen, Denmark: IWGIA.

Chakma, Trimita (2020) "A Rapid Assessment Report: The Impact of COVID-19 on Indigenous and Tribal Peoples in Bangladesh," *International Working Group on Indigenous Affairs (IWGIA)*, 10 August.

Chambers, David Wade (2020) "Native American Road Systems and Trails," *Udemy* (accessed September. 24, 2013).

Chang, Emily Nyen (2001) "Engagement Abroad: Enlisted Men, U.S. Military Policy and the Sex Industry, 15 *Notre Dame Journal of Law, Ethnics & Public Policy* 621–653.

Chang, Ha-Joon (2000) *Kicking Away the Ladder: Development Strategy in Historical Perspective*. London, UK: Anthem Press.

Changhoon, Ko (2007) "A New Look at Korean Gender Roles: Jeju (Cheju) Women Divers as a World Cultural Heritage," 23 *Asian Women* 31–54.

Charny, Israel W. (1999) *Encyclopedia of Genocide*. Santa Barbara, CA: ABC-CLIO.

Cheng, Sinkwan (2013) "Terrorism, Hegel, Honneth," 2 *Las Torres de Lucca* 47–67.

Chiaramonte, Jose (2010) Carlos Nation & State in Latin America: Political Language During Independence. NY: Routledge.

Chimni, B.S. (2006) "Third World Approaches to International Law: A Manifesto," *International Community Law Review* 8: 3–27.

Chimni, B.S. (2007a) "A Just World Under Law: A View From the South," 22 *American University International Law Review* 199–220.

Chimni, B.S. (2007b) "The Past, Present and Future of International Law: A Critical Third World Approach," 8 *Melbourne Journal of International Law* 499–515.

Chimni, B.S. (2010) "International Law Scholarship in Post-Colonial India: Coping with Dualism," 23 *Leiden Journal of International Law* 23–51.

Chimni, B.S. (2011) "Asian Civilizations and International Law: Some Reflections," 1 *Asian Journal of International Law* 39–42.

Chomsky, Noam (1996) *Powers and Prospects: Reflections on Human Nature and the Social Order.* Boston, MA: South End Press.

Chomsky, Noam (2000) *Rogue States: The Rule of Force in World Affairs.* London, UK: Plutobooks.

Chomsky, Noam (2013) *On Anarchism.* NY: The New Press.

Chomsky, Noam (2020) *Internationalism or Extinction.* England, UK: Routledge.

Chomsky, Noam & Michel Foucault (2006) *The Chomsky-Foucault Debate: On Human Nature.* NY: New Press.

Chomsky, Noam, Lois Meyer, & Benjamin Maldonado (2010) *New World of Indigenous Resistance: Noam Chomsky and Voices from North, South, and Central America.* San Francisco, CA: City Lights Open Media.

Chulov, Martin (2017) "More Than 92% of Voters in Iraqi Kurdistan Back Independence" *Guardian,* 27 September.

Churchill, Ward (1993) *Struggle for the Land: Indigenous Resistance to Genocide, Ecocide, and Expropriation in Contemporary North America.* Monroe, ME: Common Courage Press.

Churchill, Ward (1994) *Indians Are Us? Culture and Genocide in Native North America.* Monroe, ME: Common Courage Press.

Churchill, Ward (1996) *From a Native Son: Selected Essays in Indigenism, 1985– 1995.* Boston, MA: South End Press.

Churchill, Ward (1997) *A Little Matter of Genocide: Holocaust and Denial in the Americas 1492 to the Present.* San Francisco, CA: City Lights Publishers.

Churchill, Ward (1999) *Acts of Rebellion: The Word Churchill Reader.* London, UK: Routledge.

Churchill, Ward (2002) *Struggle for the Land: Native North American Resistance to Genocide, Ecocide and Colonization.* San Francisco, CA: City Lights Books.

Churchilkl, Ward (2003) *Perversions of Justice: Indigenous Peoples and Angloamerican Law.* San Francisco, CA: City Lights Books.

Churchill, Ward (2004) *Kill the Indian, Save the Man: The Genocidal Impact of American Indian residential Schools.* SF, CA: City Lights Publishers.

Churchill, Ward & Jim Vander Wall (2001) *COINTELRO Papers: Documents from the FBI's Wars Against Dissent in the United States*. Boston, MA: South End Press.

Cirkovic, Elena (2006) "Self-Determination and Indigenous Peoples in International Law," 31 *American Indian Law Review* 375–399.

Clark, Lynette (2007) "To the Lakota Nation," *Alaskan Independent Party: Alaska First- Alaska Always*, 21 December.

Clark, Wesley(2007) *A Time to Lead: For Duty, Honor and Country*. NY: Palgrave Macmillan.

Clastres, Pierre (1989) *Society Against the State: Essays in Political Anthropology*. Cambridge: Zone Books.

Clinton, Greg (2016) *Puerto Rico and the Spanish-American War*. NY: Cavendish Square Publishing, LLC.

Cochran, Charles L. & Hungdah Chiu (2019) "U.S. Status of Forces Agreements with Asian Countries: Selected Studies," 7 *Occasional Papers/Reprints Series in Contemporary Asian Studies* 1–144.

Cohen, Felix S. (1953) "The Erosion of Indian Rights," 62 *Yale Law Journal* 348–390.

Cohen, Li (2020) "Australian Bushfire Smoke Killed More People Than the Fires Did, Study Says," *CBS News*, 20 March.

Colorado Community Rights Network (2019) *Lafayette Climate Bill of Rights* (accessed 14 November 2019), available at https://cocrn.org/lafayette-climate-bill-rights/.

"Community Environmental Legal Defense Fund: Bringing Real Democracy and Protection to communities and Their Environments" (2016) *Radical Ecological Democracy*, 6 April.

Community Environmental Legal Defense Fund (2020) Community Rights Do-It-Yourself Guide to Lawmaking (accessed 15 May 2020), available at https://celdf.org/diyguide.pdf.

"Community Shaken by Woman's Murder" (2018) *Mexico News Daily*, 24 January.

Constitution of the Oglala Sioux Tribe (1935), https://narf.org/nill/constitutions/oglala_sioux/index.html (accessed 15 March 2019).

Constitution of the Oglala Sioux Tribe of the Pine Ridge Reservation (amended, 18, December, 2008), https://narf.org/nill/constitutions/oglala_sioux/oglalaconst.pdf (accessed 15 March 2019).

Convention on Biological Diversity (2007) "What's the Problem?" (accessed 22 October 2020), https://www.cbd.int/impact/problem.shtml.

Corntassel, Jeff & Cheryl Bryce (2012) "Practicing Sustainable Self-Determination: Indigenous Approaches to Cultural Restoration and Revitalization," 18 *The Brown Journal of World Affairs* 151–162.

Council on Foreign Relations (2020) "Civil War in South Sudan," 18 June, available at https://www.cfr.org/global-conflict-tracker/conflict/civil-war-south-sudan.

"Court Awards Record Damages for U.S. Noise Pollution at Kadena Air Base" (2017) *Japan Times*, 23 February.

Crawford v. United States, 212 U.S. 183 (1908).

Crawford, Quinton Douglas (2005*) Knowledge for Tomorrow: A Summarized Commentary of World History, Nature, Health, Religion, Organized Crime, and Inspiration for the Youth*. NY: IUniverse.

Cregan, Fionuala (2015) "Mapuche Leader Found 'Not Guilty' in Unprecedented Trial in Argentina," *Intercontinental Cry*, 6 November, available at https://intercontinentalcry.org/mapuche-leader-found-not-guilty-in-unprecedented-trial-in-argentina/.

Cruetzig, Felix (2017) "Govern Land as a Global Commons," Nature, 30 May.

Cullinan, Cormac (2001) *Wild Law: A Manifesto for Earth Justice*. Jackson, VT: Chelsea Green Publishing.

"Cultural Survival, Observations on the State of Indigenous Women's Rights in Mexico: Alternative Report Submission" (2018), available at https://www.culturalsurvival.org/sites/default/files/CEDAW_Report_Mexico_2018.pdf.

Cumbers, Andrew (2015) "Constructing a Global Commons in, Against and Beyond the State," 19 *Space and Polity* 62–75.

Cupples, Julie (2913) *Latin American Development*. NY: Routledge.

Da Costa, Pedro Nicolaci (2020) "Native Americans Are Being Hit Hard by Coronavirus, An Echo of Colonial Pandemics That Nearly Wiped Them Out," *Market Watch*, 13 March.

Dadouch, Sarah (2017) "Damascus Rejects Iraqi Kurdish Independence Referendum," *Reuters*, 25 September.

Danaher, Kevin (1994) *50 Years is Enough: The Case Against the World Bank and the International Monetary Fund*. Boston, MA: South End Press.

Danver, Steven (2012) The Native Peoples of the World: An Encyclopedia of Groups, Cultures, and Contemporary Issues. Armonk, NY: Sharpe Reference.

Darian-Smith, Eve (2010) *Religion, Race, Rights: Landmarks in the History of Modern Anglo-American Law*. Oxford, U.K.: Hart Publishing Ltd.

Darlington, Shasta, Jose Brito, and Flora Charner (2020) "Report: Brazil's Indigenous People Are Dying at an Alarming Rate from Covid-19," *CNN*, 24 May.

Dawson, John Philip (1960) A History of Lay Judges. Cambridge, MA: Harvard University Press.

Day, Richard J.F. (2005) *Gramsci is Dead: Anarchist Currents in the Newest Social Movements*. London, UK: Pluto Press.

Death, Carl (2014) *Critical Environmental Politics*. NY: Routledge.

"Declaration of the World Trade Organization (WTO) and Indigenous Peoples: Resisting Globalizations, Asserting Self-Determination" (2013) *IPMSDL*, 6 December. available at https://www.wto.org/english/thewto_e/minist_e/mc9_e/indigenous_peoples_declaration.pdf.

Delbruck, Jost (2002) "Prospect for a 'World (International) Law?' Legal Developments in a Changing International System," 9 *Indiana Journal of Global Legal Studies* 401–431.

Defense Manpower Data Center, (2019) Number of Military and DoD Appropriated Fund (APF) Civilian Personnel Permanently Assigned by Duty Location and Service/Component.

Dekdeken, Sarah K. Julius Caesar Daguitan and Abigail B. Anongos (2013) "Declaration: World Trade Organization (WTO) and Indigenous People: Resisting Globalization, Asserting Self-Determination", available at https://www.wto.org/english/thewto_e/minist_e/mc9_e/indigenous_peoples_declaration.pdf.

DeLoughrey, Elizabeth M. (2019) *Allegories of the Anthropocene*. Durham, NC: Duke University Press.

Denyer, Simon (2016) "Tibetans in Anguish as Chinese Mines Pollute Their Sacred Grasslands," *Washington Post*, 26 December.

Derichs, Claudia & Andrea Fleschenberg (2010) *Religious Fundamentalisms and Their Gendered Impacts in Asia*. Berlin, Germany: Friedrich-Ebert-Stiftung.

Desierto, D. A. (2008) "A Postcolonial International Law Discourses on Regional Developments in South and Southeast Asia," 36 *International Journal of Legal Information* 387–431.

Dhooge, Lucien J. (2010) "Aguinda v. Chevron-Texaco: Discretionary Grounds for the Non-recognition of Foreign Judgments for Environmental Injury in the United States," 28 *Virginia Environmental Law Journal* 241–298.

Diamond, Jared (1991) *The Third Chimpanzee: The Evolution and Future of the Human Animal*. NY: HarperCollins.

Diamond, Jared (1997) *Guns, Germs, and Steel: The Fates of Human Societies*. NY: W.W. Norton & Co.

Diamond v. Chakrabarty, 447 U.S. 303 (1980).

Dickinson, Torry (2019) "Peace Activists Have Been Protesting Korea's Navy Base in Jeju for 12 Years!? *Friends Peace Teams*, 21 October

Dietzel, Erik, Gordian Schudt, Verena Krahling, Mikhail Matrosovich, and Stephan Becker (2017) "Functional Characterization of Adaptive Mutations During Ebola Virus Outbreak," 91 *Journal of Virology* 1–13.

Dippie, Brian W. (2020)"American Indians: The Image of the Indian," *National Humanity Center* (accessed 15 May 2020) available at http://nationalhumanitiescenter.org/tserve/nattrans/ntecoindian/essays/indimage.htm.

Dixon, Robyn (2020) "Russia Stands to Benefit as Middle East Tensions Spike After Soleimani Killing," *Washington Post*, 6 January.

DNA Web Team (2016) "Struggle for Independence Will Continue Till Kashmir Gets Freedom, Says Pakistan High Commissioner Abdul Basit," *DNA INDIA*, 14 August, available at http://www.dnaindia.com/india/rep ort-pakistan-s-independence-day-dedicated-to-kashmir-s-azadi-this-year-says-high-commissioner-abdul-basit-2244894.

Dobson, David (1997) *Irish Emigrants in North America*. Baltimore, MD: Cleaerfield Publishing Company.

Doherty, Ben & Kate Lamb (2017a) "Banned West Papua Independence Petition Handed to UN," Guar*dian*, 27 Sept.

Doherty, Ben & Kate Lamb (2017b) "West Papua Independence Petition is Rebuffed at UN," *Guardian*, 29 September.

Dressler, Wolfram and Bram Buscher (2008) "Market Triumphalism and the So-Called CBNRM 'Crisis" at the South African Section of the Great Limpopo Transfrontier Park," 39 *Geoforum* 452–465.

"Drinking at USF 'Official Event' is Regarded as Party of 'Official Duty'" (2011) *Japan Press Weekly*, 14 April.

Drugmand, Dana "N.H. Town Passes Law Recognizing Right to a Healthy Climate," *Climate Liability News*, 14 March.

Dunbar-Ortiz, Roxanne (2006) "What Brought Evo Morales to Power?" *Counterpunch*, 10 February, available at https://www.counterpunch.org/2006/02/10/what-brought-evo-morales-to-power/.

Dunbar-Ortiz, Roxanne (2014) *An Indigenous Peoples' History of the United States*. Boston, MA: Beacon Press.

Dunbar-Ortiz, Roxanne (2018) *Loaded: A Disarming History of the Second Amendment*. San Francisco: City Lights Books.

Dunleavy, Harry (2019) *Irish Immigration to Latin America*. Red Bank, NJ: Newman Springs Publishing.

Dupuy, Kendra, Scott Gates, Havard M. Nygard, Ida Rudolfsen, Siri Aas Rustad, Havard Strand, & Henrik Urdal (2017) "Trends in Armed Conflict, 1946–2016," *EthZurich: Center for Security Studies*, 22 June, available at https://www.prio.org/utility/DownloadFile.ashx?id=1373&type=publicationfile.

Durrhelm, David N. (2010) "Bioterrorism: Being Prepared But Not Paralyzed," 90 *Issues* 15–17.

Dutton, Yvonne M. (2010) "Bringing Pirates to Justice: A Case for Including Piracy within the Jurisdiction of the International Criminal Court," 11 *Chicago Journal of International Law* 201–245.

Eder, James F. (1993) "Indigenous Peoples, Ancestral Lands and Human Rights in the Philippines," *Cultural Survival*, June.

El Consejo Indio de Sud America (2018) *PUEBLO INDIO* (accessed 21 November 2018), available at http://www.puebloindio.org/CISA/cisa.htm.

Elegant, Naomi Xu (2020) "Before the New Coronavirus, There was SARS, and MERS: Do Epidemics Ever Really End?" Fortune, 29 February.

Elisseeff, Vadime (1999) *The Silk Roads: Highways of Culture and Commerce*. Paris, France: UNESCO.

Elmore, Jonathan (2020) *Fiction and the Sixth Mass Extinction: Narrative in an Era of Loss*. Lanham, MD: Lexington Books.

Epstein Graham, et al. (2013) "Diagnosing Oceanic Commons ICCAT and the Atlantic Bluefin Tuna," Commoners and the Changing Commons: Livelihoods, Environmental Security, and Shared Knowledge, the Fourteenth Biennial Conference of the International Association for the Study of the Commons, http://dlc.dlib.indiana.edu/dlc/bitstream/handle/10535/8879/EPSTEIN_1150.pdf?sequence=1&isAllowed=y (accessed 22 October 2020).

Eslava Luis & Sundhya Pahuja (2012) "Beyond the (Post) Colonial: TWAIL and the Everyday Life of International Law," 45 *Journal of Law and Politics in Africa, Asia and Latin America* 195–221.

Espinosa, Nayeli E. Ramirez (2015) "Consulting the Indigenous Peoples in the Making of Laws in Mexico: The Zirahuen Ampara," 32 *Arizona Journal of International & Comparative Law* 647–670.

Evers, Sandra J.T.M. and Mary Kooy (2011) *Eviction from the Chagos Islands: Displacement and Struggle for Identity Against Two World Powers*. Netherlands: Brill Publishers.

"Ex-U.S. Base Worker Appeals Life Sentence for Killing Okinawa Woman" (2017) *Japan Times*, 12 December.

"ExxonMobil Reports Papua New Guinea Discovery" (2018) *Rigzone*, 16 January, available at https://www.rigzone.com/news/exxonmobil_reports_papua_new_guinea_discovery-16-jan-2018-153157-article/.

Eyre, Makana (2019) "Why India Just Stripped 1.9 Million People of Citizenship," *Nation*, 10 Sept.

Fabricant, Nicole (2012) *Mobilizing Bolivia's Displaced: Indigenous Politics and the Struggle over Land*. Chapel Hill, NC: University of North Carolina Press.

Fareed, Rifat (2018) "Kashmir Tension Persists After Shopian Killings," *Aljazeera*, 2 April, available at https://www.aljazeera.com/news/2018/04/kashmir-tension-persists-shopian-killings-180402145339013.html.

Fearon, James D. (2003) "Ethnic and Cultural Diversity by Country," 8 *Journal of Economic Growth* 195–222.

Fenelon, James V. (1998) *Cultricide, Resistance, and the Survival of the Lakota (Sioux Nation)*. NY: Routledge.

Fenn, Elizabeth (2020) "Biological Warfare in Eighteen-Century North America: Beyond Jeffrey Amherst," 86 *the Journal of American History* 1552–80.

Ferguson, Sarah (2019) "Heavy Monsoon Rains Drench Rohingya Refugee Camps in Bangladesh," *UNICEF*, 9 July.

Fernandez, James & John Herzog (2914) "Farewell Lord Jeffrey Amherst: Debate Over Amherst College's Institutional Anchorage in History," 30 *Anthropology Today* 7–9.

"Filipino Activist Claims He Was Given Weapons, Tortured At SFO" (2018) *CBS SF Bay Area*, 24 April, available at https://sanfrancisco.cbslocal.com/ 2018/04/24/filipino-activist-claims-he-was-given-weapons-tortured-at-sfo/.

"First Nations Sign Anti-Pipeline Declaration in Calgary Wednesday" (2016) *Global News*, 17 May, available at https://globalnews.ca/news/3459305/ first-nations-sign-anti-pipeline-declaration-in-calgary-wednesday/.

Flanagan, Richard (2020) "Australia is Committing Climate Suicide," *NY Times* 3, January.

Flassy, Don A. L. (2019) "Constitution Vis-à-vis Constitution Indonesian 1945 Versus Papuan 1999," 2 *Humanities and Social Science Research* 53–94.

Fleck, Dieter (2018) *The handbook of the Law of Visiting Forces.* Oxford, U.K.: Oxford University Press.

Fong, Jack (2008) *Revolution as Development: The Karen Self-Determination Struggle Against Ethnocracy.* Boca Raton, FL: BrownWalker Press.

Ford, Henry Jones (1915) *The Scotch-Irish in America.* Princeton, NJ: Princeton University Press.

Foreign Investment in Iraqi Kurdistan (2017) *Aleph Policy Initiative*, 4 February, available at https://alephpolicy.org/foreign-investment-in-iraqi-kurdistan/.

Forero, Juan (2002) "New Role for U.S. in Colombia: Protecting a Vital Oil Pipeline, *NY Times*, 4 October.

Forino, Giuseppe Jason von Meding, & Thomas Johnson (2017) "Religion Is Not the Only Reason Rohingyas Are Being Forced Out of Myanmar," *The Conversation*, 11 Sept., available at https://theconversation.com/religion-is-not-the-only-reason-rohingyas-are-being-forced-out-of-myanmar-83726.

Forster, Stig., Wlfgang J. Mommsen, and Ronald Robinson (1988) *Bismarck, Europe and Africa: The Berlin Africa Conference 1884–1885 and the Onset of Partition.* Oxford, UK: Oxford University Press.

Fox, Michael (2020) "Brazil's Indigenous Peoples Fight COVID-19 in Their Territories Amid Government Neglect," *The World*, 4 September.

Freeman, Andrew (2019) "Amazon Fires Could Accelerate Global Warming and Cause Lasting Harm to a Cradle of Biodiversity," *Washington Post*, 21 August.

Frisso, Giovanna Maria (2019) "Third World Approaches to International Law: 'Feminists' Engagement with International Law and Decolonial Theory," in *Research Handbook on Feminist Engagement with International Law*, eds. Susan Harris Rimmer & Kate Ogg (Northampton, MA: Edward Elgar Publishing), pp. 479–498.

"Fukkigo 574-Ken, Oinawa Beigunjin, Gunzoku Kyoaku Hanzai [Since the 1972 Reversion to Japan, 574 Criminal Cases by U.S. Military Personnel and Their Dependents]" (2016) *Ryukyu Simpo*, 20 May.

Fukurai, Hiroshi (2010) "People's Panels vs. Imperial Hegemony: Japan's Twin Lay Justice Systems and the Future of American Military Bases in Japan," 12 *Asian-Pacific Law & Policy Journal* 95–142.

Fukurai, Hiroshi (2011) "Japan's Quasi-Jury and Grand Jury Systems as Deliberative Agents of Social Change: De-Colonial Strategies and Deliberative Participatory Democracy," 86 *Chicago-Kent Law Review* 789–829.

Fukurai, Hiroshi (2012) "Lay Prosecution of U.S. Military Crimes in Japan by Prosecutorial Review Commissions and the Saiban-in Trial." In Harry N. Scheiber & Tom Ginsburg, eds., *Japanese Legal System: An Era of Transition.* Berkeley, CA: Robbins Collection, pp. 131–160.

Fukurai, Hiroshi (2018) "Fourth World Approaches to International Law (FWAIL) and Asia's Indigenous Struggles and Quests for Recognition under International Law," 5 *Asian Journal of Law and Society* 221–231.

Fukurai, Hiroshi (2019) "Original Nation Approaches to 'Inter-National' Law (ONAIL: Decoupling of the Nation and the State and the Search for New Legal Orders," 26 *Indiana Journal of Global Legal Studies* 199–261.

Fukurai, Hiroshi & Richard Krooth (2003) *Race in the Jury Box: Affirmative Action in Jury Selection.* Albany, NY: SUNY Press.

Fukurai, Hiroshi & Zhuoyu Wang (2014) "People's Grand Jury Panel and the State's Inquisitorial Institutions: Prosecution Review Commissions in Japan and People's Supervisors in China," 37 *Fordham International Law Journal* 929–971.

Fukushima, Annie Isabel & Gwyn Kirk (2013) "Military Sexual violence: From Frontline to Fenceline," *Institute for Policy Studies*, 17 June, https://ips-dc.org/military_sexual_violence_from_frontline_to_fenceline/ (accessed 22 October 2020).

Gadoua, Renee K. (2013) "Anniversary Recalls Water as Sacred Source of Life," *Washington Post*, 31 July.

Galeano, Eduardo (1997) *Open Veins of Latin America: Five Centuries of the Pillage of a Continent.* NY: NYU Press.

Galinda, Gabriela (2019) "Nearly 40% of Flemish Would Vote for Independence," *The Brussels Times*, 17 December.

Gamba, Laura (2020) "Coronavirus Hitting Indigenous Tribes Hard in Brazil," *AA*, 24 July, https://www.aa.com.tr/en/americas/coronavirus-hitting-indigenous-tribes-hard-in-brazil-/1920595.

Gander, Kashmira (2020) "Smoke From Australia's Fires Has Traveled 6,800 Miles Across the Ocean to Chile," *Newsweek*, 7, January.

Ganguly, Sumit (2002) *Conflict Unending: India-Pakistan Tensions Since 1947.* NY: Columbia University Press.

Garfield, Richard (2008) "The Epistemology of Law." In Barry S. Levy and Victor W. Sidel, eds., *War and Public Health.* Baltimore, MD: John Hopkins University Press, pp. 23–36.

Garfield, Seth (2001) *Indigenous Struggle at the Heart of Brazil: State Policy, Frontier Expansion, and the Xavante Indians, 1937–1988*. Durham, NC: Duke University Press.

Garroutte, Eva Marie (2001) "The Racial Formation of American Indians: Negotiating Legitimate Identities Within Tribal and Federal Law," 25 *American Indian Quarterly* 224–239.

Gathii, James Thuo (2008) "Third World Approaches to International Economic Governance," in *International Law and the Third World: Reshaping Justice*, eds. By Richard Falk, Balakrishman Rajagopal & Jacquelin Stevens (NY: Routledge), pp. 255–268.

Gathii, James Thuo (2011) "TWAIL: A Brief History of Its Origin, Its Decentralized Network, and a Tentative Bibliography," 3 *Trade Law. & Development* 26–48.

Gathii, James Thuo (2019) "The Agenda of Third World Approaches to International Law (TWAIL)," forthcoming in Jeffrey Dunoff & Mark Pollack, eds. *International Legal Theory: Foundations and Frontiers*. Cambridge, MA: Cambridge University Press, https://papers.ssrn.com/sol3/papers.cfm?abstract_id=3304767 (accessed 22 October 2020).

Gathii, James Thuo (2020) "The Promise of International Law: A Third World View," https://uichr.uiowa.edu/assets/Documents/GathiiGrotiusLecture2020.pdf (accessed 22 October 2020).

Gathii, James & Celestine Nyamu (1996) "Reflections on United States-Based Human Rights NGO's Work on Africa," 9 *Harvard Human Rights Journal* 285–296.

Gathii, James, Antony Anghie & Obiora Okafor (2013) "Africa and TWAIL," *African Yearbook of International Law* 9–13.

Geer, Curtis M. (1904) *The History of North America: The Louisiana Purchase and the Westward Movement*. Boston: Adamant Media Corporation.

Gellately, Robert & Ben Kiernan (2003) *The Specter of Genocide: Mass Murder in Historical Perspective*. NY: Cambridge University Press.

Gellman, Barton (2020) *Dark Mirror: Edward Snowden and the American Surveillance State*. NY: Penguin Press.

"General Command of the EZLN, First Declaration of the Lacondona Jungle: EZLN's Declaration of War, Today We Say 'Enough is Enough! (Ya Basta!)'" (1993), available at http://woocommerce-180730-527864.cloudwaysapps.com/wp-content/uploads/2014/03/1st-Declaration-of-the-Lacandona-Jungle.pdf.

Generalitat de Catalunya (2012) Biodiversity in Catalonia: The Challenge of Conservation, available at https://www.qlf.org/wp-content/uploads/2016/10/biodiversity-in-catalonia.pdf.

Geranios, Nicholas K. (2004) "Study Finds Dangerous Waste Near Indian Reservations," *Sun Local*, 28 November.

Gibbons, Ann (2012) "Bonobos Join Chimps as Closest Human Relatives," *Science*, 13 June.

Gilbert, Jeremie (2016) *Indigenous Peoples' Land Rights Under International Law*. Boston, MA: Brill Nijhoff.

Gill, Lesley (2011) *The School of the Americas: Military Training and Political Violence in the Americas*. Durham, NC: Duke University Press.

Ginsburg, Tom (2012) "Constitutionalism: East Asian Antecedents," 88 *Chicago-Kent Law Review* 11–31.

Glaholt, Eileen (2020) "California Indians and Genocide: Indian Genocide is not a Myth," *Sacramento Bee*, https://www.sacbee.com/opinion/letters-to-the-editor/article35247189.html (accessed 22 October 2020).

Glenn, H. Patrick (2007) *Legal Traditions of the World: Sustainable Diversity in Law*. Oxford, U.K.: Oxford University Press.

Global Alliance for the Rights of Nature (2015) "Video: International Rights of Nature Tribunal Introduction, Global Alliance for the Rights of Nature," available at https://therightsofnature.org/rights-of-nature-tribunal-paris/.

Gocke, Katja (2014) "Indigenous People in the Nuclear Age: Uranium Mining on Indigenous Lands." In Johnathan L. Black-Branch & Dieter Fleck, eds., *Nuclear Non-Proliferation in International* Law. NY: Springer. pp. 199–224.

Godelmann, Iker Reyes (2014) "The Zapatista Movement: The Fight for Indigenous Rights in Mexico," *Australian Institute of International Affairs*, 30 July.

Goldman, Michael (1998) *Privatizing Nature: Political Struggles for the Global Commons*. London, U.K. Pluto Press.

Goldstein, E Bruce (2009) *Sensation and Perception*. Boston, MA: Cengage Learning.

Gonzalez, Juan (2011) *Harvest of Empire: A History of Latinos in America*. NY: Penguin Books.

Gonzalez, Luisa (2020) "Coronavirus Threatens the Survival of Colombia's Indigenous Wayuu," *NBC News*, 13 August.

Goran, Baxtiyar (2018) "US Continues Military Assistance for Kudistan's Peshmerga Forces," *Kurdistan24*, 14 February.

Gordon, Seth (2014) "Indigenous Rights in Modern International Law From a Critical Third World Perspective," 31 *American Indian Law Review* 401–426.

Gottlieb, Gidon (1993) *Nation Against State: A New Approach to Ethnic Conflicts and the Decline of Sovereignty*. NY: Council of Foreign Relations Press.

Gould, Eliga H. (2014) *Among the Powers of the Earth: The American Revolution and the Making of a New World Empire*. Cambridge, MA: Harvard University Press.

Gover, Kevin (2017) "Greater Numbers Than Any Ethnic Group and Have Since the Revolution," *Huffington Post*, 6 December.

Gowrinathan, Nimmi & Kate Cronin-Furman (2017) "Rapists in Blue Helmets: The Crimes of UN Peacekeepers," *Environmentalists Against War*, 2 May.

Goyes, David Rodriguez(2016) "Land-Grabs, Biopiracy and Inversion of Justice in Colombia", 56 *British Journal of Criminology* 558–577.

Gozzi, Gustavo (2019) "Transcivilizational International Law Against the System of International Relations: Onuma Yasuaki's Normative Choice," 9 *Asian Journal of International Law* 170–176.

Graff, Peter (2011) "Berber Culture Reborn in Libya Revolt," *Reuters*, 11 July.

Grahn-Farley, Maria (2008) "Neutral Law and Eurocentric Lawmaking: A Post-colonial Analysis of the U.N. Convention on the Rights of Child," 34 *Brooklyn Journal of International Law* 1–32.

Grandin, Greg (2015) "What the Media Don't Cover When Colombian Women are Raped by Members of the US Military," *The Nation*, 7 April.

Gray, Fred D. (1998) *The Tuskegee Syphilis Study: An Insider's Account of the Shocking Medical Experiment Conducted by Government Doctors Against African American Men*. Montgomery, AL: New South Books.

Greenberg, Joel (2014) *A Feathered river Across the Sky: The Passenger Pigeon's Flight to Extinction*. NY: Bloomsbury Publishing.

Greenfield, Patrick (2017) "Preliminary Results Show 90% in Favor of Independence," *Guardian*, 2 October.

Grey, Sam (2011) "Decolonisation as Peacemaking: Applying Just War Theory to the Canadian Context," 4 *International Journal of Critical Indigenous Studies* 21–29.

Griggs, Richard (1992) "The Meaning of 'Nation' and 'State' in the Fourth World," *CWIS Occasional Paper #18*.

Griggs, Richard & Peter Hocknell (1995a) "Fourth World Faultlines and the Remaking of 'Inter-National' Boundaries," 3 *IBRU Boundary and Security Bulletin* 49–58.

Griggs, Richard & Peter Hocknell (1995b) "The Geography and Geopolitics of Europe's Fourth World," 3 *IBRU Boundary and Security Bulletin, Winter* 59–67, available at available at http://citeseerx.ist.psu.edu/viewdoc/download?doi=10.1.1.177.155&rep=rep1&type=pdf.

Grimal, Francis (2013) *Threats of Force: International Law and Strategy*. NY: Routledge.

Grisham v. Hagan, 361 U.S. 278 (1960).

Gussen, Benjamin Franklen (2017) "A Comparative Analysis of Constitutional Recognition of Aboriginal Peoples," 40 *Melbourne University Law School* 867–904.

Habermas, Jurgen (1998) "The European Nation-State: On the Past and Future of Sovereignty and Citizenship," Public Culture 10(2): 397–416.

Habermas, Jurgen (1999) "The European Nation-State: On the Past and Future of Sovereignty and Citizenship." In Ciaran Cronin & Pablo De Greiff, eds.,

The Inclusion of the Other: Studies in Political Theory. Cambridge, UK: Polity Press. pp. 237–245.

Haley, Stein (2005) "Intellectual Property and Genetically Modified Seeds: The U.S., Trade, and the Developing World," 3 *Northwestern Journal of Technology and Intellectual Property* 151–178.

Halili, Maria Christine (2004) *Philippine History.* Manila, Philippines: Rex Book Store.

Hall, Anthony J. (2003) *The American Empire and the Fourth World: The Bowl with One Spoon.* Montreal, Canada: McGill-Queen's University Press.

Han, Rimwha & Soonhee Kim (2003) "Jeju Women's Lives in the Context of the Jeju April 3rd Uprising," 17 *Asian Women* 21–37.

Hansen, Mogens Herman (1991) *The Athenian Democracy in the Age of Demosthenes: Structure, Principles, and Ideology.* Oxford, UK: Bristol Classical Press.

Hansen, Terri (2020) "How Covid-19 Could Destroy Indigenous Communities," *BBC*, 27 July.

Haqqani, Husain (2018) "Aggressive Indian Posture, Kashmir Human Rights Violations Feed Extremism: Husain Haqqani," *South Asian Media Journal*, 13 April, available at http://southasiajournal.net/aggressive-indian-posture-kashmir-human-rights-violations-feed-extremism-husain-haqqani/.

Harari, Yuval Noah (2015) *Sapiens: A Brief History of Humankind.* NY: HarperCollins.

Harari, Yuval Noah (2020) "Yuval Noah Harari: The World After Coronavirus," *Financial Times*, 19 March.

Hardin, Garrett (1968) "The Tragedy of the Commons," 162 *Science* 1243–1248.

Harfuch, Andres, Mariana Bilinski & Andrea Ortiz (2016) "El Jurado Indígenas en Argentina [Argentina's Indigenous Jury]," *Juicio por Jurados y Procedimiento Penal*, 25 (2016), available at http://inecip.org/wp-content/uploads/JxJ-JusBaires-JuradoIndigena.pdf. The English version is available at http://inecip.org/wp-content/uploads/Argentina%C2%B4s-Indigenous-jury-by-Harfuch-Bilinski-and-Ortiz-6.pdf.

Harlan, Bill (2017) "Lakota Sioux Secede from US, Declare Independence," *Common Dreams*, 21 December, https://www.commondreams.org/news/2007/12/21/lakota-sioux-secede-us-declare-independence.

Harris, Shane & Matthew W. Aid (2013) "Exclusive: CIA Files Prove America Helped Saddam as He Gassed Iran," *Foreign Policy*, 26 August.

Harrison, Guy P. (2010) *Race and Reality: What Everyone Should Know About Our Biological Diversity.* NY: Prometheus Books.

Haskell, John D. (2014) "TRAIL-ing TWAIL: Arguments and Blind Spots in Third World Approaches to International Law Scholarship," 27 *Canadian Journal of Law and Jurisprudence* 383–415.

Hatcher, Sarah M. et al. (2020) "COVID-19 Among American Indians and Alaska Native Persons – 23 States, January 31–July 3, 2020: Morbidity and Mortality Weekly Report," *CDC*, 28 August.

Hawkins, Michael C. (2011) "Managing a Massacre: Savagery, Civility, and gender in Moro Province in the Wake of Bud Dajo," 59 *Philippine Studies* 83–105.

Heath, Joseph (2018) "The Citizenship Act of 1924: An Integral Pillar of the Colonization and Forced Assimilation Policies of the United States in Violation of Treaties," *Onandaga Nation*, 7 June, https://www.onondaganation.org/news/2018/the-citizenship-act-of-1924/.

Hedges, Chris (2010) *Death of the Liberal Class*. NY: Nation Books.

Hedges, Chris and Joe Sacco (2012) *Days of Destruction, Days of Revolt*. NY: Bold Type Books.

Hedgpeth, Dana (2020) "The Irish are Repaying a Favor From 173 Years Ago in Native Americans' Fight Against Coronavirus," *Washington Post*, 13 May.

Heidbuchel, Esther (2007) *The West Papua Conflict in Indonesia: Actors, Issues and Approaches*. Berlin, Germany: Die Deutsche Bibliothek.

Herman, Edward S. & Noam Chomsky (1988) *Manufacturing Consent: The Political Economy of the Mass Media*. NY: Pantheon Books.

Hernandez, Brianna Nicole (2020) "Sexual Abuse in UN Peacekeeping: The Problem of Viewing Women as a 'Quick Fix,'" *E-International Relations*, 20 February.

Herrera, Jose Israel (2015) "The Challenge of the Cultural Diversity in Mexico Through the Official Recognition of Legal Pluralism," 4 *The Age of Human Rights Journal* 60–80.

Herring, D. Ann & Alan C. Swedlund (2010) *Plagues and Epidemics: Infected Spaces Past and Present*. NY: Berg.

Heydarian, Richard Javad (2017) "'Marawi Duterte: Liberated' from ISIL-Linked Fighters," *Al Jazeera*, 18 October, available at https://www.aljazeera.com/news/2017/10/duterte-marawi-liberated-isil-linked-fighters-171017071213300.html.

Hill, Cameron (2013) "Myanmar: Sectarian Violence in Rakhine – Issues, Humanitarian Consequences, and Regional Responses," *Parliamentary Library*, 24 July, available at http://parlinfo.aph.gov.au/parlInfo/download/library/prspub/2613925/upload_binary/2613925.pdf;fileType=application/pdf.

Hiltermann, Joost R. (2008) "The 1988 Anfal Campaign in Iraqi Kurdistan," *SciencesPo*, 3 February.

Hippolyte, Antonius R. (2016) "Correcting TWAIL's Blind Spots: A Plea for a Pragmatic Approach to International Economic Governance," 18 *International Community Law Review* 34–52.

"History of Earth Jurisprudence" (2020) *The Ecozoic Times* (accessed 15 May 2020), available at https://ecozoictimes.com/ecozoic-movements/earth-jurisprudence/history-of-earth-jurisprudence/.

Ho-Chunk Nation Legislature (2015) "Acknowledgement of General Council Resolution 9/19/2015-09 and Legislative Action Regarding the Resolution to Amend the Constitution and Provide for the Rights of Nature," 20 October.

Hodges, Richard & David Whitehouse (1983) *Mohammed, Charlemagne and the Origin of Europe*. Ithaca, NY: Cornell University Press.

Hoffman, frank (2014) "On No-So-New Warfare: Political Warfare v. Hybrid Threats," *War on the Rocks*, 28, July.

Hong, Christine (2020) *A Violent Peace: Race, U.S. Militarism, and Cultures of Democratization in Cold War Asia and the Pacific*. Stanford, CA: Stanford University Press.

Hooks, Gregory & Chad L. Smith (2004) "Treadmills of Destruction: National Sacrifice Areas and Native Americans" 69 *American Sociological Review* 558–575.

Hooks, Gregory & Chad L. Smith (2005) "Treadmills of Production and Destruction: Threats to the Environmental Posed by Militarism," 18 *Organization & Environment* 19–37.

Hooks, Gregory & Chad L. Smith (2012) "Treadmills of Destruction Goes Global: Anticipating the Environmental Impact of Militarism in the 21st Century," in *The Marketing of War in the Age of Neo-Militarism*, eds. Kostas Gouliamos & Christos Kassimeris. NY: Routledge, pp. 60–83.

Horne, Gerald (2014) *The Counter Revolution of 1776: Slave Resistance and the Origin of the United States of America*. NY: NYU Press.

Horne, Gerald (2015) *Confronting Black Jacobins: The U.S., the Haitian Revolution, and the Origins of the Dominican Republic*. NY: NYU Press.

Horning, Audrey J. (2013) *Irish in the Virginia Sea: Colonialism in the Britain*. Chapel Hill, NC: The University of North Carolina Press.

Hoyle, Lindsey (2014) " Command Responsibility: A Legal Obligation to Deter Sexual Violence in the Military, 37 *Boston College International & Comparative Law Review* 353–388.

Hughes, Roland (2018) China's Uighurs: All You Need to Know on Muslim 'Crackdown," *BBC News*, 8 November.

Huisman, Nick (2019) "EU Fails to Meet 2020 Targets Against Biodiversity Loss," *European Wilderness Society*, https://wilderness-society.org/eu-fails-to-meet-2020-targets-against-biodiversity-loss/ (accessed 22 October 2020).

Human Rights Watch (2002) *The 2002 Report*, available at https://www.hrw.org/legacy/reports/2002/bosnia/Bosnia1102-11.htm.

Human Rights Watch (2017) *World Report 2017: Events of 2016*, available at https://www.hrw.org/sites/default/files/world_report_download/wr2017-web.pdf.

Human Rights Watch (2018) *World Report 2018: Events of 2017*, available at https://www.hrw.org/world-report/2018.

Hume, David (2020) "Of the First Principles of Government," (accessed 15 May 2020), available at https://www.constitution.org/dh/pringovt.htm.

Hurley, Vic (2011) *Jungle Patrol, the Story of the Philippine Constabulary 1901–1936*. Salem, OR: Cerberus Books.

Haskell, John D. (2014a) "The Turn to History in International Legal Scholarship" in Jean D'Aspremont & Tarcisio Gazzini, Andre Nolkaemper & Wouter Werner, eds, *International Law as a Profession* (Cambridge, UK: Cambridge University Press.

Huskell, John D. (2014b) "TRAIL-ing TWAIL: Arguments and Blind Spots in Third World Approaches to International Law," 27 *Canadian Journal of Law and Jurisprudence* 383–414.

Hyppolyte, Antonius R. (2016) "Correcting TWAIL's Blind Spots: A Plea for a Pragmatic Approach to International Economic Governance," 18 *International Community Law Journal* 34–52.

Iankova, Katia, Azizul Hassan & Rachel L'Abbe (2016) *Indigenous People and Economic Development*. NY: Routledge.

Ibrahim, Azeem (2016) *The Rohingyas: Inside Myanmar's Hidden Genocide*. London, UK: Hurst & Co Ltd.

Ibrahim, Azeem (2017) "Why the Rohingya Can't Yet Return to Myanmar," *NY Times*, 6 December.

ICC Canada (2012) *ICC's Beginning, Inuit Circumpolar Council Canada*, available at http://www.inuitcircumpolar.com/iccs-beginning.html.

Iglesias, Elizabeth M. (1999) "Mapping Intersections of Critical Race Theory, Postcolonial Studies and International Law," 93 *Proceedings of the Annual Meeting of the American Society of International Law*, 225–226.

Ignatius, David (2020) "Russia's Scavenger Diplomacy is in Full Effect in the Middle East: It's Approach is a taunt at the United States, as Opposed a Grand Strategy," *Washington Post*, 7 May.

Igoe, J. & D. Brockington (2007) "Neoliberal Conservation: A Brief Introduction," 5 *Conservation and Society* 432–449.

"Indicted U.S. Base Worker Accepts an Involuntary Manslaughter Plea" (2012) *Weekly Japan Update*, 27 January.

INEGI (2015) "Resultados Definitivos de la Encuesta Intercensal 2015." *Aguascalientes, AGS: INEGI*, 8 December. available at http://www.inegi.org.mx/saladeprensa/boletines/2015/especiales/especiales2015_12_3.pdf.

Institute for Policy Studies (1999) "Women and the U.S. Military in East Asia," 1 March.

Institute for the Study of Human Rights (2017) *Indigenous people's Rights and Unreported Struggles: Conflict and Peace.* NY: Columbia University.

International Court of Justice (ICJ) (1986) "Reports of Judgements, Advisory Opinions and Orders: Case Concerning Military and Paramilitary Activities in and Against Nicaragua," available at https://www.icj-cij.org/files/case-rel ated/70/070-19860627-JUD-01-00-EN.pdf.

International Court of Justice (2004) "Legal Consequences of the Construction of a Wall in the Occupied Palestinian Territory, Advisory Opinion of 9 July, 2004," available at https://www.icj-cij.org/files/case-related/131/131-200 40709-PRE-01-00-EN.pdf.

International Indian Treaty Council (1974), *Declaration of Continuing Independence,* https://history.hanover.edu/courses/excerpts/260continuing.html.

"International Rights of Nature Tribunal, Final Verdict: Fifth International Rights of Nature Tribunal, Gathered in the City of Santiago De Chile, December 05, 2019: Resolution No.5/2019." (2019) 5 December, available at https://therightsofnature.org/wp-content/uploads/2020/03/VER DICT-TRIBUNAL-Chile-English-.pdf.

"Iran, Turkey Pledge to Stop Iraqi Kurdistan Independence from Taking Hold" (2017) *CBC News,* 4 October, available at http://www.cbc.ca/news/world/ iraq-rouhani-turkey-erdogan-meeting-1.4327874.

Isenberg, David (2010) "It's Déjà vu for DynCorp All Over Again," *Huffington Post,* 6 December.

Isenberg, David (2019) *Shadow Force: Private Security Contractors in Iraq.* Westport, CT: Praeger.

Iskandar, Pranoto (2016) "Democracy and International Law in the Post-Colonial World," 3 *Indonesian Journal of International and Comparative Law,* 799–806.

Ito, Kazuyuki & Ryuichi Yamashita (2018) "Tempers Flare Between Police and Protesters to Henoko Move," *Asahi Shimbun,* 23 April.

IWGIA Mission Statement (2018) *International Work Group for Indigenous.* (accessed 21 November 2018), available at https://www.iwgia.org/en/.

James, C.L.R. (1938) *The Black Jacobins: Toussaint L'ouverture and the San Domingo Revolution.* U.K.: Secker & Warburg Ltd.

Jandt, Fred E. (2012) *An Introduction to Intercultural Communication: Identities in a Global Community.* LA, CA: Sage.

Janis, M.W. (1984) "Jeremy Bentham and the Fashioning of 'International Law'," 78 *American Journal of International Law* 405–418.

"Japan Wants U.S. Choppers Grounded as Accident in Okinawa Leaves LDP Reeling Ahead of Election," (2017) *Japan Times,* 13 October.

"Japan's Falling Food Self-Sufficiency," (2019) Japan Times, 20 August.

"Japanese Man Died After Vehicle Collision with AAFES Employee on Okinawa" (2011) *Stars and Stripes,* 13 January.

Jaramillo, Juan Camilo (2019) "Entire Police Forces Continue to be Arrested in Mexico," *InSight Crime*, 21 August.

"Jeffrey Amherst and Smallpox Blankets: Lord Jeffrey Amherst's Letters Discussing Germ Warfare Against American Indians" (2020), https://people.umass.edu/derrico/amherst/lord_jeff.html (accessed 22 October 2020).

Jensen, Derrick (2002) *A Language Older than Words. White River Junction*. VT: Chelsea Green Publishing.

Jensen, Derrick (2007) *Thought to Exist in the Wild: Awakening from the Nightmare of Zoos*. Santa Cruz, CA: Novoice Unheard.

Johansen, Bruce Elliott (1998) *The Encyclopedia of Native American Legal Tradition*. Westport, Connecticut: Greenwood Press.

John, Tara (2019) "Jakarta Floods Leave Dozens Dead and 60,000 Displaced," *CNN*, 2, January.

Johnson, Chalmers (2004) *Sorrows of Empire: Militarism, Secrecy, and the End of the Republic*. NY: Metropolitan Books.

Johnson, Chalmers (2008) *Nemesis: The Last Days of the American Republic*. NY: Metropolitan Books.

Johnson, David T. & Mari Hirayama (2019) "Japan's Reformed Prosecution Review Commission: Changes, Challenges and Lessons," 14 *Asian Journal of Criminology* 77–102.

Johnson, David T. & Dimitri Vanoverbeke (2020) "The Limit of Change in Japanese Criminal Justice," 49 *Journal of Japanese Law*, 109–165.

Johnson, David T., Hiroshi Fukurai, & Mari Hirayama (2020) "Reflections on the TEPCO Trial: Prosecution and Acquittal after Japan's Nuclear Meltdown," 18 *The Asia-Pacific Journal: Japan Focus*, 15, January, https://apjjf.org/2020/2/Johnson.html (accessed 22 October, 2020).

Johnston, Eric (2012) "SOFA: A Source of Sovereign Conflicts," *Japan Times*, 31 July.

Jones, Collin (2021) "The Island That Ate the Constitution," 42 *Liverpool Law Review* (forthcoming).

Jones, Donna (2019) "Healing Memories Recall California Mission Heritage," *Santa Cruz Sentinel*, 11, September.

Jones, James H. (1993) *Bad Blood: The Tuskegee Syphilis Experiment: The Modern Classic of Race and Medicine Updated with an Additional Chapter on the Tuskegee Experiment's Legacy in the Age of AIDS*. NY: Simon & Schuster, Inc.

"Just 8 Men Own Same Wealth as Half the World" (2017) *OXFAM International*, 16 January.

Kahn, Brian (2020) "An Estimated 1.25 Billion Animals Have Perished in Australia's Bushfires," *Gizmodo*, 8, January.

Kamal, Sultano, Elsa Stamatopoulou & Myrna Cunningham Kain (2020) "International Chittagong Hill Tracts Commission: Indigenous Peoples in Chittagong Hill Tracts Experiencing Human Rights Violations," *International Working Group on Indigenous Affairs* (IWGIA), 26 June.

"Kashmir Graves: Human Rights Watch Calls for Inquiry" (2011) *BBC News*, 25 August, available at http://www.bbc.com/news/world-south-asia-14660253.

"Kashmir: Indian Forces Open Fire on Pro-Independence Protesters" (2018) *Democracy Now!*, 2 April, available at https://www.democracynow.org/2018/4/2/headlines/kashmir_indian_forces_open_fire_on_pro_independence_protesters.

Kelly, James J. (1994) "Article 27 and Mexican Land Reform: The Legacy of Zapatista's Dream," 25 *Columbia Human Rights Law Review* 541–570.

Kelly, Michael J. (2010) "The Kurdish Regional Constitution Within the Framework of the Iraqi Federal Constitution: A Struggle for Sovereignty, Oil, Ethnic Identity, and the Prospects for a Reverse Supremacy Clause," 114 *Penn State Law Review* 707–808.

Kelly, Michael J. (2013) "The Pre-History of Piracy as a Crime & Its Definitional Odyssey," 46 *Case Western Reserve Journal of International Law* 26–42.

Kelly, Stephanie (2013) "Testing Drugs on the Developing world," *The Atlantic*, 27 February.

Keong, Choy Yee (2020) *Global Environmental Sustainability: Case Studies and Analysis of the United Nations' Journey Toward Sustainable Development.* Cambridge, MA: Elsevier Inc.

Kerr, George H. (2000) *Okinawa: The History of an Island People.* Tokyo, Japan: Tuttle Publishing.

Keun-Gwan, Lee (2018) "International Law in a Transcivilized World: By Onuma Yasuaki." 87 *British Yearbook of International Law* 292–295.

"Keystone Pipeline Leak in South Dakota About Double Previous Estimate" (2018) *Reuters*, 7 April.

"Keystone XL Pipeline: Why Is It So Disputed?" (2017) *BBC News*, 24 January, available at http://www.bbc.com/news/world-us-canada-30103078.

Khan, Samia Liaqat Ali (2010) "Poverty Reduction Strategy Papers: Failing Minorities and Indigenous People," *Minority Rights Group International*, available at https://minorityrights.org/publications/poverty-reduction-strategy-papers-failing-minorities-and-indigenous-peoples-july-2010/.

Khosla, Madhav (2009) "TWAIL Discourse: The Emergence of a New Phase," 9 *International Community Law Review* 291–304.

Kil-Un, Hyun (2007) *Dead Silence and Other Stories of the Jeju Massacre.* Manchester, UK: Eastbridge.

Kim, Heewon (2019) *The Struggle for Equality: India's Muslims and Rethinking the UPA Experience.* Cambridge: Cambridge University Press.

Kim, Soonhee (2016) "Jeju Island Women Divers' Association in South Korea: A Source of Social Capital," 9 *Asian Journal of Women's Studies* 37–59.

Kirby, Ben (2020) "US Native Tribes and Ireland's 170-Year-Old Connection is Renewed in the Pandemic," *Vox*, 13 May.

Kirk, Donald (2013) *Okinawa and Jeju: Bases of Discontent*. NY: Palgrave MacMillan.

Kiyani, Asad G. (2016) "Third World Approaches to International Law," 109 *American Journal of International Law Unbound* 255–259.

Kiyani, Asad G., John Reynolds & Sujith Xavier (2016) "Foreward, Symposium The Third World Approaches to International Law, Cairo, Egypt," 14 *Journal of International Criminal Justice* 915–920.

Klein, Alice (2020) "2019 Was Australia's Hottest and Driest Year on Record," *New Scientist*, 8 January.

Klieforth, Alexander Leslie & Robert John Munro (2004) *The Scottish Invention of America, Democracy and Human Rights: The History of Liberty and Freedom From the Ancient Celts to the New Millennium*. NY: University Press of America.

Kloppe, Adam (2015) "The Louisiana Purchase and the Constitutionalism of Thomas Jefferson," *Missouri Historical Society*, 17 March.

Kluge, Emma (2020) "How the World Failed West Papua in Its Campaign for Independence," *The Jakarta Post*, 24 January.

Knight, David B. (1983) "The Dilemma of Nations in a Rigid State Structured World." In Nurit Kliot & Stanley Waterman, eds., *Pluralism and Political Geography: People, Territory and State*. NY: Routledge, pp. 114–137.

Kohut, David R. & Olga Vilella (2010) *Historical Dictionary of Dirty Wars*. Toronto, Canada: The Scarecrow Press, Inc.

Koskenniemi, Martti (2001) *The Gentle Civilizer of Nations: The Rise and Fall of International Law*. Cambridge, UK: Cambridge University Press.

Kramarae, Cheris & Dale Spender, (2000) *Routledge International Encyclopedia of Women: Global Women's Issues and Knowledge*. NY: Routledge.

Kramer, Paul A. (2006) *The Blood of Government: Race, Empire, and the United States and the Philippines*. Chapel Hill, NC: The University of North Carolina Press.

Kramer, Paul A. (2011) "The Military-Sexual Complex: Prostitution, Disease and the Boundaries of Empire During the Philippine-American War." *The Asia-Pacific Journal: Japan Focus*, 25 July, https://apjjf.org/2011/9/30/Paul-A.-Kramer/3574/article.html (accessed 22 October 2020).

Krishan, Yuvraj (2002) *Understanding Partition: Separation, Not Liquidation*. Mumbai, India: Bharatiya Vidya Bhawan.

Kronowitz, Rachel San et al. (1987) "Toward Consent and Cooperation: Reconsidering the Political Status of Indian Nations," Harvard Civil Rights-Civil Liberties Law Review 22: 507, 613–614.

Kropotkin, Peter (1902) *Mutual Aid: A Factor of Evolution*. Manchester, NH: Extending Horizons Books.

Kovach, Gretel C. (2013) "Cal Guard Soldiers Heading to Afghanistan," *San Diego Union-Tribune*, 17, January 2013.

Kulchyski, Peter (2017) "The Creation of Nunavut," *Canada's History*, 11 August, https://www.canadashistory.ca/explore/politics-law/the-creation-of-nunavut.

Kulp, Scott A. & Benjamin H. Strauss (2019) "New Elevation Data Triple Estimates of Global Vulnerability to Sea-Level Rise and Coastal Flooding," *Nature Communications*, 29 October.

Kuper, Leo (1981) *Genocide: Its Political Use in the Twentieth Century*. New Haven, CT: Yale University Press.

Kuzmarov, Jeremy (2017) "American Complicity in Indonesian Killings Runs Deep," *Huffington Post* 18 October, available at https://www.huffingto npost.com/entry/american-complicity-in-indonesian-killings-runs-deep_us_5 9e81584e4b0153c4c3ec537.

La Follette, Cameron & Chris Maser (2017) *Sustainability and the Rights of Nature: An Introduction*. Boca Raton, FL: CRC Press.

LaDuke, Winona (1983) "Preface." In *Marxism and Native Americans* (Ward Churchill), pp. viii.

LaDuke, Winona & Sean Aaron Cruz (2013) *The Militarization of Indian County*. Callaway, MN: Lakwa Enewed.

LaDuke, Winona (2019) "The Rights of Wild Rice," *In These Times*, 21 February.

Lagsa, Bobby (2017) "Liberated and Angry: Months of Fighting Drove the Oslamic State from the Philippine City of Marawi But Left Behind Distrust and Destruction," *Washington Post*, 9 December.

Lakota Freedom Delegation (2007) " A Declaration of Independence from the USA," *Counterpunch*, 21 December, https://www.counterpunch.org/2007/12/21/a-declaration-of-independence-from-the-usa/.

Lam, Maivan Clech (2000) *At the Edge of the State: Indigenous Peoples and Self-Determination*. NY: Transnational Publishers, Inc.

Landsman, Ned C. (2014) *Scotland and Its First American Colony, 1683–1765*. Princeton, NJ: Princeton University Press.

Lang, Johannes (2010) "Questioning Dehumanization: Intersubjective Dimensions of Violence in the Nazi Concentration and Death Camps" 24 *Holocaust and Genocide Studies* 225–246.

Langevin, Michael (2016) *The Secrets of Amazon Shamans: Healing Traditions from South America*. Hertford, NC: Crossroad Press.

Langenheim, Johnny (2010) "The Last of the Sea Nomads," *Guardian*, 9 September.

Larson, Krista & Paisley Dodds (2017) "UN Peacekeepers in Congo Hold Record for Rape, Sex Abuse," *AP*, 23 September.

Laszlo, Tony (2002) "Japan's Homogeneous Diversity," *Japan Times*, 20 January.

Lavoto, Robert (2015) "COP21: International Rights of Nature Tribunal Finds Corporations, Governments Guilty of Crimes Against Nature," *Alernet*, 10 December, available at https://www.alternet.org/environment/cop21-intern ational-rights-nature-tribunal-finds-corporations-governments-guilty-crimes.

Layton Robert & Peter Ucko (2000) *The Archeology and Anthropology of Landscape: Shaping Your Landscape*. London, UK: Routledge.

Lazard, Olivia (2020) "The EU Must Fight the Collapse of Biodiversity," *Carnegie Europe*, https://carnegieeurope.eu/2020/10/19/eu-must-fight-collapse-of-biodiversity-pub-82986 (accessed 22 October 2020).

Lee, Pam Tau, Terry Valen, & Rhonda Ramiro (2018) "Allow Jerome Succor Aba Entry to the US Now!" *New York Committee for Human Rights in the Philippines (NYCHRP)*, 18, April.

Lee, Patrick A. (2013) *Tribal Laws Treaties and Government: A Lakota Perspective*. Bloomington, IN: iUniverse.

Leitenberg, Milton (2006) "Deaths in Wars and Conflicts in the 20th Century," *Cornell University Peace Studies Program Occasional Paper #29*, available at https://www.clingendael.org/sites/default/files/pdfs/200 60800_cdsp_occ_leitenberg.pdf.

Lemkin, Raphael (2011) *Lemkin on Genocide*. Lanham, MD: Lexington Books.

Leonard, David L. (2002) "Extinct Birds by Errol Fuller: Hope is the Thing with Feathers: A Personal Chronicle of Vanished Birds by Christopher Cokinos," *The Auk*, 119: 574–577.

Lerner, Sharon (2020) "How the Environmental Lawyer Won a Massive Judgment Against Chevron Lost Everything," *The Intercept*, 29 January.

Li, Ming (2019) "Transcivilizational Perspective: A Legitimate and Feasible Approach to International Law," 9 *Asian Journal of International Law* 165–169.

Lie, John (2001) *Multi-Ethnic Japan*. Cambridge, MA: Harvard University Press.

Lim, Chin Leng (2008) "Neither Sheep Nor Peacocks: T.O. Elias and Postcolonial International Law," 21 *Leiden Journal of International Law* 295–315.

Lindenmayer, David, Stephen Dovers, & Molly Harriss Olson (2008) *Ten Commitments: Reshaping the Lucky Country's Environment*. Collingwood, Canada: CSIRO Publishing.

Lindsay, Brendan C. (2012) *Murder State: California's Native American Genocide, 1846–1873*. Lincoln, NE: University of Nebraska Press.

Linzey, Thomas (2009) *Be the Change: How to Get What You Want in Your Community*. Layton, UT: Gibbs Smith Publisher.

Liptak, Adam (2005) "U.S. Says It Has Withdrawn from World Judicial Body," *NY Times*, 10 March.

"List of International Oil Companies in Iraqi Kurdistan" (2018) *Iraq-Business News* (accessed 8 May 2018), available at http://www.iraq-businessnews. com/list-of-international-oil-companies-in-iraqi-kurdistan/.

Lopez, Oscar (2020) "A Town Torn Apart: Mexico's Indigenous Communities Fight for Autonomy," *Place*, 2 January.

Lopez, Robert Sabatino (1966) *The Birth of Europe*. NY: M. Evans.

Lou, Ethan (2017) "TransCanada's $15 Billion U.S. Keystone XL NAFTA Suit Suspended," *Reuters*, 28 February.

Louisiana Purchase Treaty (1803), http://www.classzone.com/books/am_05_ shared/pdf/psource/TAS03_6_201c_PS.pdf (accessed 15 March 2019).

Lovelace, Douglas (2016) *Hybrid Warfare and the Gray Zone Threat*. NY: Oxford University Press.

Lu, Denise & Christopher Flavelle (2019) "Rising Seas Will erase More Cities by 2050, New Research Shows," *NY Times*, 29, October.

Ly, Boreth (2019) *Traces of Trauma: Cambodian Visual Culture and National Identity in the Aftermath of Genocide*. Honolulu, HI: University of Hawaii Press.

Lynas, Victor (1998) "Papua New Guinea Seen as 'Last Frontier,'" *Oil & Gas Journal*, 17 August, available at https://www.ogj.com/articles/print/vol ume-96/issue-33/in-this-issue/exploration/papua-new-guinea-seen-as-391 ast-frontier39.html.

Lyons, Kate (2018) "Catalan Referendum: New Caledonia's Independence Referendum: What You Need to Know," *Guardian*, 1 November.

MacDonald, Kenneth (2010a) "Business, Biodiversity, and the New 'Fields' of Conservation: The World Conservation Congress and the Renegotiation of Organizational Order," 8 *Conservation and Society* 256–275.

MacDonald, Kenneth (2010b) "The Devil is in the (Bio)Diversity: Private Sector "Engagement and Restructuring of Biodiversity Conservation," 42 *Antipode* 159–184.

Mackenzie, B.B. (2005) *Alaska Curiosities: Quirky Characters, Roadside Oddities and Other Offbeat Stuff*. Guilford, CT: Globe Pequot Press.

Mackey, Robert (2009) "Pakistan's British-Drawn Borders," *NY Times*, 5 May.

Macpherson, Elizabeth & Julia Torres Ventura (2019) "The Tour to Save the World: Colombia Wins the Yellow Jersey for the Rights of Nature," *IUCN, International Union for Conservation of Nature*, 3 September.

Maestre-Andres, Sara, Laura Calvet-Mir, & Evangelia Apostolopoulou (2018) "Unravelling Stakeholder Participation on Conditions of Neoliberal Biodiversity Governance in Catalonia, Spain," 36 *Politics & Space* 1299–1318.

Magnus, Amanda (2017) "Environmental Groups and Ho-Chunk Nation Take Western Wisconsin Frac Sand Mine to Court," *Wisconsin Public Radio*, 21 June.

Mahmud, Tayyab "Geography and International Law: Towards a Postcolonial Mapping," 5 *Santa Clara Journal of International Law* 525–561.

Maluwa, Tiyanjana (2020) Reassessing Aspects of the Contribution of African States to be Development of International Law Through African Regional Multilateral Treaties," 41 *Michigan Journal of International Law* 327–416.

Manganyi, N. Chabani and Grahame Hayes, Garth Stevens, and N. Ndebele (2019) *Being Black in the World*. Johannesburg, South Africa: Wits University Press.

Manuel, George & Michael Posluns (1974) *The Fourth World: An Indian Reality*. Toronto, Canada: Collier-Macmillan Canada, Ltd.

Marques, Anatonio & Leonardo Rocha (2015) "Bolsonaro diz que OAB so defende bandido e resera indigena e un crime [Bolsonaro Says OAB Only Defends Bandit and Indigenous Reservation and a Crime]," *Campo Grande News*, 22 April.

Marquina, Cira Pascual & Chris Gilbert (2020) *Venezuela the Present as Struggle: Voices from Bolivarian Revolution*. NY: Monthly Review Press.

Marino, Angela (2018) *Populism and Performance in the Bolivarian Revolution of Venezuela*. Evanston, IL: Northwestern University Press.

Maron, Dina Fine (2016) "Ebola's West African Rampage Was Likely Bolstered by a Mutation," *Scientific American*, 3 November.

Marshall, Tyler (1986) "World Court Rules U.S. Aid to Contras is Illegal," *LA Times*, 28 June.

Martin, Summer Lynn (2014) *Ecosystem-Based Management for the Oceanic Commons: Applying the Concepts of Ecosystem Services, Indicators, and Trade-off to Make Informed Decisions*. Ph.D. Dissertation at the University of California, San Diego.

Martineau, Anne-Charlotte (2016) "Concerning Violence: A Post-Colonial Reading of the Debate on the Use of Force," 29 *Leiden Journal of International Law* 95–112.

"Mary and Carrie Dann of the Western Shoshone Nation" (2020) *The Right Livelihood Foundation* (accessed 15 May 2020), available at http://www.ind ians.org/articles/shoshone-indians.html.

Mason, R. Chuck (2015) "Status of Forces Agreement (SOFA): What Is It, and How Has It Been Utilized?" available at https://fas.org/sgp/crs/nat sec/RL34531.pdf.

May, James R. & Erin Daly (2019) *Global Judicial Handbook on Environmental Constitutionalism*. Cambridge, UK: Cambridge University Press.

Mazerolle-McGill, Frederique (2020) "Indigenous People Bear The Brunt of Pollution," *Futurity*, 20, May.

McCoy, Alfred W. (2003) *The Politics of Heroin: CIA Complicity in the Global Drug Trade, Afghanistan, Southeast Asia, Central America, Colombia.* Chicago, IL: Lawrence Hill Books.

McCoy, Alfred W. (2009) *Policing America's Empire: The United States, the Philippines, and the Rise of the Surveillance State.* Madison, WI: University of Wisconsin Press.

McCuen, John J. (2008) "Hybrid Wars," 88 *Military Review* 107–113.

McElroy v. United States ex rel Guagliardo, 361 U.S. 281 (1960).

McElvaney, Kevin (2019) "The Murders of Indigenous Activists in the Amazon Continue to Rise," *Yale Environment 360*, 17 December.

McFadden, Robert D. (2012) "Russell Means, Who Clashed With Law as He Fought for Indians, Is Dead at 72," *NY Times*, 22 October.

McGee. Thomas D'Arcy (1855) *A History of the Irish Settlers in North America: From the Earliest Period to the Census of 1850.* Boston, MA: Horart & Robbins.

McGrath, Timothy (2014) "This Map Shows What Europe Will Look Like if Every Separatist Movement Gets Its Own Country," *The World*, 17 September.

McKenna, Thomas M. (1998) *Muslim Rulers and Rebels: Everyday Politics and Armed Separatism in the Southern Philippines.* Berkeley, CA: University of California Press.

McLeod, Melissa, Jason Gurney, Ricci Harris, Donna Cormack & Paula King (2020) "COVID-19: We Must Not Forget About Indigenous Health and Equity," 10 *Australia and New Zealand Journal of Public Health* 253–256.

McMullan, Thomas (2018) "Only Dramatic Action Can Save Us from the Sixth Mass Extinction," *Wired,* 1 November.

McNeish, John-Andrew (2013) "Extraction, Protest and Indigeneity in Bolivia: The TEIPNIS Effect," 8 *Latin American and Caribbean Ethnic Studies* 221–242.

McNutt, Kristen (2005) "Sexual Violence against Iraqi Women by US Occupying Forces," *the UN Commission on Human Rights*, March, Geneva, https://meaningfulworld.com/our-work/un/sexualized-violence-against-iraqi-women-by-us-occupying-forces (accessed 22 October 2020).

Means, Russell (2008) *Petition for Recognition of Lakotah Sovereignty.* 8 February, http://danco.org/amer/Petition.pdf.

Means, Russell (2010) "UN Listening Session is US Smokescreen," 18 March, http://www.republicoflakotah.com/2010/russell-means-un-listening-session-is-us-smokescreen/.

Means, Russell (2020) "For America to Live, Europe Must Die," https://archive.org/stream/ForAmericaToLiveEuropeMustDie/foramericatolive_read_djvu.txt (accessed 22 October 2020).

Mendal, Sudip Kumar, Sourav Bhattacharya and Dhrubo Jyoti Sen, "Coronavirus: COVID-19 is Now a Pandemic," 1 *ACTA Scientific Pharmacology* 2–7.

"Mendoza, Argentina: Governor Suarez Announced the Expansion of the Jury to More Crimes and the Implementation of the Civil Jury" (2020) *AAJJ*, 9 May.

Merriam-Wester Dictionary (2018), available at https://www.merriam-webster.com/dictionary/fourth%20world.

Mexican Constitution (1917), available at https://www.constituteproject.org/constitution/Mexico_2015.pdf?lang=en.

Mgbeoji, Ikechi (2006) *Biopiracy: Patents, Plants, and Indigenous Knowledge*. Vancouver, Canada: University of British Columbia.

Michelson, Karin (2008) "Taking Stock of TWAIL Histories," 10 *International Community Law Review* 355–362.

Michelson, Karin, Ibironke Odumosu, & Pooja Parmar (2008) "Foreword, Situating Third World Approaches to International Law (TWAIL): Inspirations, Challenges and Possibilities," 10 *International Community Law Review* 351–353.

Milam, Robin R. (2014) "First Global Tribunal on Rights of Nature Hears 9 Cases," *GARN*, 17 January.

Milko, Victoria & Clare Hammond (2019) "The World's Largest Refugee Camp is Becoming a Real City," *Citylab*, 27, September.

Miller, Kerby Alonzo (1976) *Emigrants and Exiles: The Irish Exodus to North America From Colonial Times to the First World War*. NY: Oxford University Press.

Miller, Robert J. et al. (2010) *Discovering Indigenous Lands: The Doctrine of Discovery in the English Colonies*. Oxford, UK: Oxford University Press.

Ministry of Foreign Affairs of Japan (2020) "Agreement Regarding the Status of Forces Agreement in Japan," (accessed 15 May 2020), available at https://www.mofa.go.jp/region/n-america/us/q&a/ref/2.html.

Minahan, James B. (2016) *Encyclopedia of Stateless Nations: Ethnic and National Groups Around the World*. Santa Barbara, CA: ABC-CLIO.

Miranda, Lillian Aponte(2010) "Indigenous Peoples as International Lawmakers," 32 *University of Pacific Journal of International Law* 203–263.

Miroff, Nick (2013) "On Mexico's Western Front, Cartel Violence Escalates," *Washington Post*, 25, July.

Mitchell, Jon (2010) "Postcard From … Takae: In the Jungles of Northern Okinawa, Protests Against Planned U.S. Helipads Reach a Crisis Point," *Foreign Policy In Focus*, 5 October, available at https://fpif.org/postcard_fromtakae/.

Michell, Jon (2018) "U.S. Marine Corps Sexual Violence on Okinawa," 16 *The Asia-Pacific Journal: Japan Focus*, 1–9, 1 February.

Mobie, Nora (2020) "Native American Tribes Have Been Hit Harder by COVID-19. Here is Why," *Great Falls Tribune*, 5 August.

Moens, Barbara (2020) "The Flemish Nationalist Exist Strategy," *Politico*, 11 May.

Mogato, Manuel & Simon Lewis (2017) "U.S. Forces Assist Philippines in Battle to End City Siege," *Reuters*, 6 June.

Montenegro, Raul A. & Carolyn Stephens (2006) "Indigenous Health in Latin America and the Caribbean," 367 *The Lancet* 1859–1869.

"Moon Voices Regret Over Dispute Over Building of Naval Base," (2019) *Korean Herald*, 11 October.

Moran, Katy, Steven King & Thomas Carlson (2001) "Biodiversity Prospecting: Lessons and Prospects," 30 *Annual Review of Anthropology* 505–526.

"More Than 92% of Voters in Iraqi Kurdistan Back Independence" (2017) *Guardian*, 28 September.

Morin, Brandi (2017) "Where Does Canada Sit 10 Years After the UN Declaration on the Rights of Indigenous Peoples?" *CBC*, 13 Sept.

Mort, Terry (2018) *Thieves' Road: The Black Hills Betrayal and Custer's Path to Little Bighorn*. Amherst, NY: Prometheus Books.

Morris, Madeling (1996) "By Force of Arms, Rape, War, and Military Culture," 45 *Duke Law Journal* 651–781.

Morris, Stephen D. (1991) *Corruption & Politics in Contemporary Mexico*. Tuscaloosa, AL: University of Alabama Press.

Morris, Stephen D. (2009) *Political Corruption in Mexico: The Impact of Democratization*. Boulder, CO: Lynne Rienner Pub.

Moss, Margaret P. (2015) *American Indian Health and Nursing*. NY: Springer Publishing Company.

"Movement Rights, Rights of Nature and Mother Earth: Rights-Based Law for Systemic Change" (2017), available at https://www.ienearth.org/wp-con tent/uploads/2017/11/RONME-RightsBasedLaw-final-1.pdf.

Murdoch, Alexander (2009) *Scotland and America, c.1600-c.1800*. NY: Palgrave Macmillan.

Murphy, Sean D. et al. (2019) "Closing Plenary: International Law as an Instrument for Development: Remarks," 113 *American Society of International Law Proceedings* 389–400.

Mutua, Makau (2000) "What is TWAIL?" 94 *The American Society of International Law Proceedings* 31–40.

Mutua, Makau (2009) "The Transformation of Africa: A Critique of Rights Discourse," in Felipe Gomes Isa & oen de Feyter, eds, *Human Rights and Diversity: International Human Rights Law in a Global Context* (Bilbao: University of Deusto Press), pp. 899–901.

Mutua, Makau & Anton Anghie (2000) "What is TWAIL?" *Proceedings of the ASIL Annual Meeting*, 94: 31–38.

"MWR to Host a Trip to Jeju Island" (2017) *Chinhae MWR*, 15 August, https://korea.stripes.com/community-news/mwr-host-trip-jeju-island.

Nairn, Allan (1995) "A Discussion of the Guatemalan and the CIA," Interview on Charlie Rose with Elliot Abrams, Robert Torricelli and Allan Nairin, 31 March, https://www.youtube.com/watch?v=1ig0YvJCh5w (accessed 22 October 2020).

Nairn, Allan (2013) "Exclusive: Allan Nairn Exposes Role of U.S. and New Guatemalan President in Indigenous Massacres," *Democracy Now*, 19 April.

Nairn, Allan (2016) "18 Ex-Military Guatemalan Leaders Arrested for Crimes against Humanity During U.S.-Backed Dirty War," *Democracy Now*, 8 January.

Nagle, Luz E. (2010) "Corruption of Politicians, Law Enforcement, and the Judiciary in Mexico and Complicity Across the Border," *Small Wars & Insurgencies*, 21: 95–122.

Nakatani, Ryota (2017) "External Adjustment in a Resource-Rich Economy: The Case of Papua New Guinea," *International Monetary Fund, Working Paper*, No. 17/267.

Natarajan, Usha (2012) "TWAIL and the Environment: The State of Nature, The Nature of the State, and Arab Spring," 14 *Oregon Review of International Law* 177–201.

Natarajan, Usha, John Reynolds, Amar Bhatia & Sujith Xavier (2016) "Introduction: TWAIL-On Praxis and the Intellectual," 37 *Third World Quarterly* 1946–1956.

Natarajan, Usha, John Reynolds, Amar Bhatia & Sujith Xavier (2019) *Third World Approaches to International Law: On Praxis and the Intellectual*. London, UK: Routledge.

National Investment Promotion Facilitation Agency (2020) "Highest Recoverable Reserves of Crude Oil and Natural Gas in India" https://www.invest india.gov.in/state/assam (accessed 15 May 2020).

"Native American Lands and Natural Resource Development" (2011) *Natural Resource Governance Institute*, 15 June.

Nauman, Talli (2019) "Oglala Sioux Tribe Keeps Up Fight Against Uranium Mine," *Native Sun News Today*, 8 February.

Nazaryan, Alexander (2016) "California Slaughter: The State-Sactioned Genocide of Native Americans," *Newsweek Magazine*, 17 August.

Nebelkopf, Ethan & Mary Phillips (2004) *Healing and Mental Health for Native Americans: Speaking in Red*. Long Beach, CA: Native Nations Law and Policy Center.

Nebrija, Antonio de (1492) Gramatica de la lengua castellana [Castilian Grammar], available at https://www.ensayistas.org/antologia/XV/nebrija/.

Neeson, Jeanette M. (1996) *Commoners: Common Right, Enclosure and Social Change in England, 1700–1820*. NY: Cambridge University Press.

Negri, Stefania (2017) "Unethical Human Experimentation in Developing Countries and International Criminal Law: Old Wine in New Bottles?" 17 *International Criminal Law Review* 1022–1048.

Nesiah, Vasuki (2003) "The Ground Beneath Her Feet: 'Third World' Feminism," 4 *Journal of International Women's Studies* 30–38.

Nesiah, Vasuki (2016) "Local Ownership of Global Governance," 44 *Journal of International Criminal Justice* 985–1009.

Neuhauser, Alan (2016) "TransCanada Sues White House for Rejecting Keystone XL," *US News*, 6 January.

Neuwirth, Rostam J. (2018) *Law in the Time of Oxymoron: A Synaesthesia of Language, Logic and Law.* NY: Routledge.

Neuwirth, Rostam J. (2020) "GAIA 2048: A 'Glocal Agency in Anthropocene': Cognitive and Institutional Change as 'Legal Science Fiction,'" in, Kolsky, Meredith, et al., *A Post-WTO-International Legal Order: Utopian, Dystopian and Other Scenarios.* Cham, Switzerland: Springer, pp. 71–93.

Neuwirth, Rostam J., Alexandr Svetlicinil, & Denis De Castro Halis (2017) *The BRICS-Lawyers' Guide to Global Cooperation.* NY: Cambridge University Press.

"New Caledonia's Independence Referendum: What You Need to Know" (2018) *Guardian*, 1 November.

Newcomb, Steven T. (2008) *Pagans in the Promised Land: Decoding the Doctrine of Christian Discovery.* Golden, CO: Fulcrum Publishing.

Ngugi, Joel (2002a) "The Decolonization-Mobilization Interface and the Plight of Indigenous Peoples in Post-Colonial Development Discourse in Africa," 20 *Wisconsin International Law Review* 297–351.

Ngugi, Joel (2002b) "Making New Wine for Old Wineskins: Can the Reform of International Law Emancipate the Third World in the Age of Globalization," 8 *UC Davis Journal of International Law and Policy* 73–106.

Nicholson, Blake (2016) "Keystone XL Pipeline Faces Opposition From 'Historic Union' of Canada, U.S. Indigenous Tribes," *CBC*, 17 May, available at http://www.cbc.ca/news/canada/calgary/keystone-xl-pipeline-indigenous-opposition-1.4117445.

Nielsen, Marianne O. & Karen Jarratt-Snider (2020) *Traditional, National, and International Law and Indigenous Communities.* Tucson, AZ: University of Arizona Press.

Nietschmann, Bernard (1994) "The Fourth World: Nations Versus States." In George J. Demko & William B. Wood, eds., *Reordering the World: Geopolitical Perspectives on the Twenty-First Century.* Boulder, CO: Westview Press, pp. 227–242.

Nihon Heiwa Iinkai [Japanese Peace Commission] (2017) "Okinawa deno Beikaiheitaiin ni yoru Inshuunten Shibojiko ni Kogisi, Beigunkichi no Tekkyo o Motomeru [The Elimination of U.S. Military Bases in Okinawa Due to

Drunk-Driving Accidents Resulting in Deaths and Injuries by U.S. Marine Soldiers]," 20, November, available at http://j-peace.org/2011/statement/pdf/insyujiko_kougi171120.pdf.

Nilsson, Greta (2005) *Welcome to the Endangered Species Handbook*. Washington D.C.: Animal Welfare Institute.

Niranjan, Ajit (2020) "Countries Pledge to Reverse Destruction of Nature After Missing Biodiversity Targets," *DW*, 28 September.

Noack, Rick (2014) "These 8 Places in Europe Could be the Next to Try for Independence," *Washington Post*, 18 September.

Nobel, Justin (2018) "The Rights of Nature Movement Goes on Trial," *Rolling tone*, 10, January.

Nock, Albert J. (1935) *Our Enemy, the State*. Scotts Valley, CA: Createspace Independent Publisher, available at https://famguardian.org/Publications/OurEnemyTheState/OurEnemyTheState-byAlbertJKnock.pdf.

Nolan, Cathal J. (2006) *The Age of Wars of Religion, 1000–1650: An Encyclopedia of Global Warfare and Civilization*. Westport, CT: Greenwood.

Nordhaus, William D. (1994) *Managing the Global Commons: The Economics of Climate Change*. Cambridge, MA: MIT Press.

Norrell, Brenda (2012) "Russell Means: Warrior for the People," *Counterpunch*, 26 October.

Norton, Andrew (2020) "Coronavirus and Climate Change Are Two Crises That Need Humanity to Unite," *Climate Home News*, 12 March.

Nugrahanto, Mohamad Radytio (2018) "Understanding American Genocide and Enslavement of Philippines," *World Bulletin*, https://www.worldbulletin.net/news-analysis/understating-american-genocide-and-enslavement-of-philippines-h203247.html (accessed 22 October 2020).

Nunn, Nathan & Nancy Qian (2020) "Columbian Exchange: A History of Disease, Food, and Ideas," 24 *Journal of Economic Perspectives* 163–188.

Ocampo, Ambeth R. (2018) "Samar, the 'Howling Wilderness'," *Inquirer.Net*, 19 December.

Odumosu, I (2008) "Challenges for the (Present/) Future of Third World Approaches to International Law," 10 *International Community Law Journal* 467–477.

Official Gazette (2014) Document: Enhanced Defense Cooperation Agreement Between the Philippines and the United States, Article II (4), available at http://www.officialgazette.gov.ph/downloads/2014/04apr/201 40428-EDCA.pdf.

Ogle, George & Dorothy Ogle (2012) *Our Lives in Korea and Korea in Our Lives*. Bloomington, IN: Xlibris Corporation.

O'Grady, John (1935) "Irish Colonization in the United States," 19 *Studies: An Irish Quarterly Review* 387–407.

Ohnesorge, John K.M. (2007) "Developing Development Theory: Law and Development Orthodoxies and the Northeast Asian Experience," 28 *University of Pacific Journal of International Economics* Law 219–308.

"Oil Giant Chevron Urged to Cut Ties with Burmese Military Junta" (2007) *Democracy Now!*, 12 October, available at https://www.democracynow.org/2007/10/12/oil_giant_chevron_urged_to_cut.

Ojeda, Lorena "Mexico: Communities Up in Arms," *Berkeley Review of Latin American Studies*, (Spring, 2014):, available at https://clas.berkeley.edu/research/mexico-communities-arms.

Ojeda-Garcia, Raquel, Irene Fernandez-Molina & Victoria Veguilla (2016) *Global, Regional and Local Dimensions of Western Sahara's Protected Decolonization: When a Conflict Gets Old*. Granada, Spain: Palgrave Macmillan.

Okafor, Obiora Chinedu (2005) "Newness, Imperialism, and International Legal Reform in Our Time: A TWAIL Perspective," 43 *Osgoode Hall Law Journal* 171–191.

Okafor, Obiora Chinedu (2008) "Critical Third World Approaches to International Law (TWAIL): Theory, Methodology, or Both?" 10 *International Community Law Review* 371–378.

Okafor, Obiora Chinedu (2016) "Praxis and the International (Human Rights) Law Scholar: Toward the Intensification of TWAILian Dramaturgy," 33 *Windsor Yearbook Access to Justice* 1–35.

Okafor, Obiora Chinedu, T. Adebola & Basema Al-Alami (2019) "Viewing the International Labour Organization's Social Justice Praxis Through a Third World Approaches to Internatonal Law Lens: Some Preliminary Insights," in *ILO 100: Law for Social Justice*, eds. By George P. Politakis, Tomi Kohiyama & Thomas Lieby (Geneva: International Labour Organization), pp. 101–122.

O'Keefe, Mike (2012) *Custer, the Seventh Cavalry, and the Little Big Horn: A Bibliography*. Norman, OK: The Arthur H. Clark Company.

"Okinawa Prosecutors Indict U.S. Base Employee" (2011) *House of Japan*, 25 November.

Olsen, Dale A. & Daniel E. Sheehy (1998) *South America, Mexico, Central America, and the Caribbean*. NY: Garland Publishing, Inc.

Olson-Raymer, Gayle (2014) "Americanization and the California Indians: A Case Study of Northern California," *Humboldt State University's Department of History*, http://gorhistory.com/hist383/CaliforniaIndians.html (accessed 22 October 2020).

O'Malley, Vincent, Bruce Stirling & Wally Penetito (2013) *The Treaty of Waitangi Companion: Maori and Pakeha from Tasman to Today*. Auckland, New Zealand: Auckland University Press.

"One in Three Bavarians Want Independence from Germany, Poll Shows" (2017), *The Local*, 17 July.

Onuma, Yasuaki (1997) "Towards an Intercivilizational Approach to Human Rights: For Universalization of Human Rights Through Overcoming of a Westcentric Notion of Human Rights," 7 *Asian Yearbook of International Law* 21–81.

Onuma, Yasuaki (2000) "When was the Law of International Society Born? An Inquiry of the History of International Law from an Intercivilizational Perspective," 2 *Journal of the History of International Law* 1–66.

Onuma, Yasuaki (2003) "International Law in and with International Politics: The Functions of International Law in International Society," 14 *European Journal of International Law* 105–139.

Onuma, Yasuaki (2017) A *Transcivilizational Perspective on International Law: Questioning Prevalent Cognitive Frameworks in the Emerging Multi-Polar and Multi-Civilizational World of the Twenty-First Century.* Leiden, Belgium: Martinus Nijhoff Publishers.

Ortiz, Jorge L. and Ryan W. Miller (2020) "Coronavirus live Update: Global Cases Top 5M: Donald Trump Says He Has Almost Completed Hydroxychloroquine Regimen: 93K US Deaths," *Post Crescent,* 20 May.

Orwell, George (1938) *Homage to Catalonia.* London, UK: Secker & Warburg.

Osman, Abdullahi (2007) "Cultural Diversity and the Somali Conflict: Myth or Reality," 7 *African Journal on Conflict Resolution* 93–133.

Ostrom, Elinor (1990) *Governing the Commons: The Evolution of Institutions for Collective Action.* Cambridge, U.K.: Cambridge University Press.

Otis, John (2015) "Colombians Accuse US Soldiers and Officials of Sexual Assault and Rape," *Time,* 15 April.

Pagliarini, Andre (2019) "What Indigenous Rights Have to Do with Fighting Climate Change," *The New Republic,* 7 August.

Paige, Jeffrey M. (2020) *Indigenous Revolution in Ecuador and Bolivia, 1990–2005.* Tucson, AZ: University of Arizona Press.

Palacin, Carlos and Juan Carlos Alonso (2018) "Failure of EU Biodiversity Strategy in Mediterranean Farmland Protected Areas," 42 *Journal of Nature Conservation* 62–66.

Palmer, Stephen E. (2003) "Visual Perception of Objects," in Healy, Alice F. and Robert W. Proctor, *Handbook of Psychology: Experimental Psychology.* Hoboken, NJ: John Wiley and Sons.

"Pandemics, Climate Change and UN Reform" (2020) *Global Geneva,* 19 May.

Pappas, George D. (2017) *The Literary and Legal Genealogy of Native American Dispossession: The Marshall Trilogy Cases.* NY: Routledge.

Pariona, Amber (2018) "The World's 17 Megadiverse Countries," *WorldAtlas,* 25 July.

Park, Young (2012) *The Dark Side: Immigrants, Racism, and the American Way.* Bloomington, IN: !Universe.

Parker, Jean (2009) "The History of the Communist Party's Support for Aboriginal Struggles," *Solidarity,* 21 April.

Perkins, John (2016) *The New Confessions of an Economic Hit Man.* Oakland, CA: Berrett-Koehler Publishers.

Pellan, Mael (2013) "Independence of Brittany and Why Bretons Will Never be French: Their Values and Ours," *7 Seizh,* 17 October.

Pereltsvaig, Asya (2015) "Brittany, Another Independence-Seeking European Region," *Languages of the World,* 18 November.

Perry, Matthew C. (1968) *The Japan Expedition 1852–1854: The Personal Journal of Commodore Matthew Perry.* Washington, D.C.: Smithsonian Institution Press.

"Petition to Naha Prosecution Review Commission" (2011) 25 April, filed by Attorney Toshio Ikemiyagi (on file with the author).

Petroski, William (2013) "Debate Heats Up Over Keystone Pipeline's Gas Price Impact," *Consumer Watchdog,* 15 July.

Pfister, Tom (2018) "Gaining Ground From Reclaimed Abandoned Mine Lands," *Forbes,* 3 September.

Phan, Peter C. & Jonathan Ray (2014) *Understanding Religious Pluralism: Perspectives from Religious Studies and Theology.* Eugene, OR: Pickwick Press.

"Philippines Signs Historic Peace Agreement With Muslim Group" (2014) *DW,* 27 March, available at http://www.dw.com/en/philippines-signs-historic-peace-agreement-with-muslim-group/a-17523091.

Phillips, Tom (2019) "'He Wants to Destroy Us': Bolsonaro Poses Gravest Threat in Decades, Amazon Tribes Say," *Guardian,* 26 July.

Phillips, Valerie (2007) "Indigenous Rights, Traditional Knowledge, and Access to Genetic Resources: New Participants in Future International Law Making," 101 *American Society of International Law,* Proc. 319–323.

Phillips, Valerie (2014) "Indigenous Rights, Traditional Knowledge, and Access to Genetic Resources: New Participants in Future International Law Making," *University of Tulsa Legal Studies Research Paper* (No. 2008-05).

Pietari, Kyle (2016) "Ecuador's Constitutional Rights of Nature: Implementation, Impacts, and Lessons Learned," 2016 *Willamette Environmental Law Journal* 37–94.

Pindjak, Peter (2014) "Deterring Hybrid Warfare: A Chance for NATO and the UE to Work Together," *NATO Review,* 18 November.

Piper, Ross (2009) *Extinct Animals: An Encyclopedia of Species That Have Disappeared During Human History.* Westport, CT: Greenwood Press.

"Plan to Build Base Off Nago in 1960s Got OK by U.S. Top Brass, Document Reveals" (2016) *Japan Times,* 4 April.

Poling, Gregory and Conor Cronin (2018) "The Dangers of Allowing U.S.-Philippine Defense Cooperation to Languish," *War on the Rocks,* 17 May.

"Ponca Nation of Oklahoma to Recognize the Rights of Nature to Ban Fracking" (2018) *GARN*, 29 January.

Prashad, Vijay (2020a) *Washington Bullets*. New Delhi: LeftWord Books.

Prashad, Vijay (2020b) "Why Cuban Doctors Deserve the Nobel Peace Prize," *Counterpunch*, 27 August.

"Press Release: Colombia Supreme Court Rules That Amazon Region is 'Subject of Rights'" (2018) *CELDF*, 4 April.

"Press Release, Dept. of Public Information, State of the World's Indigenous Peoples" (2010) *U.N. Press Release DPI/2251*, 14 January.

"Press Release: Lakota Language Now Critically Endangered" (2016) *Wayback Machine*, 18, February, available at http://lakhota.org/lakota-language-critically-endangered/.

Pressly, Linda (2016) "Cherán: The Town That Threw Out Police, Politicians, and Gangsters," *BBC News*, 13 October.

Prestre, Philippe G. Le (2003) *Governing Global Biodiversity: The Evolution and Implementation of the Convention on Biological Diversity*. London, UK: Routledge.

Preston, Paul (2007) *The Spanish Civil War: Reaction, Revolution and Revenge*. NY: W.W. Norton & Company.

Pritchard, Justin & Reese Dunklin (2018) "U.S. Military Children Who Commit Sex Assault Abroad Rarely Prosecuted: Records," *Global News*, 30 December.

"Private Mercenary Firm TigerSwan Compares Anti-DAPL Water Protectors to "Jihadist Insurgency" (2017) *Democracy Now!*, 31 May, available at https://www.democracynow.org/2017/5/31/private_mercenary_firm_tigerswan_compares_anti.

"Protesters Rally One Year After Start of Henoko Coastal Work" (2018) *Daily Manila Shimbun*, 26 April.

Quesada, Alejandro de (2014) *The Spanish-American War and Philippine Insurrection: 1898–1902*. Oxford, U.K.: Osprey Publishing.

Rai, Nay & Zayar Tun (2017) "Ministry to Drill for Rakhine Fuel," *Eleven*, 14 January.

Rajagopal, Balakrishnan (2000a) "From Resistance to Renewal: The Third World, Social Movements, and the Expansion of International Institutions," 41 *Harvard International Law Journal* 529–578.

Rajagopal, Balakrishnan (2000b) "Postdevelopment as a Vision: From a Third World Approach to International Law," 94 *Proceedings of the American Society of International Law* 306–307.

Rajagopal, Balakrishnan (2003) *International Law from Below: Development, Social Movement, and Third World Resistance*. Cambridge, UK: Cambridge University Press.

Rajagopal, Balakrishnan (2006) "Reshaping Justice: International Law and the Third world: An Introduction," 27 *Third World Quarterly* 711–712.

Rajagopal, Balakrishnan (2013) *International Law from Below: Development, Social Movements and Resistance*. NY: Cambridge University Press.

Ramadhan, G.A. (2019) "The Development of Concept of Territory in International Relations," 20 *Global: Jurnal Politik International* 120–135.

Ramina, Larissa (2018b) "Third World Approaches to International Law and Human Rights: Some Considerations," 5 *Revista de Investigacoes Constitucionais* 261–272.

Ramina, Larissa (2018a) "Framing the Concept of TWAIL: Third World Approaches to International Law," 32 *Justica Do Direito* 5–26.

Ramirez, Deborah A. (1994) "The Mixed Jury and the Ancient Custom of Trial by Jury De Medietate Linguae: A History and Proposal for Change," 74 *Boston University Law Review* 777–818.

Ramsden, Che (2015) "International Rights of Nature Tribunal: Pachamama vs. 'Macho Papas,'" *Open Democracy*, 9 December.

Recinos, Ada (2014) "First International Tribunal on Rights of Nature: Inaugural Session in Ecuador Admits Nine Cases," *Amazon Watch*, 21 January.

Recinos, Ada (2019) "New Report: European and North American Companies Support Soy, Cattle, and Timber Companies Responsible for Recent Surge in Amazon Deforestation," *Amazon Watch*, 25 April.

"Reaching Indigenous Youth With Reproductive Health Information and Services" (1999) *In Focus*, February, available at http://www2.pathfinder.org/pf/pubs/focus/IN%20FOCUS/Indigenous.htm.

Reed, David (2013) *Structural Adjustment, the Environment and Sustainable Development*. NY: Routledge.

Republic of Lakotah (2008) *Petition for Recognition of Lakotah Sovereignty*, https://web.archive.org/web/20080411181412/http://www.republicofla kotah.com/docs/Petition.pdf (accessed 15 March 2019).

Resendez, Andres (2016) *The Other Story: The Untold Story of Indian Enslavement in America*. NY: Houghton Mifflin Harcourt.

Reverby, Susan M. (2012) *Tuskegee's Truth: Rethinking the Tuskegee Syphilis Study*. Chapel Hill, NC: University of North Carolina Press.

"Revised Brazilian Forest Code May Lead to Increased Legal Deforestation in Amazon" (2019) *Phys.org*, 7 January.

Reynolds, John (2017) " Emergency, Colonialism and Third World Approaches to International Law," in *Empire, Emergency and International Law*. Cambridge: Cambridge University Press, pp. 7–35.

Rice, Condoleezza & Robert Gates (2008) "What We Need Next in Iraq," *Washington Post*, 13 February.

Rifkin, Mark (2009) "Indigenizing Agamben: Rethinking Sovereignty in Light of the 'Peculiar' Status of Native People," 73 *Cultural Critique* 88–124.

"Rights of Nature and Mother Earth: Rights-Based Law for Systemic Change" (2017) *Indigenous Again*, 13 November, available at http://indigenousagain. com/rights-nature-mother-earth-rights-based-law-systemic-change/.

Robins, Simon (2016) *Dirty Wars: A Century of Counterinsurgency*. Gloucestershire, UK: The History Press.

Robinson, William I. (2008) *Latin America and Global Capitalism: A Critical Globalization Perspective*. Baltimore, MD: The Johns Hopkins University Press.

Rodriguez, Junius P. (2002) *The Louisiana Purchase: A Historical and Geographical Encyclopedia*. Santa Barbara, CA: ABC-CLIO.

Rodriguez, Luis Nuno & Sergiy Glebov (2009) *Military Bases: Historical Perspectives, Contemporary Challenges*. Amsterdam, Netherlands: IOS Press.

Rogers, Sarah (2014) "Frustrated Nunavut Protesters Look to Federal MP for Support," *NUNATSIAQ Online*, 23 July, available at http://www.nunatsiaq online.ca/stories/article/65674frustrated_nunavut_protesters_look_to_fede ral_government_for_support/.

Rogin, Josh (2020) "State Department Cables Warned of Safety Issues at Wuhan Lab Studying Bat Coronavirus," *Washington Post*, 14 April.

Romero, Simon & Clifford Krauss (2011) "Ecuador Judge Orders Chevron to Pay $9 Billion," *NY Times*, 14 February.

Roper, Willem (2020) "Navajo Nation Hit Hard by COVID-19," *Statista*, 26 May.

Rosane, Olivia (2019). "Typhoon Kills 28, Displaces More Thank 50,000 in the Philippines," *EcoWatch*, 27 December.

Rosendal, G. Kristin (2013) *The Convention on Biological Diversity and Developing Countries*. London, UK: Kluwer Academic Publishers.

Rosete, Maurice (2016) *Queen Liliuokalani: The Overthrow of the Hawaiian Kingdom*. Scotts Valley, CA: Createspace Independent Pub.

Ross, Alf (2006) *A Textbook of International Law*. Clar, NJ: The Lawbook Exchange, Ltd.

Roth, Robin and Wolfram Dressler (2012) "Market-Oriented Conservation Governance: The Peculiarities of Place," 43 *Geoforum* 363–366.

Rousseau, Jean-Jacques (1753) "Against Arbitrary Authority," available at https://www.cooperative-individualism.org/rousseau-jean-jacques_against-arbitrary-authority-1753.htm.

Rowland, Ashley Jon Rabiroff, and Yoo Kyong Chang (2011) "U.S. Bases Blamed for Oil-Tainted Groundwater in S. Korea," *Starts and Stripes*, 8 June.

Roy, Ash Narain (1999) The Third World in the Age of Globalisation: Requiem or New Agenda? London, UK: Zed Books.

Ryang, Sonia (2000) *Koreans in Japan: Critical Voices from the Margin*. NY: Routledge.

Ryser, Rudolph C. (2012) *Indigenous Nations and Modern States: The Political Emergence of Nations Challenging State Power.* NY: Routledge.

Ruey, Tethloach (2017) *The South Sudanese Conflict Analysis: Conflict Profile, Causes, Acors and Dynamics.* Munich, Germany: GRIN Verlag.

S!PAZ (1995), available at http://www.sipaz.org/1995-6/?lang=en.

Salazar, Egla Martinez (2012) *Global Coloniality of Power in Guatemala: Racism, Geocide, Citizenship.* NY:Lexington Books.

Salazar, Giovanna (2015) "The Cherán Indigenous Community's Remarkable Road to Self-Rule in Mexico," *Our World,* 24 April.

Salim, Mustafa et al. (2017) "Tillerson Says Kurdish Independence Referendum is Illegitimate," *Washington Post,* 29 September.

Salva, Ana (2020) "The Coronavirus Pandemic Has Put Asia's Indigenous Communities Under Serious Pressure," *Equal Times,* 9 October.

Sander, Ernest (1995) "From Operation Gatekeeper to Operation Hardline: What's in a Name?" *Associated Press,* 9 May.

Sands, Susan (1991) "West Papua: Forgotten War, Unwanted People," *Cultural Survival,* June, available at https://www.culturalsurvival.org/publications/cultural-survival-quarterly/west-papua-forgotten-war-unwanted-people.

Santos, Boaventura de Sausa (1998) "Participatory Budgeting in Porto Alegre: Toward a Redistributive Democracy," 26 *Politics & Society* 461–510.

Santos, Renato Antunes Dos, Denis Osorio Severo & Maria da Graca Luderitz Hoefel (2020) "Bolsonaro's Hostility Has Driven Indigenous Peoples to the Brink," *Nature,* 19 August.

Saha, Tushkar Kanti, (2010) *Textbook on Legal Methods, Legal Systems and Research.* India: Universal Law Publishers.

Scanlan, Melissa K. (2016) *Law and Policy for a New Economy: Sustainable, Just, and Democratic.* Northampton, MA: Edward Elgar Pub.

Schirmer, Daniel B. (1997) "Sexual Abuse and the U.S. Military Presence: The Philippines and Japan," *Monthly Review,* 1 February.

Scherr, Caitlyn (2016) "Chasing Democracy: The Development and Acceptance of Jury Trials in Argentina," 47 *University of Miami Inter-American Law Review* 316–353.

Schipani, Andres (2010) "Grassroots Summit Calls for International Climate Court," *Guardian,* 23 April.

Schuele, Waleria (2015) "Giving Nature Legal Rights, Tribunal Puts Environmental Damage on Trial," *ProJourno,* 4 December.

Scott, James (2010) *The Art of Not Being Governed: Ab Anarchist History of Upland Southeast Asia.* New Haven, CT: Yale University Press.

"SD Mines Researchers Trace Pollution from Historic Northern Hills Mine Tailings Hundreds of Miles Downstream (2018) *South Dakota Mines,* 20 July.

Sebua, Melvin C. (2012) "Philippines Discover Deposits of Oil and Gas in Mindanao," *RHSSS Foreign Ministry,* 31 January, available at https://therhsssnews.wordpress.com/2012/01/31/philippines-discover-deposits-of-oil-and-gas-in-mindanao/.

Seck, Sara L. (2011) "Global Ecological Integrity and Third World Approaches to International Law," in *Globalisation and Ecological Integrity in Science and International Law*, eds. Laura Westra & Klaus Bosselmann & Colin Soskolne. Newcastle, UK: Cambridge Scholars Publishing, pp. 165–187.

Seton, Kathy (1999) "Fourth World Nations in the Era of Globalisation: An Introduction to Contemporary Theorizing Posed by Indigenous Nations," 4 *The Fourth World Journal* 49–69.

Shaffer, Gregory (2012) "International Law and Global Public Goods in a Legal Pluralist World, 23 *European Journal of International Law* 669–693.

Shen, Simon (2017) "Is Bavaria Likely to Break Off From Germany?" *Ejinsight*, 3 August.

Shenon, Philip (1991) "Philippine Senate Votes to Reject U.S. Base Renewal," *NY Times*, 16, September.

Shesgreen, Deirdre (2020) "'Gross Misjudgment': Experts say Trump's Decision to Disband Pandemic Team Hindered Coronavirus Response," *USA Today*, 18 March.

Shevory, Thomas C. (1994) *John Marshall's Law: Interpretation, Ideology, and Interest*. Westport, CN: Greenwood Press.

Shiva, Vandana (2000) "North-South Conflicts in Intellectual Property Rights," 12 *Peace Review* 501–508.

Shiva, Vandana (2003) "Biopiracy: Need to Change Western IPR Systems," *World-Inforostructure*, http://www.se.edu/nas/files/2018/08/A-NAS-2017-Proceedings-Smith.pdf (accessed 22 October 2020).

Shiva, Vandana (2005) *Earth Democracy: Justice, Sustainability, and Peace*. Cambridge, MA: South End Press.

Shohat, Ella (1992) "Notes on the 'Post-Colonial,'" *Social Text*, No. 31/32, pp. 99–113.

Sinclair, Guy Fiti (2018) "Toward a Postcolonial Genealogy of International Organizations Law," 31 *Leiden Journal of International Law* 841–869.

Singh, Prabhakar (2010) "The Scandal of Enlightenment and the Birth of Discipline: Is Post-Colonial International Law a Science?" 12 *International Community Law Review* 5–34.

Singh, Prabhakar & Benoit Mayer (2014) *Critical International Law: Postrealism, Postcolonialism and Transnationalism*. Oxford, U.K.: Oxford University Press.

Sjostedt, Matilda Eriksson (2020) "The Role of Environmental Institutions in Producing and Reproducing Conditions for Neoliberal Biodiversity Conservation," 2 *Journal of International & Public Affairs*, https://www.jipasg.org/posts/2020/9/6/the-role-of-environmental-institutions-in-producing-

and-reproducing-conditions-for-neoliberal-biodiversity-conservation (accessed 22 October 2020).

Skouteris, Thomas (2012) "Engaging History in International Law" in David Kennedy & Jose Maria Beneyto, eds, *New Approaches to International Law: The European and American Experiences*. Hague, Netherlands: TMC Asser Press, pp. 99–122.

Sleeper-Smith, Susan, Juliana Barr & Jean M. O'Brian (2015) *Why You Can't Teach United States History Without American Indians*. Chapel Hill, NC: The University of North Carolina Press.

Smith, David L. (2011) *Less Than Human: Why We Demean, Enslave, and Exterminate Others*. NY: St. Martin's Griffin.

Smith, David Michael (2019) "Counting the Dead: Estimating the Loss of Life in the Indigenous Holocaust, 1492-Present," *Wayback Machine*, http://www.se.edu/nas/files/2018/08/A-NAS-2017-Proceedings-Smith.pdf (accessed 22 October 2020).

Smith, Donald B. (2018) Deskaheh (Levi General), Dictionary Canadian Biography (accessed 21 November 2018), available at http://www.biographi.ca/en/bio/deskaheh_15E.html.

Smith, Gar (2009) "In Ecuador, Tree Now Have Rights," 23 *Earth Island Journal*, winter, available at https://www.earthisland.org/journal/index.php/magazine/entry/in_ecuador_trees_now_have_rights/.

Smith, Joseph (2012) *The Spanish-American War: Conflict in the Caribbean and the Pacific 1895–1902*. NY: Routledge.

Sobel, Alex (2019) "West Papua: The World's Forgotten Injustice," *Red Pepper*, 8 April.

Solano, Xochitl Leyva (2007) "Indigenismo, Indianismo and 'Ethnic Citizenship' in Chiapas," 32 *Journal of Peasant Studies* 555–583.

Soloff, Andalusia Knoll (2018) "After Long Fight for Self-Government, Indigenous Town of Cherán, Mexico Ushers in New Council," *NBC News*, 4 September.

Sopher, David E. (1965) *The Sea Nomads: A Study Based on the Literature of the Maritime Boat People of Southeast Asia*. Singapore: Lim Bian Han.

Sottek, T.C. & Janus Kopfstein (2013) "Everything You Need to Know about PRISM," *The Verge*, 17 July.

South, Nigel (2007) "The 'Corporate Colonization of Nature': Bio-Prospecting, Bio-Piracy and the Development of Green Criminology," in Beirne, Piers & Nigel South (eds), Issyes in *Green Criminology*, Devon, U.K.: Willan Pub., pp. 230–247.

Sovacool, Benjamin K. et al (2013) *Energy Security, Equality and Justice*. London, UK: Routledge.

Sprague, Donovin Arleigh and Rylan Sprague (2015) *Standing Rock: Lakota, Dakota, Nakota Nation*. Charleston, SC: Arcadia Publishing.

Srivastava, Mehul & Najmeh Bozorgmehr(2017) "Turkey, Iran and Iraq Pledge to Act Jointly Against Kurdistan," *Financial Times,* 5 October.

Starblanket, Tamara (2018) *Suffer the Little Children: Genocide, Indigenous Nations and the Canadian State.* Atlanta, GA: Clarity Press.

Stares, Justin (2009) "Flanders Encouraged to Seek Independence from Belgium by EU's Growing Power," *The Telegraph,* 28 June.

"States with the Highest Number of Homicides in Mexico in 2019" (2020) *Statista* (accessed 15 May 15).

Statute of the international Tribunal of Mother Earth (2015), available at https://therightsofnature.org/wp-content/uploads/Statute-of-the-International-Tribunal-of-Mother-Earth-Rights4Dec2015.pdf.

Stephan, Maria & Jacob Mundy (2006) " A Battlefield Transformed: From Guerilla Resistance to Mass Nonviolent Struggle in the Western Sahara," 8 *Journal of Military and Strategic Studies* 1–32.

Steininger, Rolf (2003) *South Tyrol: A Minority Conflict of the Twentieth Century.* NY: Routledge.

Stern, Paul C. (2011) "Design Principles for Global Commons: Natural Resources and Emerging Technologies," 5 *International Journal of the Commons* 213–232.

Stevens, Michelle L. (2007) "Iraq and Iran in Ecological Perspective: The Mesopotamian Marshes and the Hawizeh-Azim Peace Park," in Saleem H. Ali, ed., *Peace Parks: Conservation and Conflict Resolution,* MA: MIT Press, pp. 313–331.

Stiglitz, Joseph (2000) "The Insider: What I Learned at the World Economic Crisis," *New Republic,* 17 April.

Stone, Ashley M. (2019) "Introduction to Third World Approaches to International Law," 20 *Oregon Review of International Law* 333–334.

Subcomandante Marcos & John Ponce De Leon (2011) *Our Word is Our Weapon: Selected Writings.* NY: Seven Stories Press.

Sulish, Clive(2017) "Bombing of Basque Town of Gernika Commemorated in Dublin," *RebelBreeze,* 2 May.

Sullivan, Sian (2005) "Reflection on 'New' (Neoliberal) Conservation (With Case Material from Namibia, Southern Africa," 2 *Africa e Orienti* 102–115.

Sullivan, Sian (2006) "The Elephant in the Room? Problematizing 'New' (Neoliberal) Biodiversity Conservation," 33 *Forum for Development Studies* 105–135.

Sullivan, Sian (2009) "Green Capitalism and the Cultural Poverty of Constructing Nature as Service-Provider," 3 *Rural Anthropology* 18–27.

Suny, Ronald Grigor (2001) "Constructing Primordialism: Old Histories for New Nations," 73 *Journal of Modern History* 862–896.

Suzara, Aileen (2004) "Activist Debra Harry Speaks on Indigenous Peoples' Movement to Challenge Biocolonialism," *Indigenous Peoples Council on*

Biocolonialism, 23 April, available at http://www.ipcb.org/publications/other_art/holyoke.html.

Swanson, Timothy (1999)"Why is There a Biodiversity Convention? The International Interest in Centralized Development Planning," 75 *International Affairs* 307–331.

Sweeney, Chris (2019) "The World's 30 Strangest Military Bases," *Popular Mechanics*, 7 October.

"Systematic Rights Violations Taking Place in Indian Held Kashmir: Human Right Bodies" (2012) *Pakistan News Releases*, 24 May.

Taber, Jay (2014) "Equals Not Subordinates, Intercontinental Cry," *IC*, 27 April, available at https://intercontinentalcry.org/equals-subordinates/.

Tainter, Joseph A. (1988) *The Collapse of Complex Societies*. NY: Cambridge University Press.

Takaki, Ron (2008) *A Difference Mirror: A History of Multicultural America*. NY: Little, Brown and Company.

Tantikanangkul, Walaiporn and Ashley Pritchard (2016) *Politics of Autonomy and Sustainability in Myanmar*. NY: Springer.

Tebay, Neles (2005) "West Papua: The Struggle for Peace with Justice," *CIIR*, available at https://www.progressio.org.uk/sites/default/files/West_Papua_2005.pdf.

"Texaco/Chevron Lawsuits (re Ecuador)" (2020) *Business & Human Rights Resource Center* (accessed 15 May 2020), available at https://www.business-humanrights.org/en/texacochevron-lawsuits-re-ecuador.

"The Double Crisis: How Climate Change Impacts Aggravate Dealing with Coronavirus in Countries of the Global South" (2020) *PreventionWeb*, 14 April.

"The ICSID Convention Enters into Force in Iraq" (2016) *Herbert Smith Freehills: Public International Law Notes*, 7 January, available at https://hsfnotes.com/publicinternationallaw/2016/01/07/the-icsid-convention-enters-into-force-in-iraq/.

"The Latest: UN Regrets Iraq's Kurds Went Ahead With Vote" (2017) *U.S. News*, 25 September, available at https://www.usnews.com/news/world/articles/2017-09-25/the-latest-turkey-says-it-rejects-iraWqi-kurds-referendum.

The Montevideo Convention on Rights and Duties of States Adopted by the Seventh International Conference of American States, Montevideo (1933), available at https://treaties.un.org/doc/Publication/UNTS/LON/Volume%20165/v165.pdf.

The PRC Resolution Statement (2011) 27 May (on file with the author).

Thiongo, Ngugi wa (1986) *Decolonizing the Mind: The Politics of Language in African Literature*. London, UK: James Currey Ltd.

Thompson, Ruth (1987) *The Rights of Indigenous Peoples in International Law: Selected Essays on Self-Determination.* Saskatoon, Canada: University of Saskatchewan, Native Law Center.

Tilly, Charles (1975) *The Formation of National States in Western Europe.* Princeton, NJ: Princeton University Press.

Tobin, Brendan (2016) *Indigenous Peoples, customary Law and human Rights: Why Living Law Matters.* London, UK: Routledge.

Toensing, Gale Courey (2008) "Withdrawal from US Treaties Enjoys Little Support from Tribal Leaders," *Indian Country Today,* 4. January.

Tomei, Manuela (2005) *Indigenous and Tribal Peoples: An Ethnic Audit of Selected Poverty Reduction Strategy.* Geneva, Switzerland: International Labour Office.

Tomuschat, Christian, Atilia Lux de Coti & Alfredo Balsells Tojo. (1999) "Guatemala: Memory of Silence: Report of the Commission for Historical Clarification," *Guatemalan Commission for Historical Clarification,* February.

Torio, Lisa (2016) "Can Indigenous Okinawans Protect Their Land and Water from the US Military?" *The Nation,* 20 December.

Toyosaki, Satoshi & Shinsuke Eguchi (2017) *Intercultural Communication in Japan: Theorizing Homogenizing Discourse.* NY: Routledge.

Tran, Hugo (2014) "Fighting for Brittany: Autonomy in a Centralised State," *Open Democracy,* 5 December.

Tritten, Travis J. & Chiyomi Sumida (2012) "American on Okinawa Gets 18 Months in Prison for Vehicle Manslaughter," *Stars & Stripes,* 22 February.

"Tribal Health Board: Native Americans Hit Hard by COVID-19" (2020) *AP,* 26 June, https://apnews.com/article/0f44f46abf994293acded741ff0dd403.

Tsurumi, E. Patricia, (1990) *Factory Girls: Women in the Thread Mills of Meiji Japan.* Princeton, NJ: Princeton University Press.

Tucker, Arnold (2011) *The Encyclopedia of North American Indian Wars, 1607–1890.* Santa Barbara, CA: ABC-CLIO.

Tucker, Mary Evelyn John Grim, and Andrew Angyal (2019) *Thomas Berry: A Biography.* NY: Columbia University Press.

"Turkey Balks at Arming Kurds Against ISIS" (2014) *Associated Press,* 19 October.

Turnbull, Stephen (2009) *The Samurai Capture a King: Okinawa 1609.* Oxford, UK: Osprey Publishing.

"TWAILR Founding Statement: Third World Approaches to International Law Review" (2016), https://twailr.com/about/founding-statement/ (accessed 22 October 2020).

Tzouvala, Ntina (2019) "A False Promise? Regulating Land-Grabbing and the Post-Colonial State," 32 *Leiden Journal of International Law* 235–253.

Ubieta, Enrique (2019) *Red Zone: Cuba and the Battle Against Ebola in West Africa.* Australia: PathFinder Press.

Ugochukwu, Basil (2016) "Global Governance in All Its Discrete Forms: The Game, FIFA, and the Third World," 33 *Windsor Yearbook of Access to Justice* 199–228.

"Ukraine Separatists Declare Independence: Leaders of Eastern Donetsk and Luhansk Regions Declare Independence After Claiming Victory in Sunday's Self-Rule Vote" (2014) *Al Jazeera*, 12 May.

UNCTAD (2020) "Fact Sheet on Investor-State Dispute Settlement Cases in 2018" (Accessed 15 May 2020).

"UN Security Council Opposes Kurdish Independence Vote" (2017) *FRANCE24*, 22 Sep., available at http://www.france24.com/en/201 70922-united-nations-security-council-says-opposes-kurdistan-iraq-independe nce-vote.

United Nations (1960) "Declaration on the Granting of Independence to Colonial Countries and Peoples, Adopted by General Assembly Resolution 1514 (XV) of 14 December 1960," https://www.un.org/en/decolonization/dec laration.shtml (accessed 15 March 2019).

United Nations (1969) "Vienna Convention on the Law of Treaties," http:// legal.un.org/ilc/texts/instruments/english/conventions/1_1_1969.pdf (accessed 15 March 2019).

United Nations (2007) United Nations Declaration on the Rights of Indigenous Peoples, available at http://www.un.org/esa/socdev/unpfii/docume nts/DRIPS_en.pdf.

United Nations (2008a) Achieving Sustainable Development and Promoting Development Cooperation: Dialogues at the Economic Social Council, available at https://www.un.org/en/ecosoc/docs/pdfs/fina_08-45773.pdf.

United Nations (2008b) "Israel's 'Enormous Web of Unlawful Practices' Devastating Palestinian Society, Palestine's Observer Says, as Fourth Committee Debates Situation in Territory," 4 November.

United Nations (2010) "State of the World's Indigenous Peoples (SOWIP)," 14 January.

United Nations (2012) "Oceans: The Lifeline of Our Planet: Anniversary of the United Nations convention on the Law of the Sea: 20 Years of Law and Order on the Oceans and Seas (1982–2002)," https://www.un.org/depts/ los/convention_agreements/convention_20years/oceansthelifeline.htm#% 93Common+Heritage+of+Mankind%94+in+the+international+seabed+area (accessed 22 October 2020).

United Nations (2016) "Special Committee on Decolonization Approves Texts Calling Upon United States Government to Expedite Self-Determination Process for Puerto Rico," 20 June, https://www.un.org/press/en/2016/gac ol3296.doc.htm (accessed 15 March 2019).

United Nations Commission on Human Rights (1982) "Report of the Sub-Commission on Prevention of Discrimination and Protection on Its 34th

Session: Study of the Problem of Discrimination Against Indigenous Populations," 10 March.

United Nations Department of Economics & Social Affairs (2004) "Workshop on Data Collection and Disaggregation for Indigenous Peoples: The Concept of Indigenous Peoples: Background Paper Prepared by the Secretariat of the Permanent Forum on Indigenous Issues," 19–21 January.

United Nations Department of Economics & Social Affairs (2018) "About Us," 21 November, available at http://csonet.org/index.php?menu=77.

United Nations Department of Economics & Social Affairs (2020) "COVID-19 and Indigenous Peoples," https://www.un.org/development/desa/indigenouspeoples/covid-19.html (accessed 22 October 2020).

United Nations Development Programme (2011) *Human Development Report 2011*. NY: Palgrave Macmillan.

United Nations Educational, Scientific and Cultural Organization (UNESCO) (2020) "Natural Sites in Madagascar, China and Korea Inscribed on UNESCO World Heritage List," https://whc.unesco.org/en/news/358 (accessed 22 October 2020).

United Nations High Commissioner for Refugees (UNHCR) (2009) *Global Trend: Refugees, Asylum-Seekers, Returnees, Internally Displaced ad Stateless Persons*.

United Nations Information Service (UNIS) (2020) International Law, available at http://www.unis.unvienna.org/unis/en/topics/international-law.html.

United Nations Permanent Forum on Indigenous Issues (2019) *Indigenous People, Indigenous Voices, Factsheet* (accessed 15 May 2020), available at https://www.un.org/esa/socdev/unpfii/documents/5session_factsheet1.pdf.

United Nations Statistics Division (2019) *Methodology: Standard Country or Area Codes for Statistical Use (M49)* (accessed 14 November 2019), available at https://unstats.un.org/unsd/methodology/m49/.

"United States: Address Role of U.S. Military in Fueling Global Sex Trafficking" (2013) *Equality Now*, 2 March, https://www.equalitynow.org/united_states_address_role_of_u_s_military_in_fueling_global_sex_trafficking (accessed 22 October 2020).

United States Department of the Air Force (1996) *Military Operations Other Than War*. Secretary of the Air Force.

Universal Declaration of the Rights of Mother Earth (2010), available at https://therightsofnature.org/universal-declaration/.

Upham, Frank K. (2018) *The Great Property Fallacy: Theory, Reality, and Growth in Developing Countries*. London, UK: Cambridge University Press.

U.S. Census Bureau (2010) *The American Indian and Alaska Native Population*.

U.S. Census Bureau (2017) "American Indian and Alaska Native Heritage Month: November 2017," Newsroom, 6 October, https://www.census.gov/newsroom/facts-for-features/2017/aian-month.html.

"U.S. Civilian Worker in Okinawa Indicted for Fatality" (2011) *Asahi Shimbun*, 25 November.

U.S. Constitution (1787), available at https://constitutionus.com/.

U.S.-Colombia Defense Cooperation Agreement (2009), 4 November, available at https://www.securityassistance.org/blog/us-colombia-defense-cooperation-agreement.

U.S. Declaration of Independence (1776), https://history.state.gov/milestones/1776-1783/declaration.

U.S. Department of Defense (2020) "DOD Helps Fight Ebola in Liberia and West Africa" (accessed May 15 2020), available at https://archive.defense.gov/home/features/2014/1014_ebola/.

U.S.-Japan Status of Forces Agreement (2019) (last accessed 29 November), available at https://www.nichibenren.or.jp/library/en/document/data/140220_2_opinion.pdf.

"US Military Constructing New Base in Iraq's Kurdish Region: Report" (2017) *PressTV*, 22 August.

"US Shows a Copy of the Ryukyu-US Treaties and Letters by Commodore Perry" (2018) *Ryukyu Shimpo*, 20 November, available at http://english.ryukyushimpo.jp/2015/04/04/17747/.

"U.S. Soldier Gets 100 Years for Iraq Rape, Killings" (2007) *KLTV*, 23 February.

U.S. v. Wood, 299 U.S. 123 (1936).

USAID (2018) "Ambassador Kim Announces PHP 1.35 Billion Marawi Response Project: For Immediate Release," 16 October, available at https://www.usaid.gov/philippines/press-releases/oct-16-2018-ambassador-kim-announces-php135-billion-marawi-response-project.

Vaktania, Saurabh (2019) "Mumbai Receives Record Monsoon Rains in 2019," *India Today*, 16, September.

Valdmanis, Richard (2015) " Green Group's Unconventional Fight Against Fracking," *Reuters*, 28, June.

Van Dyke, Jon M. (2008) *Who Owns the Crown Lands of Hawai'i?* Oahu, HI: University of Hawaii Press.

Velasco, Luis Francisco Valle (2013) *The Rights of Mother Earth in Bolivia*. Scotts Valley, CA: CreateSpace Independent Publishing.

Vanhullebusch, Matthias (2015) "The International Court of Justice's Advisory Jurisdiction on Self-Determination," 1 *Sri Lanka Journal of International & Comparative Law* 25–48.

Vargas, Michael A. (2018) *Constructing Catalan Identity: Memory, Imagination, and the Medieval*. London: Palgrave Macmillan.

Vaughn, Bruce (2010) "Indonesia: Domestic Politics, Strategic Dynamics, and U.S. Interests," 31 January, available at https://heinonline.org/HOL/P?h=hein.crs/crsmthaatep0001&i=1.

Vermont Declaration of Independence, Second Vermont Republic (1777), http://vermontrepublic.org/vermont-declaration-of-independence/ (accessed 15 March, 2019).

Vidal, John (2011) "Bolivia Enshrines Natural World's Rights with Equal Status for Mother Earth, *Guardian,* 10 April.

Villamor, Felipe (2017) "Philippines Extends Martial Law in South for Another Year," *NY Times* 13 December.

Vine, David (2015a) *Base Nation: How U.S. Military Bases Abroad Harm America and the World.* Dallas, TX: Metropolitan Press.

Vine, David (2015b) "My Body Was Not Mine, But the US Military's: Inside the Disturbing Sex Industry Thriving Around American Bases," *Politico,* 3 November.

Vogler, John (2012) "Global Commons Revisited," 3 *Global Policy* 61–71.

Vovin, Alexander (2013) "From Koguryo to T'amna: Slowly Riding South with the Speakers of Proto-Korean," 15 *Korean Linguistics* 222–240.

Wallace Scott (2019) "Murder in the Amazon Heightens Fears for Isolated Tribes," *National Geographic,* 27 September.

Wallerstein, Immanuel (2004) *World-Systems Analysis: An Introduction.* Durham, NC: Duke University Press.

Ward, Brian (2018) "Socialism, Solidarity and the Indigenous Struggle," *Socialist Worker,* 12 September.

Washinawatok, Ingrid (1998) "International Emergence: Twenty-One Years at the United Nations," 3 *New York city Law Review* 41–57.

Watanabe, Toru & Chiho Watanabe (2019) *Health in Ecological Perspectives in the Anthropocene.* NY: Springer.

Watson, Fiona (2018) "Bolsonaro's Election is Catastrophic News for Brazil's Indigenous Tribes," *Guardian,* 31 October.

Watson, Irene (2016) *Aboriginal Peoples, Colonialism and International Law.* NY: Routledge.

Watson, Irene (2018) *Indigenous Peoples as Subjects of International Law: We Were Here First.* NY: Routledge.

Watts, Jonathan (2017) "Battle for the Mother Land: Indigenous People of Colombia Fighting for Their Lands," *Guardian,* 28 October.

Webb, Stephan H. (2004) *American Providence: A Nation with a Mission,* NY: Continuum.

Webster, J. Clarence (1931) *The Journal of Jeffrey Amherst.* Toronto, Canada: The Ryerson Press.

"Western Sahara Environment: Current Issues" (2019) *Indexmundi*, 7 December, available at https://www.indexmundi.com/western_sahara/enviro nment_current_issues.html#google_vignette.

"West Papua: Petition Calling for Self-Determination Handed Over to UN" (2019) *UNPO*, 30 January, https://unpo.org/article/21351.

Weigmann, Katrin (2015) "The Ethics of Global Clinical Trials," 16 *EMBO Report* 566–570.

Weiner, Michael (2004) *Race, Ethnicity and Migration in Modern Japan: Imagined and Imaginary Minorities*. London, UK: Routledge.

Westerman, Ashley (2020) "Over 120,000 People Remain Displaced 3 Years After Philippines' Marawi Battle," *NPR*, 23 October.

Whakatupua, Tutohu (2012) "Agreement Between Whanganui Iwi and the Crown." 30 August, available at https://www.govt.nz/dmsdocument/3706. pdf.

Whaley, Floyd (2013) "Shadows of an Old Military Base," *NY Times*, 26 April.

Wheeler, Skye (2020) "UN Peacekeeper has a Sexual Abuse Problem, *Human Rights Watch*, 11 January.

"White Earth Band Enacts First-of-Its Kind Rights of Nature Law" (2019) *IC Magazine*, 7 February.

Wijkman, Magnus (1982) "Managing the Global Commons," 36 *International Organization* 511–536.

Wilfley, Lebbeus R. (1904) "Trial by Jury and 'Double Jeopardy' in the Philippines," 13 *Yale Law Journal* 421–429.

Williams, Dana M. (2017) *Black Flags and Social Movements: A Sociological Analysis of Movement Anarchism*. Manchester, UK: Manchester University Press.

Williams, Richard Allen (2007) *Eliminating Healthcare Disparities in America: Beyond the IOM Report*. Totowa, NJ: Humana Press.

Williams, Timothy (2019) "Legal Rights for Lake Erie? Voters Ohio City Will Decide," *NY Times*, 17 February.

Wilson, Thomas M. & Hastings Donnan (1998) *Border Identities: Nation and State at International Frontiers*. NY: Cambridge University Press.

Winchester, Mark (2009) "On the Dawn of a New National Ainu Policy: The 'Ainu' As a Situation Today," 41 *Asian-Pacific Journal* 1–19.

Wing, John & Peter King (2005) "Genocide in West Papua? The Role of the Indonesian State Apparatus and a Current Needs Assessment of the Papuan People" available at https://sydney.edu.au/arts/peace_conflict/docs/WestPa puaGenocideRpt05.pdf.

Wither, James K. (2016) "Making Sense of Hybrid Warfare," 15 *Connections* 73–87.

Wolf, Eric R. (2010) *Europe and the People Without History*. Berkeley, CA: University of California Press.

Wolfe, James and Lesli J. Favor (2015) *Understanding the Iroquois Constitution*. Berkeley Heights, NJ: Enslow Publishers, Inc.

Wolfe, Jeremy, Keith R. Kluender, Dennis M. Levi, Linda M. Bartoshuk, Rachel S. Herz, Roberta L. Klatzky, Susan J. Lederman & Daniel M. Merfeld (2008) *Sensation and Perception*. Sunderland MA: Sinauer Associates.

Wolfe, Patrick (1999) *Settler Colonialism and the Transformation of Anthropology: The Politics and Poetics of an Ethnographic Event*. London, UK: Cassell.

Wolfe, Patrick (2006) "Settler Colonialism and the Elimination of the Native," 8 *Journal of Genocide Research* 387–409.

Wong, Edward (2016) "Tibetan Monk, 18, Dies After Self-Immolation to Protest Chinese Rule," *NY Times*, 3 March.

Woo, Grace Li Xiu (2003) "Project, Canada's Forgotten Founders: The Modern Significance of the Haudenosaunee (Iroquois) Application for Membership in the League of Nations," *LGD 2003*, (1) at n. 19, available at https://warwick.ac.uk/fac/soc/law/elj/lgd/2003_1/woo/.

Wood, Johnny (2018) "Why Asia-Pacific is Especially Prone to Natural Disasters," *World Economic Forum*, 6 December.

Woodard, Stephanie (2017) "Warnings from First Americans: Insidious Changes are Underway That Will Affect Us All," *In These Times*, 5 October.

Work, L. Susan (2010) *The Seminole Nation of Oklahoma: A Legal History*. Norman, OK: University of Oklahoma Press.

World Trade Organization (2017) "Members Welcome Iraq's Firm Intention to Resume Formal WTO Accession Negotiations," 17 November, available at https://www.wto.org/english/news_e/news17_e/acc_irq_17nov17_e.htm.

World People's Conference on Climate Change and the Rights of Mother Earth (2010), available at https://therightsofnature.org/universal-declaration/.

Wright, Kate (2020) "Rhythms of Law: Aboriginal Jurisprudence and the Anthropocene," 31 *Law and Critique* 293–308.

Wyk, Gary van (2019) *Our Anthropocene: Eco Crisis*. NY: Center for Book Arts.

Yamada, Masahiko (2018) *Tane wa Donaru? Shushi-ho Haishi to Shubyo-ho Unyo de [What Happens to Seeds? The Abolition of the Main Crop Seeds Act and the Promulgation of the Seedling Act]*. Tokyo, Japan: Saizo.

Yamaguchi, Mari (2017) "Okinawa Boy Injured After Window Falls Off U.S. Marine Helicopter," *USA Today*, 13 December.

Yamamura, Eiji (2008) "The Role of Social Capital in Homogeneous Society: Review of Recent Researches in Japan," *MPRA Paper*, No. 11385, 8 November.

Yamamoto, Kana (2015) "The Myth of 'Nihonjinron', Homogeneity of Japan and Its Influence on the Society," CERS Working Paper 2015.

Yang, Changyong, et al. (2020) *Jejueo: The Language of Korea's Jeju Island*. Honolulu, HI: the University of Hawaii Press.

Yashadhana, Aryati, Mellie Pollard-Wharton, Anthony B. Zwi & Brett Biles (2020) "Indigenous Australians at Increased Risk of COVID-19 Due to Existing Health and Socioeconomic Inequities," 1 *The Lancet Regional Health: Western Pacific*, 1 August, https://www.thelancet.com/journals/lanwpc/article/PIIS2666-6065(20)30007-9/fulltext.

Yeung, Jessie (2020) "The US Is Halting Funding to the WHO: What Does This Actually Mean?" *CNN*, 16 April.

Zabludovsky, Karla (2012) "Reclaiming the Forests and the right to Feel Safe," *NY Times*, 3 August.

Zapatista as Political and Cultural Practice," 29 *Humboldt Journal of Social Relations* 6–37.

Zargham, Mohammad (2017) "U.S. Does Not Recognize Kurdish Independence Vote in Iraq: Tillerson," *Reuters*, 29 September.

Zartner, Dana (2029) "How Giving Legal Rights to Nature Could Help Reduce Toxic Algae Blooms in Lake Erie," *The Conversation*, 10 September.

Zaw, Htet Naing (2017) "Ethnic States Win right to Draft Constitutions," *Irrawaddy*, 12 May, https://www.irrawaddy.com/news/burma/ethnic-states-win-right-draft-constitutions.html.

Ziegler-Otero, Lawrence (2004) Resistance in an Amazonian Community: Huaorani Organizing Against the Global Economy. NY: Berghahn Books.

Zucchino, David (2017) "After the Vote, Does the Kurdish Dream of Independence Have a Chance?", *NY Times*, 30 September.

Zunes, Stephen & Jacob Mundy (2010) *Western Sahara: War, Nationalism, and Conflict Irresolution*. Syracuse, NY: Syracuse University Press.

INDEX